AUSTRALIA: WORLD OF DIFFERENCE

AUSTRALIA: WORLD OF DIFFERENCE

JOHN BÉCHERVAISE

RIGBY

Edited by Peter Wade
Designed by Joy Eckermann

National Library of Australia
Cataloguing-in-Publication entry

Béchervaise, John.
  Australia: world of difference.
  Rev. ed.
  Previous ed. : Adelaide : Rigby, 1967.
  Includes index.
  ISBN 0 7270 1836 1.
  1. Australia—Description and travel—1967–
  I. Title.

919.4'0463

RIGBY PUBLISHERS • ADELAIDE
SYDNEY • MELBOURNE • BRISBANE • PERTH
NEW YORK • LONDON • AUCKLAND
This edition first published 1983
Text copyright © 1983 John Béchervaise
Photographs copyright © 1983 individual photographers
Typeset by ProComp Productions Pty Ltd, Blair Athol, South Australia
Colour separations by Lasercolor, Adelaide, South Australia
Printed by Griffin Press Limited, Netley, South Australia

THE WIDE VIEW

To many praises of the lovely earth—
No more divided in the minds of men,
However nations strive for sovereignty—
I add another: benediction spun
From breadth and beauty of Australia,
Her precious freedom and virility;
An invocation many voices blend,
Addressing all who, by her favour won,
Have been admitted to her sanctuary;
Who, marching forward with courageous eyes
Scanning the future, feel her eager heart
Bearing them on through pulsing arteries
To noble destinies and purposes,
Not limited by inward turning sight,
But dedicated to humanity;

And men of older lands who understand
That bounties, which possess their noblest songs,
In distant countries, yet unvisited,
May also blossom; that hearts turned,
Gladly, at last (as once the heart of Rome,
To alien island or the plains of Gaul)
From ancient home to anxious colony,
May find at last an anchorage as fair,
Holding at length a double wisdom there:
Traditional knowledge from a treasured past
And vital union with a virgin soil.

—from WIDE HOMELAND
by the author

IT WOULD BE IMPOSSIBLE TO NAME all who have helped me in the writing of *Australia: World of Difference*. Many, whose knowledge has illuminated my travels through the years, are mentioned both in the text and in the notes. To my companions on innumerable excursions and expeditions I will always owe both delight and gratitude.

For help, along the track or through discussion or correspondence, I am grateful to the following: Mr Rolf Baldwin, Mr C. Warren Bonython, Mr Alex Burns, the late Prof. Tom Cherry, Prof. Kathleen Fitzpatrick, Mrs Neilma Gantner, Miss Jean Galbraith, Mr Einar Hay, Mrs L. Luckman, the late Mr P. Crosbie Morrison, the late Dr Charles Mountford, Mr Ken Peake-Jones, Mr Vincent Serventy, the late Dr T. G. H. Strehlow, Dr J. H. Willis, and the Directors of several State and Commonwealth Libraries and Museums. To the Trustees of the National Museum, Melbourne, I am indebted for permission to use the late Sir Baldwin Spencer's outstanding photographs of Aranda tribesmen.

To my wife, Lorna Fearn, and to Mr Rolf Baldwin, much thanks for the reading and correction of typescripts and proofs.

Acknowledgments for quotations used in the text are made to the following:

Kipling, Rudyard: 'The Flowers' (Mrs George Bambridge and Methuen & Co. Ltd).

Lawrence, D. H.: *Kangaroo* (William Heinemann and Lawrence Pollinger Ltd and estate of the late Mrs Frieda Lawrence).

Paterson, A. B.: 'Black Swans' (Angus & Robertson Ltd).

Strehlow, T. G. H.: *Aranda Traditions* (Author and Melbourne University Press).

J.M.B.
Belmont, January, 1983

Contents

NOTE: It is impossible always to be consistent in following the conventions of scientific nomenclature, especially in quotations. Some follow the older manner of using capital initials for specific names. Well-known generic names, unless used in a definitive sense, are used in roman type and without capitals or italics; they have become part of the vernacular.

In the chapter, *The Old Australians*, the word 'Aborigines' (singular 'Aboriginal') is capitalised as denoting the *race* of Aboriginal Australians. Not all anthropologists follow this convention: occasionally it seems better not to be strict in this usage also. The plurals 'Aboriginals' and 'Aborigines' are both commonly used.

In quotations, measurements of all kinds are not normally metricated.

CHAPTER 1

The Wide View

AUSTRALIA HOLDS NO EXTREMES in altitude, latitude, or physiography; she possesses the most stable land mass and the most equable climate on earth. Yet, looking closer, there is a world of difference between this wide view of Australia and the detailed image where, to the surprise of even those who know her best, infinite and unexpected diversity continually appears. The broad, slow transitions between major physical and climatic regions; their characteristic vegetation, associated soil changes, and the general measure of occupancy and industry; all these may be found most explicitly in contemporary studies of geography and of the other natural sciences. They will be mentioned here only as they form the sombre or brilliant backgrounds linking typical Australian entities and accents, made familiar by the passage of time.

Even in prehistoric times the ecologies of all continents except Australia included man as a dominant force. To attain this position, it had been necessary for him to discover, for his safety, weapons effective against the great carnivores, and to cultivate certain plants as crops. Australia, without the hazards of dangerous beasts, nor the security of a staple plant diet for the Aborigines, developed in isolation, largely as a non-human sanctuary. Divergent and different animals and plants, distinctive from those of the rest of the world, flourished in communities through which the lean, nomadic tribes of man passed only on sufferance. For scores of millennia, man's acquiescence in his indifferent, unchanging environment found no expression in agriculture or permanent settlement. The records of countless generations faded on the walls of rock-shelters, and were overlain.

When, late in history, men from the Old World at last defined the shores of *terra australis*, their European eyes could discover only strangeness: mild, harmless creatures of astounding agility and incredible shape, incapable of domestication; trees so far outside experience as to seem gaunt, aloof, and even awe-inspiring, their huge columnar trunks the reservoirs of white tributaries in the sky; brilliant flowers that heralded no sustaining fruits for man; undergrowth either prickly, dry, and unkempt, or dank and gloomy, with tree-ferns reminiscent of a carboniferous age. Colours formed new, unimagined combinations, unlike those of any other landscape. Greys, fawns, and olive-greens predominated, providing a subtle foil for many-coloured, jewel-like birds in their own special element of hot, clear sunshine, through which they flashed and called to each other with strong, strange notes . . .

The first European explorers turned away, as from a land actively inimical, or passively indifferent to human beings; those who came later, including Captain Cook, not unnaturally evaluated its potential as a canvas that might be scraped clean and repainted in colours more flattering to man's traditional taste; as soil that might be stripped and cultivated for imported seeds; as pasture that might sustain herds of foreign cattle that could be milked, or yoked, or mustered easily for slaughter. Any animals, human or otherwise, that might contest a new order, could be driven back into the limitless unknown, if necessary beyond mountains so intensely blue that their colour became their name. Any plant that offended the European vision of landscape and agriculture could be destroyed. If there was inevitability in much of the change, much also was initially indefensible. Officially, it has taken two centuries to accord, even in theory, the Aborigines' fundamental right to their own territories and culture. If, indeed, as historical analogies reveal, ultimate blending of our Australian peoples occur, then, for the Aborigines, it must be part of a process of self-determination.

'New Holland is a very large Tract of Land. It is not yet determined whether it is an Island or a main Continent: but I am certain that it joins neither to Asia, Africa, nor America,' wrote William Dampier, the first Englishman to visit Australia, in 1688. He was quite unimpressed.

William Dampier, from the oil painting by William Dobson

'The Land is of a dry sandy soil, destitute of Water, except you make Wells. . . . We saw no Trees that bore Fruit or Berries. We saw no sort of Animal, nor any Track of Beast, but one . . .' The old freebooter called the Aborigines he saw 'the miserablest People in the World,' who, 'setting aside their Humane shape . . . differ but little from Brutes'.[1]

A second voyage by Dampier did not change his opinion. 'If it were not for that sort of pleasure which results from the discovery even of the barrenest spot upon the globe,' he asserted, 'this coast of New Holland would not have charmed me much . . .'[2]

Eighty-two years before Dampier, Australia had been sighted by a Dutchman, Willem Jansz—and subsequently, of course, by others—'who was searching vaguely for the great south land but mainly for countries with spices, and gold, and souls to rescue from heathenism. . . . And when other seamen stumbled on the great south land they found neither spices, nor gold, nor men interested in trade, but flies, savages, and little water . . .'[3]

If we accept the presumed provenance of the remarkable 'Dieppe' maps, particularly of the so-called 'Dauphin' world map (1536), it would seem plausible that the Portuguese discovered and mapped the eastern coast of Australia more than two centuries before the voyage of Captain Cook.[4] The Portuguese monopoly in the Spice Islands, the Moluccas (Maluku), in the early sixteenth century—one hundred years before the Dutch came to Ambon—provided ample opportunities for exploration by intention or chance. That discoveries remained secret is understandable in the polarised light of Portuguese and Spanish rivalry. Similar cartographic secrecy existed between British and American sealers in the years following Cook's discoveries in the sub-Antarctic. Magellan, himself, had served his country in the East Indies before defecting to Spain and (1520–21) leading his five Spanish vessels on the notable voyage of discovery which, though first circumnavigating the world, cost the life of the leader and four of his five ships.

Because we now have the full picture, the wide view, the history of the Dutchmen and conjectures concerning the Portuguese make fascinating reading. Both were often blown off course, particularly when taking advantage of the westerlies on their way to the East Indies. It is well known that the Dutch, over-reaching their meridian and making a landfall of the west coast, remained unmoved by any possibilities of a future in their discoveries. Three generations of Dampier's countrymen, also, were unstirred by his description of New Holland, although his *New Voyage Round the World* ran through many editions. It is a coincidence that another eighty-two years passed between Dampier's first voyage and the sighting of Australia by Captain Cook, this time on a coast as far from his English predecessor's landfall as it was possible for a ship to be.

Cook described no Eden in his summing up. 'But the Country itself,' he wrote, 'so far as we know doth not produce any one thing that can become

Captain James Cook, from an engraving of the original oil painting by N. Dance

an article in trade to invite Europeans to fix a settlement upon it. However this Eastern Side is not that barren and miserable country that Dampier and others have described the Western side to be.'[5] How could he look upon the Pacific Coast with any other eyes? His supply lines—timbers, time, and fortitude all holding—were extended through endless months, and perhaps 25 000 kilometres.

Under such conditions, it is easy to be prejudiced amid the unfamiliar, even though Cook's 'botanical gentlemen'[6] might be in their element. There is insufficient time for contemplation, or for the discovery of new values in beauty in the exploration of a strange land. One may be excited, intrigued, elated, fearful; seldom completely at ease. But Cook envisaged a potential, the realisation of which alone made New Holland habitable by the generations of men and women who, from security of tenure, ultimately discovered an enchantment that they would not have surrendered for all the traditional loveliness of Europe. Cook went on to say, '. . . it can never be doubted but what most sorts of Grain, Fruits, Roots etc. of every kind would flourish here were they once brought hither, planted and cultivated by the hand of industry and here are Provender for more Cattle at all seasons of the year than can be brought into this Country . . .'[7]

The process that commenced in the last quarter of the eighteenth century has been sustained for two hundred years, with an increasing confidence in Australia's future as a great, productive country where, today, with the benefits of both new and conventional sources of energy, no problems, even of water conservation and reticulation, seem insuperable. In an age where little is incredible, Australian cities continue to grow; everywhere new suburbs eat up the marginal paddocks, space is multiplied by many-storied buildings . . . and still, somehow, the exploding population is reflected in the advancing hectares of crops and the increase of flocks and herds still conquering the proud old communities of plants and animals that, through endless time, had maintained a delicate, perfect balance with their environment.

Where will it all end? For a few fortunate generations there will remain places beyond the ends of roads. Presumably, the National Parks will be safeguarded from the inevitable spread of agriculture and grazing, at least for very many years, and, according to their size and management, and a consequent ability to maintain ecological unity, preserve some of the old Australia in its natural state. The realisation of the value and the necessity of such reserves has been too belated and sporadic to save some of the ancient areas most truly representative of the land as it once existed, and, of course, the survival of animals, especially outside their ancestral haunts, has become equally tenuous. Population and environment are necessarily concomitant. A dominant species retains its supremacy by modifying the ecology of which it is part. Any species, including *Homo sapiens*, may become too populous for its balanced, healthy growth.

If, however, land usage in Australia is carried to its logical maximum, there will still be immense areas of marginal territory, belonging 'to a time in the earth's history before fertility as we know it existed,'[8] which may remain uncultivated and of little economic interest except for mining.

The transmutation of Australia from a sensitive non-human state of balance to an immensely rich cropping place and stamping ground for homocentric millions is inevitable, and as morally justifiable as the ascendancy of Man. Yet, curiously enough, the more we follow this seemingly inevitable movement, the more we mourn that which we destroy, the more desperately we try to conserve what we may of our Australian heritage, and the further we are prepared to travel in search of a virgin environment. Through seven generations of Europeans in Australia—seven generations of new Australians (or new Settlers)—there have always been those who apprehended the land, who breathed its air, watched its taut shadows, sought its disciplines with delight and humility . . . and discovered a new freedom. In part this was doubtless manifest as a function of their increasing security. The literature of the early settler begins to reflect this only when the crops are assured; the migrant listens for the authentic Australian accent when he stands on the edge of his clearing, as though he needed just a little space to take in the sound and the vision.

In the beginning it was scarcely conceivable that the territories of one colony should ultimately adjoin those of the next, that roads and railways should make movement itself secure; that, at last, the entire continent would be comprehensible as a unity, speaking clearly in spite of its many voices.

The records made by the explorers or early settlers of any distinctively Australian thing or theme—a koala observed by Governor Phillip, a dry creek bed by Robert O'Hara Burke, a gum tree by William Dampier, or a high column of residual rock by Charles Sturt—are all overlaid many times by the subjective and objective impressions of others, by history and, ultimately, by their existence in creative literature. For centuries such developments occurred in isolation; they were not related, for few had considered them except as solitary wonders in a vast, quite amorphous space existing in a word or in a map, but not in any comprehensible whole. But if the whole is greater than its parts, it is because it shows the relationship between these parts.

Slowly the gaps in the continent's history and geography were filled in: the gaps between Cook's landfall at Botany Bay, and the Dutchmen's arid sightings along the north-western coasts; between the arrival of the First Fleet, and the crossing of the Blue Mountains; between the forlorn expedition of Burke and Wills, and the modern roads and airways that traverse country once even more hazardous than that faced by the overlanders; hitherto unknown ground was gradually forced to yield to a measure of security, and its frightening aspects became beautiful. Where security is seasonal, or dependent on the vagaries of climate, as is the case in much of the cattle country and in some of that given to sheep, a characteristic fatalism has developed in those who have survived disaster. It is natural that, even in the fat years, there should be some reserve. In the expanses of the Inland, Australia frequently presents together 'her beauty and her terror.'[9]

Nevertheless, the taut, sensitive, Australian shapes and colours, the olive-grey bush, all that once seemed remote, detached, non-human, too finely spun, has lost its strangeness and, to those who know it from the intimacy of childhood, has become compellingly familiar. So that, though Australians now travel abroad to the fields, villages, and cities of their ancestors—very often of their present kinsmen—and are enchanted with them, yet they continually return to their homeland. What to the first colonisers may have seemed the 'maniacal laughter' of the kookaburra has become one of the warmest of all dawn choruses, and the carolling of the Australian magpie, an evocation of values holding a clarity and a freedom that, for many, make of Europe an antipodes.

The words of Marcus Clarke, less than a century ago, may show the beginning of the transition:

> In Australia alone is to be found the Grotesque, the Weird, the strange scribblings of Nature learning how to write. Some see no beauty in our trees without shade, our flowers without perfume, our birds who cannot fly, and our beasts who have not yet learned to walk on all fours. But the dweller of the wilderness acknowledges the subtle charm of this fantastic land of monstrosities.[10]

Incidentally, there was never a false implication than in the phrases

Top: Robert O'Hara Burke, leader of the Great Northern Exploration Expedition, 1860–61. *Centre:* William John Wills, second in command. His journal recorded the expedition's tragic journey. *Bottom:* Charles Sturt, discoverer of the Darling River and among other areas the Stony Desert which bears his name

12

concerning flightless birds and shadeless trees; the words of the poet, too, are false, 'in lands where bright blossoms are scentless, and songless bright birds.'[11] The scents of wattle, boronia, sassafras, and many others are as appealing, and as subtle as any lovely scents in nature, and birdsongs are equally varied.

A year or two after the first World War, the sensitive and keen observer, D. H. Lawrence, is able to see things on two different levels. He knows what the bush means to Australians. and because he does not have to undertake the hard, blunt life of the first settlers; because he finds waiting him all the means of living the contemplative life, he can write:

> The curious sombreness of Australia, the sense of oldness, with the forms all worn down low and blunt, squat. The squat-seeming earth. And then they ran at last into real country, rather rocky, dark old rocks, and sombre bush with its different pale-stemmed full-leaved gum-trees standing graceful, and various healthy-looking undergrowth, and great spiky things like yuccas. As they turned south they saw tree-ferns standing on one knobbly leg among the gums, and among the rocks ordinary ferns and small bushes spreading in glades and up sharp hill-slopes. It was virgin bush, and as if unvisited, lost, sombre, with plenty of space, yet spreading grey for miles and miles, in a hollow towards the west. Far in the west. the sky having suddenly cleared, they saw the magical range of the Blue Mountains. And all this hoary space of bush between. The strange. as it were, *invisible* beauty of Australia, which is undeniably there, but which seems to lurk just beyond the range of our white vision . . . And yet, when you don't have the feeling of ugliness or monotony . . . you get a sense of subtle, remote, *formless* beauty more poignant than anything ever experienced before.[12]

New values are gradually entering into the universal currency of educated people wherever they are. It becomes possible to explain the Australian vision. Now immigrants often find it extraordinarily quickly, and start off without handicap in their new surroundings, partly because the vision has entered literature at every level, partly because they identify themselves with a population that takes its views completely for granted. So the work of almost any contemporary Australian writer, wherever his scene is set, shows the full integration that has permitted Australians to enter into a spiritual ecology with their environment. Randolph Stow, for instance, writes of this integration in the far north:

> From the water flagged with lily leaves, lilies flowering among them, birds rose in sudden stages with a clatter of wings. Ibis and white cranes climbed slowly, wild ducks sped low over the water with a confused whistle, and wheeled, and returned, and flew off again. Geese trailed their long cry over the plain, a single black jabiru following.
>
> Before they had gone the children were already in the water, floundering among the lilies, crying to one another of the coolness of it and of its richness in ducks and flowers. The small children danced naked in the shallows with shining skins. The others, in brief pants, some girls in their dresses, dolphined among the lily stems.
>
> Gunn, seated on one arm of a baobab grown after centuries to resemble a clump of gigantic bagpipes, watched them with contentment. In the rays of the low sun the petals of lilies shone almost translucent against the shadowed hill, the far bank with its leaning pandanus. In that light the lily pads and the reeds glowed green as malachite, the water glistened, rock burned redly on the hilltop. Smooth as a fish. her wet hair flattened, a brown child turned in the water with her arms full of flowers.
>
> He had brought a book with him, meaning to read there, to show Helen that he was not letting his brain lie fallow, but he could only sit and look at the

children and the water and the flowers, in a mind-draining peace. *Annihilating all that's made*, he recalled from more studious days, *to a green thought in a green shade.*[13]

Here, all the strangeness has disappeared, even from the jabiru and baobab. There is visible beauty, and 'mind-draining peace.' Many of the forms once considered strange, perhaps 'all worn down low and blunt and squat,' here breathe their new vitality.

Australia has no mountains attaining a permanent snow-line, no great rivers pulsing trade and ideas between her inland and the world at large, no busy estuaries assembling river-borne produce for world trade; her range of latitudes is such that the noon sun, even in winter, is everywhere high in the sky; twilight is brief; dawn and dusk everywhere are decisive, from Cape York to southern Tasmania (where the latitude is comparable with that of Rome and Oporto). No gigantic canyons speak of millennia still bearing away cubic kilometres of the earth's crust to the surrounding ocean, and no Australian Niagaras thunder over high precipices. Not a single active volcano reponders the landscape, nor do blizzards and typhoons ravage it. Every tree in Australia, over 8 million square kilometres of the continent, may be simultaneously sunlit. The mountains are so old that time has rounded them so that they resemble sleeping dinosaurs with, here and there, a skeleton showing ribs and vertebrae. Rising starkly, these show the foundations of still more ancient worlds.

Our western plateau is one of the foundation blocks of the earth's surface, that has remained unchanged in these parts for at least a thousand million years, while the contiguous crust of the earth has folded and buckled against it, forming high, stark mountains piercing the clouds, or, sinking below oceans which have submerged parts of Australia many times, become the sea-floor. Many such movements occurred long before mammals existed there, or, indeed, anywhere on the planet. Other geologically ancient, and stable, regions of Australia include much of the Kimberleys and the Barkly Tableland.

Today, far and wide, we may discover the old sea-evidence: a shark's tooth still polished, in the mesozoic limestone overlaid by lava from the grassy, long-dead volcanoes of Anakie, deep in my local Barrabool Hills, or, in the famous Harper's Hill area of New South Wales, not far from Maitland, shells and starfish preserved in volcanic ash or sandstone deposited over earlier glacial debris perhaps 200 million years ago. Much more recent ocean sediments are found in the Mount Lofty Ranges of South Australia.

We may stand at the foot of some high cliff in the Musgrave Ranges, the oldest of all existing Australian mountains and, our imagination spurred by knowledge, think of them islanded by sea that receded before the continent had any shape recognisably suggestive of its present coastline. I have sat on the harsh undulating summit of Ayers Rock at sunset, looking south to these mountains, and the shadows deepening on the plain have become 3000 square kilometres of dark blue sea. The wind rising through the shadowy mulgas below has brought me the sound of its waves. How very old Australia is ... The rock on which I linger—almost too long for a safe starlit descent— includes between its crystals some unchanged pebbles, rounded by water before the earth bore life; for Ayers Rock, though so largely metamorphosed as superficially to resemble granite, is a monolith reconsolidated from the stuff of earlier mountains that were completely worn away.[14]

That inexorable forces and cataclysmic movements shaped the world is less apparent over much of Australia than anywhere else on earth, for nowhere else have the great attritions so completely planed the surface, laid low the mountains, and silted up the old sea gulfs. When you stand overlooking the Grand Canyon of Arizona, you are conscious of the immensity of the air *below*, replacing, in the ravines of the Colorado River, vast but comprehensible masses of solid land. In miniature, the traveller may see something similar in the Blue Mountains, but, in many parts of Australia, the process has been carried so far that you look up from the plain at sparse residual flat-tops such as Mt Conner, and contemplate the air *above* occupying the space of incalculable volumes of an older land surface the merest fragments of which remain. Australia might perhaps be described as the oldest tellurian.

Every Australian sunrise is a Pacific noon, and the light leaves no part of the Australian Continent until the sun is far to the westward over the Indian Ocean on its way to Africa. How easily in these modern times we may follow its course, for almost three hours, over an eighth of the world's circumference, between our eastern and western meridians. We may take the itinerary that three hundred years have compiled, watching the sun cast its shortest shadows, first along the golden Pacific beaches and the headlands between Bundaberg and Newcastle, penetrating the eastern forests clothing the Great Divide, from the towering mountain eucalypts of the south to the palms of Cape York. The sickle of noon will span far western Australia, beyond the grass-trees and baobabs, along Dampier's coast, while the afternoon is still warm along the Pacific surf.

The mind's eye desires the wide view that may embrace Australia as a whole, yet, even while comprehension finds unity, memory and imagination catch upon bright facets of experience and history. If you have lived long in Australia, travelled widely, and collected many memories, you may travel with the sun as it unites in its beams the great cities with the farthest outstation shanties, the cool sea with the strange desert, the bush with the jungle. Those who do not know Australia, who live, perhaps, in America or Europe, or even a long way off in time—the sort of distance that lies between, say, Sydney and the country 'back o' Bourke'—should try first to take the wide view, see the continent as a whole, and relate this first impression to any knowledge that later comes their way.

The Australian continent offered no easy ingress to its discoverers and early settlers. The west coast of the Dutchmen and Dampier, provided no physical obstacles, but it was hostile plain and plateau, incredibly arid and drought-stricken. Who would have dreamed that, to follow the course of the Tropic of Capricorn, from west to east over the Australian mainland, would entail travelling more than 3000 kilometres without seeing a single permanent river? No one has ever made that precise journey, but its piecing together over the last century has cost much effort and endurance, and many lives.

Explorers setting out from the more fertile east, on the other hand, encountered rugged mountain country everywhere from south to north. Ultimately this was shown to constitute Australia's Great Divide, a complex series of continuous ranges parallel with, and, for the most part, within 80 kilometres of the coast. With an average altitude of 1250 metres in the south, the ranges curve round into Victoria, and extend to Tasmania through the island chain of Bass Strait. Several massifs rise to between 1500 and 1800 metres and culminate in Mt Kosciusko (2230 metres)[15] but, further north, the mountains mostly become lower. and those topping 1500 metres are less frequent. The Great Divide reaches the tip of Cape York Peninsula as low hills.

Because of its thirty degrees of latitudinal range, and its generally abundant rainfall, the Great Divide presents wide diversity of climate and vegetation— from the snowfields of a long winter in the south, with their characteristic lacquered snow-gum, to the tropical rain-forests of Queensland.

It was this mountain barrier, the Blue Mountains, that for many years defied the aspirations of the first colonists, until Gregory Blaxland, William Lawson, and William Charles Wentworth (then only a youth) made the first successful crossing in 1813. Soon after, Surveyor George Evans led the way to settlement beyond the narrow coastal strip to which the colony of New South Wales had been confined for more than twenty years. Time has since yielded the wide view, and shown that, compared with the Great Divide, all other Australian highlands are localised, though by no means insignificant. For instance, the Flinders and Mt Lofty Ranges, which on the continental scale appear isolated, form a chain something over 650 kilometres in length. Although the Eastern Highlands, 3700 kilometres long, and averaging with their foothills, about 160 kilometres in breadth, represent a zone of intense folding and uplift that occurred in the late Tertiary Period, vulcanism and faulting have occurred, and these, combined with the effects of massive erosion by both ice and water, are evident in various regions of the Great Divide.

All mountains concentrate rainfall within more or less permanent channels. The Great Divide separates all the short, eastern rivers reaching the Pacific Ocean from those that flow into the Murray[16] system, those disappearing into the west, or occasionally flowing into Lake Eyre, and those entering the Gulf of Carpentaria.

Regular flights between capitals make it easy to contemplate the whole length of the Great Divide in clear air. As the light touches the crests of the ranges, almost simultaneously on the Victorian Alps and the tops of the Atherton Tableland, 2000 kilometres apart, an immense shadow, gradually intensifying to the west, must lie over the whole time-levelled continent. It will take about an hour for the sunlight to leap across the cattle country of Queensland and over the Simpson Desert to gild the lonely MacDonnells and Musgraves; and then thirty minutes or so to prick the Flinders Ranges[17] in the south. Breakfast in Brisbane will mark the time when the dawn light catches the Hamersley Ranges 300 kilometres inland from the Indian Ocean. Here are some magnificent rockscapes such as that of Wittenoom Gorge, once famed for its deposits of blue asbestos. Like those of the Kimberleys, the mountains here show almost horizontal bedding in residual flat-tops, or mesas, and the typical terraces where weathering has been resisted by harder layers. The gentler hills of the south-west, so vital to settlement there, without which the country must differ little from that along the Bight, would also catch the sun about two hours later than the tops of the Great Divide. Incidentally, even the desert city of Kalgoorlie, centre of the once fabulous goldfields, owes its vitality to the pipeline that conveys water 560 kilometres from the Darling Range in the south-west.[18]

But let us return to the Great Divide. There, in the south, still catching the early morning light, is the ice-sculpted pillar of Frenchmans Cap, rising from the Tasmanian lakelands; to its summit we shall climb by Moore's Track and Philps's Lead;[19] we must pause by those tranquil, sequestered tarns in the valleys. But expediency, and the demands of industry for hydro-electric power, have engulfed unique glacial tarns and river gorges, with their delicate marginal ecology, so that some who contemplate the great south-west wilderness may reason, 'this is why we, the lucky ones, who knew the south-west before the great changes of the past decade, are so concerned that as much as possible of the region should be set aside as a national park and wilderness area, so that others, in the years ahead, may capture something of the wonder, adventure and joy of discovery that was granted to us'.[20] And the same might be said of so much of Australia, last of all settled continents, other than Antarctica.

Swiftly we may scan all Tasmania—isle of lakes and mountains—and

John Oxley, an explorer in New South Wales and who is better known for his discovery of Moreton Bay and the Brisbane River

glance beyond to the mainland. It is easy to distinguish Wilsons Promontory, a knobbly granite pointer to the south, showing the way to the hill-tops, now islands—Rodondo, the Kent Group, Flinders Island, and the rest, of the former Bassian Isthmus. Westward the coast is beginning to catch the sun... Western Port Bay . . . Phillip Island, where thousands of Victorians holiday and make excursions to see the penguins, koalas, and seals . . . Port Phillip, and Melbourne at its head, awakening to a spring morning as fresh as the wattle-blossom that makes gold clouds in the Dandenongs edging the plain. Eastward the Ninety-Mile Beach of southern Victoria, raised by the currents that have swept for a mere 20 000 years through Bass Strait, is so uniform, holding in the beautiful Gippsland Lakes.

If we allow ourselves more than a passing glimpse it is impossible not to linger. We may pick out and name Buller, Howitt, Buffalo, Feathertop, and a hundred other mountain summits, many still white with winter; and great Kosciusko, beyond the Snowy River gorges and the youthful Murray. We may see the bright cusped reservoirs filling the blue-green valleys—the Hume Dam is said to hold more water than Sydney Harbour. We may look down on self-conscious Canberra,[21] the city that has grown to order . . . and, beyond the Blue Mountains, follow the edge of the sea. Sydney Harbour and Broken Bay are drowned valleys, intricate rifts in the long Pacific coast, where surf-fringed beaches and other attractions make a picnic ground equal in length to the distance between London and Moscow.

Descend for a moment to watch the bursting ferries, and the stream of cars on Sydney's Harbour Bridge; hear the roar of traffic surging away up Pitt Street. Admire the great sails of the Opera House,[22] making air of concrete . . .

The toothed mountains—250 kilometres inland from Port Macquarie, across the great forests flanking the Oxley Highway—are the Warrumbungles, old Pliocene volcanoes. John Joseph Oxley explored the Macquarie River that, with the Castlereagh, flows west from the Great Divide. In the year 1818, the most logical hypothesis, in the absence of any corresponding river mouths to disgorge the inland rivers, was that they flowed on to an inland sea. On 3 July 1818, Oxley wrote:

> Towards the morning the storm abated, and at daylight we proceeded on our voyage. The main bed of the river was much contracted, but very deep, the waters spreading to the depth of a foot or eighteen inches over the banks but all running on the same point of bearing. We met with considerable interruption from fallen timber, which in places nearly choked up the channel. After going about twenty miles, we lost the land and trees; the channel of the river, which lay through reeds, and was from one to three feet deep, ran northerly. This continued for three or four miles further, when although there had been no previous change in the breadth, depth and rapidity of the stream for several miles, and I was sanguine in my expectations of soon entering the long sought for Australian sea, it all at once eluded our further pursuit by spreading on every point from north-west to north-east, along the ocean of reeds which surrounded us, still running with the same rapidity as before.
> . . . if an opinion is to be hazarded from actual experience, mine is decidedly in favour of our being in the immediate vicinity of an inland sea, or lake, most probably a shoal one, and gradually filling up by immense depositions from the higher lands, left by the waters which flow into it . . .[23]

Oxley was too late in geological time to find his sea; he was right concerning the existence of 'immense depositions from the higher lands.' Of the Great Divide, he wrote on the same day, 'It is most singular, that the highlands of this continent seem to be confined to the seacoast, or not to extend to any great distance from it . . .' and it is impossible not to agree.

Aerial seascape of the Port Campbell National Park, Victoria

Rugged coastline near Loch Ard Gorge, the site of many shipwrecks

Sea mist over the Twelve
Apostles at sundown

The Island Arch, one of the
many offshore stacks in
the Port Campbell National
Park, Victoria

Up near the Queensland border rises abrupt Mt Warning, named by Captain Cook, and noted by every coaster since; behind are the MacPherson Range and the Lamington Plateau. The dense rainforest country up here, in certain areas of the mountains that define the boundaries of the northern States for 320 kilometres, is as different from the bush further south as a spray of orchids is from a branch of wattle.

The high eucalypts of the southern foothills and Gippsland have here given way to jungle, mossy antarctic beech,[24] massive figs with their strange aerial root systems, ancient cycads, araucarias, and many other species, still including some eucalypts and angophoras. As we allow our minds and eyes to stray north up the Great Divide, along the Carnarvons and the Warrego Range, past the red sugar lands between them and the sea, to the highlands behind Cairns, we may watch the dawn light catching the breakers along 1500 kilometres of the Great Barrier Reef. We will take in flat cays, palm-girt and white-fringed reefs, and pools forming brilliant patterns . . . and the tall continental islands inshore, like the Whitsunday Group, and Hinchinbrook, with their jungled peaks rising from casuarina-fringed beaches, lovely as any morning in the heart of man. Of the Hinchinbrook Passage, the famous British anatomist and zoologist, Professor Wood Jones, is claimed to have said, 'It would be worth considering if the Federal Authorities could make it possible that the entire population of Australia should make an annual pilgrimage of the Hinchinbrook Pass.'[25]

We shall catch the gleam of several considerable waterfalls in the northern Great Divide, and note innumerable striking features of the north-eastern fringe of Australia. Cities, townships, farms, forests, seashore, mountains, islands and coral reefs, and the wide Pacific itself, all follow the direction of the Great Divide. The light leaps the mountains and warms the western plains, from the Brigalow to the Mallee.[26]

In the first hour of Australian noons, the sun crosses the meridians of all the eastern capitals from Brisbane to Adelaide; it crosses the Great Divide, from the broad backs of hills where perhaps the winter snows still lie in the south, to those clad in the rainforest jungles north of Townsville, and, gradually, the greens of the coast and ranges become the cloud-shadowed, inconstant colours, fawn and green and red according to the season, of the sheep- and cattle-lands beyond. It is a tremendous transition, this hour's movement of the sun that, in its sweep, lights the city worker bustling up Martin Place or Wickham Terrace, and the full-blooded Aborigines of the plains. (There are still some 45 000 Aborigines in the State of Queensland alone, including probably 30 000 with one or more non-Aboriginal ancestors. The problem of definition is considerable, though increasing numbers claim the status that the Aborigines, as such, have gained.)

In that first hour the sun embraces many of the largest sheep and cattle stations, areas grazing the majority of Australia's 25 million beef and dairy cattle and her 150 million sheep;[27] the same warm benediction finds the shyer marsupial creatures of the bush, plain, and desert, and the other highly specialised animal life so much of which is unique. This wide view can give no more than the great tonal changes, the living transitions . . . the broad sweeping strokes of the canvas whose detail had been examined first with astonishment, blending fascination with horror, then with the growing detachment of security, and finally with the love of the generations for whom it became the familiar texture of home.

The capital cities give way inland to the bush towns . . . noon in Canberra is half an hour from Broken Hill; it is noon where long roads meet in Cloncurry, noon along the famous, arid Birdsville Track, before it is midday in Adelaide. Almost imperceptibly the land changes from green to tawny, from beige to cinnabar, as the bush gives way to the Mallee, and the Mallee to the Mulga;[28] only in the far north does a broad band of heavy vegetation follow the coast. The river system of the Murray, stretching away up to Queensland via the Darling and the Warrego, up the Lachlan, through the irrigation lands of the Murrumbidgee, nourished in the south by the Victorian tributaries fed from the alps, gleams brightly, the silver veins of a continent. But below, also, is the Lake Eyre Basin, the desolation that is the dead finish of the less determinate western rivers—the Barcoo and the Cooper, the Diamantina and the Georgina. Occasionally they may flow, kilometres wide, down over the plains; and Lake Eyre may become, for a few seasons, a vast stretch of salt water; but in a year or two it has all evaporated, leaving a sad expanse of gleaming salt.

For nearly an hour the noon sun dwells above the Great Australian Bight, on the old sea-bed that is the Nullarbor,[29] on the red quietness of the central plains and mountains that occupy 1·25 million square kilometres, on the Northern Territory, from Alice Springs to Darwin; from the Musgrave Ranges, over the desert tors, Ayers Rock and Mt Olga, beyond the MacDonnells, up to the cattle country of Wave Hill, Victoria River, the Katherine; to Rum Jungle . . . to Arnhem Land, one of the last sanctuaries of stone-age man, and the mining place of radio-active minerals.

Nothing drains to the west from the Barkly Tableland, south of the Gulf of Carpentaria; from the MacDonnell and Musgrave Ranges of the Centre; or from the mountains of South Australia. All these regions should be considered if one is to appreciate Australia's world of difference. The detailed view, for instance, will reveal the quite exceptional topography of Wilpena Pound in the Flinders Ranges, where there is residual evidence of massive pressure from all directions causing a vast elevated depression completely surrounded by the remnants of high ranges. The 'tangled labyrinth of rounded rocky tors, without discernible pattern, in which the compass is the only guide'[30] that comprises the red gneissic Musgraves, with their ghost gums and hidden waters; the memorable Standley Chasm and Palm Valley of the MacDonnells; and the elevated promised land of the ancient Barkly Tableland that drains into the Gulf of Carpentaria and the shadowy, intermittent Georgina: to many of these places I shall refer more fully in the later chapters of this book, but their story will go on for ever. They have passed from the strange to the beautiful; they have entered, both by pen and brush into the familiar 'universe of discourse' of innumerable Australians who have never visited them; and, little by little, they are reaching the limitless sea of creative literature whose waters can support for ever all the craft that may venture there.

And then there comes the enormous West . . . Kalgoorlie, after the railway across the Nullarbor has ruled an almost straight line for 800 kilometres . . . the Kimberleys in the north, Broome and the pearling coast, and in the south-west, the fertile corner of Australia that balances each of the eastern States in turn, and possesses qualities as distinctive as any. Perth is one of Australia's most lovely cities, the capital of a State as large as western Europe.

The first Australian noon sun shines down on Cook's landfall . . . Thursday, 19 April 1770; and her last on that of William Dampier . . . 4 January 1688. Between these lies the continent which each discovered after his fashion, and which neither could possibly know. If the dates had been reversed, the settlement of Australia might conceivably have been advanced by three generations. The space that lay between the two landings, to be slowly revealed through the years, is our World of Difference.

[1] Dampier: *A New Voyage Round the World*, chap. 16. The first edition was published in 1697; that from which the extract is quoted is the edition of 1729.

[2] William Dampier made his first visit (1688) in the pirate ship *Cygnet*; in 1699, as commander of the *Roebuck*, he had intended rounding the Horn, and so reaching the east coast of New Holland. Had he done so, he would probably have anticipated Cook's discoveries; however, the season and other factors conspired against him, and he returned by his original route, round the Cape of Good Hope.

[3] From *Sources of Australian History*, selected and edited by M. Clark (*World's Classics*, O.U.P. 1957); chap. 1, 'The Discoverers,' p. 1. The Dutch discoverers were aboard the *Duyfken*, which sailed down the western coast of what was later named Cape York Peninsula.

[4] In *The Secret Discovery of Australia* (Souvenir Press, 1977), K. G. McIntyre sets out the available material, examines evidence and, by converting the original maps to Mercator's Projection, shows their apparently close resemblance to modern maps of our east coast. George Collingridge's *The First Discovery of Australia and New Guinea* (1895; a 1982 edition being published by Pan Books (Australia) Pty Ltd), with a Foreword by K. G. McIntyre, and an Introduction by Professor O. H. K. Spate, was published first when Australian historians were not prepared to accept his thesis. A further important work on our early history is *The Discovery of Australia—the Charts and Maps of the Navigators and Explorers*, by T. M. Perry (Nelson, 1982).

[5] From the original *Journal* of the first voyage of Captain James Cook, in the National Library, Canberra.

[6] The phrase, I think, was Flinders', but typifies the gentle condescension that explorers and navigators of the period often felt towards scientists.

[7] See note 5, above.

[8] From *My Australia*, by M. Barnard Eldershaw (Jarrolds, London), from the chapter, 'Before Dawn.'

[9] The phrase is from the poem, 'My Country,' by Dorothea Mackellar.

[10] Quoted by C. B. Christesen, in *Australian Heritage* (Longmans, Green & Co.).

[11] From 'A Dedication' (Bush Ballads and Galloping Rhymes), by Adam Lindsay Gordon, 1833–1870.

[12] From *Kangaroo*, by D. H. Lawrence (William Heinemann Ltd, 1923), chap. 5.

[13] From *To the Islands*, by Randolph Stow (Macdonald, London, 1958), chap. 3.

[14] Perhaps part of the older Musgrave Ranges. See *The Face of Australia*, by Charles F. Laseron (Angus & Robertson, Sydney, 1953).

[15] Kosciusko, the highest Australian mountain, was named by Count Strzelecki, after his great countryman, in 1840, while the explorer was making a journey south through the mountains to the region he called Gippsland, named for Sir George Gipps, the Governor of N.S.W. (See also chap. 12, note 30.)

[16] The Murray River was named by Captain Charles Sturt, in 1830, after the then English Secretary of State for War. It had previously been named at a higher point by Alexander Hume, and should, perhaps, still rightly bear his name.

[17] Matthew Flinders was searching for a great river mouth, or a strait, to explain the destination of Australian rivers, when he sailed northward up Spencer Gulf in 1802. While he was exploring the head of the gulf, very disappointed that it was not the promised estuary, Robert Brown, the botanist, led a party including the artist, William Westall, into the mountains which Governor Gawler named after Flinders, in 1839.

[18] The Goldfields Water Supply Scheme, an exceedingly bold venture, piping water to Kalgoorlie from the Mundaring Weir, in the Darling Ranges, was completed in 1902. Before its construction, water was sold on the goldfields for anything from 4d to 2s 6d per gallon. C. Y. O'Connor, who directed the construction, had asserted that water could be supplied to Kalgoorlie for 3s 6d per thousand gallons. It is difficult to equate these figures with present-day prices. Even now, in drought, water may sell at cents per litre.

[19] See chap. 5, 'Tasmanian Lakelands.'

[20] From 'We the Lucky Ones', in the *Tasmanian Tramp*—J. S. L. The *South-West Book* (Australian Conservation Foundation, 1978) which quotes the extract, is, as Sir Mark Oliphant writes, a 'remarkable book . . . a compendium of information about Tasmania's South-West'.

[21] The site of Canberra was selected in 1908 for a federal capital, but, as a planned city, it was established swiftly after the first World War. The first meeting of the Commonwealth Parliament to take place in Canberra was that opened in May 1927, by the late King George VI, then Duke of York.

[22] The interesting, and still controversial, design of the Sydney Opera House is mentioned later (chap. 11, note 11).

[23] From 1812, Oxley was Surveyor-General of Lands in N.S.W. His hypothesis of an inland sea was considered feasible for nearly forty years, and it was not finally disproved

until John McDouall Stuart reached the centre of the continent in 1860. The relevant portions of Oxley's journal are given in Kathleen Fitzpatrick's *Australian Explorers* (*World's Classics*, O.U.P., 1958).

[24] The Queensland antarctic beech is closely related, botanically, to the Tasmanian *Nothofagus cunninghamii*, and, with species in Tierra del Fuego, they are considered to have had a common origin in time, hence the attributive 'antarctic.'

[25] Professor Frederic Wood Jones (1879–1954), F.R.S., held the Chairs of Anatomy, first in Adelaide and later in Melbourne. His broad interests included, especially, sea birds and the Australian Aborigines.

[26] The 'Brigalow' is the name given to large areas of the Queensland plains with their growth of a bushy acacia, brigalow (*A. harpophylla*). The 'Mallee' is an area and the common name of several species of bushy eucalypt; the 'Mulga' covers the areas of growth associated with an acacia (*A. aneura*).

[27] The estimated numbers of cattle, sheep and pigs in Australia in 1981 were, respectively, 25 170 000, 133 396 000, and 2 427 000— *Year Book, No. 66.* The cattle had almost doubled in numbers over forty years, while the sheep remained fairly constant.

[28] See note 26, above.

[29] Nullarbor, meaning 'no trees,' not an Aboriginal name.

[30] Charles F. Laseron: *The Face of Australia* (Angus & Robertson, Sydney, 1953).

CHAPTER 2

Cliffs, Coasts, and Islands

Nor, of the land alone, shall poems be fashioned:
Wherever racing breakers leap and fall,
Her seamen from Cape Everard to Leeuwin,
By north and south will net the ocean voices,
Enmeshed like silver fishes in the haul. . . .
—from WIDE HOMELAND

IN THE ARTS AND LITERATURE, the moving sea has been presented as a sentient power, moody and capricious; or as an emotionless, lifeless force in unheeding nature. Yet, because man is part of nature, he will always find in the sea a symbol of his own energy. Possessing from the beginning the most powerful and constant of all visible movements, its work in building and shaping the earth's surface is generally apparent, even in parts of Australia from which it receded hundreds of millions of years ago. I may look up from my writing to the tawny Barrabool Hills formed of rocks laid down more than a hundred million years ago by the Jurassic seas; these hills still contain plentiful fossil evidence of the life of those ancient waters.

The shore-line is a changing frontier. In a human lifetime, though the dunes may advance, a cliff-edge crumble, a beach vary, a tide reach a level unknown in memory, the sum of change is minute. The coast reveals the grand strategy in geological time, a chronology that may be conceived but not fully comprehended by man.

Rivers and glaciers have worn down mountains to provide the ocean's bed, and always the sea has made it smooth and enriched it with shells, and hidden between its successive sheets the still recognisable remains of marine creatures. Yet, in turn, the ocean's beds have been raised and drained, making new coastlines that challenge the waves to seek reclamation. The cliffs, such as those bounding hundreds of kilometres of the Great Australian Bight, reveal the ancient sediments, always with their irrefutable time scale. The limestones of the Nullarbor Plain have changed little since they emerged from the sea that covered them in Tertiary times. Deep below the surface of the plain the strata have provided channels of drainage to the Bight, in many places allowing the formation of the great caverns, which today are among the many attractions of this intriguing region.[1]

In other places, the sea has invaded the land and reached the hills that are now its capes and headlands. Some of these, and many of our loveliest islands, are of granite, rock formed deep below the surface of the earth, and subsequently denuded by weather and time. Wilsons Promontory, the southern cornerstone of Australia, and the islands of Bass Strait exemplify these formations, but they occur as notably in places ranging from Hinchinbrook Island in North Queensland to the Archipelago of the Recherche off the south coast of Western Australia. Other promontories and islands reveal

24

volcanic rocks, reminders that the fiery girdle of the Pacific once held a more westerly perimeter.

Most romantic and, for many, most lovely are the coral coasts—the reefs, cays, and atolls of the north and west. Their formation is also associated with changing sea-levels,[2] for the foundations of the reefs frequently lie at depths too great for coral growth. The slow rise of sea-levels has been matched by that of the living reefs. If the unity of the entire ocean adds a common element of romance to all seashores, for the scientist it provides invaluable evidence of correlation.

Australia's coastline varies in height, substance, and character; it is unique in being breached by no large, navigable rivers—a circumstance that led to the most persistent theories of inland seas.[3] The world map emphasises the relatively smooth, unbroken boundaries of Australia, and one may easily envisage both the long ocean beaches which have made surf-riding a national summer pastime, and such high continuous cliffs as bound the greater part of the south coast. Less apparent on the map are the shallow drowned valleys such as Sydney Harbour, Port Phillip Bay, and King George Sound, providing protected waters for yachtsmen and hundreds of kilometres of tranquil seaside for family holidays.

Top left: Searching for a landing space, Rodondo Island, 1947. *Bottom left:* Scrambling up the rocks of Rodondo Island. *Top right:* Rodondo Island seen from the air, 1947. *Bottom right:* The group departs from Rodondo Island

Some of my happiest adventures have been on the crags and islands of the Australian coast. It would be impossible, I think, to confuse one's memories with those of the margins of other oceans, yet, recalling any of a hundred occasions, I find there is a universal quality that links all contacts with the sea. Mountains, also, tend to be reminiscent of a delight common to all high places of rock, or ice and sky.

Some years ago, I fulfilled a minor ambition by landing on Rodondo Island, a steep granite pyramid in Bass Strait, just south of Wilsons Promontory.

As I climbed up the rough stone to a place flat enough to support a tent, I could easily have been scrambling on a buttress of the Cornish cliffs, yet, just where the hand found its next hold, instead of tufted thrift, there quivered a sunlit everlasting flower, as unmistakably different as the melaleucas on the cliff-top were from oaks or beeches. The cry of the gull wheeling round my head was also different, as though its accents had been modified by innumerable successive changes of latitude. But, by and large, there is not much difference between the atmosphere of a sun-warmed beach in the Mediterranean, anywhere from Gibraltar to the Bosphorus, and one at Mordialloc or Cottesloe . . . except for the voice of birds and people. The beach sands of Australia are mostly superior to those of the Riviera.

Australia is the only continent that may be fairly easily circumnavigated. Unfortunately, few coastal vessels now provide opportunities for this. To list the interests of such an itinerary would be a lengthy task. The low, yet rugged, limestone coast of Western Australia is as fascinating as the granite and gneissic formations of the extreme south-west; the stratified cliffs of the Bight, matched by the sandstone edge of western Victoria, provide the impressive ramparts of a continent. Harder sandstones of the east coast, such as those forming the Heads of Sydney Harbour, or those facing the Timor Sea in the far north-west, show further variations on this theme. Columnar basalt and dolerite make another characteristic and forbidding definition of

Left: Collecting saltwater from the sea, 60 metres below the camp on Rodondo Island. *Top right:* The steep cliffs of Rodondo Island, a granite island in Bass Strait. *Bottom right:* Rodondo Island, as seen from Wilsons Promontory

26

some parts of the Australian coast, notably in the Point Danger and Fingal region near the Queensland border, and along the southern part of the Tasman Peninsula, and at Cape Raoul.

The Tasmanian cliffs of columnar dolerite, in places 180 metres high, mark a sunken coast. The same sheet of volcanic rock may be linked with the dolerites of Tasmania's high mountains of the northern tableland. An ultimate contrast is presented by the low, mangrove coasts of northern Australia. No State lacks sandy coasts, dunes, and ocean beaches, and plentiful safe and sheltered sands for children.

Where might one start, and where finish, along a coast which no lifetime could exhaust of interest; which, for everyone, holds a separate series of delight and interest? A hundred volumes would be needed to list all the haunts which might be chosen. Rather than generalise in terms of quality, it is better, I think, to be selective, knowing that one's choice is paralleled by innumerable rival delights. The illustrations of this book will, for many, extend in time and space beyond their margins.

All the scenes mentioned or depicted have been transmuted from the unfamiliar, inhospitable, and sometimes frightening barriers that confronted the early explorers—Dampier, Cook, Flinders, Eyre—who looked inward upon an unknown continent, to places of majesty, beauty, and tranquillity, reached by roads from prosperous cities and a flourishing inland. A love of islands would influence my choice. Islands and peninsulas . . . where the sea woos the land. But, even so, it is difficult to choose between, say, South Australia's Kangaroo Island—with the glories of Flinders Chase, the wonderful granite scenery of the Remarkables,[4] and of the great capes—and the Archipelago of the Recherche, off the south-western coast of Western Australia—through which I once sailed 1600 kilometres, landing on many beautiful and desolate islands. In Australia we are very fortunate in possessing so much that is natural and unspoilt. It is easy to find untrodden coves and beaches anywhere from the headlands and islands near Port Stephens, in New South Wales, all the way to the coral beaches of the Abrolhos Islands of Western Australia, several thousand kilometres round the coast, either way.

Ultimately, I think, I would decide in favour of the great granite headlands and sequestered coves of Wilsons Promontory which I explored as a boy, places which led to endless adventures, whose echoes I have found in many parts of the world. Yet, if I am to start in the south, then, perhaps more logically, I shall first revisit the south-eastern coast of Tasmania, a dramatic cross-section of time itself. And then, in the other chapter in which I speak of the sea, I shall return to Queensland's tropical Hinchinbrook Island, and to the pure coral of the Barrier Reef islands. These four facets may serve as samples of our coasts and islands.

South of the narrow Eaglehawk Neck, joining the Tasman and Forrestier Peninsulas, you may see a hundred prehistoric sea-floors upraised, revealed clearly in layer after layer of the cliffs. There, today's ocean thunders in from the south, undermining and blasting what once lay in its dark, still depths. And there you may consider how these grim places have been matched in briefer time by human events, and claimed by our literature.

Between 200 and 300 millions of years ago, in the Permian Period when the horizontal rocks of the Tasman Peninsula were formed beneath the invading sea, Australia was probably already defined as a continent. Vast ice-sheets were formed over many parts of the land, especially in the east, and sinking of the earth's crust allowed the sea to cover areas that had not been submerged for millions of years. Glacial beds, containing rock debris of distant origin, are clearly visible in north-western Tasmania, where, also, older rocks show scars left by the abrading ice. Today, less than 3500 kilometres to the south, a similar ice-cap bounds this same ocean. I stand on the cliffs and, despite the clamour of the contemporary sea, find my mind trying to comprehend the 'vast eternity' that lies in past and future; that may contain and create these buff and grey strata, and perhaps dissolve them completely away.

The first time I visited the Tasman Peninsula, I was alone on a day of storm, when the fascination of spray-filled abysses, roaring and booming like Judgement Day, almost overcame my awe. Here was the power of the southern sea pitting its strength against the bedded rocks of the world; and an observer could so easily be drawn into the conflict . . . on through the hard, mad spray . . . down a steep place into the pulsing sea. Twice more I came to these places with friends, on clean, rollicking days, when the sunlight ruled lines along the walls of the Blowhole, and even irradiated the surge which raced in under Tasman's Arch. But, on a summer's day, when you can find a seat that is warm, surrounded by scented and secure scrub, you may yet find yourself pressing against the rock, and clutching the heath, as a force equal to several thousands tonnes' weight seems to shake the earth.

The action of a breaker crashing on an open beach is comprehensible (though it may exert a force of 30 tonnes to the square metre!). In the Blowhole, near Pirate's Bay, a wave's enormous force is confined and accelerated, so that it not only mounts vertically, as in a huge kettle about to boil over, but defeats gravity altogether, and flings itself high in the air. Though you are amazed, somehow you share the exultation of the striking sea, rising as though it would overflow the earth. It is the horrible ebbing that appals most, the sobbing withdrawal, the terrible falling of the water, that leaves emptiness and the imagination to race in pursuit, knowing that they will be met halfway in the darkness by the inescapable surge.

Tasman's Arch is sublime as a rock-form, a natural bridge of hard strata usually remaining clear of the invading seas which, nevertheless, will eventually demolish it. Because its shape is more easily seen, it is less intimidating than the Blowhole, which is basically of the same form. Charles Barrett, a great lover of Tasmania, considered that the description of Tasman's Arch by Robert Johnston, the geologist, was 'unlikely ever to be bettered.'[5]

'It is a fearful sight,' he writes, 'to look down nearly two hundred feet into boiling cauldrons at Tasman's Arch, which is situated some considerable distance inland on a heathy slope, rising seaward, clothed with shrubs and trees, and giving no indication to the traveller, from the landward side of the neighbourhood of the great open sea beyond. On peering down over the giddy rim of this inland chasm, a giant arch is seen at a lower level, composed of the mudstone beds, fully one hundred and sixty feet[6] in height, disclosing a monster tunnel communicating with the open sea . . .'

A much earlier description of the remarkable natural features of Tasman's Peninsula was provided by Anthony Trollope, the famous novelist who visited the area more than ninety years ago.[7] After discussing the convict settlement which at that time was the only reason for habitation on the peninsula, he writes:

> Then we went farther on, riding our horses where it was practicable to ride, and visited two wonders of the place—the Blow-Hole and Tasman's Arch. The Blow-Hole . . . did not puff nor blow when I was there; but we were enabled by the quiescence of the sea to crawl about among the rocks, and enjoyed ourselves more than we should have done had the monster been in full play. Tasman's Arch, a mile farther on, is certainly the grandest piece of rock construction I ever saw. The sea has made its way in through the rocks, forming a large pool or hole, some fifty yards from the outer cliffs, the descent into which is perpendicular all round; and over the aperture stretches an immense

natural arch, the supports or side pillars of which are perpendicular. Very few even now visit Tasman's Arch; but when the convict establishment at Port Arthur comes to an end, as come to an end I think it must, no one will ever see the place. Nevertheless it is well worth seeing, as may probably be said of many glories of the earth which are altogether hidden from human eyes.

What would Trollope think today? The thousands who visit Tasman's Peninsula each year will certainly not limit their itinerary to the natural wonders of Eaglehawk Neck and Pirate's Bay. Twenty kilometres down the road is Port Arthur and the ruins of the penal settlement from which even a sunny day and a century's growth of soft deciduous trees cannot quite dispel a feeling of horror. In the brutal days of lashings, starvation, and solitary confinement, fierce dogs guarded the Eaglehawk Neck, and the chances of a prisoner's escape were so small that Governor Arthur called the peninsula 'nature's natural penitentiary.' It is almost a hundred years since Marcus Clarke's classic, *For the Term of His Natural Life*, was published. Two of the most exciting chapters of the novel are devoted to the perilous escape of John Rex, to whom Clarke gives unexpected sanctuary on the brink of terror. Rex, racing over the dangerous headlands, is pursued through the darkness by guards and dogs.

> The darkness had increased with the gale. The wind ravaging the hollow heaven, had spread between the lightnings and the sea an impenetrable curtain of black cloud. . . . The shrieking which he had heard a few moments ago had ceased, but every now and then dull but immense shocks, as of some mighty bird flapping the cliff with monstrous wings, reverberated around him, and shook the ground where he stood. He looked towards the ocean, and a tall misty Form—white against the all pervading blackness—beckoned and bowed to him. He saw it distinctly for an instant, and then, with an awful shriek, as of wrathful despair, it sank and vanished. Maddened with a terror he could not define, the hunted man turned to meet the material peril that was close at hand. . . .

The story then tells of the encounter with the dog; of how Rex flung it off and advanced:

> . . . the terror at his heels drove him on. . . . The column disappeared; and in a lull of wind, uprose from the place where it had been, such a hideous medley of shrieks, laughter, and exultant wrath, that John Rex paused in horror. Too late. The ground gave way—it seemed—beneath his feet. He was falling—clutching, in vain, at rocks, shrubs, and grass. The cloud-curtain lifted, and by the lightning that leaped and played about the ocean, John Rex found an explanation of his terrors, more terrible than they themselves had been. . . . Suddenly the bottom of the abyss seemed to advance to meet him; or, rather, the black throat of the chasm belched a volume of leaping, curling water, which mounted to drown him. Was it fancy that showed him, on the surface of the rising column, the mangled carcase of the dog?

It is not possible to match the fictional and actual terrains, and there are other coastal features that may have entered into Clarke's composite picture; but, as the inspirational source of the scenes so vividly described, the Blowhole and Tasman's Arch are precise.[8]

Close to Eaglehawk Neck, at sea-level, near the northern end of Pirate's Bay, a strange fragment of an old ocean floor is revealed; the sediments formerly overlying it have been carried off by the sea. Much of the horizontal surface is criss-crossed by intriguing grooves, the majority set precisely at right angles. These have been produced perpendicularly to the plane of the original bedding, by ancient stresses in tension or torsion, or by contraction.

Left: Tessellated pavement on Tasman Peninsula, southern Tasmania.
Bottom left: The narrow isthmus of land at Eagle-hawk Neck, Tasmania.
Bottom right: The famous Tasman Arch at Eagle-hawk Neck

One of the many blowholes
in the cliffs of the Tasman
Peninsula, Tasmania

Port Arthur, a penal settlement on the southern edge
of the Tasman Peninsula.
Noted for its brutality to
convicts, it is now a
mellow ruin and a popular
tourist attraction

The resultant cracks have been filled with iron-bearing natural cements somewhat softer than the bed-rock itself. Scoured out by the sea, these bear a remarkable resemblance to masonry. The effect is heightened, literally, as the varying hardness of successive strata allows differential wearing, and gives depth to the structure. Well named the Tessellated Pavement, this feature demonstrates the same sort of action, on a small scale, as that which has created the other natural wonders of Tasman's Peninsula.

'That a man has written a book of travels in Montenegro, is no reason why he should never have been to Richmond . . .' Nor, indeed, still holding to the philosophy of R.L.S., why he should not possess as much delight in the familiar hills and streams of his own country as in those of strange foreign lands. Wherever I have travelled, in the Old world or the New—and in that ageless *terra nullius*, Antarctica—it has always been the more buoyantly for the hope that I should return to the places of boyhood, none better known or loved than Wilsons Promontory.

Truly a seaward extension of mountains, with further island outriders between the mainland and Tasmania, the promontory was discovered by George Bass, in 1798, during his memorable *Tom Thumb* voyage of exploration, of which Matthew Flinders subsequently wrote with unstinted praise: 'A voyage expressly undertaken for discovery in an open boat, and in which six hundred miles of coast, mostly in a boisterous climate, was explored, has not, perhaps, its equal in the annals of maritime history.'[9]

Bass, having sailed down the coast of New South Wales, adding to Cook's discoveries, followed 'the low, level and sandy coast' of the Ninety-Mile Beach early in January, then continued into the heavy sou'-westerly swell far enough to discover the existence of a strait between the mainland and Van Diemen's Land. He thought the high granite promontory behind which he sheltered must be the land sighted by Tobias Furneaux,[10] Cook's Second-in-Command during his second, circum-polar, voyage, but Flinders knew this could not be so, and subsequently recommended that Governor Hunter call it 'Wilsons Promontory.'[11]

Top: George Bass, explorer of the South Coast of New South Wales and who circumnavigated Van Diemen's Land. *Centre:* Matthew Flinders, friend and companion to Bass, is noted for his circum-navigation of Australia 1801–03

Matthew Flinders gives a characteristically succinct description:

> From Jan. 26 to Feb. 1,[12] Mr Bass was detained by eastern gales from proceeding on his return. The boat lay in *Sealers' Cove*, whilst he occupied the time in examining Wilson's Promontory. The height of this vast cape, though not such as would be considered extraordinary by seamen, is yet strikingly so from being contrasted with the low, sandy land behind it; and the firmness and durability of its structure make it worthy of being, what there was reason to believe it, the boundary point of a large strait, and a corner stone to the new continent. It is a lofty mass of hard granite, of about twenty miles long, by six to fourteen in breadth . . . Looking from the top of the promontory to the northward, there is seen a single ridge of mountains, which comes down, out of the interior country, in a southern direction of the promontory; but slopes off gradually to a termination . . . it leaves a space of twelve or sixteen miles of low, sandy land between them. This low land is nearly intersected by a considerable lagoon on the west, and a large shoal bay, named *Corner Inlet*, on the east side; and it seems probable that this insulated mass of granite has been entirely surrounded by the sea at no very distant period of time.

Towards the end of 1800, Lt Grant, in the *Lady Nelson*, passed through the strait for the first time from the west, and, in February 1802, Lt Murray, in the same vessel, entered Port Phillip Bay, and took possession of the region 'in the name of his sacred Majesty George the Third.' The flag—used for the first time in a newly discovered place in the British Dominions—was the Union Jack, commemorating the union of Great Britain and Ireland.

Top: The high surf beaches of the southern coast are used increasingly for surfing championships. This is Johanna Beach, near Cape Otway, Victoria. *Centre left:* The mouth of Roaring Meg Creek, a vigorous stream on the west coast of Wilsons Promontory. *Centre right:* The South Gippsland Hills. Once heavily timbered, the hills have become an area of extensive dairying. *Bottom left:* The Mussolini Rocks, on the northern slopes of Mount Boulder, Wilsons Promontory. *Bottom right:* Lichen-covered rocks at Sealers Cove, Wilsons Promontory

Little has changed along the east coast of Wilsons Promontory since the days of Bass, Flinders, Grant, and Murray. Recently, I repeated, after a quarter of a century, one of the old courses of my boyhood, a tough hike down the length of the 'prom,' landing from a fishing boat near Mt Singapore and traversing, from Corner Inlet, the spiky flanks of Mt Hunter and the everglades below, to the coast on the east; thence, by the beaches, coves, and headlands, to the lighthouse on one of the most southerly points, with a homing *via* the Tidal River. The route touched or intersected twenty former journeys, many through scrubs trackless to this day. Each beach and bay, each ridge and tor, each peaty stream, even the gulf of racing air separating me from the delectable granite islands of Bass Strait, seemed to echo the wit and laughter of those who were my companions through the years.

In older days we usually took a train to Fish Creek or Foster, and walked 80 kilometres by beach and bush to the southernmost tip of Australia; once we walked all the way from Korumburra. So today's South Gippsland Highway whirls me past remembered campfires encircled by the white, ring-barked gums which for so long maintained a watch over the increasing herds. There are few of the old giants left now. In fact, over the years the whole face of South Gippsland has been very much changed; though digressions are still tempting in this country, where bald hills may seem more mysterious than the tunnelled bush.

The motor road to the Tidal River holiday camp makes a judgement by default of much lovely moorland country beyond the Hoddle Hills and Yanakie. Though it made a pretty hard first day, and we often enough cursed the stony way between Fish Creek and Shallow Inlet, we found joy in its clothing of bright heath, orchids, and dwarf banksia, in its marshlands, its strange, slow estuaries and warm dunes. Later, when we were longer of purse and shorter of time, we had to become more selective of our delights, and then we drove an upright grand 'A' Model Ford to the Darby River. Our best route lay along the firm beach sands to the west of the isthmus, though it often meant waiting three hours for the tide.

Anyway, at the Inlet, once we had quietened the immense Irish wolfhounds which seemed as resentful of company as their masters were glad, the Winchesters made waiting no hardship. The old fishermen had great eyes for beauty, and imaginations that fitted their desolation of sand, sea, and abrupt tussock grass. They collected and sold nautilus shells, and surged us through and through with tales of Johnny Nabtoes, the monster shark of Shallow Inlet. I never saw a shark in these waters but, for the rest of my life, as a result of the gleam in old George's eye, I have regarded them as the natural habitat of the most voracious species.

Of the promontory, more than of most places recurrent in my wandering years, I have found that to write of the past is to write of the present. On the southern slopes of the broad valley crossing to Waterloo Bay stand the huge Mussolini Rocks—one like an Easter Island effigy of the dictator—christened long before their namesake was discredited. The mouth of Roaring Meg, on the west coast, has not changed a boulder since I stood there agog with discovery of the big granite faces, the leaping stream in the ravine, and the little beach . . . ten thousand days ago. Further along the coastal uplands trending east, the clutching hakea and low she-oak still spread out from the clean little forests of gum, and are still as suddenly intersected by the route to the lighthouse. The old tracks, edging crabwise in the granite gravel as successive lines were deeply eroded, may still be found, but the limited access road, for supplies, maintenance, fire control, and emergencies, has become the usual walking route.

There is still an air of expectancy about that last kilometre round the flanks of South Peak. At dusk one thinks of vanished tribes and of unwritten myths; every great standing stone seems a relic of ancient hillside dolmens. It is obvious that the plateau must soon end. Two small near-by capes possess half a minute more latitude: these are the most southerly knuckles of the Australian mainland. Glimpses of the sea, and of the whale-back islands, bring them tantalisingly close, until it seems that the coast must fall away as an immense cliff. Then comes the astonishing view of the final yellow-stone tongue a hundred metres below, frothed with pale surf, and bearing the old white tower and clustered keepers' houses. The settlement was established in 1859.

At Refuge Cove, which is a tough scramble round the coast from the lighthouse, the bent banksia still strains out over the high tide. A conical island to the south is Rodondo, above whose steep cliffs, under a giant melaleuca, there still waits a low wall of stones to shelter a high campfire.[13]

When, the other day, we pressed through the dense paperbark swamp below Mt Hunter, the trees so close that every metre was a vertical vice to grip our packs, the air so heavy with the exciting smell of decay that it pervaded all other impressions, I thought of the commandos who were trained there for Pacific service in the second World War. I wondered how many others had tasted the torments of Chinaman's Swamp in the intervening years. It was thought by some of Spencer Chapman's men that nothing of the tropical jungles ever compared with the swamp. It is a viewless, clutching place, where faith is needed that the eastern beaches really lie beyond; yet I like it, this little end-of-the-world where, outside my own team, I have never met a fellow adventurer. If you are going that way, you may prefer to stick to the spurs of Mt Hunter; though the way is longer, it probably costs less in discomfort and uncertainty.

Not all promontory ridges provide such easy going as they might appear to offer from a distance. Only a few kilometres south-west of Hunter is the Vereker Ridge which we followed once to the summit of Mt Latrobe.[14] In that youthful tussle with a mountain, we frequently took turns at cutting a tunnel through the woven scrub and wire-grass. It was a memorably slow journey — 11 kilometres in five days! The first three were waterless except for the yield of occasional patches of damp moss. An encounter with post-bushfire regrowth ended in a cloudy deluge that washed out the world beyond our bleak ridge. After this, the warm chalet at the Darby River seemed doubly attractive. This was later destroyed by fire, and never rebuilt; but of course the amenities of Tidal River are now available. Necessarily so, today's hikers through the beautiful, accessible areas are constrained to keep to narrow, well-formed tracks, so that the wilderness they seek, and the balanced ecology of flora and fauna, may be preserved.

On one memorable visit to Wilsons Promontory, we butted through ninety minutes of contrary wind and tide to a small beach below Mt Singapore. Somewhere here, according to local report, there were once a few fishermen's huts and even a public house. Only a few broken bricks remain of the settlement. We crossed the tip of the north-eastern cape that runs out towards Snake Island and almost encloses Corner Inlet, then gained the sands of an unnamed beach, and made camp.

For the next few days we kept to the coast as much as possible until we reached Sealers' Cove — where Surgeon Bass's boat lay sheltering in 1798. The place hasn't changed. There are two main beaches, the Three Mile and the Five Mile, that help the traveller on his way to Sealers' Cove. They are separated by 5 kilometres of small rocky bluffs jutting from high moorland. Between the southern end of the longer beach and Sealers' Cove is a massive hill, 520 metres high and densely forested. It falls abruptly to the sea on a front of between 5 and 6 kilometres where immense rocks provide a sufficiently hard alternative route.

This page and facing page: Wilsons Promontory
Top left: Looking into the rising sun over Corner Inlet at Foley's Beach. *Top right:* Norman Bay, looking north from the Oberon Saddle on the western coast of the promontory. *Bottom left:* The Tidal River area is a popular place to camp.

Facing page, top left: Even a thistle head becomes a thing of beauty when it houses a cobweb jewelled by morning dew. *Top right:* Sealers Cove on the east coast. The stream now entering the cove at the southern end was diverted by the build-up of beach sands to run parallel with the beach. *Centre left:* Crested Terns at Sealers Cove. *Centre right:* The beautiful Refuge Cove on the eastern coast. Almost landlocked, it is a memorable anchorage for small craft with its clean beach backed by green forest. *Bottom left:* Black-tailed Wallaby at Sealers Cove. *Bottom right:* A further view of Refuge Cove

The attractions of this part of the promontory are manifold, especially in clear, sunny weather. The beaches are seldom visited; other than members of my own parties, I recall meeting few on the broad sands of the Five Mile. They are places to forget time, where you may rest your pack and absorb sunshine and scenery, run naked in the surf, and feel that you own the Pacific. It is folly not to linger. All the coves and beaches of the promontory appear much shorter than they are. The boulders of the headlands show up clearly end to end, deceiving the eye and luring you on. No philosopher, however, hurries over a promontory beach or grows impatient of its length. Each beach has its own texture and colour; the swift arcs from the breakers race up the shelving sands, depositing bright shells, snatching at footprints and weaving inestimable patterns and, for sustained delight, a destination continues to recede with one's approach.

Movement on headlands requires care, but the granite co-operates with planned paces, providing a better grip than any other rock. You may leap ravines where successive waves impound the complaining surf, press through narrow gaps between monoliths, and find cavernous ways between boulders so ponderous that they engender formless fears, apprehensions as old as the night. Progress is a continuity of problems and solutions with penalty scores against mere strength. The ups and downs of a day aggregate hundreds of metres and, with a pack adding 15 to 20 kilograms to one's weight, a pause is never more appreciated. Every now and then special problems are solved, and one rests in satisfaction. There are a few places, especially between the Five Mile and Sealers' Cove, where the shortest routes require confidence and good balance, where a slip leads straight into turbulent deep water. Occasionally a light rope line is worth its weight for sustaining packs or confidence.

It is extraordinary how one retains memories of these gymnastic journeys. I have come upon a rock which I have not consciously thought of for ten years and, in the meeting, known instant recognition. Here we rested on just such a day as this . . .

My preference for a camping site is on the edge of a promontory bluff. There is frequently a tidal estuary at each end of a beach, and usually a few crystal tributaries trickle from the headland a little upstream; in all cases good drinking water is reasonably close.[15] All the beaches of Wilsons Promontory are backed by bush, and often there is ample driftwood to use as supplementary fuel. On some nights during this last hike, when our tents stood firmly under the honeysuckle[16] trees, and we had cooked our food, we refuelled bright fires with odd spars and ribs and staves found on the beach. We undressed and rolled in the black water, feeling the salt in our scratches. Then we ran back to the fire of driftwood, and dressed by flames that held wisps of orange and green. For one night, some of us camped in a tiny embrasure of the cliffs between two beaches. It was an exciting place for a fine night's bivouac, with a jet of sweet water at the end of a torch-lit scramble, in a minute jungle where, since its beginning, only the animals had come to drink. We discovered flat places to spread sleeping bags, and slept warmly amid huge firelit rocks above the sea.

There is a certain quality in Australian camping that I have never found elsewhere. The bush above the lonely bays and beaches along the east coast of the Promontory provides a special essence of delight, always worth discovering or re-finding.

I experience a particular joy known only in contemplating a combination of granite cliffs and she-oak trees facing a sunrise over the sea. The trees grow miraculously from clefts in the rocks, and drop their soft brown needles to form mats. The light is Eden-fresh and clear, revealing the texture of both rock and ancient trees: long sharp shadows, not mellow like those of evening, bar the granite; there is an essence of Australian dawn that is unique, though the setting is reminiscent of some steep Mediterranean coasts. One may sit motionless in contemplation, scanning the glorious sea, and turn to discover a mild-eyed wallaby sharing unafraid the peace of the morning. There is no other time when living creatures are at once so calm and eager.

We spent less than twenty-four hours revisiting the lighthouse settlement[17] and receiving its traditional hospitality. The organisation of the station has changed with the years. As vessels now make their own radio contacts with Australian ports, keepers are no longer required to record passing shipping, nor must they row out weekly, in all weathers, to catch provisions lowered hastily from a wallowing coaster. (In times past, landsmen marvelled to watch the lantern of Headkeeper Hugh Dickson disappear in the troughs of waves, as he sculled out in the darkness before the dawn, to meet the old *Tambar*.) Today, a diesel-powered craft under contract slips across from Port Albert with stores, and there is a road and jeep, instead of the old 'flying-fox,' to hoist them up from the landing. Helicopters, also, are used when necessary in the exchange of personnel.

When, many years ago, the lookout building was blown away in a great gale, its replacement was deemed unnecessary. People who last visited it between the wars miss that polished cabin with the great brass telescope (through which, as a boy, I gazed at inaccessible Rodondo for hours on end) and the neatly furled signal flags, the morse-lamp, and the keeper-on-watch. How the wind roared round that high bridge, thrumming the stout cables that held it to the rock! But still the broad beams from the round white tower sweep 50 kilometres of sea, and patches of light, escaping through the prisms, race effortlessly up and over the rocks and cottages. As they pass, each wind-sculpted stone leaps to vigilance above the southern sea. I do not think the southern road has changed the promontory's essential character. Roads and railway lines through undeveloped areas have the curious property of leaving their margins even less disturbed than when their courses were marked by less definite, pause-on-the-way routes. I was interested to see that, despite the ferocity of wind, there was still considerable vegetation between the buildings and boulders of South-East Point, including some robust blue-gum thickets (*Eucalyptus globulus*) which have always given delight by their winter flowering. The Promontory has its own times and seasons.

When I first knew the Tidal River, it was so tightly gladed with scrub that it seemed preferable to wade through the estuary, or swim at high tide, rather than to attempt an upstream crossing. The present holiday camp, visited annually by thousands, was unimaginable in those days; but it is good to see the delights of Wilsons Promontory so widely shared, and under so prudent an arrangement. To stand on the top of Mt Oberon is to witness how little, really, has been alienated; to walk even as far as Oberon Bay is to realise that a few kilometres of foot-track leave the majority of people behind. The ideal design of a National Park probably includes a one-way, circular access road, and a judicious pattern of footpaths. In the 40 000 hectares of the Wilsons Promontory National Park, more than 600 species of native plants, and eighty-three of birds have been noted.

Today's management of Wilsons Promontory National Park sensitively combines the two great factors which might so easily be mutually inimical — the conservation of its grandeur and ecology and the area's immense popularity. Accommodation at Tidal River, in lodges or at campsites, with all necessary amenities, is excellently maintained. Typical and representative aspects of the promontory are accessible by good walking tracks from the centre, and a splendid museum and educational centre has served hundreds of thousands of visitors since it was opened in 1982.

Top: The lighthouse at Wilsons Promontory on South East Point guides shipping passing through Bass Strait. *Bottom left:* The long beach of Waterloo Bay on the eastern coast. *Bottom right:* The lighthouse was built of local granite on South East Point by convicts in 1859

Top left: The head-like rock on Pillar Point looks out over Leonard Bay to Norman Island, Wilsons Promontory. *Top right:* Many bays along the shores of Wilsons Promontory National Park are popular for either, swimming, fishing, or hiking. *Centre left:* Sealers Cove was once used by sealers in the nineteenth century. *Bottom:* Tidal River flows into Norman Bay on the western coast of Wilsons Promontory

[1] It is probable that successive changes of sea-level have occurred, and that some of the erosion may have been caused by sea water. There has also been much discussion as to whether the formation of the Nullarbor caverns was by the action of vadose or phreatic water, i.e. by seepage of water above the water-table, or by the effects of that below.

[2] An apparent change of sea-level may be caused by the subsidence or elevation of the land surface. Eustatic movements are absolute sea-level changes caused by distant earth movements, or by the accumulation or melting of ice-sheets. Through the latter cause, over millions of years, sea-level variations of several hundred metres have occurred.

[3] Captain Charles Sturt commenced his inland explorations of 1844–46 with the strong conviction 'that the interior was occupied by a sea of greater or lesser extent . . .' After his return he wrote: 'I am still of the opinion that there is more than one sea in the interior of the Australian continent, but such may not be the case.'—*Narrative of an Expedition into Central Australia*, 1849, chap. 1.

[4] The Remarkables are a series of huge granite rocks, fantastically hollowed by weather, on the south coast of Kangaroo Island, not far from Cape de Couédic.

[5] Quoted, *Isle of Mountains* (Cassell & Co. Ltd, 1944).

[6] Approx. 50 metres. Quoted references are usually left unmetricated.

[7] *Australia and New Zealand*, two vols. (Chapman and Hall, London, 1873).

[8] *For the Term of His Natural Life*, first issued in book form, 1874.

[9] Matthew Flinders: *A Voyage to Terra Australis* (London, 1814).

[10] The Furneaux Group, including Flinders I., Cape Barren I., etc., is separated from N.E. Tasmania by the narrow Banks Strait.

[11] 'In compliment to my friend, Thos. Wilson, Esq. of London'—Flinders, Introduction to *Voyages*. There have been other attributions: See article, 'Around Tidal River,' L. H. Smith (*Walkabout*, February 1953).

[12] 26 January is a propitious date in Australia's history. Exactly 171 years earlier, in January 1627, the 'South Coast of the *Great* South Land was accidentally discovered by the ship *Gulde Zeepaard*, outward bound from the Fatherland, for the space of a thousand miles.' Flinders also quotes the Dutch account. On 26 January 1788, Phillip raised the British flag at Sydney.

[13] See 'Rodondo Report' (*Walkabout*, June 1947); also accounts of landing and living on Rodondo Island (*Wild Life*, March and April 1947). The author landed on the island in the previous summer with a small party of boys from Geelong College, and L. P. Greenhill and T. Riddell; the island was occupied for nine days.

[14] 'The Ascent of Mount Latrobe,' an account of this venture, was published in the Melbourne *Argus*, 14 July 1934.

[15] Camping, on the well-known and popular routes, is now confined to suitable sites with water, fuel, and other facilities, and permits to camp must be obtained from the authorities at Tidal River.

[16] Honeysuckle trees: Banksias, see chap. 4. The florets forming the characteristic 'bottlebrush' blooms are, individually, shaped a little like the flowers of honeysuckle.

[17] The Wilsons Promontory Lighthouse, 84 metres above the sea, was built in 1859 on the south-east extremity of the headland facing Bass Strait, after the loss of two vessels, the *Cionnel* and the *Domain*. Before its provision of a warning beacon visible for more than 30 kilometres, the abrupt granite projecting more than 40 kilometres further south than the rest of South Gippsland, was the scene of many wrecks. Cape Otway, 160 kilometres south-west of Melbourne, was even more notorious. There are now well over 200 lighthouses to assist navigation of the Australian coast; about a quarter are manned, the rest automatic. There is a stretch of 1600 kilometres, along the Great Australian Bight, without lights, but shipping passes far to the south of coastal dangers.

CHAPTER 3

Tall Gums and Golden Wattles

Where still the muted, moon-pale ghosts attest,
In silent grief, or dreaming, arms outcast,
An ancient royalty, we shall invest
Our faith with time's proud destiny of trees.

—*from* WIDE HOMELAND

MOST AUSTRALIANS ARE CITY-DWELLERS, separated by walls, roofs, and pavements from sky, weather, natural vegetation, and the uncultivated earth. But no urban population in the world may so easily and freely exchange its city amenities for the pleasures of wild shrublands and forests which, in spite of their wide regional differences, we call everywhere 'the bush.'

Half a day from the city! You may pitch your tent, or draw up your caravan by a clear hill stream overhung by ferns, roll out your bedding, and camp, without cost or permit, among the aromatic gums and wattles. Listen quietly; you will distinguish the clear calls of many native birds, and perhaps you will recognise them, and discover their owners. Be patient and watch carefully: you may see the swift, curling wake of a platypus cut the reflections at the bend of a creek, a sleepy grey koala clamped to the high smooth arms of a gum, or a wallaby, alert for instant flight, peering at you inquiringly over a bank of heath or hop-bush. At night there is life everywhere around you—possums large or small, flying foxes, perhaps a ponderous wombat careless of disturbance, or kangaroos bounding through the undergrowth. Breathe deeply, and to the prevailing scent of the bush, varying with place and season, will be added the subtle flavour of the earth itself.

For the Australian there is a deep satisfaction, an affirmation of values, and an absolution from temporal folly. For the visitor, the attraction may be more subliminal than overt, and he may be very puzzled and think, as D. H. Lawrence did, in strange terms of 'invisible beauty,' perhaps feel something of the atavistic fears and fantasy this old land may still inspire in a sensitive newcomer.

Every kind of bush has its own delight, whether it is dappled by the hot sun filtering through gleaming leaves, or in shadow, cool and sombre, or even in rain or mist. It may be forest, with pale trunks so tall that, in perspective, they form starred rays from every zenith, with a lower storey of sassafras, hazel, and blackwood; or it may be northern 'brush,' casting a green twilight in which elk-horn ferns and cascades of cream and orange tree-orchids make vivid accents on the mossy beeches; or, again, it may be sandy coastal scrubs of banksia, she-oak, melaleuca, and tea-tree, within sounds of the waves. The bush may be dense or open, jungle or parkland, precipitous mountain or level plain; in every region is to be found a distinctive Australian flora.

A knowledge of the subtleties of the bush comes slowly through the years; it is the accumulation of lore rather than learning, received unhurriedly and communicated gently.

Top: River Red Gums on the Murray River at Echuca, Victoria. *Centre left:* Ironbark and Golden Wattle trees on the Victorian goldfields. *Centre right:* A typical fern gully in southern Victoria; this one on Wilsons Promontory

Left: Ferns of southern Victoria. *Facing page:* Tall eucalypts, such as Mountain Ash, produce the high, elongated trunks which are a function of light-seeking growth in dense forest in Victoria and southern New South Wales

'There's not much difference,' the bushman will tell you, 'between a manna gum and a candlebark. I reckon they're easy enough to confuse!' But then he will quietly explain the differences between the two; and never again will you forget.

'Well, generally, the bark at the base goes up higher on the manna,' he will explain, 'and when it's shed, the winter trunk shows grey patches . . . never the warm reds and yellows of the candlebark. Almost as though the trunk gets a touch of the sun! Of course, you can be sure, if you see the stumpy powder blue juvenile leaves: the manna's leaves are always long and narrow.' You may have learnt that 'juvenile' in this context does not cover the young leaves, the new growth of the mature tree, though it does describe the new growth from a lopped or broken branch, or from a dismembered trunk.[1]

'What about the one over there, beyond the peppermint?' you may ask, secretly a little proud, not having sniffed its crushed leaves, that you can refer with assurance to this eucalypt,[2] distinguishing it by the persistent, rather fine-grained bark that covers even the upper limbs and smaller branches.

'Oh, swamp gum, I'd say. Notice the whitish look in the foliage. The leaves have twisted edges and are broader.'[3] For the first time, you notice the whole mass of the tree standing out quite clearly from the higher messmate beyond the stream. Knowledge gives a new richness to the bush. Above the deep green blackwoods and arching tree-ferns, the shimmering, almost opaque swamp gum branches are isolated for ever from the vertically hanging, shining messmate leafage, where the depths are full of shadow. You know the messmate trunk; already you have teased kindling from its soft red fibres, dry enough even after a week's rain.

After a while, your senses are more acute in the bush. The soft, persistent chattering, high above the creek, is separated from the sounds of wind and water. A pair of crimson rosellas scream ecstatically, and swoop marvellously down the invisible airways, finding an extra dimension between the interlacing trees, where the sun catches a million transparent red gum tips.

'Nothing like this, I reckon,' smiles your companion. It could be anywhere. Nothing like the bush anywhere—the wonderful Australian bush that captures the hearts of all who enter its territory of gums and wattles, anywhere between the Darling Range and Cape York; or from southern Tasmania to the Kimberleys. However, in the hearts of men, lonely and insecure, it was not always so.

In the beginning, it was the trees that owned the land. It was with aboriginal trees, not tribes, that the old settlers struggled long and persistently to gain security beyond the landfalls of the First Fleet.[4] For the right to cultivate millions of hectares in the higher rainfall areas of Australia, the battle was fought relentlessly, without quarter, by felling and ringbarking, by grubbing and burning, by every means contesting the ancestral territories of the trees. Now it is we who own the land, but during the long campaign, the trees have also triumphed after their fashion, for now, among the majority of Australians, the old hatred and fear is replaced by a genuine love of them, and, often, a conscious national pride in forms and foliage that are peculiarly our own.

The old vision, eternally seeking and, if necessary, creating, echoes of Europe, had to be clarified by a generation of sensitive Australian artists to whom the gums and wattles, the brittleness of the bush, its infinitely subtle colours, and the essential golden quality of Australian light and distance, were all exciting and wonderful, newly realised, raw material, to be absorbed and recommunicated. A number of fine painters had preceded them in Australia, yet, in the earlier men, vision was separated from the landscape by traditional concepts of ideal forms, by prejudice, and by mental processes

46

that conditioned not only opinions, but the very images of tree-structure and foliage.

> The strictly topographical and scientific interest of the explorers provided the earliest pictures of Australia. Pelsart, the Master of the *Batavia*, and Vlamingh, who had named the Swan River, both left records, written and pictorial, of seventeenth century events. Cook's Sydney Parkinson; Tobin of *The Providence*; William Westall, companion to Matthew Flinders—to mention three only—carried on this work of recording a new continent, and, inasmuch as they all possessed genuine artistic talent, their pictures were not merely documents. The dispassionate scientific approach was most accurate with close botanical and zoological studies; with the troubled natives and the unfamiliar trees, even the most faithful recorder was lost outside his period-vision. Unconsciously, perhaps, he interpreted our trees through preconceived, inborn, oak-and-elm forms, through Gainsborough techniques; and our primitive aboriginals as the morally noble, physically perfect, and socially contented creatures of Jean Jacques Rousseau.[5]

Almost a century of transition followed. Conrad Martens, arriving in Sydney in 1835, and carving for himself a home in the bush north of the harbour, became the first great Australian painter. To study his luminous, romantic landscapes in the fine Sydney collections[6] is to be transported into a picturesque, distant, and half-fanciful world. Martens selected those aspects of form, light, and colour that his mind permitted, and, of these, made gracious pictures, creating of a strange, frightening continent a place that might be loved.

Another considerable painter, William Charles Piguenit, born in Hobart at about the same time as Martens arrived, penetrated far into the bush, and along the rugged ridges of southern Australia, especially of Tasmania. A romantic flavour lingers in his work, but it is beginning to embrace a new idiom.

By the time Louis Buvelot, the distinguished Swiss painter, arrived in 1865, the gum trees no longer needed transmutation in order that they might appeal to civilised man. It is true that Buvelot was very selective in his subjects, but in his canvases there is no covert distaste for the eucalypt, little adaptation of its qualities to make the tree aesthetically acceptable; and there is no nostalgia for old world landscapes. Within a year of Buvelot's death, the youthful Heidelberg School—Tom Roberts, Frederick McCubbin, Arthur Streeton, Charles Conder, and the rest—were exhibiting in Melbourne.

Never again was the Australian bush to be scorned for its native accents: the clean white gum, rising naked and virile from golden clouds of wattle; ancient tree-ferns, verdant and graceful; the giants of the West, jarrah and karri; the beech, myrtle and sassafras, glittering in deep shadow—all spoke, at last, in a language that was not only intelligible, but noble. Whispering casuarinas, banksias, and melaleucas by the sea; red-gum of river and plain; mallee, mulga, myall, and brigalow of the marginal lands; the harsh, ridgy, arid scrubs beloved of blackboy and wattle—all these would gradually reveal an absolute beauty.

In South Australia, Hans Heysen devoted years to the study of eucalypt physiology, expressed the trees' character, and revealed to a receptive people their splendour of contour. His success preluded the 'cult of the gum tree' and, for a time, the twisted, mottled trunks, their fluent strength and pendulous foliage became a somewhat uncontrolled passion. The representations, characteristically, were soon more highly prized than the original; as a friend once rather caustically remarked, 'People all over the suburbs are cutting down their gum trees, and hanging them up on their walls!'

William Dampier, from an engraving of the original oil painting by T. Murray

If the first visitors to Australia were not enthusiastic about trees that differed so markedly from their traditional conceptions of tree-forms and tree-behaviour, at least their distaste was soundly buttressed by economic and practical considerations. There was no machinery, and no power beyond men's muscles, to subdue the trees, to conquer the stubborn grain of their wood to fashion planks and beams. The trees of New South Wales were not proper trees: they were evergreen but sparse of foliage; they shed their bark, and bore no edible fruit; their knotty, hard timber was entirely unresponsive to building needs; their only virtue seemed to be in the gum they exuded.

'They are about the bigness of our large Apple-trees,' Dampier had written of those on the west coast, 'and about the same height: and the Rind is blackish, and somewhat rough. The Leaves are of a dark Colour; the Gum distils out of the Knots or Cracks that are in the Bodies of the Trees.'[7] James Cook, naturally, was familiar with William Dampier's descriptions, and soon found gum trees for himself.

'We found 2 sorts of Gum,' he wrote, 'one sort of which is like Gum Dragon and is the same as I suppose Tasman took for gum lac; it is extracted from the largest tree in the woods. . . . The Woods do not produce any great variety of Trees, there are only 2 or 3 sorts that can be call'd Timber; the largest is the Gum Tree which growes all over the Country, the Wood of this Tree is too hard and ponderous for most common uses.'[8]

Even after the arrival of the First Fleet, the gum of the eucalypt seems to have been its only virtue. When fish and fresh vegetables were in desperately short supply, Phillip wrote:

> In the dysentery, the red gum of the tree which principally abounds on this coast, was found a very powerful remedy. The yellow gum[9] has been discovered to possess the same property, but in an inferior degree.
>
> The tree which yields the former kind of gum is very considerable in size and grows to a great height before it puts out any branches. The red gum is usually compared to that called *sanguis draconis*, but differs from it by being perfectly soluble in water, whereas the other, being more properly a resin, will not dissolve except in spirits of wine. . . . The leaves are long and narrow, not unlike those of a willow.[10]

The name 'gum tree' has struck through the centuries, and been applied as a common generic name to species of eucalypt in which the gum is not at all conspicuous. Certainly, most Australians use the words 'gum tree' without any thought of their original connotation.

To the original settlers, so many of whom were transported from Britain against their will, the strange, inhuman trees that marched towards the distant ranges were by turns passively indifferent and actively malignant. In an unfamiliar race, whether of men or trees, only the dominant characteristics are observed. So there seemed an awful sameness about the trees that crowded round the unhappy, tenuous settlement. Slowly the areas of arable land increased as the forced labour of convict gangs attacked their iron-barked trunks. Long after conscription was only an evil memory, the same dogged battle was fought for many of the farmlands of Australia. The trees occupied the land that seemed best for cultivation, but their heavy trunks resisted the axe and, with the means at his disposal, the settler was unable to convert them into useful timber; the stumps were too numerous for him to remove.

'At Rose Hill,' David Collins wrote, in January 1789, 'the people were principally employed in clearing and cultivating land; but the labour of removing the timber off the ground when cut down, very much retarded the best efforts of the people so employed.'[11]

Facing page: The Karri is a true eucalypt tree, limited to a small area of south-western Western Australia. It is a tall and majestic tree, and when the bark is shed it displays varying colours of orange, yellow, grey, and white, giving rise to its botanical name *Eucalyptus diversicolor*

49

Left: Young eucalypts in the Dandenongs, Victoria. Mountain Ash, *Eucalyptus regnans,* is the most common species. *Facing page top and centre left:* There are endless shades of colour of the cross-polinated Western Australian flowering gums. *Centre right:* Mulga, *Acacia aneura,* is a typical tree of central Australia. *Bottom left:* Fern Gully, Victoria, on the Great Divide. *Bottom right:* Candlebark (Jubilee Lake, Daylesford, Victoria), one of the many smooth-trunked eucalypts which shed their bark constantly to reveal clean, white trunks

'At Sydney,' the same author states, of June 1791, 'the little ground that was in cultivation belonged to individuals; the whole labour of the convicts employed in clearing ground having been exerted at Parramatta . . .'

With the daily floggings and frequent executions, with the food shortages while awaiting relief ships from the other side of the world, with the back-breaking toil, it was little wonder that some of the convicts sought a desperate freedom in the dense, uncooperative bush. Many just disappeared without trace. They entered the forest and found themselves surrounded by indistinguishable, innominate trees; and, however far they penetrated, torn, parched, and fearful, they found that the same terrible trees had pursued them, until they were driven mad. Their final asylum, where their bones rested for ever, were the iron-stone ravines of the hills, beyond which 'an impassable barrier seemed fixed to the westward.'

> It might have been supposed, that the fatal consequence of endeavouring to find in the woods of New South Wales, a place where the means of life could be obtained without labour, had been sufficiently felt by the convicts who had tried it, to have deterred others from rushing into the same error, as they would doubtless acquaint the new comers with the ill success which had attended all their schemes of that nature.[12]

However, some desperate characters continued to attempt concealment, the more daring making forages into the settlement until, inevitably, they were shot down, or recaptured and punished with a savagery reflecting the insecurity of the administration.

It was not, of course, only the vengeful vegetation that troubled the colony. Capricious weather, flies, ants, shallow and poor soil, heathen savages, and homesickness made 'a country and a place so forbidding and so hateful as only to merit execration and curses.'[13] But it is interesting to note that, by 1795, in Governor Hunter's time, along the Hawkesbury, the value of trees as timber was already becoming recognised. '. . . the Governor, among other colonial regulations, thought it necessary to direct, that no timber whatever should be cut down on any ground which was not marked out on either the banks or creeks of that river: and, in order to preserve as much as possible such timber; as might be of use for building or for naval purposes, he ordered the king's mark to be immediately put on all such timber . . .'[14]

The realisation that there were vast open plains in Australia, ranging from useless deserts to lightly timbered and fertile parklands, such as Major Thomas Mitchell, in 1836, called *Australia Felix*, came as the boundaries of the denser bush clothing the foothills of the Great Divide were slowly delineated.

> Nothing, therefore, can be more cheering than to burst at once into an open and delightful country, after having been for some time entangled, perplexed, and wearied in threading the recesses of a scrubby and gloomy forest. Then the impediments that have hitherto prevented his progress, and bewildered him, are all in his rear, and he sees the unveiled face of Nature . . .[15]

To individuals, each decade brought a change in outlook, and yet, for more than a century, there lingered a Europo-centric vision that attempted to 'idealise' the scene, producing strange cultural hybrids such as we have noted in the work of the artists, and which existed as strongly in the literature of the time, typically among the early novelists, including Henry Kingsley, Marcus Clarke, and Rolf Boldrewood.

Almost two centuries have passed since Cook, Phillip, and Hunter. There is still land that may be cleared, still canvas that is being scraped clean of the tones of *terra australis* and re-primed with new, cultivated shades of *terra verte*, assisted by fertilisers, trace elements, irrigation, and machinery. Now bulldozer and chain-saw, mechanical power and chemicals, give man virtual supremacy, but the trees of the Australian bush, of the forests, jungles, and plains, have attained a different status, demanding consideration; not only aesthetically, but intrinsically, as a resource they are of immense value.

Following the indiscriminate destruction of the trees, which so often brought retribution in erosion and flood, came a period of milling and of uncontrolled exploitation. Timber prices were attractive, and forests, unprotected by any effective policy of conservation, were mined rather than farmed. Happily, most State authorities are now conscious of this evil, and increasingly, milling is restricted to mature trees, selected and marked by forestry experts. Policies, both of planting and allowing for natural regeneration, are being formulated in attempts to meet the needs of the future. It cannot yet be assured that expediency will not ravish forests and parklands, but at least this can no longer happen without powerful voices arousing the conscience of the community.

In every State there are dynamic and well-informed conservation groups, opposed without compromise to exploitation of unique areas wherever they exist. The world production of newsprint, cartons, and other paper products entails the daily destruction of thousands of trees. For this reason, many forests and bushlands, and much they support and modify, including aspects of climate and atmosphere, may be under threat. What are the alternatives? How may today's prodigality affect the future? A conservationist is as powerful as the question he poses.

In taking the wide view of the continent, there are aspects which enter every sweep of vision, every area of contemplation: of these one might instance the ubiquitous eucalyptus genus . . . or the wallaby-like marsupials. Everywhere in Australia there is some kind of gum tree,[16] some kind of wattle, and some kind of wallaby or kangaroo. Such may be regarded as common Australian symbols accompanying the many unique subjects confined to specific regions, and yet they also possess forms which may not exist outside a special environment.

Every Australian has his own favourites among the trees: his choice may be influenced by childhood associations, or it may depend on mature, objective judgment independent of reminiscence. But reflection shows us all that, in some context, trees are likely to be recalled when the heart is restless, or when any of the senses find the world unprofitable.

Many of our trees are austere, compared with those fringing our ancestral European fields; yet it is in such places that the Australian exile will miss them most poignantly. Our evergreens, accompanied by different qualities of light, by their own subtleties of scent and colour; even of sounds, are elsewhere unknown; these cannot be exported with their seed. The wind in leaves and branches speaks with a voice as characteristic of the tree as the singing of its sheltering birds.

Some kind of eucalypt, with leaves gleaming in the sky is bound to be remembered: a great sufficient red-gum of the plains or river flats; or a patient coolibah with faith in the dry creek bed; or a mountain ash, taut and monumental of trunk in the company of giants; these are all Australian symbols. Many an expatriate has burnt a few aromatic gum leaves from his homeland, and discovered a compound sensory delight. The carolling of the magpie that 'overflows like bubbling water,' the blue haze of the ranges, perhaps the texture of broad slabs of sun-warmed granite . . . the smoke of gum leaves may be redolent of any of a thousand memories. In many food parcels received during the 'blitz' on London and the Home Counties, I found a few gum leaves to provide an incense that recalled an old tranquillity.

54

Facing page top: The South Gippsland Hills supports an extensive dairying industry in Victoria. *Bottom left:* Grazing land in the Barrabool Hills of Victoria in a good season. *Bottom right:* The Barrabool Hills after a long season of drought.

This page top: Sheep . . . grazing anywhere at sunrise. Australia's sheep population generally ranges from 135 to 140 million, a number exceeded only by the U.S.S.R. *Bottom:* The Barwon River, near Geelong, Victoria. This river slides past Geelong, having been diverted by massive lava flows in geologically recent times, and flows out to sea at Barwon Heads on the south coast

Many will recall John Morrison's moving story called *The Incense Burner*. The old man Burroughs had just died in a poor London lodging house; his landlady tells of the parcel of 'herbs' he had received on the very morning of his death.

> 'Where've they taken him?'
> But I didn't hear her reply.
> Because that something which had been tickling my nostrils got right inside, and I lifted my head like a parched bullock scenting water, and stared along the passage, and sniffed, and licked my lips—and drew in a mighty inhalation that filled my lungs and sent me dizzy with the sickness that had been eating into me for five mortal weeks. . . .
> Burning gum leaves! Oh, shades of the bush and smell of my home!

I have never attempted to discover whether any kind of tree on earth, in a genus so easily recognisable, possesses such extraordinary diversity of shape, size, timber, bark, flower, and seedbox as the eucalypt. Or, for that matter, whether any of the other well-known trees have adapted themselves, in the long course of their evolution, to conditions ranging from extremes of desert, in some years completely rainless, to jungles where the annual rainfall may reach 4000 millimetres; from inland plains where daily shade temperatures may exceed 38°C for months on end, to mountain gullies where the deep winter snow drifts may persist in high summer. It may be so, though I doubt it. Throughout the world there are some 300 known species of oak, of which not one is indigenous to Australia. Australia carries considerably more species of eucalypt than there are oaks in the whole world; and not a single species of eucalypt is indigenous to any other continent. Nowadays, of course, they are well known in practically all Mediterranean-type climates, from California to the Black Sea; particularly the vigorous blue gum (*E. globulus*) which, in a given area, with the aid of sunshine and water, is capable of converting air into timber more rapidly than perhaps any other tree.

It was the sage Baron Ferdinand von Mueller, designer of Melbourne's splendid Botanic Gardens, who observed that the same species could be utilised in draining swampy country; for his suggestion that these gums be used in an attempt to reduce the malarial menace of the Pontine Marshes, he had his long list of honours for scientific work increased by the bestowal of a Papal Knighthood.[17]

'By their fruits ye shall know them,' was an oft-quoted maxim of the baron, and, indeed, a study of the seed-cases of the eucalypts will greatly help in identifying them. The blossoms of all gum trees resemble each other in so far as there are no petals, but, from a characteristic cup—which may in turn vary almost infinitely with species, in shape, size, and manner of growth, being loosely clustered in most cases—seems to explode a brush of filaments and stamens, circular, not unlike the bloom of a thistle. Often these tasselled cups are sweetly perfumed and rich in nectar; indeed, the eucalypts produce many excellent honeys.

That of the yellow box (*E. melliodora*), named for the colour of its timber immediately beneath the bark, is most delectable. Of it, my old friend, Tarlton Rayment,[18] once wrote:

> Travel through the forest in the summer when a million bees are singing a melody of industry in the nectar-laden air. The atmosphere is drenched with a delicious perfume, for the blossoms are flowing over with riches. The sweet harvest of the Yellow Box is sought far and wide, for the ripe honey is most delectable and dense, and laden with the unforgettable scent of the flowers of the forest. It is the joy of the bee-farmer, for it fills his hives with honey unsurpassed in the markets of the world.

56

Top left: Trunk of scribbly gum *Eucalyptus rossi*, growing on Capital Hill, Canberra. *Top right:* Flowering eucalypt, Mt Disappointment, Victoria. *Centre right:* Blossoms of *Eucalyptus* sp. *Bottom left:* Young spotted gum at Tathra, south coast of New South Wales. *Bottom right:* Ghost gum *Eucalyptus papuana* in MacDonnell Ranges, central Australia

the typical foliage, every leaf brilliantly reflecting the intense light. The propensity of many eucalypts to turn their hanging leaves edge-on to the sun so that they shine like knife-blades—thereby, of course, reducing transpiration and consequent loss of moisture—is well seen in the desert species when the air is still. But the ghost gum is a wonderful sight both by day and night; eerie, perhaps, to the senses sharpened almost preternaturally by the vastness and the silence of the shadowy flanks of the Musgraves or MacDonnells, with the stars so close and brilliant overhead. By day, the tree is etched brightly against the warm rocks, like a river receiving light in every tributary twig, and pouring it through cascading shadows down the ravines.

It is no wonder that even men who have hated the capricious, cruel droughts of the Centre, and held most precarious existence until its bounty has returned, will still pause in silent admiration of a tree.

As appealing as the ghost gum is the gimlet gum of the western plateau, whose clustered mallee stems are often polished like the patina on an ageing penny; or, at another extreme, the snow gum of the south-eastern alps, with smooth trunks twisted and lacquered with reds, greens, and yellows, sometimes all together. I doubt if there is any bole more lovely than that of the snow gum.[20] It provides brilliance on a misty day, colours gleaming from trunks half-hidden beneath branches bowed with snow; and, no matter how often you come upon a striking example, it seems to offer benignity as well as beauty.

And then there are the spotted gums, *maculata*, and the like, with patterned trunks; and the fragrant *citriodora*, the lemon-scented gum. Both these possess a special evocative quality. Beneath each ponderous limb you will notice the convolutions and wrinkles so smoothly contained within the skin of the tree that they resemble tensed flesh, straining against gravity to raise arms into the sky.

Yet, if there is variation in the minute beauty of filament and torus, and character in bark and bole, there is also an absolute and total character in each of several prevailing forms of the tree as a whole. Some combination of leaf, trunk, and foliage, gives every Australian assurance that any one of 500 species[21] is a eucalypt. Without the close and familiar things—a leaf, or a gum nut, or a strip of delicate bark, picked up from the strewn ground—it would be impossible for the layman to recognise that the immense, aloof mountain ash, rising 75 metres in a white column, sparsely crowned, close and yet infinitely distant from his neighbour on the southern Great Divide, is in any way related to the whip-stick scrub of the Mallee. The scrubby thickets that clothe the sand-plains and the little deserts of the borderlands that lie between Victoria and South Australia, or cover the infinite plains of the west immediately the Nullarbor Plain loses its authority, show the ultimate difference of form: the bushy mallees give way reluctantly to the central mulgas.

As different also, of course, are the river red-gums and coolibahs[22] which are almost traditionally 'tree' in form, squat of trunk and spreading of branches, in spite of their great size; they possess sufficient living room in open places, and do not compete so obviously for light and life. Their numbers have always been dependent on climatic factors that occasionally permit sufficient consecutive seasons to favour the growth from seed to sapling in the spaces left vacant by trees that have died, or in the margins where the old giants are declining. In one lifetime, it is hard to observe the operations of such an equilibrium, and there are men of the red-gum plains who swear that the climate has altered, and that the existing titans are the last of their race, and will never be replaced. Certainly man, in grazing his animals, has everywhere decreased the chances of natural regeneration of all plant species.

The mountain ash (*E. regnans*) is one of the most remarkable trees in the world. There are still living trees close to 90 metres in height, and two, at Marysville, in Victoria, and at Maydena, in Tasmania,[23] were known to exceed this stature. Many stumps of older trees with girths, head-high from the ground, of 15 and 18 metres, have been authenticated. It is probable that some of the largest trees in the virgin bush reached over 100 metres, but there is no acceptable record by actual measurement of anything beyond 99·5 metres.[24] Numerous photographs of immense hollow trunks exist, some large enough to be used, in the early days, as stables and barns.

Although the terrible, haunting strangeness of the forests of the Great Divide has given way to a delight in their grandeur, and to the exploitation of their valuable timber, the feeling of wonder that such immense living columns should rise, cylindrical and branchless for half their height, to culminate in such a feather capital of foliage, still persists. There is nothing hidden amid the remote graceful upper branches, glittering against the sky with daytime stars. The immense virility of trees that rise through the centuries, side by side in magnificent competition, to raise such ponderous trunks bearing crowns so small, to outstrip, by many metres, the competition of all lesser species, becomes a bewildering phenomenon, matched only perhaps by that of some of the great soft-wooded sequoias on the other side of the Pacific. Yet the latters' trunks seem more functional, with their branches lower to the ground. A stand of *Eucalyptus regnans*, a hundred uniform trees, seems to hold a collective character, a vast, upsurging, yet static demonstration of energy and fecundity perfectly balanced against time and tempest. While other trees stress their variety in eccentricities of trunk and limb, these great gums keep their small differences to themselves, in their lofty heads, beyond the prying of the most mature blackwoods and wattles. Even lower are the struggling hazels; and yet they too dwarf a lower stratum of tree ferns and densely matted undergrowth along the streams.

Other species of eucalypt, woollybutt, and messmate of the east, karri of Western Australia, may closely rival the height of the white mountain ash. They all appalled the settler who, struggling for open pasture, attacked them relentlessly. He found that, though he could not force them to retreat, he could kill them standing; and countless thousands were ringbarked, to be blackened by fire, and blanched by weather while the scrub was cleared from their feet and replaced by fodder for cattle. They bristled many of the otherwise bare ridges of the dairying country, stark reminders of the primordial forests, for several decades. Now, few are left in the obedient farmlands of the man-made landscapes, but, in the timberlands of the ranges, they are still to be seen, although the greatest may have been milled, or destroyed by fire. Today, whenever trees are felled and 'snigged out' to the mills, there is a beginning of regeneration. Ancient forest that has reached equilibrium, of course, possesses a constant tree population through the ages; any seed that germinates is early doomed unless one of the patriarchs falls and makes room for it.

As we have already seen, everywhere in Australia there are eucalypts and acacias—gum trees and wattles—that have adapted themselves to every circumstance from coast to coast. While preserving some quite dominant family characteristics, in detail they reveal innumerable different features. Who would not recognise the kinship of the wattles, though they may range from the feathery cootamundra (*Acacia baileyana*) of the south-east, with its sprays of myriad fluffy yellow balls promising release from winter, to the bright little golden-globed wattle (*A. nervosa*) of the Darling Ranges in the far west? There is never a month when some kind of Australian wattle is not offering its soft furry blossoms and warm, unforgettable fragrance to the sun. Both hues and scents vary considerably, the former from white, through pale

Mountain ash forest in heavy mist in the Dandenong Ranges in Victoria

Top left: Mountain ash forest in the spring, Dandenongs, Victoria. *Top right:* Tree ferns weighed down by snow in mountain ash forest, Victoria. *Bottom:* Several species of Acacia are commonly called 'Golden Wattle'. Most have flattened leaf-stalks (phyllodes) which function as leaves

creams and light lemon yellow, to saffron and deep orange; the latter through a range of sweet scents to some that appeal more to pollen-bearing insects than to man.

The name *Acacia* is derived from the Greek, and refers to some prickly members of the very large genus growing in Egypt. Australian wattles, in maturity, either, like the cootamundra, retain the feathery true-leaf foliage of the seedling, or develop broad, parallel-veined phyllodes (or flattened stems) as in the blackwood (*A. melanoxylon*), famous for its timber, its evergreen shelter, and warmly scented white or cream downy blossom. There are several Australian species of acacia that are well armed with prickly leaves.

The largest members of the family are forest trees, 45 metres or more in height; the smallest are aromatic shrubs of less than half a metre. Some species provide timber, others gum for both adhesive and medicinal purposes, some shelter and emergency fodder, and others, such as the sweet-scented black wattle (*A. decurrens*, and other similar species), bark rich in tannin for the processing of leather.

As a national emblem, wattle has no rivals. Not only is the genus ubiquitous but, in form, scent, and range of colour, it is recognisable everywhere. Adam Lindsay Gordon caught not only the spirit of the flower, but of a prevailing bush atmosphere when he wrote:[25]

> In the Spring, when the wattle gold trembles
>   'Twixt shadow and shine,
> When each dew-laden air draught resembles
>   A long draught of wine;
> When the sky-line's blue burnish'd resistance
> Makes deeper the dreamiest distance,
> Some song in all hearts hath existence,—
>   Such songs have been mine.

[1] In most eucalypts, the foliage of the young trees differs from that of maturity; there is often a sudden change as the tree gains sapling size. The juvenile leaves are often more ovate, and glaucous, and arranged in stemless pairs. Later the distinctive blue-bloomed foliage gives way to the characteristic adult leaves, long, green, and shining. In a few species the blue foliage is retained (e.g. *E. macrocarpa*, the Kalgoorlie rose). The juvenile leaves of the manna gum closely resemble those of the adult. The candlebark is *E. rubida*; and the manna gum *E. viminalis*.

[2] The distinction cited is not infallible; there are several 'peppermints' including the mountain ash (*E. regnans*) with smooth barks. The peppermint-oil is characteristic, and the numerous small flowers that grow along the branches rather than at the tips. *E. radiata* is the common peppermint mentioned.

[3] The swamp gum is *E. ovata*.

[4] The First Fleet sailed in May 1787, and arrived at Botany Bay on 18 January 1788. On 26 January the British Flag was first flown at Sydney. The fleet comprised the two 'king's ships,' H.M.S. *Sirius*, commanded by Arthur Phillip, and the armed tender, *Supply*, under Henry Ball, with six transports and three store ships.

[5] Slightly adapted from the author's lecture notes on Australian Painting, published by the Council of Adult Education, Melbourne, 1950.

[6] Notably in the Mitchell Library, and in the William Dixson Gallery, Sydney.

[7] Dampier: *A New Voyage Round the World*, chap. 16.

[8] Cook: *Journal of the First Voyage of Captain James Cook*, the original in the National Library, Canberra. Many passages are quoted in *Sources of Australian History*, selected and edited by M. Clark (*World's Classics*, O.U.P., 1957).

[9] The yellow gum plant was not a eucalypt, but a grass-tree, mentioned in another chapter. Phillip wrote: 'The yellow gum as it is called, is strictly a resin, not being at all soluble in water: in appearance it strongly resembles gamboge, but has not the property of staining. The plant that produces it is low and small, with long grassy leaves . . .' (from *Phillip's Voyage to Botany Bay*, 1788; chap. 7).

[10] Phillip: ibid., chap. 7.

64

Facing page. Top left: Early black wattle *Acacia decurrens*. Top right: Blackwood seeding, New South Wales; curved seed pods and brilliant orange and black seeds make a lovely and unusual pattern. Bottom left: Nealie, a wattle, *Acacia rigens*. Bottom right: Spreading wattle, *Acacia genistfolia*

[11] Collins: From *An Account of the English Colony in New South Wales, from its first settlement in January, 1788, to August, 1801.* (T. Cadell and W. Davies, London, 1804.) All the Collins extracts are quoted from the same source.

[12] Collins, ibid.

[13] One of Governor Phillip's officers: quoted by A. G. L. Shaw: *The Story of Australia* (Faber & Faber, 1955).

[14] Collins: See note 11.

[15] From an article signed W.R.G., in *The Saturday Magazine*, London, for 16 July 1836.

[16] Eucalypts can endure in country with less than 230-millimetre rainfall only where they follow stream-beds or find soakage, as, for instance, at Ayers Rock. In the shade of rainforests, also, eucalypts will not thrive.

[17] Baron Sir Ferdinand Jacob Heinrich von Mueller, 1825–96. This great explorer-botanist landed in Adelaide in 1847. He became the first Government Botanist at Melbourne in 1853. Although the Melbourne Botanic Gardens existed, the Baron added to them enormously, and established the first Herbarium. In 1869, at the Baron's suggestion, Archbishop Goold carried seeds of *E. globulus*, a Tasmanian species, to Rome. The ensuing growth enabled the draining and subsequent use of much swamp land. After twenty years, von Mueller was relieved of the Directorship of the Melbourne Botanic Gardens when it was officially decided to make the gardens 'more aesthetic'; but he remained Government Botanist.

[18] Tarlton Rayment (*Walkabout*, January 1943). Tarlton Rayment died in June 1964. The author expresses his indebtedness for information, advice, and friendship in past years.

[19] The generic name *Eucalyptus* arises from these caps which so firmly surmount the buds. From the Greek, *eu*, well, and *kalypto*, I cover. Botanically, the cap is known as the operculum. The famous eucalyptus oil is contained in the leaves, and is obtained by soaking the leaves in pits, before distillation.

[20] The snow gum is *E. niphophila*; there is a lowland form known as white sally. A small species of eucalypt, *alpina*, is found only in the Victorian Grampians. The alpine ash (*E. delegatensis*) is the very tall timber species known as woollybutt.

[21] Some botanists concede a greater, some a lesser, number of species, according to whether they recognise fine genetic differences. The extremists have sometimes been termed the 'splitters' and 'lumpers.'

[22] A huge coolibah (*E. microtheca*), at Monkira Station, in the Diamantina, has a trunk circumference of 14 metres, a foliage girth of 229 metres, and a height of about 30 metres.

[23] The tree found in the Styx River area, near Maydena, was measured in 1956 at 98·2 metres; the Marysville tree was 92 metres in 1930. It is reported that the former tree was felled for pulping.

[24] In 1888, the tallest tree that could be found was a white mountain ash (*E. regnans*) 99·5 metres high, at Noojee. The record height of 114·4 metres, for a tree at Thorpdale, appears less well authenticated.

[25] Adam Lindsay Gordon: 'A Dedication.' (From *Bush Ballads and Galloping Rhymes.*)

CHAPTER 4

Blackboys
and Kangaroo Paws

A land of softly blended shades and perfumes
Which senses cherish, subtle, unforgotten,
However long the years, or far the journey.
— *from* WIDE HOMELAND

ALTHOUGH MOST OF OUR TREES are very different from those of Europe and America, they frequently bear the same names; this must be very confusing to the visitor or the new settler. He hears of ash, box, and beech; of oak, cedar, and pine; and none of these bears much resemblance, let alone botanical relationship, to the trees the names recall. But because, from childhood, the Australian has generally read a great deal of descriptive British and American literature, and is familiar with overseas scenery as depicted in innumerable films and illustrated papers, he is not usually puzzled.

There has, however, been a relatively slight flow of reciprocal information, as most Australians discover when they first go abroad. Most of us know that the British rowan tree is called the mountain ash; that none of our pines is much like those of Europe, though some are conifers;[1] that the beautiful trees we in Australia call oaks, are seldom mentioned without an attributive: the *silky* oak is a golden-flowered grevillea—some of our most handsome natives, the *she*-oaks, *bull*-oaks, and *desert* oaks are *casuarinas*,[2] while Australian or Tasmanian oak is a term applied to the timber of the big eucalypts, but not to the trees. The box trees, again, invariably carry an essential adjective, generally a colour. These are eucalypts with heavy persistent bark—unlike that of those trees usually called gums; the brush box, however, is the splendid *Tristania conferta*, a close relative of the eucalypts. The Australian beeches are sufficiently related to their namesakes to be so described botanically, but they all flourish in such specialised haunts that there can be no confusion. Nearly all the kinds of trees that flourish in Europe have long since been imported to our country. They are entirely familiar; many are popular as street trees, and are also found in private and public gardens. There is seldom any confusion, nor any necessity to be specific; an oak, without further definition, is an English oak; similarly an elm is never confused with the tropical crowsfoot 'elm' of Queensland,[3] nor the walnut of the tropical scrubs,[4] with the imported species bearing edible nuts.

The reason for the similarity in naming often lies in the character or colour of the timber. The wood of the silky oak has a 'rose' not unlike that of quercus; our cedar[5] provides a fine red timber related to the mahoganys—hard, and excellent for furniture; our ash is white and straight grained. Some of the Australian pines, especially those of Tasmania, produce straight-grained softwoods of remarkable durability;[6] superficially, these resemble the northern pines in texture. The genus Callitris are trees of very ancient lineage; they

Facing page: Ferns in beech forest. *Top:* The edge of a myrtle forest. *Bottom left:* Fern fronds uncurling; one of the most beautiful curves to be seen in the Australian bush. *Bottom right:* Forest on the Gordon River, Tasmania

are often called cypress pines because they possess needle-like foliage, and bear conical seed capsules. Throughout the Inland, they rival in number even the eucalypts and acacias. The famous Murray pine is found in most dry parts of temperate Australia as far as the Centre; there are several other species, all easily recognisable as belonging to the genus.

As Australian as her inland skies are the casuarinas[7] we call she-oaks. There are far fewer species than there are of acacia, yet the characteristic veiled, green-grey foliage, varying somewhat in density, is found from the coral seas to the red Centre, from south-east to north-west. The foliage consists of slender, wiry branchlets on which the leaves are quite inconspicuous, minute tufts encircling the nodes that give the growth its characteristic flexibility. Where the branchlets are long, they give the species a weeping or drooping appearance, as in *Casuarina stricta*. In season, the massed effect of the inconspicuous male flowers gives the whole tree a splendid golden-brown cloak; the female flowers become the typical fine-toothed woody cones. In all details of flower and foliage the various species show considerable variation. The desert oak (*C. decaisneana*) is the finest shade tree of central Australia.

In many parts of the Great Divide, where there is sufficient rainfall, in areas ranging from Queensland to Gippsland, also in the mountains of Tasmania, there are jungled tree communities of many species. In Queensland and New South Wales, they include many of the hard, beautifully grained and coloured timbers used for furniture, panelling, and veneers. For species distinct from their namesakes, again we have familiar names: red cedar, silky oak, tulipwood, walnut, rosewood,[8] and many more. The same bush contains several pines, such as the broad-leafed kauri, the bunya, and the hoop pine.[9] Tasmanian pines are equally valuable: Huon, King William, celery top, and pencil[10] are typical of species becoming too scarce as timber for any but highly selective uses.

The cold rain forests of Tasmania, apart from their ubiquitous eucalypts and acacias, are little less diversified than those of the tropical north. In both, species of beech persist, the giant antarctic beech (*Nothofagus moorei*) in Queensland, and *Nothofagus cunninghamii*, in the higher latitudes. Some of the specimens in the MacPherson Range of Queensland are considered to be thousands of years old, and the appearance of their gnarled and mossy trunks firmly supports such a belief. The late Arthur Groom, who knew the Lamington National Park in the Range better than most, once wrote.[11]

> . . . it was not difficult to realize that at 3,800 feet elevation, some of the dark and mysterious monsters had been alive a year for every foot I stood above sea-level. Their small leaves had dropped to carpet the ground and had been swept away by torrential rains throughout the centuries from the days of King David. They were old at the coming of Christ. No one knows how far back in the dawn of creation, their predecessors crowded the McPherson forests. From the original tree in every acre or so family circles had suckered outwards, so that in the fogs and swollen hanging mosses of early morning, you may imagine all the goblins of childhood story using them as hosts.

All Australian beech forests are deeply shadowed, mossy places where the fancy may play with the strange distorted trunks, and find infinite delight in brightly coloured fungus and lush ferns. The *Nothofagus* species mentioned are evergreen,[12] but in the period of spring growth, the young leaves of the southern species are a brilliant russet colour, extraordinarily fresh and jewel-like, the complete contrast to trunks so venerable. In the north, the beech forests are hosts to orchids, bright mosses, lichens, and ferns; they share with the whole forest a wealth of joyous birds—currawongs and magpies, brightly coloured parrots, yellow-robins, whip-birds. There are sudden transitions in the rainforests; in the north, beech may give way to gums and she-oaks, to open forest country, or to a stand of sinister climbing figs[13] whose strangling roots still clutch some long dead support, or perhaps to crowsfoot elms with their immense root-buttresses. Although progress through the Tasmanian beech forests, compared with that through less shaded bush, is relatively easy, the abrupt change to a button-grass plain is generally as welcome as it is unexpected—if only for its light and air.

It is certainly not my purpose to attempt a botanical treatise, or to compile a catalogue. Both would be beyond my capabilities and the scope of this book. Our trees and our flowers have many associations; they are an integral part of our history, our literature, and of the very character of Australia. As typically Australian as the quiet creatures, the possums and koalas that still inhabit their heights, as the vivid birds of their varied foliage, to us their interest may never be exhausted.

If conservation measures are vital among the tall eucalypt forests of the south, no less is the urgency of preserving characteristic large areas of tropical rainforest in the north.[14] Recent research claims that such moist, close vegetation once covered Australia, and that the sclerophylls (hard-leafed plants) that now dominate the Australian flora have evolved from the luxuriant rainforests of Carboniferous periods. Because much of the jungle country has been cleared successfully for pasture and crops, much more is in jeopardy.

Ignorance afforded some bliss, I think, to the early map-makers who used strange beasts, drawn large, to span their unknown lands. Thus an old chart of van Neck's voyages to the East Indies gives Capricornia over to the ponderous elephant; for, in the European mind, no specifically Australian fauna was yet imaginable. And yet there was, all the time, a veritable pachyderm flourishing in our tropical north although it belonged to the vegetable kingdom. This tree which was to remain on the waiting list of discovery for more than two hundred years was the baobab, or boab, *Adansonia gregorii*, whose brothers (*A. digitata*) were at home in Africa and perhaps, as expatriates, in some other tropical regions. How baobabs became established in Australia is, as a botanical friend once wrote, 'for ever bound up in geological antiquity . . . the only reason that can be advanced is that they once enjoyed a much wider distribution throughout the world, but have long since died out from intervening countries like Arabia, India, etc.'[15]

As we have seen, Australia provides extraordinary contrasts in tree forms; at one extreme, surely, must stand these venerable, fat, and friendly baobabs. With grey, swollen trunks, frequently much broader than they are high, as though expanded to bear a special burden of gravity, they squat, bulging and wrinkled like aged elephants, tree survivors from an age before Adam. Their natural region is restricted to the ancient Kimberley area of north-west Australia and in general they range a coastal strip about 160 kilometres wide, from the King Sound to western Arnhem Land.

Frequently, their vast boles, often exceeding 20 metres in circumference, are hollow, with openings, sometimes enlarged by man, inviting creatures that would exchange the outside world of hard light for their deep, safe shadow. And man himself has been swift to accept their sanctuary, though such tenancies as that of Harry Layman, of the Lennard River country, who was reported to have used a tree as his home for twenty years, must be exceptional. There still stands at Wyndham a famous gaol baobab, one of several within which unwilling Aboriginal guests were once chained, in the days when they were fierce, feared, and too often fettered. The hollow interior of this tree would accommodate at least a dozen men; at its widest it is about 4 metres across.

Top left: Desert oaks on the Gibson Desert, Western Australia. The timber has an oak-like grain but the tree belongs to the Casuarina genus.
Top right: A silky oak in full bloom; these trees are actually grevilleas of the Proteaceae family.
Bottom: Lichen on a bright boulder in the uplands of Tasmania. *Facing page:* The baobab, *Adansonia gregorii*, in the Kimberleys, Western Australia

Although the botanical name of the Australian baobab commemorates that of the explorer, Augustus Charles Gregory, and was probably bestowed by Baron Ferdinand von Mueller, who accompanied his North Australian Expedition of 1855–56, the trees had certainly been discovered by men of H.M.S. *Beagle* some sixteen years earlier. Commander John Stokes, in his *Discoveries in Australia*,[16] refers to them as 'gouty stem trees.' In 1839, the *Beagle*, in which the famous Charles Darwin had recently voyaged (leaving our shores 'without sorrow or regret'),[17] navigated the Victoria River for 80 kilometres, from the sea to Holdfast Reach (where she lost two anchors); land and boat parties traced the river much further. It is interesting to recall that, at this time, men still believed strongly in the existence of an inland sea draining out, perhaps, by one of these north-western rivers. The name of the *Beagle*, carved on an ancient baobab at the Reach, was at least partly visible for more than fifty years.[18] Inscriptions by Gregory, who made an adventurous voyage upstream in the schooner *Tom Tough*, in 1855–56, were reported as being still legible nearly a hundred years later.[19]

Baobabs, immune to the ravages of white ants, may reach a very great age, and 'are doubtless among the world's oldest living organisms'; yet, apparently, they may fall suddenly and mock the legend of immortality that has been applied to them.[20] I do not know of any authoritative dating estimates of the age of Australian baobabs; an African example in Senegal was considered to be more than 5000 years old.

The grotesque old baobab not only offers shade from the fierce sun, and shelter from the monsoonal summer rains; it also has the unexpected beauty of pale deciduous foliage and white heavy-scented blossom, gourd-like fruit containing a pulp of refreshing acidulous flavour, edible seeds, and a great capacity for holding water in its cavities. The rainy season of the north-west monsoon, concentrated through the summer months from December to March, fills shaded hollows, and these may provide drinking water for long afterwards; however, the pithy substance of the tree itself, if compressed, will yield a clear, potable fluid.

The list of the tree's virtues has been extended to include its gum and its fibres. No one ever wrote with greater enthusiasm of the baobab than Ernestine Hill, and the fine descriptive passage in her *Great Australian Loneliness*,[21] includes all the excellent qualities of this 'Caliban of a tree . . . friendly ogre of the great North-west.'

Somewhat resembling baobabs, the bottle-trees (*Brachychiton rupestris*) of the Queensland scrub country are of a different family (Sterculia). The trunks of these trees are so valuable as stock food that, when clearing new land, the bottles are always left standing as an emergency food supply against the days of drought. The trunks may be chopped up and fed directly to stock. The explorer, Ludwig Leichhardt, in southern Queensland, wrote:[22] 'Fine large bottle-trees (Sterculia) were frequent: the young wood of which, containing a great quantity of starch between its woody fibres, was frequently chewed by our party.' Bottle-trees are swifter growing and shorter lived than the baobabs. John Gilbert, who, in June 1845, met a tragic death at the hands of the Aboriginal attackers of one of Leichhardt's camps in northern Queensland, wrote enthusiastically in his journal of the bottle-trees as being upwards of fifteen feet—4·5 metres—in circumference, and all shaped like soda-water bottles. He had no doubt that the fleshy white pith of the tree would preserve human beings from hunger for a considerable time; this it has indeed done on many occasions; though, perhaps not being sufficiently famished on the occasion I tried it, I did not find it greatly to my taste.

I return to the baobab. What I have dreamed about often enough, especially in places where only memory can sustain such joys, is merely lying beneath a baobab in bloom . . . when a honey fragrance, heavy lazy air, and

74

the huge old solidity of the tree combine to create a peace at once sensuous and serene.

Though we may find Australian eucalypts thriving in southern France, Italy, California, even in Cornwall; though Australian wattle (in the northern hemisphere invariably called mimosa, for it resembles some of the Mediterranean species) is grown in Provence and sold from flower-stalls in Piccadilly, or outside the Madeleine, there are many trees and shrubs for which home thoughts from abroad can receive no such vital stimulus. If I think of a grass-tree, its appearance, or the tantalising resin-nectar of its tall flower spike, then, wherever I am, for confirmation I must return all the way to Australia.

No genus of Australian plant can have a much wider distribution than *Xanthorrhoea*.[23] In the West, its members are invariably called 'blackboys'; in South Australia, the Aboriginal 'yacca' or 'yucca' is fairly common, and 'grass-tree' is usual in the eastern States. All the sixteen species possess common characteristics, although some are endemic to certain areas of the continent, and generally to individual States. They all wear grass skirts and flourish fine plumes above the waist; when they bloom—which may be fairly regularly with some species, or seldom with others—they send up tall spear-heads of many tightly packed white florets on a clean shaft. One of the Western Australian grass-trees, *Kingia australis*, resembles the *Xanthorrhoea*, but flowers with several independent globular 'drum-stick' heads.

The brittle, grass-like leaves gradually fall away from the inner skirt, leaving a sort of ring by which extent the main stems of some species of the plant appear to lengthen each year. Any examination of the trunk of a tall grass-tree must impress one with its evidence of vast age, a characteristic which it shares with the northern cycads—probably the world's most primitive seed-bearing plants. Although highly resinous—the name *Xanthorrhoea* refers to the yellow, flowing gum—and inflammable, blackboys seem to be stimulated by fire, and flower best after the bush has been burnt. In Western Australia particularly, the theory that periodical fire has become a natural factor in the ecology of a region, has been advanced by several credible authorities. It certainly seems to have charred the stems of xanthorrhoea so frequently and with so little harmful effect as to have suggested that local popular name of this purely Australian genus. The black trunks, sometimes leaning or divided, strike strange attitudes, and, surmounted by plumes and erect spears, are an adequate starting-point for the imagination. Today, it is only in the far north that the old tribes may be glimpsed among the grass-trees.

It does not seem improbable that there should be numerous grass-trees hundreds of years old; their appearance bears out notions of pre-history. What does seem strange is that they belong to the natural order Liliaceae.

The resin that is obvious in all species, especially in the closely packed bases of leaves that remain after the main fronds have fallen away, has several uses, and from some species (such as *X. tateana*, common on Kangaroo Island, in the entrance of Gulf St Vincent, South Australia) it is extracted for commercial use. The Aborigines melted out the gum and used it as an adhesive, or, mixed with clay, as a filling for their artefacts. It will yield additives for explosive compositions used in pyrotechnics; it may be refined to produce picric acid or used as a base for hard lacquers and varnishes. Industrial alcohol has also been distilled from the trunk of xanthorrhoea. Bees are much attracted by the heavy, sweet smell of the flower spikes; they are also said to gather the resin and use it in hive-building, though the flavour it imparts to honey is too distinctive to be welcomed by apiarists. The leaves, rectangular or rhomboid in section, and in some species no thicker than a match, look as though they would be admirable for weaving, but they are too brittle.

Facing page: Ancient cycads in the Finniss River area of the Northern Territory. *Top left:* Grass-tree in the Flinders Ranges of South Australia; this species is a member of the lily family. *Top right:* This grass-tree is almost 6 metres high and was photographed in the northern Grampians, Victoria. *Bottom:* These examples of grass-trees are from Wilsons Promontory, Victoria

Some species of grass-tree such as *X. australis*, common in south-eastern Australia—seldom develop a stem. The spreading blue-green crowns of their long, still leaves remain below the eye-level of anyone walking through the bush. I have often tried to analyse the reasons for the quite beautiful effect of flickering light that appears in the sunlit plumes as one passes, even on a still day. It is doubtless a function of their symmetry, of the rigidity of the long arching leaves, and of their sharp, square section causing each spike to have bright and shadowed facets that suddenly seem to change as one moves. Often there is an appearance of fine radial jets of green light.

It is generally believed that grass-trees flourish in poor, arid soils, which may explain why, even in the more populous States, so many areas of bush in which they grow remain unexploited. With the increasing use of trace elements, it has been suggested, much grass-tree upland may be made productive. Fortunately, at the same time, we have an increasing appreciation of our unique flora, and one begins to have faith that sufficient areas of national park will be gazetted to preserve all species of grass-tree. It is worth remembering that, in an emergency, the small white heart of the lower crown of most (probably all) grass-trees is edible, if not particularly palatable. It is as well that it is not a delicacy, for its removal kills the plant.

Grass-trees are susceptible, along with a great many trees and shrubs to the fungus disease phytophthora, or 'die-back'. This destructive parasitic fungus appears to be extending its range in Australia, and has caused considerable concern. Gravels, disturbed or transported by earth-moving machinery, may spread the disease; it may be carried downhill along channels of natural drainage.

The difference between Australian and other flora has been stressed ever since the first explorers began to exchange facts for the fantasy that had so long screened *terra australis*. Dampier's collection of plants, now nearly three hundred years old, still rests in the herbarium at the University of Oxford. Sir Joseph Banks and Dr Solander, Cook's botanists, were intrigued and enchanted by the flora of the east coast; their specimens also still exist. An important stage in the scientific study of our flora was reached in 1810, with the publication of the *Prodromus Florae Novae Hollandiae* by the indefatigable botanist, Robert Brown, who sailed with Matthew Flinders, in the *Investigator*.[24] Several later works by great resident botanists, especially those of Baron Sir Ferdinand von Mueller, continued to elucidate the genera and their constituent species which now are known to number up to 14 000. The great *Flora Australiensis* of George Bentham was completed in 1878. Upon these scholarly bases rests another century of botanical research.

The flora of Australia has developed in isolation for many millions of years, perhaps since the southern land-masses drifted apart from some hypothetical Gondwanaland, existing before any of the continents had been differentiated. The theory may explain the common elements in what has sometimes been termed the Antarctic Flora,[25] so named, not for our contemporary south polar ice-cap, but for a vast, conjectural land-mass long since submerged, but which may have joined regions today as distinct as those separated by the Indian Ocean.

Such speculation helps to explain, for instance, the virtual monopoly shared between South Africa and Australia of the Proteaceae (which, for us, include the well-known genera of the hakeas, banksias, and grevilleas); while the antiquity of the link might be assumed from the fact that neither country has now a single common genus of this distinctive family. Another very ancient bond, typified by the beech trees and many of the lesser rainforest genera, seems to exist with New Zealand and South America; this has been called the Andean element. If the botanical relationship connotes ancestry inhabiting common territory, its age must be of an order that has yet permitted the subsequent evolution of the world's most distinctive endemic flora, older, probably, than even the first appearance of the ancient marsupials.[26]

The unique quality of our trees, so different from those of the other continents, is matched by the whole range of Australian shrubs and annuals, which includes many of nature's most intriguing and extravagant forms. Wherever you wander in Australia, there are plants to accent her most memorable landscapes, from the ice-sculpted peaks of Tasmania to the opalescent plains and deserts of the Northern Territory. Which are its most vivid and persistent images? Time and again you recall scenes associated with some wildflower, see it windswept on the edge of the snow drifts, enlivening the coastal dunes, starring the plain, floating over the topical lagoon . . .

Any selection of these evocative plants must be personal. Some will call to mind the flowers of their home State, even of the countryside of their particular district. Others will think of the outstanding glories of one of the great natural regions. Fifty years ago, J. H. Maiden wrote:[27]

> Australia has three grand types of flora—the brilliant inflorescences of the dry sandy plains of Western Australia; the luxurious vegetation of eastern Queensland and New South Wales and the alpine plants of Tasmania. South Australia, the north-west of Victoria, and the vast western plains of New South Wales and Queensland approximate to the botanical conditions of the western State. Many Tasmanian or allied plants extend to south-eastern Australia generally, viz, most of Victoria and the south-eastern portion of New South Wales, the flora of Victoria being intermediate in character. The rain forests of western Tasmania are unique, and on the mainland are most closely approached by those of the Cape Otway district of Victoria.

The whole range of traditional flower forms that have delighted mankind since we first became aesthetically aware are found among the Australian flora. There are thousands of all shapes and sizes with corollas of every hue; all the daisies' rayed petals reflecting the sun; the olearias; the immortal stars of the everlastings, white, rose, and yellow; the fire-weeds, the groundsels, and the golden billy buttons; these may be found practically everywhere in Australia. Innumerable are the pea-flowers; the lilies and irises; the flowers that correspond to the convolvulus, the violet, and the rose; the campanula, and other bells of every imaginable shape; the mints and veronicas—all have many representatives. Look for a labiate, and there is the beautiful eastern Christmas bush, with pale lilac lips and throat, spotted with deep orange; ask for a snapdragon, and we can offer any number of the family, open-mouthed in invitation to the bee. Consider the clematis or the buttercup, the gentian or the geranium; they are known and loved by children here, just as they are known and loved everywhere, by all who share the clear vision of the young.

The great Myrtle family includes, as well as the eucalypts and other genera too numerous to mention, the tea-tree, the bottle-brushes, and the exquisitely scented thriptomenes. Everyone knows the tea-tree, the genus Leptospermum—bushes and trees with clouds of small round flowers, pale or ruddy, with all five petals circular, one or more stamens to each, surrounding a honey cup from which the pistil stands erect for pollination. The experimental use of the small, stiff leaves among the early settlers gave it the name that is often corrupted to 'ti-tree.' Some of the more brilliantly flowered species are now common in many southern gardens.

The bottle-brushes of the melaleucas, of calothamnus, and of the callistemons—white, yellow, crimson, scarlet—are most familiar Australian flower forms which, as with the eucalypts and wattles, provide globes, brushes, and plumes of stamens stressing the essential reproductive function

Top: Silver snow daisies *Celmisia longifolia* in the mountains of south-east Australia. *Bottom left:* Parsnip daisies *Trachymene glaucifolia* on the sandhills of inland Australia. *Bottom right:* Callistemon, a typical Australian bottlebrush

of the flower, and are sufficiently glorious in scent and colour to be attractive without a display of petals.

Among the wholly Australian genera of the Proteaceae, the banksias, grevilleas, and hakeas have already been mentioned. The term 'bottle-brush' is also often applied to the flowers of the banksias, the majority of which flourish in Western Australia. Each floret of hundreds, or even thousands, in the brush is shaped rather like that of the honeysuckle, and the trees are often known familiarly by this name. The perianths, which take the place in this bloom of petals and sepals, vary enormously with species; they bear conspicuous styles, and are clustered in splendid cones or cylinders ranging in colour from pale yellow to flame or crimson. In the largest kinds, these distinctive flowers may grow to a length of 25 or more centimetres; they are succeeded by characteristic woody banksia cones, the follicles of which gradually open like mouths; as a result of this resemblance, together with the appearance of their gnarled and knobbly trunks, the bushes have become friendly bogeymen and great favourites with Australian children.

Although the panicles of the grevilleas and hakeas are often as uniformly clustered as those of the banksias, forming magnificent torches and candles, catkins and fleeces, many of them are less regular, more wayward and spiderlike. The vegetation of the hakeas is frequently spiky; the Proteaceae as a whole, not only vary in stature, but display immense differences of foliage, ranging from holly-shaped grey-green leaves to needle-like forms. Any short list of the finest Australian flowers would include the waratahs, of the genus *Telopea*, also a clan of the antipodean Proteaceae. The flaming torch of the New South Wales species, its clustered florets surmounting a rose of scarlet petals, is one of the world's most distinctive blossoms.

Right across the continent, we find the heaths, and, although some are restricted to small areas, as a family they form another typical keynote of the Australian flora. In Tasmania, the Richeas predominate, and the majority of these are endemic of the isle of mountains. One species, *R. scoparia*, shows extraordinarily beautiful colour variation; in the same highland thicket you may see spikes ranging through white, cream, pink, yellow, and orange to deep red. The genus includes the giant heath, *pandanifolia*, which grows to a palm-like 'tree' often 6 metres high. In Victoria, south of the Divide, the white, pink, and red heaths follow the verges of the roads; they comprise a most distinctive flora of the drier bush beyond the ranges. There are heaths in every State of Australia, with bells long and tubular; with finely recurving mouths, as in the Styphelia, whose species range from the Pacific to the Indian Ocean; with open, fluffy, shorter flowers, as in the beard-heaths (Leucopogon); heaths as exquisite as the astroloma, of Western Australia, with short crimson bells partly opening as bright pink stars to reveal a characteristic circular tuft of down within the corolla.

When you consider Australian orchids, you are faced with a range far richer than might be expected of a continent renowned for its highly specialised xerophilous vegetation. Among the 700 or more known species, it is the small terrestrial orchids that offer endless fascination to many of our keenest nature-lovers. The epiphytes grow on ferns and tree-trunks; conforming more closely perhaps to the world conception of 'orchid,' with strange, conspicuous labellum and column, curious design, delicate colour and texture, endless diversity of structure, they often rise in long, graceful sprays that seem to be nourished directly from the heavy air. There are only half a dozen epiphytes in the south, but, increasing through northern New South Wales, they number more than a hundred in Queensland.

Greenhoods, nodding and shy, shell-like, banded; and leek-orchids, sun-orchids, and helmets; all the graceful little horned orchids and spiders, and others of their kind—hooded, musky, spotted, black of tongue—are familiar

81

Top left: Lavender grevillea
G. lavandulacea in
Victoria. *Top right:* A
handsome member of the
Banksia genus of the
Proteaceae family. *Centre
left:* An isopogon or cone
bush, another member of
the Proteaceae family.
Centre right: Pink sea-
heath, *Frankenia* sp.,
common in arid saline
conditions. *Bottom left:*
Grevilleas, of many
species, flourish in most
parts of Australia. *Bottom
right:* The beauty of holly
grevillea seen close up

Top left: Nodding greenhood orchid *Pterostylis nutans. Top right:* Candle heath *Richea continentis* is found in alpine spagnum bogs in Victoria and New South Wales. *Centre left:* Pink heath *Epacris impressa*, the floral emblem of Victoria. *Centre right:* Wax flower, found in dry country; this specimen from Castlemaine, Victoria. *Bottom left:* Veined helmet-orchid *Corybas dilatatus* in Tasmania and Victoria. *Bottom centre:* Parson's bands (orchid) *Eriochilus cucullatus;* all Eastern States. *Bottom right:* Leopard orchid *Diuris maculata;* all Eastern States

to all who are prepared to seek them, and stoop to make their acquaintance. Only in size are they less grand than any of their tropical relations; and those who know them best would consider this smallness, which concentrates their fascinating beauty and structure, enchanting. The miniature leopards and tigers, and their proud sisters, purple *Diuris punctata* and the vanishing *alba*; the duck orchids; the minute flies and mosquitoes: all these offer as absolute and rare a quality of beauty as may be discovered in the most patrician and pampered lady's slipper or *Cymbidium*.

But in a brief consideration of Australian wildflowers, one is bound to be eclectic, and to attempt description of a few brilliant, curious, and outstanding genera whose common factor is that they arouse wonder and delight, and, ideally, a curiosity that can only be satisfied by much wandering and a study of the systematic botanical handbooks.[28]

It is doubtful whether any convincing organic form, whether of plant or animal, may be imagined except as compounding elements of existing, or known natural entities. The medieval artists tried to create unearthly monsters, but always ended up with an incredible zoological pastiche. I cannot recall an instance of their successfully blending plant and animal forms, with the exception, perhaps, of some of the Scythian and Celtic non-representational decoration. The snapdragon, already existed, and a hundred other reminiscent flowers, including Shakespeare's 'long purples . . . our old maids do dead men's fingers call them.' Yet, if a catalogue of the entire world's most unusual flowers were compiled, the kangaroo paws of Western Australia would certainly be entered. Nor, if grace and beauty were criteria, would they be denied.

These flowers, of which there are eight kinds—all peculiar to the rich sand-plain flora of the south-west—are aptly named, particularly the furry buds of one species.[29] They are brown-green in colour, and in each flower head, eight or twelve showing consecutive stages of development are shaped astonishingly like miniature paws of kangaroos, swelling to the knuckles and pads, and pointed as with claws. The effect is heightened by a knee-joint but, quite extraordinarily, there is a sudden change as every soft-pelted limb flowers into brilliant vermilion that continues through the bodiless stalk. When the bud opens, the upper part of the paw is serrated and recurved, showing a pale grey-green lining from which are spread the stamens. Suddenly the limb has become a swan neck with a crested head and six fantastic pale yellow bills. One species of Anigozanthos, *viridis*, as the name states, is almost entirely green, and another, called catspaw, is small and warm all over; its little furry flowers, yellow, orange, and red, open down one side to reveal pale, saffron linings. The black kangaroo paw is of a different genus— Macropidia. Its pale green buds and stems are almost totally covered with black fur from which the soft, yellow-green flowers seem to writhe in strange ecstasy.

Among the unique and striking flowers of the inland are the Sturt pea (Clianthus) which by its common name commemorates Charles Sturt, the renowned explorer, and, by one of its specific names, the old free-booter, William Dampier, who deposited the first known specimen in the herbarium at Oxford. Each flower stalk may display five or six elongated pea flowers of intensely scarlet colouring, up to 8 centimetres long, and, in the centre of each the lower part of the wings bulges blue-black and shining, like obsidian. The flowers are set off by grey-green trailing leaves and brown-purple stems, and it is difficult to recall a more striking assemblage of colours in the whole of nature, especially in combination with the desert red earth of parts of Western and central Australia, and the deep, cloudless blue of the sky.

If you would seek a tree of gold, brighter even than any of the wattles, more brilliant than you could imagine in nature, a tree that flared in the landscape as though emitting, and not merely reflecting, light, you would find it in the nuytsia of the south-west. If you would ask for a further strangeness, you would surely be satisfied in discovering that the whole tree was a mistletoe, parasitic on the roots of other trees; and yet it has been described as perhaps the finest tree of the State. It is named after Pieter Nuyts who, bound eastward across the Indian Ocean on the *Gulde Zeepaard*, seeking, like others from his country, the isles of spice, remained too far south, and in 1627 sailed across the Great Australian Bight to the islands of St Peter and St Francis.[30]

It has been said that Australian flowers are predominantly purple and yellow: yet, if you considered some of the most exquisite flowers of our land, they would include the blue leschenaultia, also of the west, ranging from 'pale azure through caerulean to deep ultramarine,'[31] or the great blue water lily (*Nymphea gigantea*) of the Northern Territory and Queensland, or even the small blue pincushion, *Brunonia australis*, or the lobelias and wahlenbergias, the most delicate bluebells in the world, having a wide distribution throughout the continent. The flaming waratah and the glowing eucalypt *ficifolia* and the desert pea would represent the reds; the whites, yellows, and purples are legion. If you sought scent, what sweeter than that of some of the boronias, more subtle than of the vanilla or chocolate lilies, more haunting than of the early nancy, more pervading than the breath of the wattles? Though it is true that so much of Australian flora is unique, yet today, perhaps, its strangeness is a thing of the past.

[1] The genus *Callitris* which includes the Murray pine (*C. columellaris*) and several other members is included in the *Pinaceae*.

[2] She-oak, or drooping she-oak, *C. stricta*; bull-oak (sometimes bulloke), *C. leuhmannii*; desert oak, *C. decaisneana*; black oak, *C. cristata*.

[3] Crowsfoot elm, *Tarrietia argyrodendron*.

[4] Walnut, of the tropical scrubs, *Endiandra palmerstonii*.

[5] Cedar, *Cedrela toona*, not a member of the genus *Cedrus*.

[6] Huon pine, *Dacrydium franklinii*; King William pine, *Athrotaxis selaginoides*; celery top pine, *Phyllocladus aspleniifolius*; pencil pine, *Athrotaxis cupressoides*.

[7] The casuarinas are so named because their fine branch structure is reminiscent of the drooping feathers of the cassowary, Latin *casuarius*.

[8] Respectively, red cedar, *Cedrela toona*; silky oak (the northern silky oak is not a grevillea), *Cardwellia sublimis*; tulipwood, *Harpullia pendula*; walnut, *Endiandra palmerstonii*, rosewood, *Dysoxylon fraseranum*.

[9] Kauri pine, *Agathis* spp., including *robusta, microstachya*, etc.; bunya pine, *Araucaria bidwillii*; hoop pine, *Araucaria cunninghamii*.

[10] See note 6.

[11] *Walkabout*, April 1947.

[12] There is also a deciduous beech in Tasmania, *Nothofagus gunnii*, often growing in a depauperate form on wind-swept mountain-slopes, and there known as tanglefoot.

[13] The Australian figs include, besides the strangling fig, *Ficus rubiginosa*, several other species: The Moreton Bay fig, *F. macrophylla*, is much planted as a fine decorative shade-tree; *F. platypoda* is a wild, edible fig of the Inland, indigestible unless quite ripe; there are several 'climbing' figs, and most jungle species put down aerial roots which finally reach the ground and help support the tree. *F. bengalensis*, the banyan, is well known for this kind of growth, and has been established in Australia.

[14] In the 1970s ten or twelve sensitive, rare habitat areas in the wet tropical lowlands of North Queensland were set aside as national parks or reserves: Melbourne *Age*, 8 January 1983.

[15] J. H. Willis, *Walkabout*, Sept. 1948.

[16] *Discoveries in Australia* (Boone, London, 1846), by Commander J. L. Stokes, who, subsequent to his work as a ship's officer on the *Beagle*, took over its command.

[17] Charles Darwin sailed as naturalist on the *Beagle*, during its long cruise, December 1831 to October 1836.

Top left: Kangaroo paw *Anigozanthos* sp., native of Western Australia. *Top right:* Another species of kangaroo paw. *Bottom:* Spring wildflowers in Parachilna Gorge, Flinders Ranges, South Australia

86

Top left: Flowers of kapok bush *Cochlospermum gillivraei* from Australia's tropical north. *Top right:* Nodding blue lilies *Stypandra* sp. in the Grampians, Victoria. *Centre left:* Rosy dock *Rumex vesicarius*, an introduced plant now widespread in the inland. *Centre right:* Mountain bitter-pea *Daviesia mimosoides*, found in the alpine areas of Victoria. *Bottom left:* Mimulus or monkey flower growing along banks of Barwon River, Victoria. *Bottom centre:* The breaking of the drought; small vigorous dicotyledons break through the desert when rain falls in central Australia. *Bottom right:* Grass trigger-plant *Stylidium graminifolium*, widespread in eastern Australia

[18] A. Searcy, in his *In Australian Tropics* (Geo. Robinson & Co., 1909), describes the tree during a visit in 1889.

[19] 'A. C. Gregory carved dates and messages on bottle-trees and baobabs to guide searchers, should he be lost. At least one such tree, on the Victoria River, remains to mark the expedition, which in 1856 the British Government organized, under his leadership, to explore central and northern Australia and to discover, if possible, traces of Leichhardt.' — From *Trees of Australia* (Australian National Travel Association, 1948). The publication contains a close-up photograph of Gregory's baobab.

[20] The quotation is from a letter written by J. H. Willis, and published in *Walkabout*, in September 1948. In the issue of August 1951, Elizabeth Durack describes how 'a giant of the species can, at times, keel over practically overnight.'

[21] *The Great Australian Loneliness*, by Ernestine Hill (Robertson and Mullens Limited, Melbourne, 1940). The description of a baobab occurs in chap. 10, of *Ports of Sunset*.

[22] From the Journal of Leichhardt's second expedition, 26 October 1844. *Journal of an Overland Expedition in Australia from Moreton Bay to Port Essington, a Distance of Upwards of 3,000 miles, during the years 1844–1845*, (London, 1847). The Prussian explorer, Friedrich Wilhelm Leichhardt, and his companions disappeared on an expedition which planned to cross the continent from east to west. It left Sydney in February 1848.

[23] See chapter 3, note 9. The grass-tree appears in a great many of the topographical sketches of the artists who accompanied the early explorers. The illustration of the kangaroo, that faces Captain Cook's entry of 24 June 1770 (vol. 3, *First Voyage*), depicts a few grass-trees in the background.

[24] Matthew Flinders first reached Australia in the *Reliance* on which he was serving, the vessel having been sent to convey Governor Hunter to New South Wales (1795). With the ship's surgeon George Bass, Flinders formed a partnership in exploration. Bass disappeared during a trading voyage in the Pacific in 1803. Flinders was given command of the *Investigator*, a vessel of 334 tons, and left England in July 1801. In the next two years he circumnavigated Australia and charted most of the unknown coasts. Robert Brown (1773–1858), who had been recommended by Sir Joseph Banks as Flinders' botanist, ultimately returned to England in 1805, with nearly 4000 species of Australian plants.

[25] The celebrated botanist, Sir Joseph Hooker, published his *Flora Antarctica* (1844–47); his *Flora Novae Zelandiae* (1853–55); and his *Flora Tasmaniae*, in 1860. He thought Western Australia 'was connected by land with the Cape district (of Africa) at a time when it was severed from eastern Australia.' — J. H. Maiden, in his Paper, 'Australian Vegetation,' delivered before the 'British Association for the Advancement of Science,' 1914.

[26] Several authorities have noted that by far the greater number of the known species of Proteaceae and Restiaceae are, for instance, confined to Australia and South Africa. But the absence of marsupial life in South Africa, or its evidence in fossils there, might seem to pose objections to the hypothetical land link. Maiden (see note 25) says: 'It would seem necessary almost that they (i.e. the marsupials) must have been present at the Cape and have died out, unless it is possible that Proteaceae and Restiaceae are very much older than marsupials, in which case they would have been very old indeed.'

[27] See note 25. J. H. Maiden, F.L.S., was a former Government Botanist of New South Wales, and Director of the Sydney Botanic Gardens.

[28] Most States publish, officially, handbooks of flora. Some, e.g. *Flora of South Australia* (J. M. Black), are clearly illustrated with line drawings. Information on what is currently available may be obtained from the offices of the Government Botanists, in the capital cities. The Commonwealth Government (1982) has produced an extensive set of volumes on Australian flora. Dr J. W. Willis's *Handbook to Plants in Victoria*, in two volumes (M.U.P.) is for the botanist and student. *The Flowers and Plants of Victoria*, by G. R. Cochrane, B. A. Fuhrer, E. R. Rotherham, and J. H. Willis, is a splendidly illustrated popular work, as is Jean Galbraith's *Wild Flowers of South-East Australia* (Collins). The Australian Systematic Botany Society's *Flora of Central Australia* (Reed, Wellington, 1981) will long prove a standard work. *How to Know Western Australian Wildflowers*, by B. J. Grieve and W. E. Blackall, in several parts, describes the flora of the West.

[29] *Anigozanthos manglesii*.

[30] Matthew Flinders in his journal of *Voyages*, 1801–3, quotes the Dutch recital of Nuyts' discovery: 'In the year 1627, the South Coast of the Great South Land was accidentally discovered by the ship *Gulde Zeepaard*, outward bound from the Fatherland, for the space of a thousand miles.' Nuyts Archipelago, containing the islands mentioned, lies offshore from the modern Ceduna (c. 134° E. long.).

[31] The Leschenaultia (of the family Goodeniaceae) is named after the botanist, Leschenault de la Tour, who was with Nicolas Baudin, the French explorer, a contemporary of Matthew Flinders. The colour description quoted is from C. A. Gardner's caption in the excellent volume of coloured photographs, *West Australian Wildflowers*, published by W.A. Newspapers Ltd.

CHAPTER 5

Tasmanian Lakelands

The voyagers essay, with eager Tasman,
To chart the darkness, quest on fateful seas,
Assess his daring, test his navigation:
A shrinking circle, tethering a dream.
Thrust by adversity, or tossed on surge,
By unknown capes around the unknown cores,
They search his secret islands, the blue shores
Where rolling streams from pole and tropic merge . . .

—from WIDE HOMELAND

THE FIRST FREE PERMIT TO EXPLORE new country is granted by its rivers. Where a coast is unbroken by estuaries, as is the case with so much of the Australian mainland's, there are no natural points of entry. This lack was one of the primary astonishments of *terra australis*, and it fostered visions of compensatory inland seas, immense gulfs, or, even, of dissecting straits, which could receive the drainage of the continent.[1] For a quarter of a century after the foundation of Sydney, the colonists were confined by the waters of the Pacific Ocean and by the wall of the Blue Mountains. Continental rivers were not discovered until Gregory Blaxland had led a successful expedition over the ancient Dividing Range; Surveyor George Evans then found them flowing away from the sea, through a promised land, from the far side of the mountains.[2] Another two decades were needed to solve the puzzle of the western rivers, and longer still to dispel the mirage of an Australian Mediterranean Sea. In Tasmania, insular, minute by comparison, exploration proceeded by the traditional method of delineating the river pattern, following up the associated spurs and, from their summits, obtaining bearings to test or prove surmise. The island was comprehensible; its problems were not of line of attack, but of terrain and weather.

One after another the tributary streams of the Derwent, on whose estuary Hobart had been founded in 1804, were traced through heavy bush and high moorland to a lakeland source. The northern streams, discovered by settlers at contemporary Port Dalrymple[3] and at the bridgeheads of the Van Diemen's Land Company, founded in 1825, were followed back to the same sources.

Long years of minor exploration ultimately proved that not only Hobart's Derwent and the Huon, but the Franklin, which helps the Gordon flush Macquarie Harbour in the far west; the Pieman further north; and the Mersey, Tamar, Levan, and Forth reaching Bass Strait—with many lesser streams—all sprang from a high plateau bearing ample evidence of former glaciation. This is an ancient and beautiful landscape, set with numberless natural lakes and tarns ranging in size from the sky-reflecting minutiae of the Traveller's Range above Lake St Clair, where there are several hundred in a

Top: Cradle Mountain, Tasmania, reaches to a height of 1420 metres.
Bottom left: Artist Pool, in the Cradle Mountain–Lake St Clair National Park. *Centre right:* Twisted Lakes, also part of the national park which covers over 1300 square kilometres of Tasmania and includes fifteen peaks over 1200 metres high.
Bottom right: The Walls of Jerusalem, on the central plateau of Tasmania

Dove Lake and Lake Lilla,
with Cradle Mountain in
the background. Barn Bluff
is on the right

space no larger than the city and inner suburbs of Hobart, to the Great Lake, of about 180 square kilometres.

Until the summer of 1971, at the southern end of the Frankland Range, near the sources of the Serpentine, lay the most sequestered of all Tasmania's glacial lakes. Occupying a dip behind ancient fluvio-glacial outwash, shone Lake Pedder, remote and far beyond the end of roads. To reach Lake Pedder on foot entailed a long rough hike, taking days on exiguous tracks through heavy scrub and button-grass. In summer, however, when the surface was lowered, it was easily accessible to those who were prepared to fly in small aircraft over uncompromising ridges, for then Pedder exposed its marvellous welcome, a smooth, white beach, 3 kilometres long and averaging 700 metres in width.[4]

Now, to provide a huge head of water, Lake Pedder is submerged with its pristine sands forever. Many metres overlie its original level; the new lake occupies an area twenty-five times that of the original. The impounded waters are linked by a canal to those of the Gordon, the whole estimated in volume to exceed twenty-seven times that of Sydney Harbour.

Preternaturally clear are my memories of Lake Pedder, with its age-old seasonal fluctuations, its specialised flora, its solitary grandeur—especially in stormy weather when clouds boiled over the deep-blue surrounding ranges. No one ever better recorded the 'vanished splendour of this once unique place' than Olegas Truchanas, who lost his life in the Gordon River Gorge on 6 January 1972. His published photographs capture perfectly that small exquisite world before the flood.[5]

Some world authorities described the flooding of Lake Pedder as 'the greatest ecological tragedy since European settlement in Tasmania'. There was genuine concern over the fate of some endemic species of aquatic animals and plants. The controversy highlighted the scientists' assertion that 'a unique and extremely valuable biological asset, about which they knew next to nothing', was destroyed for all time.

Countering laments for lost wilderness, many will rightly claim that, aesthetically, the lakes formed by the immense arched walls hold both beauty and grandeur, to say nothing of facilities for recreation and water-sports of all kinds. The government's view was that the generation of more hydro-electric power was both necessary and inevitable.

Tasmania's potential for hydro-electric power—pollution free and virtually inexhaustible—had long been obvious. In the first seventy years of the twentieth century six or eight large dams had been constructed in the central highlands and the north, impounding water which, by generating hydro-electric power for mining and industry, had transformed the Tasmanian economy. There is little wonder that the Hydro-Electric Commission won great prestige and what amounted to considerable political influence. At the beginning of the 1970s there remained untapped the immense energy potential of the South-West.

Deluged annually, in some places by 4000 millimetres of rain, the South-West is drained by several complex river systems. The conservation and exploitation of these systems, notably of the Gordon, entering the sea on the west coast, and of the Huon, with its great estuary in the south-east, will remain controversial for decades.

It remains, of course, a great feat of engineering that 1800 metres of concrete and rockfill, comprising the four dams on the upper Serpentine, Huon, and Gordon rivers, may so impound water that the South-West is islanded, the high tributaries blending. The proper questions that must be asked and answered concern the ultimate uses of energy and of wilderness, are how they affect the quality of life. The problems are not peculiar to Tasmania. Every State is faced with the necessity of damming rivers, for water reticulation in cities, the irrigation of crops, and the generation of power. Questions of the conservation of natural beauty, of unique species of flora and fauna, of systems so fragile, and of values so subtle, are especially significant in our world of difference.

Still Lake Pedder is mourned. Especially below its confluence with the Franklin, the use and potential of the Gordon became the subject of the major conservation controversy of the 1980s, not only in Tasmania, but throughout Australia. The great wild river, tumbling through immense gorges, the caverns used by Aborigines tens of thousands of years ago, the specialised flora, including rare tree species as well as the minutiae, the sheer beauty and remote grandeur of the place . . . could these be sacrificed, so that future generations might but dream of a primordial wilderness, its very landscape species extinct?

Listed, in 1982, as a region recommended for preservation by the World Heritage Committee, along with places such as the Grand Canyon, the Serengeti National Park, the Great Barrier Reef, and the Sagamartha National Park containing Mt Everest, the South-West of Tasmania remains one of the rare absolutes in our scales of values.[6]

Tasmania will always have some of the loveliest highlands and lakelands in the world. Roads now speed the visitor close enough for him to sample their delight with little effort; but the true feast is spread, according to taste, along the tracks beyond; by tranquil pools, in open acres of cushion plant, or bright, heath-like richeas; or up on the clean brown dolerite and gleaming quartzite peaks.

I am beginning to lose count of the times I have packed my rucksack, dubbined my boots days in advance of departure, and, in joyous anticipation, contemplated the swift flight over Bass Strait to Burnie or Devonport, and the road, by way of Sheffield, to the northern end of the Cradle Mountain and Lake St Clair Reserve. Soon enough you fly out from Port Phillip Heads, leaving behind a continent; about 320 kilometres of water provide a world of difference, yet, over Bass Strait, land is not long out of sight. You run out of airway sooner than of the rolling road which follows, and, taking a ridge above the Forth River, eventually stop where the Austrian naturalist, Gustav Weindorfer,[7] and his wife, settled in 1912. The rest of the way is by track for about 65 kilometres, undulating above the tree-line and down into forests; to places shadowed only by cloud, and to valleys where there is abundant shelter, plenty of clear, running water, and ample wood for campfires.

The serrated skyline of Cradle Mountain, seen from any distance, offers an immediate promise to anyone who likes scrambling on rock; and this expectation is always exceeded, whether he takes a boot-marked track, or finds a route for himself among the huge dolerite prisms; whether he spends an hour reaching one of the bristly summits, or a long day working along the ridge to the Little Horn, 370 metres above Dove Lake. In all directions are fine, distinctive mountains of about 1500 metres, and clear memorable lakes. The usual route lies southward, down beyond stumpy Barn Bluff to Lake Windermere where there is an excellent shelter hut, built of split pine slabs and palings.

There is plenty of vigorous walking in the next stage, even without attempting the alluring escarpments of Mt Pelion West or Mt Oakleigh. On both these, incidentally, I have been almost cragfast; once, on Pelion, in thickening dusk and sleet. But I cannot remember a time in this country that I would not gladly repeat; even the night in the Pelion Gap below Mt Ossa, when 100 millimetres of rain fell, and the soggy earth ejected staunchless fountains beneath my sleeping-bag. Most hikers will be delighted with the endemic flora, including the King William pines (nothing similar is found on the mainland), and the strange tree-heath, *Richea pandanifolia*, whose palmy

Top: Storm over Lake Pedder; south-west Tasmania has a very high rainfall, being directly in the path of the south-westerlies from the Antarctic. *Bottom:* The beach of Lake Pedder now lies deep under the waters of a dam

Top: Lake Gordon and the
Gordon Dam, Tasmania.
The actual powerhouse is
150 metres below the
building seen on the left.
Bottom: Little Horn from
Twisted Lakes, in the
Cradle Mountain–Lake
St Clair National Park

crown and upthrust flower-spike still seem defiantly tropical, as though surviving from a steamy primordial jungle. It is useful to know that their drooping dry underleaves are heaven-sent tinder in the wettest weather. For scenery, there is the immense cirque above the Forth Gorge, where it is not hard for the imagination to replace the vast glaciers of Pleistocene times; and every high point gives the eye 3000 square kilometres of ridges and valleys, blue as a Chinese woodcut. Ossa's little summit plateau offers an unforgettable view, bright with reflected sky and shadowed snow drifts, and with sweet summery euphrasia to soften both. Far away, the white pillar of the Frenchman seems phantasmal, as inaccessible as when it first lured men a hundred and fifty years ago. From side tracks, leading down out of the pointillism of great beech forests, a few kilometres further on, are the tumbling falls on the Mersey.

The naturalist will be prepared for his rewards; he will earn interest on any investment he has made in preliminary reading, as he searches for plants and animals peculiar to the region. In the shallow tarns he will certainly discover the mountain shrimp, *Anaspides*,[8] whose close relatives lived in the northern hemisphere, and have been fossilised since palaeozoic times; the botanist will find special attractions in the species described as part of the ancient 'antarctic' flora, closely linked with much to be found in the cold rainforests of New Zealand and Patagonia.

Perhaps the most spectacular part of the standard journey is the pass between the Du Cane Range and the Cathedral Mountain massif, where abrupt cliffs rise magnificently, and where you glimpse the incredibly steep arête of Geryon, and the astonishing vertical needles of the Acropolis.[9] I would wish some of my cragsmen friends from the English lakelands and Wales, or even the Sierra, could look upon those rock walls of Geryon, those gendarmes of the Acropolis; they could provide delightful problems for the best of them.

One winter, four of us travelled through these passes in deep, wet snow. We were fairly well prepared for the journey, using short 'skuds' of Burmese cedar as snow shoes, but progress was arduous, particularly where the snow lay in a deceptively flat sheet over the low, prickly richea, *scoparia*. There must be some magnificent ski runs over towards the Labyrinth, in the Du Cane Range; but, even in summer, few penetrate so far.

Incomparable Lake St Clair fills a deep glacial trough between the Traveller Range and the long spurs of Mt Olympus. You may finish the course on foot, in deep forest, for 20 kilometres round the western shore of the lake, having your attention suddenly diverted from the far view of Mt Ida's pinnacle by the sudden silver splash of a platypus near the bank, by the light of a flame-breasted robin, or the vibrant colour of fungi on a mossy log. There is an alternative route, through the Byron Gap, north-west of Mt Olympus, and down the valley of the Cuvier;[10] or the final stage, from the Narcissus River at the head of the lake, to Cynthia Bay, where the Ranger lives, may be made by boat,[11] a wonderfully tranquil ending to the hike.

Five kilometres beyond Lake St Clair, the walker reaches the Lyell Highway joining Hobart with Queenstown and Strahan on the West Coast,[12] and there he may rejoin the cultivated world. Provided he has been properly equipped, whether he has had good company along the route or travelled alone, he will have strengthened his love of life.

The journey may, of course, be taken in the opposite direction—rather more easily than when Anthony Trollope,[13] about a hundred years ago in Hobart Town, 'was very anxious to get to Lake St Clair, but did not succeed.'

'Lake St Clair,' he wrote, 'is nearly in the middle of the island . . . and is . . . wonderfully wild and beautiful. It was described to me as another Killarney but without roads.' The highway now runs 160 kilometres up from Hobart to

Top: Mount Gould and the Ducane Range from Lake St Clair, as seen from the lakeside track near Echo Point hut. *Bottom:* Sunrise at the junction of the Narcissus River and the northern end of Lake St Clair; Mount Ida is in the background

Derwent Bridge (where there is accommodation), and you may drive to the edge of the lake itself, but, beyond that point, as at Waldheim in the north, is a scene that has not changed in history.

Should you wish something more remote than the well-trodden ways of Cradle Mountain and Lake St Clair, it is only necessary to plan carefully a little marginal bypassing, to enter solitudes unbroken for years on end, immuring unvisited mountains and lakes. Cradle Mountain–Lake St Clair National Park is 125 000 hectares in area; the South-West reserves are close on 200 000 hectares. Westward from Derwent Bridge, the Lyell Highway runs across to another large reserve, holding the far-famed Frenchmans Gap within a 30-kilometre bend of the Franklin River. This terrain is perhaps more vigorous than that of the northern reserve; and there are others, all with mountains sculpted, and lakes gouged, by the omnipotent Pleistocene ice-sheets, the earliest of which may have aggregated 300 metres in thickness.[14]

For strong bush-walkers, who know what they are about, Tasmanian highlands, for centuries to come, will offer sufficient untrodden detail, some in scrub so dense that all progress must be continuous struggle . . . and this, three and a quarter centuries after those mountain regions held Abel Tasman's landfall in about latitude 42° . . . 'the wind south-westerly and afterwards with a light top-gallant breeze.'[15]

'In the afternoon, about 4 o'clock, we saw land, bearing east by north of us, at about 10 miles' distance from us by estimation; the land we sighted was very high; towards evening we also saw, east-south-east of us, three high mountains, and to the north-east two more mountains, but less high than those to the southward . . .'[16] In these words, on 24 November 1642, Abel Janszoon Tasman records the first sighting European eyes made of the 'Isle of Mountains.'[17] And, 'This land being the first land we have met with in the South Sea, and not known to any European nation, we have conferred on it the name of *Anthoony van Diemenslandt* in honour of . . . our illustrious master, who sent us to make this discovery . . .' The apt and deserved name, Tasmania was not adopted officially for 200 years (1853).

It is generally thought that Tasman's landfall was somewhere north of Cape Sorell and the inlet to Macquarie Harbour, and that two of the mountains seen were those appropriately named Heemskirk and Zeehan, 'crouched like two sentinel lions keeping watch over the seaboard,'[18] a century and a half later by Matthew Flinders, when he and George Bass were circumnavigating Van Diemen's Land for the first time, proving that no isthmus connected it with the mainland.[19] Had the weather been clearer, the intrepid Dutchman might have glimpsed the white tower of the conspicuous mountain some 50 kilometres inland, long afterwards called the Frenchmans Cap,[20] whose rock pinnacle was not climbed until 1855. In recent years the most difficult buttresses and faces have been scaled.

The crisp mountain country of Tasmania had long to wait before it was traversed by any but the hardiest or most desperate travellers, for the lower slopes, particularly, were clothed by scrub denser than could have been imagined. With roads and tracks literally excavated through living bush, and with bridges to cross the dark streams, the mountains are no longer so secluded; but you only need to probe through a few hundred metres in a new direction to encounter virgin forest and undergrowth.

After Tasman had seen those tall peaks in the reign of our King Charles I, the island remained unvisited for a century and a quarter, by which time French explorers were beginning an honourable record of exploration in the southern oceans. Had men like Bruni d'Entrecasteaux and Nicolas Baudin not been at least matched by James Cook, George Bass, and Matthew Flinders, British interests there might have been less firmly established and consolidated, for, although history has failed to justify the contemporary fears that the French planned colonies in New Holland, maps published in France after Baudin's return show Terre Napoleon stretching from the head of the Great Australian Bight to Wilsons Promontory.[21] As it was, the first settlements in Tasmania were avowedly to forestall the French. To the forced move was added forced labour, that of our darkest era of convict exploitation.

Prison establishments are, naturally, not ideal bases for exploration. The terror of the early convict gaols and settlements of Port Arthur, on Tasman Peninsula, in the south-east, and of the earlier Port Macquarie especially, in the west, was walled in by scrub, a barrier whose dimensions usually exceeded the span of all escapees' lives; for, ill-equipped in a country offering little natural sustenance, they usually disappeared for ever into the green entangling silence. Something of the atmosphere of the west coast, at that time, may be gleaned from Marcus Clarke's 'Topography':[22]

> Upon that dreary beach the rollers of the southern sea complete their circuit of the globe, and the storm that has devastated the Cape, and united in its eastern course with the icy blasts which sweep northward from the unknown terrors of the southern pole, crashes unchecked upon the Huon pine forests, and lashes with rain the grim front of Mount Direction. Furious gales and sudden tempests affright the natives of the coast. Navigation is dangerous, and the entrance to the 'Hell's Gates' of Macquarie Harbour at the time of which we are writing (1833), in the height of its ill-fame as a convict settlement—is only to be attempted in calm weather. The sea-line is marked with wrecks, the sunken rocks are dismally named after the vessels they have destroyed. The air is chill and moist, the soil prolific only in prickly undergrowth and noxious weeds, while foetid exhalations from swamp and fen cling close to the humid, spongy ground. All around breathes desolation; on the face of nature is stamped a perpetual frown.

Clarke goes on to say:[23]

> Once through the gates, the convict, chained on the deck of the inward-bound vessel, sees in front of him the bald cone of Frenchman's Cap, piercing the moist air at a height of five thousand feet; while, gloomed by overhanging rocks, and shadowed by gigantic forests, the black sides of the basin narrow to the mouth of the Gordon. The turbulent stream is the colour of indigo, and, being fed by numerous rivulets, which ooze through masses of decaying vegetable matter, is of so poisonous a nature that it is not only undrinkable, but absolutely kills the fish, which in stormy weather are driven in from the sea.

Perhaps no complex of Australian mountains has entered so frequently, as those of the area of Frenchmans Cap, into both our history and literature. Matthew Flinders' view inland from the sea is interpreted imaginatively by Ernestine Hill, in *My Love Must Wait*:[24]

> The melancholy of that brow-beaten shore prayed on Flinders' mind. Those lowering ranges were stupendous works of nature . . . awful effigies of peak and pylon defied in diabolical majesty the siege of wind and sea. To the boy from the Fens they were astonishment and horror. He kept well out from that ferocious coast, clapped on sail and frankly fled from its black despair, naming no more than two stark monoliths in memory of Abel Tasman's hero ships . . .

Flinders certainly did not see 'The Frenchman.' The weather was bad at the time and he was on a lee-shore, with well-founded fears and no obvious beaches if the worst should come to the worst. However, less than a degree further south, he noted and named peaks as bald, in the range he called De

Top: Ducane Range, Mount Gould, Mount Olympus, and Lake St Clair (under fog). *Bottom:* Mount Olympus from Cynthia Bay on Lake St Clair; the tourist view from the end of the road

Top: Frenchmans Cap from Barron Pass, the first close-up view walkers have on the track from the Lyell Highway. *Bottom:* Frenchmans Cap from the air; snow is on the mountain but frequently the white quartzite rock is mistaken from a distance for a covering of snow

Witt, never withholding the least honour from his great Dutch predecessor whose intention he thus honoured:

> The shore round the bight is high, and at the back were several bare peaks which, from their whiteness, might have been thought to be covered with snow; but their greatest elevation of perhaps 1,200 feet, combined with the height of the thermometer at 62°, did not admit the supposition . . . These peaks . . . probably Tasman named De Witt's Isles, from his distance having been too far off to distinguish the connecting land; and I therefore called the highest of them, lying in 43° 9½′ S., Mt De Witt.[25]

All communications with Macquarie Harbour, after the establishment of the convict settlements there, by Governor Sorell, in 1821, were by sea, and another century was to pass and perhaps dim some memory of its shame before the first road was forced through the scrub.[26] First to approach Frenchmans Cap from Hobart was the Government Surveyor, W. S. Sharland, in 1832. He glimpsed the splendid Lake St Clair on the way. Another surveyor, the indomitable J. E. Calder, was sent out in 1840, by Sir John Franklin, Lieutenant-Governor of Van Diemen's Land, to survey the possibilities of a road, and to prepare a path for his own expedition with his courageous wife. Calder wrote:[27]

> Indeed, Macquarie Harbour is a very unapproachable place from the land, travel to it as we may. The mountain range of the Frenchmans Cap, lying in the way, and shooting out its great spurs in every direction, leaving little choice as to the direction of a road. In whatever way we attempt to reach the harbour, in anything like a direct manner, we are met by some inferior arm of the mountain mass, to scale which is inevitable.

However, for Calder, nothing seemed impossible, and he eventually reached the summit of the main ridge. 'So close is the underwood of the western forests,' he writes, 'that my party never on an average cut more than a third of a mile a day through it; but it must be stated that we were greatly impeded by the difficult task of carrying forward provisions . . .'

Sir John and Lady Franklin, their backs turned to much lethargy and smug opposition, set out on their great trek in March 1842. The records of their journey include descriptions of the precise hazards of today's south-west— scrub almost indescribably dense, rain that sometimes persists for days or weeks, flooded rivers, and consequent delay. But David Burn, who travelled with the Franklins and kept a colourful diary, also revealed the pristine, sunlit beauty of the Tasmanian mountains. Describing the country near Frenchmans Cap, he writes:[28]

> It transcends the power of the most gifted pen; mine is wholly incompetent to convey the faintest idea of the scene that here meets the traveller's gaze. Its magnificent grandeur—its boundless extent—its infinite variety—its romantic loveliness—its pictorial wildness—the enchanting graces of its innumerable panoramic beauties, astound and delight, fresh subjects of admiration wooing the eye at every turn.

Burn considered that only water was needed to render the scene 'the most imposing . . . the world could probably produce.' The diarist, I imagine, was an admirer of the great English landscapist, J. M. W. Turner who, of course, was a contemporary. Yet, had David Burn been able to reach tranquil Lake Vera, or the lovely Tahune, or Lake Gertrude whose reflections would have enraptured him, his ultimate condition might have been satisfied.

Today, solely because of access roads, tracks, bridges, and shelter (in the

102

magnificent Cradle Mountain—Lake St Clair National Park), all impressions of Tasmania's mountains and lakes tend to be more objective. The haunting melancholy of the dripping, impenetrable scrub was partly a function of first-generation living at the world's end, of fear of the unknown, of the bleak oppression of convict history; and the alternate rhapsody, when the weather was fair and the scenery Eden-fresh, the virgin peaks shining and blue-shadowed through a golden sunhaze, was its natural converse. Even now, it is easy to share something of that dawn when man saw for the first time its splendid desolation. In the dense undergrowth, at any distance you wish to venture from the excavated trails, there will be a sense of occlusion. There may be the hopeless tangle of the beautiful baurera whose ethereal pink and white rosettes seem to float in air, but are connected by a wiry three-dimensioned net that is proof against any but the most determined effort. Or, especially in the south-west, you may still encounter the 'horizontal scrub' (*Anodopetalum biglandulosum*) which forms a mat of spars, the treacherous and rotten indistinguishable from the sound, over and in which a man will travel, for preference, 2 or 3 metres above the dank, fungus-strewn earth. No sooner does a branch of this strange tree grow tall, than it lies down and allows other branches to grow from it and in turn to become prostrate and interwoven with their kind.

I have struggled through new country and seventy hours' continuous rain in the south-west, carrying all my gear; and then, perhaps, in more fortunate days, sustained by faith in aerial photographs, I have entered the wonderful glade of a beech forest,[29] incredibly quiet, with vast shapeless trunks, mossed and shadowless in uniform gloom. an endless gallery of monumental figures, representing nothing. From time to time, heavy scrub gives way to plains of button-grass whose spiny tussocks are seldom conveniently placed as 'stepping-stones' through the marshy peat-lands in which they flourish.[30]

Ultimately the right ridge leads upward, and the vegetation ceases to waylay the climber. High, stony fells carry dwarf heaths, richeas with many-coloured bells, and exquisite pink and white boronias; there are firm cushion plants set with minute starry flowers in summer, and a multitude of berried plants and mosses, brilliant lichens, and everlasting daisies. In sheltered corries there is the red and golden Christmas bell; there is a delicate black lily that grows in unexpected places, often on exposed ledges; there are ferns and sundews. Tarns lie close to the summits of many mountains, as in glacial country elsewhere in the world. Far below, the forest is an olive-green and golden astrakhan with blue folds; endless peaks recede into the distance; often there is a glimmer from the sea that stretches uninterruptedly to Antarctica. Then it is one can appreciate the extravagant language used by David Burn, as he accompanied the Governor and his lady so long ago, for one has at least a vicarious sense of the extremes of relief and tension.

Frenchmans Cap is still a white eminence reaching cleanly and abruptly above the lesser peaks. Unmistakable in shape and hue, it is visible unexpectedly from many high parts of the island. Everyone who takes the road to Queenstown, opened just a century after W. S. Sharland first passed that way, looks across to the majestic mountain; every summer the number who stand on its summit increases. It is not only that the track to the Frenchman is defined on the surface of the earth, and need span no more than two days from the highway; it is as much that the route is known through the years, and the journey is comprehensible.[31]

When one comes to look at it, the way is direct enough—over the Franklin River and the Franklin Hills, from the main ridge of which the peaks stand clearly within one's visual compass; down to the South Loddon, a tributary of the Franklin, and along the Loddon Plains, stumbling and squelching through the button-grass. So far the trail has meandered, but now it suddenly

Left: Mount Geryon and Lake Elysia from one of the many lakes on the Labyrinth. *Above:* Dove Lake and Cradle Mountain, the view seen by those who do not venture far from their cars. *Right:* Lake Rodway, Little Horn, and the southern view of Cradle Mountain

becomes purposive, and climbs by Philp's Lead[32] to sequestered Lake Vera; thence, steeply, 300 metres by scree and ancient moraine, up to the Barron Pass.

On the first visit, you tend to rush the hurdles; the great cirque south of Vera is worth several energetic days, if weather and time permit. From the Barron Pass there is a pleasantly distinctive traverse among huge rocks, with some hidden shelter from rain, and a steady, mainly ascending valley of about a kilometre or so to the little Lake Tahune, right under the Frenchman himself. Another kilometre or so of steep scrambling, mostly on rock, lifts the hiker to the summit of one of the finest rock massifs in Australia. There would be no difficulty in bestowing superlatives on most of the route . . . unless it were raining and your feet were really sore . . .

Stand on the summit as long as you can, and gaze down over lakes and forests, to peaks that will always be remote unless you spend months in this region, to the valley of the Franklin 1250 metres below, and to the Engineer Range beyond; catch the gleam on Macquarie Harbour and the western horizon along which Tasman sailed. Everyone who visits the Frenchman remembers him in his own way. My most vivid recollection, subduing occasions of mist and driving rain, is of a summer sunset, when the age-old white rock was flushed, a great finger raised to the sky, to count the millennia, and test for ever the force of the westerlies as they encircle the world. I stood there while the sun left every other mountain within sight, and watched as each in turn flared for a moment, then became one with the blue-grey night lifting in the east. The way down to a brilliant campfire that excavated a flickering cavern in the night was accomplished easily, in a starlit euphoria. When the fire became embers, the Frenchman rose black against the stars; but he withdrew in mist during the night, and I have since seen him only from a distance.

All the early explorers, if not frankly fearing it, seem to have looked askance at the sunset coast of Tasmania. For their vessels it was a grim lee-shore where the breakers of the longest and strongest oceanic fetch conceivable crashed incessantly on the stony end of the world. Westward, in that latitude, the circumpolar West Wind Drift is uninterrupted by any land before South America—along the parallel, nearly 18 000 kilometres away. Occasionally, I have come up from the southern pack-ice through storms lasting many days, and found relative calm along the eastern seaboard of Tasmania. But, gone for ever are the dangerous days when sail could no further be shortened on masts blown bare, nor, under any sail, tack or tactic give security.[33] The effect of the westerlies is now measured mainly on land; but the rains they let fall are also a fair indication. In some parts of the Tasmanian West Coast rainfall is more than 2500 millimetres annually, a quantity exceeded in Australia only in a small area in tropical Queensland. The precipitation decreases sharply with distance from the sea; the central plateau, including the environs of Cradle Mountain and Lake St Clair, receives less than half the rainfall of Queenstown or Macquarie Harbour.

South-west Tasmania is still unsettled and sparse of roads because of the weather and the density of the scrub; yet both become less formidable wherever there is shelter and access. These are the factors that in time have made even England 'a green and pleasant land.' In Tasmania are thousands of square kilometres of country without any habitation, including some of the finest mountains and fairest lakeland of the entire island. Already some of these have been claimed by joy and pride of heritage, and constituted as the Mt Field and Harz Mountains National Parks, where their qualities may be preserved for many generations.

Through the years, explorers, whalers, prospectors, hunters, and 'piners' cutting out the valuable Huon pine-logs, have all found sanctuary at Port

Davey and Bathurst Harbour, and various tracks have been cut by determined men; but, while intention was mainly specialised and of small economic interest, almost all were lost beneath the scrub's returning tide. The area has always held an irresistible appeal for the adventurous and, in these lithe days of bush-walking and amateur exploration, not only are some of the old routes being reopened, but new ones are being established.[34] White water canoeing and rafting has become very popular on the turbulent rivers of the South-West.

A solitary trail about 100 kilometres long over the lonely Huon and Arthur plains is still the established link between the extensive, sheltered waters of Port Davey and the named *places*, Kallista and Maydena, on the road leading back to Hobart. The South Coast Track back to the road south of Geeveston is as long. New roads were built for the construction and maintenance of the Huon–Serpentine impoundment and the town of Strathgordon also is residual from that enterprise. Study any map of the South-West, and you will find few *place names* as distinct from those applied to physical features; mountains, sometimes named from a distance, lakes glimpsed from high places, and rivers disappearing in blue-hazed valleys, are the delight and the challenge—both frequently augmented by the different moods of weather and scrub. With every year comes new knowledge as ways are found through the ranges, and across the complex river systems of the Huon and Gordon.

Much is still country for the unhurried, the deliberate, and the experienced, who are prepared to take what comes and to keep moving; but the rewards are often enough in strict proportion to the difficulty. Naturally, each time a route is repeated, it becomes easier, and there can be no doubt that good tracks and robust shelter huts will some day remove from the south-west most of the bunyips—such as once howled round the Frenchmans Cap.

For several years after the second World War, the way in to the spectacular Federation Peak,[35] in the southern Arthur Range was truly a *tour de force*, beset all the way by uncertainties of route and weather, by doubt concerning river crossings, and by problems of carrying sufficient food. Much of the surrounding country, ice-gouged, remote, still revealing the innumerable moraines of the last great ice age, had been seen only from the air. Today, the peak is becoming as popular as the Frenchman; the route is well defined, and several climbing routes have been established on the mountain. It is different from the time when we waited three days before a rope could be stretched across the turbulent Picton River; when the cold west Craycroft was waded because it flowed through a tunnel in almost impenetrable scrub, and that was the easiest way; when, only a day later, moss was squeezed at the famous Porridge Camp on the final ridge; even the scramble up to the pinnacle is not quite the same climb it seemed when the summit was still virgin.

I believe that the opening up of the Tasmanian lakelands by well-defined foot-tracks must lead to a proper and better evaluation and appreciation of them. For those who will still seek the unknown and unexpected in the South-West, as in many other parts of Australia, for many generations there will be somewhat smaller blank spaces that are *terra incognita*.

It is not necessary to be a Spartan or Amazon to penetrate and love this country. Energetic young men and women each year redraw the frontiers. It is their birthright, handed down from both the remembered and the forgotten, who were not deterred by any kind of obscurity that made the way seem difficult. Hydro-electric projects have necessitated the building of new roads to the headwaters of the Gordon, Franklin and Huon rivers, with access to ways as appreciated among the noble peaks of the Frankland Range as by their namesake, writing in 1835, of the Lake St Clair country, now visited by

This page and facing page: Franklin River in south-west Tasmania, a place of rugged beauty

thousands. 'The view from this point,' he wrote, describing what he saw from the newly climbed top of Mt Olympus, 'was beyond all description: the whole of Lake St Clair lay at our feet with its beautiful bays and golden beaches,[36] and in addition we could descry at least twenty other lakes of various dimensions . . .' Anyone who has an eager heart and stout legs may, even today, share George Frankland's exaltation.[37]

[1] Of the problem, as it appeared at the beginning of the nineteenth century, Matthew Flinders wrote, in the Introduction to his *Voyages*: 'What rendered a knowledge of this part more particularly interesting, was the circumstance of no considerable river having been found on any of the coasts of Terra Australis previously explored: but it was scarcely credible that, if this vast country were one connected mass of land, it should not contain some large rivers; and if any, this unknown part was one of two remaining places, where they were expected to discharge themselves into the sea.'

[2] The old promise of delectable lands on the further side of the ranges had lured many to attempt the crossing of the Blue Mountains; but none was successful until Blaxland, Lawson, and Wentworth forced a route in 1813. Wentworth described the triumph in a poem submitted in a competition at Cambridge, in 1816:
'. . . the beauteous landscape grew,
Opening like Canaan on rapt Israel's view.'
Quoted by Prof. Ernest Scott, in his *A Short History of Australia* (O.U.P., 1916).

[3] Port Dalrymple, like Hobart, was established for fear that an unoccupied coast might be claimed and settled by the French.

[4] The last time I visited Lake Pedder was in December 1971, when C. E. R. Parsons flew R. R. Baldwin, R. Maddever, and me to the sequestered beach, so soon afterwards to be inundated. We camped by the lake for some days.—J.M.B.

[5] *The World of Olegas Truchanas* (Olegas Truchanas Publication Committee, Hobart, 1975), edited by Norman Laird, with a Memoir by Max Angus.

[6] *The South West Book—A Tasmanian Wilderness* (Australian Conservation Foundation, 1978) is essential reading for those who would wish to appreciate mutually irreconcilable views concerning the future of the South-West. Sir Mark Oliphant contributes a trenchant foreword, and sections on History, the Natural Environment, Recreation, Industry and Conservation are co-ordinated by experts in their respective fields.

[7] *Peaks and High Places*, an excellent monograph published by the Scenery Preservation Board, Tasmania, and written by I. R. Boss-Walker, pays tribute to Weindorfer, 'who built Waldheim . . . and was for many years its genial host. Weindorfer was an excellent linguist and also a close student of natural history, and made frequent contributions to scientific journals in Europe.' The booklet is also a guide, and much to be recommended to the visitor to whom good maps are also readily available from Tasmanian travel offices.

[8] The mountain shrimp, *Anaspides tasmaniae*, grows to about 6 centimetres long. The largest freshwater crayfish known, *Astacopsis franklinii*, is also found only in Tasmania. It attains a length of 50 or more centimetres and may weigh 4 kilograms.

[9] The bestowing of classical names in the area was begun, doubtless, when Mr Surveyor George Frankland climbed the mountain dominating Lake St Clair and called it Olympus, early in 1835. The nomenclature has been much criticised almost ever since; however, the name Acropolis is descriptively apt, and is quite recent, replacing the name Porcupine given by Chapman and Urquhart in 1935 (see *Peaks and High Places*, by Ian Boss-Walker).

[10] Named for the great French naturalist, Baron Cuvier, whose major work, *Regne Animal*, a systematic description of the animal kingdom, was first published in 1816. Frankland named a nearby mountain also after Cuvier.

[11] For boat transport, the Ranger, at Cynthia Bay (Derwent Bridge) should be contacted well in advance.

[12] The West Coast is so distinctive a region, climatically, physiographically, and ecologically (and, for long, socially), that the capitals are proper.

[13] Anthony Trollope, 1815–1882, the distinguished traveller and novelist, published his *Australia and New Zealand* in two volumes, in 1873.

[14] A. N. Lewis, 1933, *Proceedings*, Royal Society, Tasmania; quoted by Charles F. Laseron, in *The Face of Australia* (Angus & Robertson, 1953).

[15] Tasman quotations from *Sources of Australian History*, by M. Clark (O.U.P., 1957).

[16] Thought to be those named by Flinders, Heemskirk, and Zeehan, after Tasman's ships.

[17] *Isle of Mountains*, by Charles Barrett (Cassell, 1944); a useful, popular account of Tasmania.

[18] *For the Term of His Natural Life* (Bk II: The Topography of Van Diemen's Land), Marcus Clarke, 1874. Now available in *The World's Classics* (O.U.P.).

[19] *Flinders' Voyage* (1814: *A Voyage to Terra Australis*): quoting Bass: 'Whenever it shall be decided,' says Mr Bass in his journal, 'that the opening between this and Van Diemen's Land is a *strait*, this rapidity of tide, and the long south-west swell that seems to be continually rolling in upon the coast to the westward, will then be accounted for.'

[20] Frenchmans Cap does not seem to have been known by name by John Rolland, in 1824: however, Jorgen Jorgenson mentions it as such, in 1826. It is very unlikely that Jorgenson really saw the mountain.

In *Van Diemen's Land*, Henry Widdowson (London, 1829), says that the Cap derived its name from 'its generally being covered with snow, and bearing some resemblance to the shape of that article of dress which invariably adorns the head of a French cook.' The first record of an ascent of the final rocky summit is a Tasmanian Lands and Survey Dept. report, but, unfortunately the names of the party are not disclosed. However, the names W. Alcock Tully, Charles A. Glover, and F. N. Spong, and the date, 10 January 1857, were found carved on wood by Thomas Bather Moore, on 14 April 1887. (Communications from Archives Section, The State Library of Tasmania, Hobart, 1 May 1964.)

[21] A copy of this map is reproduced in *A Short History of Australia*, by Ernest Scott (Oxford, 1930).

[22] See note 18.

[23] *For the Term of His Natural Life* (Bk 2, chap. 2: 'The Solitary of "Hell's Gates"'), by Marcus Clarke, 1874.

[24] *My Love Must Wait*, by Ernestine Hill (Angus & Robertson, 1941).

[25] Introduction, *Flinders' Voyages*, 1814, p. 177.

[26] The first regular road service started on 1 September 1932. The official opening of the Hobart-West Coast Road was performed on 19 November 1932, by the Tasmanian Lieutenant Governor, Sir Herbert Nicholls.

[27] Quoted by Professor Kathleen Fitzpatrick, in *Sir John Franklin in Tasmania, 1837–1843* (Melbourne University Press, 1949). This is a most valuable work in the history and topography of the area.

[28] Professor Kathleen Fitzpatrick gives the source as 'Narrative of the Overland Journey of Sir John and Lady Franklin and Party from Hobart Town to Macquarie Harbour,' published in *Colburn's United Service Magazine and Naval and Military Journal* (London, 1843).

[29] See chap. 4: There are two Tasmanian beeches. *Nothofagus cunninghamii* is the forest beech, generally called myrtle in Tasmania. *Nothofagus gunnii* is a deciduous beech often growing in a depauperate, prostrate form high on the mountains, and only showing arboreal status under favourable conditions in high valleys.

[30] Button-grass, *Gymnoschoenus sphaerocephalus*.

[31] However, an article in *Walkabout*, April 1964, entitled 'Formidable Frenchmans Cap,' should serve as a warning to the inexperienced or ill-equipped hiker.

[32] Mr John Ernest Philp was commissioned by the Dept. of Works, Hobart, 6 January 1910, to cut a track connecting the Overland Track (Ouse to Linda) with the Frenchmans Cap. The work was completed by mid-March 1910. (Records in the Archives Section, State Library of Tasmania.)

[33] At Port Davey, there are still indications of the extensive graveyard that once existed there. Many of the interments were of seamen. One wooden head 'stone,' existing until recently, records the death of Patrick Bourke, who fell from aloft on the barque *Planter*, in 1872 ('Tasmania's Lonely Fjord,' by M. O'Brien, *Walkabout*, March 1948).

[34] The members of the Hobart Walking Club, one of the most active and capable bodies of its kind in Australia, have made many remarkable expeditions into south-west Tasmania. Their numbers have sometimes been augmented by enthusiasts from other States.

[35] Although the author was fortunate in leading the first ascent of Federation Peak in January 1949, he was greatly assisted by aerial photographs of the locality, and, for many years, gallant and persistent work had been performed by members of the Hobart Walking Club in cutting some of the approaches, especially on to a shoulder of Mt Picton. The very bad weather which had so frequently hampered earlier attempts, lifted for the final climb by members of the Geelong College Exploration Society.

[36] Since Frankland's time the scene is little changed, but the beaches are now usually submerged by the lake, dammed for water-conservation and hydroelectricity. In very dry summers I have walked along fine beaches on the western side (J.M.B.).

[37] Frankland's report is quoted at length in Charles Barrett's *Isle of Mountains*. The account of the 1835 expedition was published, about a hundred years later, as *Tasmania's Wonderful Highlands*.

CHAPTER 6

The Old Australians

Now from the fragments, the remnants, the whispers,
Urgent the summons of phantom Churinga:
Tribesmen shall gather from infinite shadow:
Kaitish, Binbinga, and sad Whakelbura,
Kakadu, Mara, and central Arunta—
Many the totems, and endless the dreams.

—from WIDE HOMELAND

'THE INDIANS SAT DOWN UPON THE ROCKS, and seemed to wait for our landing; but to our great regret, when we came within about a quarter of a mile, they ran away into the woods . . .' On Friday, 27 April 1770, Captain Cook records in these words his first close approach to the people and the shores of Australia.[1] On the next day he landed, not without opposition, finding it necessary to fire with small shot on the few Aborigines who, with stones and spears, courageously opposed him. The great navigator certainly intended no harm to them but, from that first east-coast meeting of Europeans and Aborigines,[2] came a mutual distrust that neither the love nor fear of the black man or the white man could ever completely allay.

Out of the cruelty and degradation that the European invasion brought to a people which had occupied Australia for fully 40 000 years,[3] gradually there arose among the Europeans a comfortable acquiescence in the thought of what might still seem inevitable, the assimilation of the Aboriginal people into the Australian population as a whole.

However, by a deeper sense of responsibility in the white, and a new pride and power of self-determination in the black, that integration, once seeming imminent, has advanced further into the future. Though perhaps analogous to some other ethnic fusions, it may be entered ultimately by the Aborigines from a position of strength and self-awareness.

So much is irrevocable; it is the pattern of history. The only ways its course could have been averted are unthinkable: that Australia had never been discovered; that no First Fleet had ever anchored in Botany Bay. Many terrible injustices were suffered by the Aborigines; for years the most significant—such as the bitter cruelty of depriving them of ancestral lands—were not even fully understood. Some dreadful massacres, by both black and white men, marked the extension of European settlement to the lonely Inland. Yet it may be assumed that the time will come when a posterity of both invaders and invaded will wish for no reversal of time.[4]

In a moving passage from the preface of her *Timeless Land*,[5] Eleanor Dark has written:

> The Australian Aboriginal had great virtues; in a fairly extensive reading I
> have been able to discover no vices save those which they learned from the
> white invaders of their land. I do believe that we, nine-tenths of whose

'progress' has been a mere elaboration and improvement of the technique, as opposed to the art of living, might have learned much from a people who, whatever they may have lacked in technique, had developed that art to a very high degree. 'Life, liberty, and the pursuit of happiness'—to us a wistful phrase, describing a far-away goal—sums up what was, to them, a taken-for-granted condition of their existence.

I have discovered little in books, and less on my journeys among Aborigines and part-Aborigines, to make me doubt the basic truth of Eleanor Dark's belief. However, the precarious conditions under which life and liberty existed were often very hard, and the constant pursuit of food was charged with difficulty and the necessity for complex ritual. As the Aboriginal was swift to discover, the art of living is not necessarily debased by technical resources.

There is now a great and increasing interest in the Australian Aborigines. This is reflected in the popular descriptive works being published, and by the fine reproductions of Aboriginal art that are now available. For many years, my interest in the Aborigines was based on the excellent works of Baldwin Spencer and F. J. Gillen,[6] and on a couple of older volumes on the now almost extinct peoples of Victoria.[7] Some years before Eleanor Dark's *Timeless Land* appeared, Professor A. P. Elkin's now standard work, *The Australian Aborigines*,[8] became available, and H. H. Finlayson's *The Red Centre*[9]—the latter providing me with dream goals that the war years only made more alluring.

Today, numerous works deal with all aspects of the Aborigines' prehistory and archaeology, physical anthropology, languages, social structure, religion, culture and mythology.[10] Contemporary welfare, education, and land rights, especially since the establishment of the Australian Department of Aboriginal Affairs (1972), when self-determination, rather than assimilation became the proclaimed government policy, have been under continual review. The Federal Government then assumed responsibility for the welfare of Aborigines in all States, the transference from regional control being virtually complete by 1976.[11] Official reports on health, welfare, education, employment and land ownership are available.[12]

In the early days, lack of security and the vast unknown made many Europeans look on our Aborigines with fear and abhorrence. Captain Cook might again be quoted:

> . . . yet we know that if any should be left on board to perish in the waves, they would probably suffer less upon the whole than those who should get on shore, without any lasting or effectual defence against the natives, in a country, where even nets and fire-arms would scarcely furnish them with food; and where, if they should find the means of subsistence, they must be condemned to languish out the remainder of life in a desolate wilderness, without the possession, or even hope, of any domestic comfort, and cut off from all commerce with mankind, except the naked savages who prowled the desert, and who perhaps were some of the most rude and uncivilized upon the earth.[13]

What a difference fifty years were to make! In 1822 Governor Macquarie stated in a report '. . . the children of the natives have as good and ready an aptitude for learning as those of the Europeans, and they are also susceptible of being completely civilized.'[14] And, at about the same time, W. H. Hovell, the explorer, writes in his Journal:

> Those are the people we generally call 'miserable wretches,' but in my opinion the word is misapplied, for I cannot for a moment consider them so. They have neither house rent nor taxes to provide, for nearly every tree will

Facing page: Ayers Rock rises over 300 metres above the surrounding sand and gravel plains. It was first reported by Giles in 1872. *Above:* Mount Olga, with Ayers Rock in the background 48 kilometres to the east. *Right:* Many caves at the base of Ayers Rock contain Aboriginal paintings concerning the Dreamtime. The Aboriginal name for the rock is Uluru

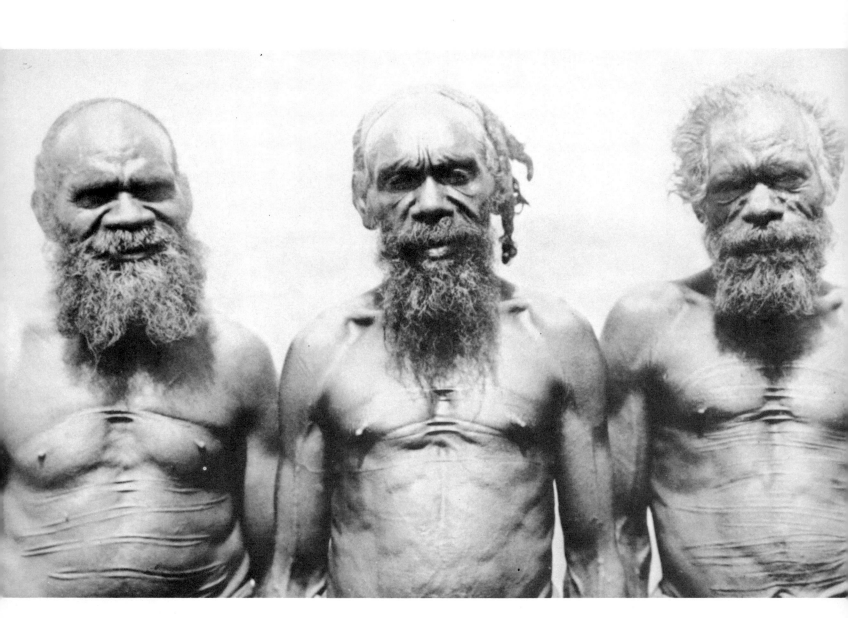

furnish them with a house, and perhaps the same tree will provide them with food. They are happy within themselves; they have their amusements and but little cares; and above all they have their free liberty.[15]

A late nineteenth century photograph of Aborigines from central Australia

'Life, liberty, and the pursuit of happiness!' Certainly whatever of these existed among the Aborigines before the arrival of the Europeans, began, after that time, to change, perhaps become more complex. Cook writes: '. . . as we saw no house, nor any remains of a house, we were inclined to believe that as these people had no clothes, they had no dwelling; but spent their nights, among the other commoners of Nature, in the open air;'[16] and Governor Phillip's chronicler, describing the cicatrices that either for decorative or ceremonial purposes scarred the bodies of the Aborigines, thought 'probably, therefore, these are marks of distinction: ambition must have its badges, and where cloaths are not worn, the body itself must be compelled to bear them.'[17] It would certainly be very difficult to persuade contemporary civilised Aborigines that their freedom and happiness would be increased by reversion to such simplicities.

It is true that many records of the Aborigines will remain for ever, and that much of the old life will even be re-enacted, probably by direct descendants of the last surviving tribes; it is certain that vast collections of stone and wooden artefacts will be treasured and endlessly described, and that Aboriginal carvings and paintings will be preserved and, at least from illustrations, become familiar to everyone. It is even probable that the numbers of dark

116

people will increase, eventually, beyond the estimations of the number that
existed in the era before the European's arrival. But they will no longer be
other than European, except, to varying degrees, in a purely physical sense;
and, as individuals, less may separate them ultimately from other Australians
than that which may distinguish two men born of the same mother.

The world of difference between the old Australians and ourselves lies
more in aspirations, skills, and traditions, than in species or, perhaps, even in
race. Several able ethnologists have recognised the Aborigines as Caucasians,
like the Aryans and Semites; certainly the typical Aboriginal cast of features
differs no more from either of the latter than theirs do from each other; and
there are individuals or family groups of Aryans, for instance, in appearance
differing only in colour of skin from Aborigines.[18] Other scientists use the
word Australoid[19] to denote a special division of mankind comprising the
Australian Aborigines and some peoples of the lands through which they may
have migrated long ago. But, however classified, they belong to *Homo
sapiens*, for whom exists no absolute canon differentiating virtues of skin
colour or of healthy physical forms. History, including that of twentieth-
century Europe, has stressed this fact a hundred times, and the future of the
world assuredly depends on its universal recognition.

The Australian Aborigines are now generally considered to have migrated
southward from Asia because of ethnic pressures originating further north,
some, quite possibly, as a result of advancing ice during the several periods
of more intense Pleistocene glaciation.[20] The same primary climatic urging

117

Facing page: Edward River country on the west coast of Cape York peninsula; the community of Aborigines there maintain a state of virtual self-determination. *Top right:* On the edge of the Gibson Desert, near Docker River, Western Australia. *Bottom right:* Aboriginal desert food; this small boy displays the results of the morning's foraging: a lizard and an echidna

would coincide, of course, with opportunities of using land bridges or island stepping-stones that, with the melting of the ice-sheets, and the consequent rise of world sea-levels, were to disappear. Separated by periods of time, immense by human standards, each peak of ice accumulation offered the means and incentives for human migrations. Evidence of the inconstancy of sea-level is often seen in coastal shelves and platforms obviously once covered by the sea, or by wave-worn cliffs now well inland from the shore.[21] These show that the seas once rose higher; but, conversely, the presence of glacial erratics on high plateaux and mountain-tops may be taken to indicate ice-levels correlated with land surfaces that have been submerged since the ice melted.[22] There appear to have been several fluctuations during the last 20 000 years. During one of the more recent inundations, Bass Strait was formed, thus cutting off the Tasmanian Aborigines from contact with the mainland whose inhabitants may themselves have by then lost their land link with New Guinea.

Because of the probability of several waves of migration over a very long period, it is not surprising that some anthropologists do not consider the mainland Aborigines physically homogeneous. Some consider that the extinct Tasmanians were of a different ethnic group, negroid or negrito, darker than most mainland peoples, and with a less developed culture. They might have been the vestiges of an earlier migratory movement forced south across the Bassian isthmus by more virile immigrants. Other pockets of various periods might have persisted on the mainland, and have caused the broad differences that seem to have existed between some Aboriginal people on the east coast and those of the Centre, or of the far west. When you consider that in spite of the migrations and conquests in Europe over the last two or three thousand years. Celtic, Nordic, Mediterranean, and other typical characteristics have survived within the general European racial unity, it would indeed be surprising to find absolute uniformity of type in Australia.[23]

Nevertheless, there are as many characteristic features of the Australian Aborigines as a whole as there are of comparable ethnic groups such as the Europeans, the Red Indians, or the Eskimos. Professor Elkin provides one of the best and most succinct descriptions ever written of the Australian Aboriginal:

> . . . no one could mistake an Aborigine. The following is a general description: chocolate-brown skin which appears black when sunburnt and unwashed; usually a low or retreating forehead and a narrow head which is sometimes keel-shaped on top; eyes deep set; eyebrow ridges sometimes very heavy but not made of a solid piece of bone as in Neanderthal man; nose, depressed at root and fairly wide at the nostrils; jaws sometimes prognathous; mouth wide, skull cap very thick; hands very slender; legs also slender and buttocks slight; very erect carriage of the body; average height about five feet five or six inches, with variations from short to tall, some individuals being over six feet. In most of these features the Australian Aborigine differs from ourselves, the Mongol and the Negro, and therefore is rightly classed, as already stated, in a special human division.[24]

Could there here be an echo of Tacitus describing another people who had been subdued; who, ultimately, would be invaded times almost without number, absorbing, and being absorbed, until they became part of a greater humanity?

Those habits, skills, values, aspirations, prejudices, and traditions, which seem so fundamentally to differentiate the Europeans and the Australian Aborigines, are acquired after birth, as a result of formal or informal education. Knowledge and tastes, fashions, manners and morals, for black man and white man alike, are transmitted only to the conscious mind,

120

however subconscious they may ultimately become. Language has controlled imitation and modified our responses to instinct, while writing has enormously intensified the process of learning, and made possible the kind of specialisation that is essential to our modern scientific advances. But it must always be remembered that 'there is no evidence that, given equal opportunities, our Aborigines are not capable of the same achievements as white Australians. Indeed there is positive evidence to the contrary and many individuals have shown themselves possessed of outstanding qualities.'[25]

For the Aborigines to be given equal opportunities they must receive from birth the same nurture and nourishment, both physical and mental, as other Australians. Where two societies are separated by social and linguistic frontiers, assimilation within one, or two, or even several generations, is only possible where it might seem appropriate or welcome to the elders on both sides of the barrier. But today the rigidity of the frontier which, in fact, with interchange of knowledge, started to yield at the beginning, has given way, leaving in its place the broad territory of the part-Aborigines who, either culturally or in blood, have also become part-Europeans.[26] A celebrated anthropologist[27] has likened the state, existing to some degree throughout most of Australia, to a continuum, at one end of which 'people are coming into contact with Europeans for the first time (. . . there are very few of these indeed); and, at the other, those who are in the process of merging entirely with the dominant groups, the Europeans (that is to say, who are assimilated and acculturated).'

The passing of the Aborigines, from a tenuous, uncertain, and highly specialised nomadic life to the comparatively colourless diffusion of civilised security, must arouse feelings which include both regret and sympathy, particularly during the transitional periods, in areas where maladjustment to such vast change is most common.

Soon after the establishment of the Federal Department of Aboriginal Affairs in 1972, a national advisory body, consisting of thirty-six 'freely elected, salaried representatives of the Aboriginal and Torres Strait Islander peoples, each coming from a separate geographic area of Australia' was set up, to advise the Government on Aboriginal opinion. By the 1980s the National Aboriginal Conference, as the body was called, had formulated proposals designed to dissolve the long-standing unrest of their people in an agreement, or 'Makarrata', with the Federal Government. The proposals included recognition of the blacks' prior ownership of Australia, land rights,[28] cash compensation, and reserved seats for Aboriginals in Parliament. The Aborigines had been forced to forsake their creeds for the materialism of the European invaders. Though there lie ahead years of frustration and apathy; though progress seem belated, this were, of its kind, assimilation indeed. Though it might be inevitable, and ultimately welcomed by all, a unique quality and way of life will have been lost.

> *Men are we, and must grieve when even the shade*
> *Of that which once was great is passed away.*

And yet, perhaps the emptiest form of regret is for the inevitable, whose course so often bears the same relation to the racial desire revealed by history, as that of will power, or total intention, to the behaviour of the individual. We often regret most bitterly what we would not change.

The disappearance of the Aborigines from the most fertile parts of the continent is a result of our own success as colonists, as founders of a great, civilised community in less than two centuries; our regret is a manifestation of our security. We have little ground for presuming that, unless the difficult frontier conditions of a century and a half ago, we should have acted much differently from our ancestors.

121

Most natural features in Kakadu National Park, Northern Territory, have a sacred meaning to the Aborigines

Facing page: Two photographs of Aboriginal food gathering, taken around the turn of the century: at the top file snakes are being transported after a day's hunting, and below is seen a fishing expedition

Our growth of interest as a nation in the Aborigines is a direct result of the extinction of the tribes. Some observers have rather cynically regarded this interest as an academic virtue, an aggrandisement for our intellectual comfort, rather than a guarantee of the protection of the few remaining full-blooded tribesmen. It is a recent fashion for any large number of people to be concerned at the possible extinction of a type or species, either of plant or of animal. Presumably a desire for the conservation of life-forms for scientific reasons has been a product of universal education, but the multifarious philosophic and other reasons motivating the primary impulses are not immediately apparent.

Perhaps the extinction of a species is a form of denial, the decreation of an objective truth, a kind of cosmic life. Pure science, considered absolutely, and in its eternal quest for greater self-awareness, is merely food for the spirit of man. Today, when a non-human species appears endangered, there is a great outcry for its preservation. Rigid protective measures are enforced by civilised communities, food provided, and therapy undertaken as necessary. If regeneration of the species occurs, even from a few isolated colonies or families, to the extent that the creature is no longer in danger of extinction, we are satisfied. Although they have been both advocated and attempted, such measures cannot be applied to the Aborigines, for they are of our own species with minds of their own, and, in the inevitable marginal no-man's-land where we have substituted social services for our former callousness and fear, the movement is spontaneously towards assimilation with the white community. If the Aborigines themselves can control the movement's pace, and the process itself, from a position of dignity, with adequate land rights, the conscience of white Australians may be eased.

Once the Aborigines were free and uncluttered by material possessions; they were immensely skilful, and possessed the pride of personal achievement in the arts of living; their aspirations did not bind them to toil and struggle for wealth and position; their traditions were venerable and meaningful. As in the matters of pigmentation and physique, there is no absolute criterion of morality; yet the Aborigines were a happy, kindly, and tolerant people, and shrank away horrified at the inhumanity they witnessed in the men of the First Fleet. When a convict, taken in the act of stealing from the Aborigines, was ordered to be flogged in their presence, 'there was not one of them that did not testify strong abhorrence of the punishment, and equal sympathy with the sufferer. The women were particularly affected, shedding tears and menacing the "executioner." '[29]

The Aborigines' visions of the world, of the meaning of life and death, of beginning, duration, and end, of property attached to person, were such as to make the ways of the settlers both comical and inexplicable.[30] The Aboriginal was bound to his tribal territories by a spiritual bond of which the first European settlers were completely ignorant. Dispossession of traditional hunting preserves was serious enough, both physically and socially, for it meant starvation, or invasion of land already carrying a capacity population; but the coincidental loss of the only home of their living spiritual ancestors, of themselves after death, and of their posterity, brought lethargy and despair. The tribes coveted no territory other than their own, and, after their fashion, regulated their increase to its capacity.[31] Deprivation of their ancient lands was less conceivable than death; localities were linked to the Dream-time in which all men had their beginnings and their reason of being, to a spiritual reality behind the sensory appearance and perception.[32] The size of tribal lands probably varied inversely with their fertility, a balance of population with food potential which must have taken many thousands of years to evolve. Though the human inhabitants were so integrated with the land that its deprivation might bring death to elderly tribesmen, the animals

Facing page and above: Aboriginal rock paintings in Kakadu National Park, Northern Territory. *Right:* Aboriginal markings in the Cave of Hands, Grampians, Victoria. The hand out-lines were obtained by blowing ochre over a hand held against the cave wall

could retreat before the press of European settlers. To the Aborigines, sheep and cattle, replacing native fauna, must have seemed theirs by right.

The desire and intention of the white men was for change, to recast the land, and to mould the future to a known, western European pattern; to compress slow time, and to rearrange space, to subdue, to catalogue, to evaluate, to compare . . . For the black man, the land was changeless in eternity, containing ever-recurring patterns, varying only with the known seasons, and, perhaps, by the caprice of spirit beings, who, in any case, could be propitiated, largely controlled, and influenced, provided the proper ceremonies were enacted.[33] The white man's actions were as inconsequent and incomprehensible as they were repugnant.

What did happen to the Aborigines who once occupied all the lands now turned to grazing and farming, to forest and watershed, to towns, cities, and suburbia? Whom Cook saw; and who later watched, at first curiously, and then with fear and apprehension, Phillip's expanding settlements at Sydney Cove?[34] Many of those to whom the dereliction of ancestral lands was spiritual annihilation died, heart-broken, hungry, and diseased; younger ones, in the days when they were spared scant food or sympathy, were driven back, fearful or apathetic, to violate the territories of strangers, where the food resources were already taxed. With them travelled the part-Aborigines who survived; but they were all caught in a spiritual no-man's-land, vacillating between the frontier hostility of tribes for whom the land was fully committed, and that of the usurpers overrunning their former homelands. They might spear a few sheep or cattle, but retribution was swift. The European's weapons were as incomprehensible as his law. Naturally, the Aborigines harried the invader whenever possible. David Collins wrote, of August 1788:

> The natives continued to molest the inhabitants whenever they chanced to meet any of them straggling or unarmed; yet, although forcibly warned by the evil and danger that attended their being thus found, the latter still continued to give the natives opportunity of injuring them. About the middle of this month a convict who had wandered beyond the limits of security fell in with a party of natives, who stripped and beat him shockingly, and would have murdered him had not the report of a musquet frightened them away . . .[35]

Perhaps they had learnt to imitate the European's methods of punishment for theft or trespass. But, in the end, they were no match for the invader who, in some parts of Australia organised 'black' hunts. It would be a mistake to think that we, under similar circumstances of fear and insecurity, would act much differently. Altruism is easily applied to distant problems, or in conditions which cannot affect our own lives.

Had all Australia been as fertile as New South Wales and Van Diemen's Land, the Aborigines would long since have been either exterminated or 'absorbed.' In Tasmania this happened; on the continent, by the time the inland plains were being grazed, the remnants of the coastal peoples, now mostly part-Europeans, and long since detribalised, had been bypassed. For many years their existence was precarious. Even in the earlier decades of the present century, they lived menially, often in degradation, in reserves and settlements, or on the fringes of the towns. Moving from humpies into houses, finding regular employment, and being assisted by Governments in increasing measure, they have since greatly improved their lot.

Throughout Australia, full citizenship is the acknowledged right of all Aborigines and part-Aborigines.[36] Legally, at least, they possess equality with other Australians in conditions of work, and the freedom to settle where opportunities are presented. A complex process, perhaps over a period of several centuries, may lead to an admixture of Aboriginal blood in virtually

Facing page: An Aboriginal rock painting in a cave at the base of Ayers Rock

128

all our distant descendants. Many people throughout the world will certainly preserve genetic traces of the old Australoid race.[37]

Although far greater consideration is now paid to the Aborigines, our cultural and economic conquest of Australia continues; its effects have been felt even among the most isolated full-bloods. In the Outback it is probable that semi-voluntary segregation may persist for a long time, although there might be no legal difference of status or privilege, and even when the Aborigines' former beliefs and way of life are completely renounced, the emergence of a bi-racial nation such as that of the United States of America is considered unlikely.[38] The ultimate pattern of assimilation may rather resemble that of Europe, where the 'aboriginal' peoples gradually blended with the invaders. But studies of the human contemporary scene cannot guarantee accurate forecasts, least of all in an age where technological progress is being made in all the over-populated countries of Asia and Africa.

It is important that the Aborigines' traditional manner of life be recorded— their social organisation, pattern of kinship, and rules of marriage; their religion, ceremony, and totemism; their methods of food-gathering and of obtaining shelter; their art and artefacts. By contrast, perhaps, such knowledge makes us more conscious of ourselves, and of our evolving civilisation. Our posterity may claim part of the culture as ancestral. Not to record all we possibly can of the Old Australians and their ethos would constitute a dereliction of our privileged position. But it is as essential to recognise the inevitability of change, and to concern ourselves as strenuously, as urgently, and as scientifically, with the processes of change that have been, and are still, overtaking the Aborigines.

Most white Australians have never seen an Aboriginal in his native state, living naked off the land, but it is doubtful whether, anywhere, the converse remains true. The few desert tribes whose isolation had survived the first quarter of the twentieth century made firm contact with the white man within the next two or three decades. After that they could never again return fully to the old dispensation, for they had glimpsed the compelling magic of a security independent of season and the unremitting anxiety of hunting; they were caught for ever in a magnetic field as powerful as that once exerted on an even more primitive society by the first fire-makers.

From the beginning it was so. Even Phillip's men, in the first weeks of 1788, found that the fears Cook had reported were replaced in the Sydney area by avid curiosity. For a generation or two, the full-blood Aboriginal felt the contrary attraction of his tribal lands and totems, of which he was born as surely as from the womb of his mother, and to which he must return for his final salvation. There were times of terror and bewilderment, when the voices of the old men who had passed echoed like doom, but, like the receding judgments of history, they became muffled and weak, until, in the end, he exchanged his ancient, harsh certainties for the slip-shod security of detribalised life on the fringe of civilisation. The tide has turned. What may happen subsequently depends on the ability of men, both black and white, to reconcile a way of life and a reason for living, and to solve some difficult human problems of economics and sociology. Clearly connected through the years with the earliest days of settlement, these are an evolving part of Australia's world of difference.

Although today the ancient territories of the Aborigines exist more in time than in space, the best having been overlaid by two hundred years of European culture and development, the people have survived successive crises, and shown that their line will not be extinguished. Much the same thing occurred with the aboriginal tribes of Britain and western Europe, or with their descendants in historical times. To use a phrase constantly quoted in older days, it is no longer a matter of 'smoothing the dying pillow' of the Aborigines, but of nourishing a new and vigorous youth, based on their right 'to determine their own futures, to retain their racial identity and traditional lifestyle or where desired to adopt wholly or partially a European lifestyle. With this choice go the rights of Aborigines as full citizens to vote, to travel freely, and to have the same freedoms as all other citizens unrestricted in any way.'[39]

Anyone who travels up through the Centre, into the west of New South Wales or Queensland, or overland between Perth and Adelaide, will meet Aborigines or part-Europeans with strongly Aboriginal features: the heavy brows, the broad nostrils, and the prominent mouths. Sometimes, especially near the country townships and stopping places, they are unprepossessing, wrapped in cast-off clothing, as ill-adapted to the fixed settlements of the white man as they are incapable of returning to their old nomadic life. Others seem to have achieved greater integration. They have a better physique, and walk more proudly even among their own people. Some, who have the appearance of being relatively settled workers—stockmen, timber-men, shearers, or builders—still periodically feel the urge to return to tribal lands, and may dismiss civilisation for periods of weeks or even months. This shows a degree of traditional orientation[40] which may not be overlaid for generations. And there are still to be seen some who are shy and marginal; bewilderment is in their eyes, and they are fearful in contemplation of a world that stretches farther than they can conceive, but into which they must eventually enter.

Curiously enough, it is in the larger towns that Aborigines and part-Aborigines are often happiest and most productive, meeting less prejudice, and gradually obtaining work of genuine intrinsic interest, rather than merely exchanging the hard work and dignity of nomadic food-gathering for what may be, relatively, an ignoble security on the edge of civilisation.

The economy of the outback station once depended on cheap Aboriginal labour, and its ethos on a maintenance of European supremacy and 'face.' Many Aborigines show great skill as cattlemen, becoming fine horsemen and excellent musterers. The strong family-group system of the Aborigines tends to survive even on a cattle station, and he is surrounded by relatives who, by ancient custom, expect to share whatever he acquires. Their presence in contrived humpies in the sandhills on the outskirts of the station area was not generally welcomed by the station manager, but he knew that his labour depended on an acquiescence in the tribal habit of holding fortune in common: even the security of his herds was contingent on the goodwill of his embarrassing guests. It is not very long, of course, since the spearing of cattle was common, though the Aborigines in their no-man's-land probably had little realisation of its significance as a crime.[41]

Today, stockmen, black or white, have the same entitlement and, particularly in the Northern Territory, very large pastoral areas are owned and controlled by Aborigines. After the passing of the Aboriginal Land Rights (Northern Territory) Act, in 1977, some 250 000 square kilometres was placed under the ownership of Aborigines. As a whole, however, Australia's original people are far from establishing a state of 'Makarrata' (normal relations following hostilities) with the Australian Government. Aboriginal freehold land, in all states except South Australia and the Northern Territory, is minimal.

After four hundred centuries of changeless, disciplined, and ordered living, integral with Australia's ecology, the Aborigines had no means of countering the devastation and dispersal caused by the white invasion. They raised their spears, as ineffectual as the defences of the small marsupials against the teeth and talons of imported cats and dogs.

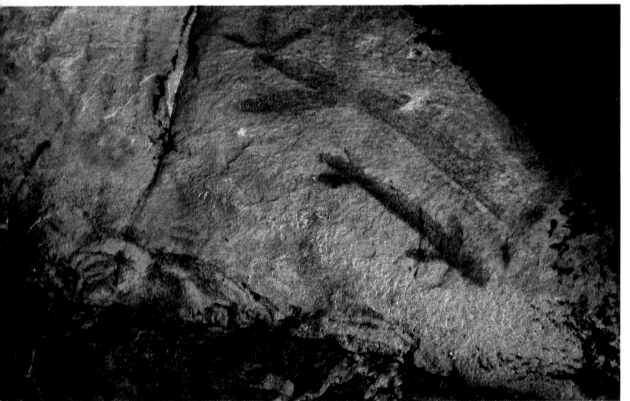

Top: Aboriginal markings on rock near Emily Gap in the ranges close to Alice Springs; these are probably tally marks of important statistics. *Bottom:* The Cave of Fishes, Grampians, Victoria; these Aboriginal paintings could be depicting fish or lizards

Top: Children play on the beach near Bamaga on the tip of Cape York Peninsula.
Bottom: Bert Bolton, en route to the Gibson Desert, speaks with an Aboriginal representative of the Docker River Settlement, close to the Western Australian border

The missions and government stations that provide sustenance, health services, education, and suitable work for the Aborigines have made, and are making, a significant contribution to the ultimate change that must finally overtake all Aborigines, or their descendants. They probably provide a frontier as inexplicable to tradition-minded Aborigines as the private stations run for profit, but, on the whole, they are sympathetic to the family group, and understand its integral part in the Aborigines' society.

In the small outback town, there is often considerable prejudice against the Aboriginal. It may be slightly conditioned by echoes of the old insecurity. Suitable work for him does not always exist, and he may have lost both his tribal organisation and the hunting skill of his fathers. He begins to realise the huge gulf between him and the European just when he has severed completely the last bridges that allowed his return to a traditional existence. This is the period of greatest danger, when dejection or apathy can be succeeded by complete moral and spiritual breakdown.[42]

Naturally, the Aboriginal of the Inland, originally master of the continent, at first took from the Europeans what seemed to him good, and continued his secret, personal inner life and beliefs, vanishing into tribal territory when seasons were favourable, or when ceremony was necessary. His dependants, though, formed closer bonds with European organisation. Another generation of young men might be drawn off for tribal initiation but, inevitably, they had absorbed less of the lore of the old men. Gradually, therefore, the social organisation must break down; the significance of its totemism, its ceremony, and its religion be forgotten. Now the process is almost complete; everywhere there is realisation that, although the Aborigines are increasing in numbers, the non-physical qualities which most distinguished them from Europeans— their beliefs, skills, and aspirations—are swiftly being forgotten.[43] It is ironical that mission Aborigines drifting to the towns find another inversion of values necessary. From the beginning, the Aborigines have found inexplicable differences between the principles and the practices of the Europeans.[44]

It would be almost impossible for an adult European to be assimilated by the Aborigines; he could never cultivate, in maturity, the perception, the alertness, the observation, and the awareness of the Aboriginal; he could hardly learn the endurance of hunger and of extremes of temperature; he would flag in the necessary, endless search for food; and he would be hopelessly clumsy in fashioning weapons and tools of stone and wood, or in attempting to create fire by friction. If he had to depend on the natural resources of Australia, he would quickly die as, indeed, under such circumstances, many Europeans have died, ever since the arrival of the First Fleet.

Yet, poorly as he would show by comparison with the Aborigines in his ability to adapt to the physical environment, even more fraught with difficulty would be his attempts to discard the mental paraphernalia of meanings and purpose in life, to clear the cluttered mind-tracks fed by second-, third-, and fourth-hand knowledge residing in the printed word, and approach more closely than his ancestors for several thousand years, the primary springs of direct apprehension. What modern man can really look at the stars, without his vision being clouded by knowledge itself; who, of the civilised races, ever feels himself as part of the living integument of the earth, part of matter that is immortal and eternal? Who, of the western world, could dare to live without possessions?

It is for the sake of his possessions that civilised man loses most of his freedom of movement; his houses and little personal plots of earth, his furniture, his dress, his gardens, all keep him from straying away; his fashions, prejudices, morals, creeds, learning—all tend to swirl him into a vortex of respectability with its great central fears of losing face and identity; of being free, of dying.

A healthy, new-born white baby, loved and cared for by Aboriginal tribes, might survive, to mature with them and to learn their skills. Precisely the same thing can certainly happen with an Aboriginal child. The areas of ultimate development might differ, but less, probably, than most of us would expect; if he were received completely without prejudice, there is no doubt that the Aboriginal child, reared from the beginning in a wholly European environment, could take his place as an adult in the community, as staunch in its beliefs, and as limited by its conventions, as his fellows.[45]

There is not the world of difference in the person, but there is an almost incredible difference in the effects of environment that, on the one hand, the European has imported—which has spread over the face of the land wherever walls strong enough may be built to enclose it, wherever minds conditioned by its creeds find the basic essentials for its survival—and, on the other, which, for tens of thousands of years, has cradled the Australian Aboriginal. If Australia had remained as Dampier and Cook discovered it, no settlers could have survived without continual sustenance from their homeland.

An interest in the primitive Aboriginal Australia is now largely historical. It would be extremely difficult for most Australians to visit one of the remnant tribes, and see fire being kindled by friction, stone weapons and tools being fashioned by pressure flaking and grinding, spears being straightened in the fire, or, with a woomera as lever, hurled astonishing distances with extraordinary precision. Everyone knows what a boomerang is—the word has entered into the language—and, occasionally, most people have the chance to see one being more or less expertly thrown at some country fair or show,[46] but few, even after a most persistent quest could see a tribesman bringing down, with one boomerang throw, several birds from a flock flying beyond the furthest fringes of civilisation. Today . . . somewhere . . . it may be happening for the last time. Yet, whether in time or space, this is an aspect of Australia which increasing numbers of people are rightly regarding as necessary for their comprehension of the southern continent.

The Aborigines, with their economy, their social organisation, their religious and artistic life, comprise a great Australian theme and region of which all but a small area exists in the past. Yet it is possible to enter this complex and splendid domain by many paths, and, once within its boundaries, to explore endlessly, gradually discovering a substratum in our world of difference as valuable as that which objectively persists.

Most Australians, with little effort, can visit places marked with carvings or paintings by the men who have long since vanished. I have spent hours looking on the designs still clearly visible in the Victorian Grampians, days wandering round Ayers Rock and Mt Olga, finding graphic representations of ancestral beings and totemic symbols. In many parts of eastern Australia, some close to Sydney, I have been fascinated by the incised linear carvings of men and animals. The famous X-ray animal symbolism of the north-west, and the fascinating paintings at Queensland's Laura are called to mind. But most of these would have been like uninterpreted dreams, vivid, often larger than life, with curiously blended elements, if I had not had enlightenment from anthropologists, some of whom have become personal friends. In the Centre, in the north-west, and in parts of the Northern Territory and Queensland—in the MacDonnell Ranges, in Arnhem Land, in the Kimberleys —it is still possible to find willing Aboriginal guides, but these are in faraway places, and include sites seldom accessible to the ordinary traveller.

The starting point for a journey into the stimulating and moving world of Aboriginal culture may be an axehead or grinding stone found by chance while digging in a suburban garden, or in cleanly broken chippings exposed by the wind in the old sand-dunes.[47] It may lead to a new and exciting interest in the fine collections of the city museums, and, inevitably, it will inspire

Dreamtime, Kakadu National Park, Northern Territory

interest in a remarkable, growing literature—the passport into a cultural realm that was long established when Britons still wore woad. Ultimately, there may come an understanding of the complex structure of the tribes, clans, and moieties, of the Aborigines' society, and of their relationship, none the less integral, with spirit beings who sustained their faith and courage through the everlasting present of their 'timeless' land. The patient observation and research, and the faithful recording of dedicated anthropologists, will allow you to witness the sacred rites which only the old men understood. You may observe the rhythmic urgency of a firelit corroboree, hear whispers of the terror of the pointed bone, or discover the sacred hiding places of the churinga.

Some of our visitors, although intrigued by the Australian scene, by so much that is freer, brighter, and so different, nevertheless find the quality of the Australian's love of country inexplicable. So often, the land seems old and harsh, or unheeding, as it did to generations of men without security, who struggled to build a new life in it. It is not easy to explain how we have accepted, and been accepted; nor how subtly we have become enthralled by forms and colour and light that seem so strange to newcomers. Yet, perhaps we have become attuned to the ancient Aboriginal vision, and even, instinctively, to something of the Dreamtime philosophy of those who once roamed over every metre of the soil we cultivate.

In his *Aranda Traditions*,[48] T. G. H. Strehlow tells of the Aborigines' love of the country's centre; and this, wherever we are, we have learnt to share:

> Mountains and creeks and springs and water-holes are, to him, not merely interesting or beautiful scenic features in which his eyes may take a passing delight; they are the handiwork of ancestors from whom he himself descended. He sees recorded in the surrounding landscape the ancient story of the lives and the deeds of the immortal beings whom he reveres; beings, who for a brief space may take on human shape once more; beings, many of whom he has known in his own experience as his fathers and grandfathers, and brothers, and as his mothers and sisters. The whole countryside is his living, age-old family tree. The account of his own totemic ancestor is to the native the account of his own doings at the beginning of time, at the dim dawn of life, when the world as he knows it now was being shaped and moulded by all-powerful hands. He himself has played a part in that first glorious adventure, a part smaller or greater according to the original rank of the ancestor of whom he is the present reincarnated form.

I list, in the course of this chapter, and in the notes following, a few of the guides who have illumined for me what would otherwise have been a shadowy field. Some of the works mentioned have extensive bibliographies, indicating how many there are to assist in such exploration. Over any of their territory one treads with deference.

[1] *An Account of the Voyages undertaken by the Order of His Present Majesty, for Making Discoveries in the Southern Hemisphere, and successively performed by Commodore Byron, Captain Wallis, Captain Carteret, and Captain Cook . . .* vol. 3 (London, 1773), p. 490. The volume is usually titled *Cook's Voyage*, vol. 3, 1773.

[2] Aborigines: The spelling of 'Aborigines' with a capital 'A' is the accepted English-language name for this race of people in Australia—Helen Sheils, Editor, *Australian Aboriginal Studies*, a Symposium of Papers presented at the 1961 Research Conference; published for the Australian Institute of Aboriginal Studies (O.U.P., Melbourne, 1963).

[3] Human remains from Lake Mungo, in western N.S.W., have been carbon-dated at about 26 000 years old, and stone tools estimated at 10 000 years older have been excavated.

There appears to have been little development in the design of stone tools through tens of thousands of years.

[4] A 'cliometric' view of history is necessary, even when evaluating the Norman (or the Roman) invasions of Britain, for example, or the upsurge of black power and influence in the Americas. The utterly indefensible forced migration of Africans was ultimately responsible for the 'westernisation' (good or bad!) of millions of blacks.

[5] *The Timeless Land*, by Eleanor Dark (Collins, London, 1944). Preface written in 1940.

[6] *The Native Tribes of Central Australia*, by Baldwin Spencer and F. J. Gillen (London, 1899); also B. Spencer: *Native Tribes of the Northern Territory of Australia* (London, 1914). A useful summary, *The Aboriginals of Australia*, was presented by Professor (later Sir) Baldwin Spencer as a Paper during the visit of the British Association for the Advancement of Science, to Australia, in August 1914. The Federal Handbook prepared for the occasion published the paper and several others.

[7] R. Brough Smyth: *The Aborigines of Victoria*, in two vols. (Melbourne and London, 1878).

[8] *The Australian Aborigines: How to Understand Them*, by A. P. Elkin, Professor of Anthropology, University of Sydney (Angus & Robertson, Sydney, 1938). The book has been reprinted several times, with important later additions and revisions.

[9] *The Red Centre, Man and Beast in the Heart of Australia*, by H. H. Finlayson (Angus & Robertson, Sydney and London, 1935).

[10] A compendious study of the Aborigines, with extensive bibliographies, is available in the *Australian Encyclopaedia* (Grolier Society, 3rd (1977) and subsequent editions). Contributing authorities include F. D. McCarthy, R. V. S. Wright, N. W. G. MacIntosh, R. L. Kirk, D. E. McElwain, S. A. Wurm, Kenneth Maddock, Ronald M. Berndt, Catherine Berndt, Alice M. Moyle, Betty Meehan, and C. D. Rowley. *Australian Aboriginal Social Organization*; by David H. Turner; *The Two Worlds of Jimmie Barker: the Life of an Australian Aboriginal, 1900–1972*, as told to Janet Mathews; *Aboriginal Land Rights: a Handbook*, edited by Nicholas Peterson, and other works are published by the Australian Institute of Aboriginal Studies. In the 'Australian Experience' Series (George Allen & Unwin), *Aboriginal Australians: Black Response to White Dominance, 1788–1980*, by Richard Broome (1982), is a valuable recent work.

[11] At the time the Queensland Government did not agree with Federal Government control of State Aboriginal affairs.

[12] Australian Government publications (1983) include: *Aboriginal Futures, Aboriginals and Islanders in Brisbane, Aboriginals in Australia Today, Aboriginals in Victoria, Australian Aboriginal Culture, The Australian Aboriginals, Gallery of Aboriginal Australia, Health Studies of Selected Disadvantaged Groups*, and *Poverty among Aboriginal Families in Adelaide*.

[13] See note 1: *Cook's First Voyage*, p. 549, describing the near-disaster of 10 June 1770, when the *Endeavour* struck a coral reef, and was badly holed.

[14] Report of Governor Macquarie to Earl Bathurst, 27 July 1822. This report is published in M. Clark's *Sources of Australian History* (O.U.P., 1957), chap. 2.

[15] W. H. Hovell, Journal, Royal Australian Historical Society, vol. 7 (1921), pp. 307–78; quoted in *A History of Australia*, by M. Barnard (Angus & Robertson).

[16] See note 1.

[17] See chap. 11, note 23.

[18] W. Baldwin Spencer, 1928, quoted in the Paper, *Physical Characteristics of Australian Aborigines*, by A. A. Abbie (in Symposium, see note 2, above): 'They (the natives) are commonly spoken of as "niggers" or "blacks", but in reality are neither "nigger" in race nor black in colour, but are long-headed Caucasians, belonging to the same race as we ourselves, only to a darker variety of it.'

[19] Australoid: See pp. 3–4, *The Australian Aborigines*, by Prof. A. P. Elkin (Angus & Robertson, Sydney, 1954).

[20] Tindale and Lindsay: *Aboriginal Australians* (The Jacaranda Press, 1963), chap. 1.

[21] In many parts of Victoria, for instance, as at Apollo Bay, and round parts of Port Phillip Bay, there are raised wave-cut platforms clearly visible a metre or more above the highest tides. The apparent uplift is frequently the result of a eustatic fall of sea-level; however, round the coasts of Australia as a whole, the major raising of old sea-floors is tectonic, that is, due to tilting, faulting, and other earth movements.

[22] Even in Antarctica, in the ranges south of Mawson, the author has discovered glacial erratics more than 60 metres above the present ice surface.

[23] Tindale, in *Aboriginal Australians* (note 20), distinguishes the Barrinean Negritoes, of northern Queensland (allied with the vanished tribes of Tasmania, and small pockets in East Gippsland and south-west Australia), the Carpentarians of the North and Centre, and the Murrayians, of Victoria and New South Wales and of the coastal areas of southern and western Australia generally. This classification is not accepted by several authorities.

[24] A. P. Elkin: *The Australian Aborigines*, op. cit.

[25] From *Our Aborigines*, a pamphlet prepared under the authority of the Minister of Territories (then Hon. Paul Hasluck who, himself, had made a study of the Aborigines), in connection with the celebration of National Aborigines' Day in Australia, 12 July 1957. One hundred and thirty years before, Governor Macquarie had said much the same (see note 9).

[26] An Aboriginal (or Torres Strait Islander) is a person of Aboriginal or Torres Strait Islander descent who identifies as an Aboriginal (or Torres Strait Islander) and is accepted as such by the community in which he lives. This definition, has, for purposes of national census, been accepted by both the Government and the Aboriginal people— *The Australian Aboriginals* (Australian Information Service Reference Paper, 1981).

[27] Ronald M. Berndt, in his Paper, *Groups with Minimal European Associations*, at the 1961 Research Conference *(Australian Aboriginal Studies*, O.U.P.).

[28] The whole question of Land Rights is complex, and a matter of widely differing State acceptance. About 500 000 square kilometres of freehold Aboriginal land exists (1983) in South Australia and the Northern Territory. In the rest of the States combined, the total is less than 150 square kilometres. The present Aboriginal population (estimates vary) is close on 180 000. *Aboriginal Land Rights—A handbook*, edited by Nicholas Petersen (Australian Institute of Aboriginal Studies, Canberra, 1981), surveys the position.

[29] W. Tench: *A complete Account of the Settlement at Port Jackson, in New South Wales* (London, 1793). Several extracts, including the account of this incident, are reproduced in M. Clark's *Sources of Australian History* (see note 14).

[30] Mrs Eleanor Dark, in the Preface to *The Timeless Land*, writes: 'The Aborigines, too, have a strongly developed sense of humour, and one cannot help suspecting that the early colonists had their legs frequently and diligently pulled.'

[31] In his Paper, *Tribal Distribution and Population* (1961 Research Conference), N. B. Tindale speaks of 'some infants who are killed at birth because they cannot be reared, as another not yet weaned is already at the mother's breast.' There are also several mentions of infanticide in *The Aborigines of Victoria* (R. Brough Smyth, 1878). The author considers infanticide may be a method 'of keeping in check the too rapid increase of a barbarous people in a region where the indigenous productions afford a very scanty supply of food.' Baldwin Spencer: 'In regard to their manner of life it must be remembered that they are pure nomads, the members of a tribe hunting over land that has belonged to their ancestors and not encroaching on that of other tribes. There are favourite hunting and camping grounds and here they will stay as long as food and water supplies are abundant, moving on to other places when these become scarce.'—*Aboriginals of Australia*, op. cit.

[32] The Dreaming, or Dreamtime: In the discussion, following E. A. Worms' paper on Religion, at the 1961 Research Conference, R. M. Berndt said 'that there was indeed much seriousness in Aboriginal religion, but there were also elements of pleasure and lightness. A further point in his observation was that sacred ancestral beings of the Aborigines were treated as equal rather than as supreme beings far removed from the everyday world. Sacred beings were included in the everyday world, while human beings were not seen as merely ordinary; there was a feeling that every person shares in the Dreaming; the Aboriginal indeed does not always regard Europeans as equals in the sense in which he treats his gods as equals.'—*Australian Aboriginal Studies*, op. cit., p. 253.

[33] Baldwin Spencer (see note 31) said: 'It is difficult to say exactly how much time is occupied by this (ceremonial), but in many tribes at least half the life of a man is spent in attendance upon, or taking part in, ceremonies of a sacred nature that only initiated men may witness, and the older a man becomes the more time he spends in this way.'

[34] W. Tench: *A Narrative of the Expedition to Botany Bay*, op. cit.: '. . . we had been but a very few days at Port Jackson, when an alteration in the behaviour of the natives was perceptible; and I wish I could add, that a longer residence in their neighbourhood had introduced a greater degree of cordiality and intermixture between the old, and new, lords of the soil. . . . The result, however, of our repeated endeavours to induce them to come among us has been such as to confirm me in an opinion, that they either fear or despise us too much, to be anxious for a closer connection.'

[35] David Collins: *An Account of the English Colony in New South Wales* (London, 1804).

[36] See note 28.

[37] '. . . a new dominant type in evolution has come to be represented by a single world-wide species instead of showing adaptive radiation into many intersterile species. Doubtless this is due to his (Man's) great tendency to individual, group, and mass migration of an irregular nature, coupled with his mental adaptability which enables him to effect cross-mating quite readily in face of differences of colour, appearance, and behaviour which would act as efficient barriers in the case of more instinctive organisms.'—*Evolution: The Modern Synthesis*, by Julian Huxley (Allen & Unwin, London; 2nd Edition, 1963); p. 354.

[38] Some figures showing that, although the population of Aborigines was increasing, the number of full-bloods had declined, were published by C. M. Tatz, of Monash University, in

140

the Melbourne *Age*, 5 June 1965. In 1947, the total Aboriginal population was estimated at 73 800 (including 27 000 half-castes); in 1964, it had increased by 39 per cent to an estimated 120 000, of which 59 000 were part-Aborigines (formerly called half-castes). These figures would seem to indicate that the full-blood population has decreased by some 4000 in 17 years. However, accurate statistics, over a considerable period of time will be necessary before absolute trends are determinable.

[39] *Aboriginals in Australia Today* (Australian Government Publishing Service, Canberra, 1981.)

[40] 'People with minimal European contact, living in remote or relatively inaccessible places, are traditionally oriented. They are not exposed to a great variety of European pressures, and then mainly to certain categories of persons (for example, missionaries, government officials, anthropologists, and stray travellers).'—Ronald M. Berndt (1963).

[41] 'In the more outlying stations, particularly in those consisting of hilly country, the natives have for some time and to his great loss, liberally helped themselves to the squattor's herd. Mr R. F. Thornton, the owner of Tempe Downs, informed me that, in the neighbourhood of Gill's Range, they were for some time killing cattle at the rate of 100 a month, a loss which no station could long endure. The *modus operandi* is for one party of natives to drive a small detachment of the herd into the bed of one of the deeply-cut rocky gorges which are numerous in the ranges, and to which the cattle may be in the habit of repairing for water in the springs or rock-holes. Another party lies in wait higher up the gorge or on the rocks above and either spears the cattle or disables them by rolling down rocks. They cut up the beasts in portions, carry them off to conveniently retired and often very inaccessible spots, eat to repletion and then move on again next day.' (From E. C. Stirling: *Anthropology: part IV. Report of the Work of the Horn Scientific Expedition to Central Australia, 1896.*)

[42] Prof. A. P. Elkin states in his Epilogue to *The Australian Aborigines*, already cited: 'Cities and large towns provide the best opportunities for this transition (i.e. from "fringe" dwelling to absorption by the white community), small country towns the least, especially if there is an Aboriginal settlement or camp in the vicinity.'

Our Aborigines (1957), op. cit. contains the following statement: 'As tribes found that settlement made their old life impossible in their own territory, social and religious organization broke down, belief in the future and the will to survive were weakened. The younger tribesmen became more amenable to and dependent upon the white man and contemptuous of the old men's knowledge and authority before they learned that they did not really share the white man's views and ways of life. Thus many of them, not entrusted with the sacred knowledge and finally disillusioned, found themselves then with no spiritual retreat.'

[43] Occasionally, half-forgotten memories are searched for 'sacred sites', when mining or industry threatens to overwhelm long vacant land. The National Aboriginal Conference, an official body meeting annually in Canberra, is more interested in land rights *per se*.

[44] In discussion concerning the contemporary scene, at the 1961 Research Conference, Mrs Fay Gale, of the University of Adelaide, quoted a Maori to illustrate this point. The Maori said: 'Well, we come from a place where spiritual values are uppermost and material things are down the most, to the city where material things are uppermost and spiritual things may be not there at all and we are all upside down.'

[45] See notes 14 and 21. *One People*, a pamphlet published by the Dept of Territories, illustrates how well integrated Aboriginal children may be in ordinary Australian schools. In 1981, about 16 000 Aboriginal children were attending secondary schools; 7200 were at technical and tertiary institutions. However, especially at primary level, there is a growing belief that opportunities should exist for alternative, specifically Aboriginal education; that not all Aboriginal children should enter the schools of 'mainstream' society.

[46] *Australian Aboriginal Studies* (1963), p. 436: 'Another phenomenon which deserves attention is what might be called neo-Aboriginalism. In North America there are people described by the term "professional Indians," that is, they are people who make a profession of being North American Indians. The same sort of thing is beginning to be seen in Melbourne and Sydney; people who have a vested interest in remaining Aborigines, even though in practically all respects their lives and attitudes may be identical with those of their white neighbours.'

[47] While the author was writing this chapter, he uncovered a well-used grinding stone, with four indented finger-grips, while digging at Wyperfield National Park (Victorian Mallee). This artefact lay at a depth of 1·2 metres. Chippings and 'microliths' of various kinds are especially common in some coastal districts where the Aborigines gathered shell-fish, or birds from lagoons banked by sand-bars. Many of the rougher fragments 'would be called Eolithic or rejected as non-human by those who had never seen a native using a pebble that he has roughly flaked to serve some temporary purpose.' (Baldwin Spencer, describing stone implements in his Paper, cited in note 31.)

[48] *Aranda Traditions*, by T. G. H. Strehlow (Melbourne University Press, 1947).

CHAPTER 7

The Dreamtime Landscapes

From Uluru's caverns, by far Etikaura,
Out of the chasms of red Katatjuta,
Over the mulga, the gibber, the gidgee
Voices are chanting the songs of the Dreamtime:
Soft is their sighing, and old is the land.

—from WIDE HOMELAND

'HALTED AT SUNSET IN A COUNTRY such as I firmly believe has no parallel on Earth's surface . . .' Such is the inscription marking the most northerly point on the official map, published in 1849, of Captain Charles Sturt's 'Route from Adelaide into the Centre of Australia.' John Harris Browne, the expedition's surgeon, is reported by his leader as exclaiming, 'Good Heavens, did ever man see such country!'

Many travellers in Central Australia today ask such rhetorical questions, and make comments as emphatic, but in sheer wonder at the vast, strange rock-forms, the incredible lights, and the bizarre colour. For the stranger there are scenes of disturbing contrapuntal beauty, where brick-red landscapes flare to crimson and shade to violet, where the colours of nature familiar to Europeans, exist merely as remarkable accents, where the air is so clear that distant mountains seem only an hour's easy walk away, and where, at night, the stars are extraordinarily close and bright. Aeons of arid weathering have exfoliated the faces of some mountains to dramatic convex profiles, plunging down featureless from the rounding of their brows; or left abrupt, scree-buttressed residuals, fragments of ancient land surfaces that, in other latitudes, rain would long since have eroded away. The prevailing ferric colour itself is provided by the static oxidation of the iron-bearing rocks.[1]

Suddenly inspired by an unfamiliar face of beauty, their senses wonderfully stimulated and alert, travellers may well echo the words of Charles Sturt; but the wheel has turned full circle; their emotions are of delight and astonishment, not of the torture of conceiving themselves, as Sturt expressed it, 'locked up in this desolate and heated region' as effectually as if they 'were ice-bound at the Pole.'[2] If they possess feelings of awe, these blend atavistic, rather than present, unease. In modern man, impressions of immensity of space and volume, having ceased to inspire fear, leave a peculiar delight. Finlayson[3] once wrote of the conditions facing the early explorers: 'A daily threat of death would spoil the charms of paradise.' Today's visitors to the Centre have the permission of water—never given freely to Sturt—and swift, reliable motor transport over well-defined roads and tracks, leading to comfortable, prepared quarters, even in some of the very regions where the explorers' visions were blighted by fears and uncertainties.

Thirst reduces men to silence. Every exhalation may be reckoned in terms of precious humidity—exchanged for the dehydrating desert air. Plants of the desert are spiky and hard, taut of form, tardy of growth, seeming merely

142

to exist between rains—such is the famous acacia known as 'dead finish';[4] or succulent, miserly of moisture, xerophytes that hoard their water in stems and leaves, with minimum transpiration. There are also the small ephemera which appear and complete their life cycles while conditions are favourable. The dead finish is incredibly gnarled and brittle, often scantily clothed, appearing generally on the verge of extinction. When, after rain, it suddenly bursts into fluffy scented blossoms, its poverty is seen to have been pretence. It is frequently the host of a brightly coloured harlequin mistletoe. Animals must pay for freedom of movement by carrying or discovering water.

For many thousands of years, through all the conceivable time of the Aborigines' Dreaming,[5] the waters of the Centre represented licence of tenure. Rain might not fall for years but, deep in the hidden clefts of Uluru, in pools or soaks between the limbs of Katatjuta,[6] perhaps at only one place in 15 000 square kilometres, the sky lay reflected, and the itinerant life came to drink. How long might it have been, reckoned in the perishing of tribes, of desperate forages pressed out beyond their points-of-no-return, before all the secret waters became part of a vital oral tradition, the wisdom of the old men? Did the climate change by slow degrees, so that permission to live was retained only by those who could survive the increasing marches between waterholes, the necessity to hunt ever more sporadic game?[7]

Australia has been completely mapped, and we know now that there is not a single permanent flowing river, nor sweet-water lake, over about 5 million square kilometres of the interior. Great 'lakes' of the Centre, such as Eyre, Mackay, Amadeus, and Neale, are almost perennially and permanently huge dry expanses of gleaming salt, sometimes encrusting evil mud particularly treacherous for wheels. It is true that once in several, perhaps many, years, the vast basin of Lake Eyre, draining 2·5 million square kilometres, receives flood waters from Cooper Creek, the Georgina, the Diamantina, and the Finke; though very seldom indeed do they all run together. I have seen the Cooper flooding down from Queensland 16 kilometres wide, and Lake Eyre seeming like an inland sea, extending for thousands of square kilometres; yet, after a year or two, all this water has evaporated. Over the Gibson Desert, the Great Victoria Desert, and much of the Nullarbor Plain, any streams marked by the cartographers are vague lines of possible drainage, with outlet neither to lake nor ocean. The land absorbs completely all the water that is not more rapidly taken up by the burning sun.

If it is beautiful, Australia's centre is still an uncertain and intractable land, where men's enterprises may flourish or fail in seasons of drought or plenty extending through years. But though, for carelessness or folly, there are many by-roads to disaster, modern communications—roads, surface and air transport, short-wave radio—and the Royal Flying Doctor Service, have ensured the safety of properly planned travel. The invisible limits of precious natural waters are no longer its boundaries: perhaps the definition of beauty is sharper when proper precautions remove anxiety.

Immense areas of the Inland, reckoned in thousands of square kilometres, have been taken up on Commonwealth lease, as cattle runs. In all of these, bores have been sunk, and artesian water, varying in quantity and quality, flows or is pumped to the surface. About 12 000 such sources of water[8] have vastly augmented those supplies which for so long were the jealously guarded preserves of the Aboriginal tribes. Modern man, with his four-wheel drive vehicles, his planned roads, and his known destinations, may usually carry sufficient potable water for his needs. Cattle, on the other hand, will not stray many kilometres from the bore-water trough, except in times of abundant rain and its consequent swift growth of succulents from seeds which may have lain dormant for years. The cattle are still enclosed by the bounds of available water, and, provided such supplies are separated by

143

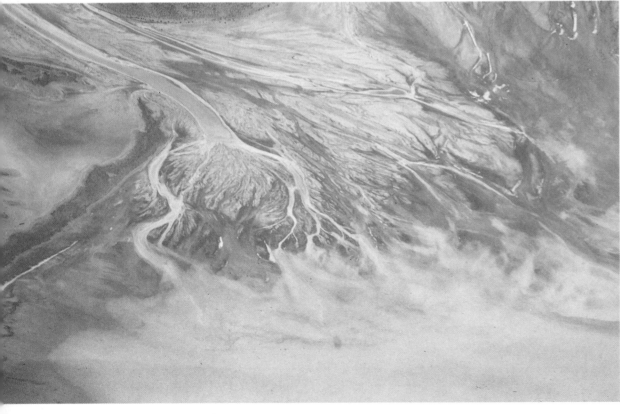

Top: Lake Amadeus, Northern Territory, named by Giles in 1872; he described it as 'an infernal lake of mud and brine'.
Bottom: Delta, Lake Frome, South Australia

Facing page: The Finke River crosses both Northern Territory and South Australia but only carries water in wet seasons; there are permanent waterholes along its course

sufficient distance,[9] stock may normally be mustered from areas which they are known to frequent.

The presence of cattle, naturally, has changed the ecology of those areas where they roam. While the country, in its original state, could recover fairly rapidly from even prolonged periods of drought, the removal of herbage by stock has created a threat of dust-bowl conditions that certainly must be heeded. Overstocking in the good years may permanently impoverish the land. A wise man once wrote that desert places become desert only by the agency of man. Certainly, since the North African cornfields blew away and left the Sahara, history has provided sufficient examples of such almost irreversible folly.

Between the polar regions and the equator, I have never seen any virgin country, even that including aboriginal tribes among its fauna, that did not seem beautiful. And very often in Central Australia, a lonely red-flanked gorge, where an oblique light aureoles each tuft of mulga grass or tussock of spinifex,[10] possesses an exquisite, haunting loveliness. The sunshine seems to flow undiluted through the foliage of the ghost gums, from tiny tributaries down through their gleaming trunks to the bright earth; it glows faintly purple in the grey mulga branches, and is totally absorbed by the dark, twisted tracery of the graceful corkwoods.[11] The desert oak[12] is also black, supporting its showers of needles above the deep pools of shade. Very strange combinations of colour in vegetation—crimson, black, and Sung green of desert pea,[13] heliotrope of emu-bush, gold of cassia, vivid greens of ghost gums and ironwood—may blend uniquely with the jasper red earth which distance may turn to coral or rose, a hidden sun to madder or maroon. Perhaps because of the stimulus provided by colour there is also a greater realisation of form. Whatever words men may use to try to capture the magic of the light reflected from the desert—'Crimson, carmine, red ochre, pink, chrome'[14] to 'fiery cinnabar'[15]—they will always speak the truth of some passing mood. In this country, especially when you wake each morning, this world that greets you may be a revelation of almost unearthly beauty.

From any of the Australian cities, you may fly within a few hours to Alice Springs,[16] that colourful and hospitable focus of inland purposes; you may watch the coastal forests and scrubs turn to mallee, the mallee to mulga, the surface of the earth becoming tawny or red, wrinkled in sandhills, smoothed in huge, white phantom lakes, broken by ranges and residuals that seem as old as the moon. From 'The Alice,' in the air, you may telescope a century into minutes. And, stimulated by knowledge of the 'Red Centre,'[17] as recorded by Sturt and Stuart, Giles, Forrest, Warburton, and Gosse, or recounted by later explorers—some, such as Spencer, Gregory, Finlayson, and the early missionaries, no less intrepid—imagination may recreate the haunting fears that accompanied men along the dry watercourses, leading into the Finke, or losing themselves before they found any destinations. Even the most exiguous meanderings are generally visible as thin lines of stoical trees, surviving on the promises of contour and gravity.

Such realisations will add colour even to the opalescent plains lying as large as half England between the ancient marginal hills on the edges of vision. For some, to be able to visualise history in its unchanged setting adds significantly to the appreciation of that setting. There is an added awareness in which the present is integrated with the millennia that have made the Dreamtime landscapes. To land in their heart, perhaps in the shadow of Ayers Rock, is an unforgettable experience.

Sturt was bitterly disappointed that he did not quite reach the geographical centre of Australia. Like the later expedition of Burke and Wills, he traversed fearful country on the eastern and northern sides of the Lake Eyre Basin. The relatively fertile grasslands in the area drained by the Finke River were

146

unknown to Sturt, as were the Musgrave and MacDonnell Ranges.

> Let any man lay the map of Australia before him, and regard the blank upon
> its surface, and then let me ask him if it would not be an honourable
> achievement to be the first to place foot in this centre.
> Men of undoubted perseverance and energy in vain had tried to work their
> way to that distant and shrouded spot. A veil hung over Central Australia that
> could neither be pierced or raised. Girt round by deserts it almost appeared as
> if Nature had intentionally closed it upon civilized man, that she might have
> one domain on the earth's wide field over which the savage might roam in
> freedom.

Sturt wrote these words at the beginning of the account of his retreat. He
summed up his opinion of the Centre in some succinct but erroneous statements towards its end:[18]

> . . . there can, I think, be no doubt as to the non-existence of any mountain
> ranges in the interior of Australia, but, on the contrary, that its central regions
> are nearly if not quite on sea-level, and that the north coast is separated from
> the south as effectually as if seas rolled between them . . . I must confess I have
> no hope of any inland fertile country.

For the remainder of the century, the interior of Australia invited
expeditions from determined explorers. Fifteen years after Sturt had won for
himself the kind of fame that could never be impoverished, a member of his
party, John McDouall Stuart, reached the heart of the continent. Laconically
he records his triumph, the ceremony on his Central Mt Sturt,[19] on 22 April
1860: 'Built a cone of stones, in the centre of which I placed a pole with the
British flag nailed to it . . . We gave three hearty cheers for the flag.'
The same fine explorer also successfully crossed Australia, from Adelaide
to the Indian Ocean near Port Darwin, in 1862, ten years before the Overland
Telegraph Line followed his route. But his great success was shadowed
rather by the tragedy of Robert O'Hara Burke and William John Wills who,
having succeeded in reaching the Gulf of Carpentaria from the south, died,
with all their party except King, on the homeward journey. Search parties by
William Landsborough, A. W. Howitt, John McKinlay, and others could not
save the overlanders but, incidentally, they considerably extended knowledge
of the region. Stuart's discovery of grasslands to the west of the Lake Eyre
Basin turned the courses of the explorers westwards in the 1870s. Ernest
Giles and John Forrest made courageous inland journeys linking the far west
with the centre, and supplementing the great trek of Eyre round the coast of
the Bight.
One hundred years after Charles Sturt's expeditions, vast tracts of Central
Australia were still inaccessible. Today, no frontiers exist for properly
equipped and well-navigated four-wheel-drive motor vehicles. Landings for
aircraft have been discovered or made in hundreds of inhospitable regions.
The climate has not changed—still, over much of the Centre, the annual
rainfall averages less than 125 millimetres—and the country can be just as
merciless as in the past to the unprepared or lost.
Too frequently, inexperienced parties have found themselves in serious
trouble; there are still occasional fatalities, especially when thirst has
conquered prudence, and caused stranded motorists to wander away from
established routes into the featureless desert. Few travellers beyond the ends
of formed roads, omit to take the cardinal precautions of carrying sufficient
fuel and water for unexpected emergencies, and of leaving a plan of their
intended movements with a responsible person. The verb 'to perish' still has
a special connotation in the Outback.

Top: A desert oak, one of the sheoak family that are actually casuarina trees.
Bottom: Padanus, Finke River, South Australia

Facing page: Ruins of abandoned homestead in sight of Mount Connor, east of Ayers Rock, Northern Territory

Yet, to those who are capable and prepared, who can muster the proper equipment and the right companions, and, upon a basis of wisdom absorbed from wide reading of the experiences of others, are determined to build their own, the Inland will always yield rewards commensurate with skill and intention. Usually, anyone who has real knowledge of the bush anywhere, anyone who is capable of sustained travel where mountain ridges are routes, and a compass course is necessary to avoid a waterless camp, can effect the necessary changes of outlook required by the arid lands, and is not likely to underestimate the desert, where a vehicle can increase the measure of both achievement and danger.

Many of the most impressive regions and features of Central Australia are now approachable by graded roads, and are annually visited by thousands of tourists. From Alice Springs one may travel in relative comfort by coach to some of the finest gorges and ravines of the MacDonnell Ranges, to such remarkable formations as Ayers Rock and the domes of Mt Olga, and within reasonable hiking distance of such splendid mountains as Sonder and Giles.

John McKinlay, who searched for Burke and Wills, and made a notable journey to the Gulf of Carpentaria wrote: 'I never beheld such fearfully grand country in my life—nothing but towers and pinnacles of sandstone conglomerate, fit for nothing but wallaby and euro; and if it is for a thousand years from this time, it can be used by no other animals but them and the natives, as it is at present.'[20] He might have been writing of places which, almost to the middle of the twentieth century, seemed just as remote . . . but which are now accessible to visitors in casual clothes and sports shoes. The 'Dig Tree' on Cooper Creek, close to where perished Burke and Wills in 1861, is as accessible as the tip of Cape York . . . or the Katherine Gorge on the other side of the 'Top End'. Safaris follow the route of Lasseter's last journey,[21] and strike even farther west into the Gibson Desert and beyond. Marble Bar, Port Hedland, Exmouth Gulf, Derby, and Wyndham; all are now within reach, yet they all bound the Dreamtime landscapes.

It was not until 1929 that the railway line which previously had ended at Oodnadatta[22] was extended to Alice Springs. For many years before that, the name Oodnadatta had spelled romance for thousands of city dwellers. It was a place of heat, dust, camels: the veritable edge of the unknown. From it the Overland Telegraph Line, linking the southern cities with Europe, extended 2000 kilometres to the Indian Ocean. Beyond Oodnadatta, men travelled by camel train and drove herds of cattle out to broad pastures between crimson ranges where the Aborigines still roamed and hunted, chanted in corroboree, and pointed the death bone at those they despised. I dreamed of visiting the Musgrave Ranges before ever I had climbed to the top of the Dandenongs.[23]

Who would have dreamed that the route of the old Ghan, as the train to Alice Springs was affectionately called, would be replaced by a new line between Tarcoola and 'The Alice' (opened on 9 October 1980), or that an extension to Darwin would be planned for somewhere round the end of the decade? Perhaps the time will come when 'The Capricornia' will rival the 'Indian Pacific'. Who would have imagined Alice Springs with 20 000 citizens, or Darwin, cosmopolitan, its wounds of war and cyclone healed, reaching perhaps three times that population?

Before the first World War, the literature of the Inland comprised the explorers' accounts, such papers as were produced by the later scientific expeditions,[24] and a few semi-popular works of which Gregory's *The Dead Heart of Australia*[25] was probably best known. However, this book is mainly concerned with the flat and desolate Lake Eyre Basin, and does not even mention Alice Springs. Even as recently as 1942, Paul McGuire says that 'north and west of the Alice is the Great Australian Emptiness.'[26] However, the late 1930s had blossomed with several descriptive and literary works, including Finlayson's *Red Centre*. The objective accounts of the heroic age of the inland explorers, and of their more scientific successors, were also overlaid by tales of the cattle stations, reports from the missionaries, novels of the important social impact of Europeans on Aborigines, some dramatic pictures from the brushes of artists enchanted by the boldness of colour and form, and by much highly imaginative fiction incorporating whispers of fabulous reefs where gold lay gleaming in the sun.[27]

For security reasons, during the war in the Pacific, a sealed road, aptly named the Stuart Highway, had replaced the dirt track which, having just grown alongside the telegraph line, fluctuated with 'The Wet' and 'The Dry' between mud and washaways, and fearfully rough and dusty corduroy. 'The Bitumen,' between Darwin and 'The Alice' carried thousands of servicemen during the war. They all passed by Central Mt Stuart; and, further north, about 100 kilometres south of Tennant Creek, they stopped to gaze at the great granite boulders known as the Devil's Marbles—the remains of mountains which have been eroded almost completely away. The weathering of granite commonly leaves rounded monoliths, often seemingly precisely balanced upon each other; occasionally actual 'rocking-stones' are discovered, which, although weighing many tonnes, may be moved slightly upon their fulcra.

Innumerable travellers over the Stuart Highway have had their imagination stirred by the Devil's Marbles. They are sufficiently spherical to seem artificial, yet it is impossible to envisage a human artificer. A ponderous sphere three times as high as a man might engender a fleeting animism in anyone; repetition adds to the response. For the European Australian, the boulders arouse fancies such as their name indicates, or suggest long-vanished giants, at war or at play. For the Aboriginal Australian, unencumbered by geological science, they were objective evidence of the creation and the Dreamtime. One legend recounts that they were eggs laid by the gigantic rainbow-serpent, 'essentially the water element in nature,'[28] whose booming cry from the marshes and waterholes over much of the continent was sometimes attributed to the fearsome bunyip. It is often difficult to obtain authoritative information on such legends.

Strangely shaped standing stones are characteristic of arid lands where an extreme range of diurnal temperatures flakes rock surfaces, removing irregularities and, inevitably, sculpting the rock they bound to curved, organic forms reminiscent of life and limb. In an introduction to a remarkable collection of Aboriginal legends,[29] published at the turn of the century, Andrew Lang wrote:

> Without our savage ancestors we should certainly have had no poetry. Conceive the human race born into the world in its present advanced condition, weighing, analysing, examining everything, except a few phenomena which happen not to chime in with the general ideas of science. . . . Barbarians did the dreaming for the world, poetry arose in their fancies, and poetry, in spite of facts and science, resolutely refuses to 'follow darkness like a dream.' . . . The Australians, just escaping from the Palaeolithic age, were among the most distinguished.

Science relates all knowledge, seeks a rational explanation for every phenomenon; the inconceivable contracts almost to nothingness; yet how eagerly would we wish to enter the Aborigines' time of Dreaming, and how sympathetically must we seek their myths and traditions.

It is certain that 'The Bitumen' led to a much greater interest in Central Australia. Before the war, a journey to Hermannsburg Mission, or to any of the now famous scenic regions near Alice Springs, was an adventure; to

151

Facing page top: Devil's Marbles, south of Tennant Creek. Northern Territory, are heaped and scattered granite boulders resting on quartz pebbles and outcrops. *Bottom:* Katherine Gorge, a popular tourist spot in the Northern Territory
This page top: The cave where Lasseter rested for some days before beginning his fateful last journey. *Centre:* The inscription outside the cave. *Bottom:* This tree is reputedly the famous 'Dig' tree on Cooper Creek where rations had been buried for Burke and Wills

KULPI TJUNTINYA

LEWIS HAROLD BELL LASSETER SHELTERED IN THIS CAVE FOR APPROXIMATELY 25 DAYS DURING JANUARY 1931. HE WAS STRANDED WITHOUT FOOD AFTER HIS CAMELS BOLTED AT A POINT 15 Km. EAST OF HERE.

ALTHOUGH WEAK FROM STARVATION HE SET OUT, ABOUT 25 TH JANUARY, TO WALK THE 140 Km. TO MOUNT OLGA, HOPING TO MEET UP WITH HIS RELIEF PARTY.

CARRYING 1.7 LITRES OF WATER AND ASSISTED BY A FRIENDLY ABORIGINAL FAMILY HE REACHED IRVING CREEK IN THE POTTOYU HILLS A DISTANCE OF 55 Km WHERE HE DIED ABOUT 28 TH JANUARY 1931.

ERECTED BY DOCKER RIVER SOCIAL CLUB INC. FOR MR. R. LASSETER
26 TH APRIL 1974

travel further necessitated an expedition. During the war, many thousands entered the astonishing portals of the Heavitree Gap—through which squeeze a road, a railway line, and a river—and arrived at 'The Alice' where, generally, they remained long enough to appreciate something of the attractions of the MacDonnells. Many discovered the literature also, and turned their minds to the ranges and outliers which might be approached from the southern terminus of the Stuart Highway.

Although within the first quarter of the century, motor cars had been used in the Centre for some notable exploratory work,[30] for general inland transport the age of the camel persisted until the second World War. Four-wheel-drive trucks were available in numbers soon after; indeed, for a long time, the provision of motor fuel was a greater problem.

I remember leaning on the rail of a vessel in convoy in the Atlantic, discussing a homecoming with a fellow Australian. My plans, at the time, envisaged a swift return to Europe after a brief period back at home. But what we dreamed of on that grey day, drawing heavily on visions of largesse, when every kind of rationing would have ceased, was the mounting of an expedition into Central Australia . . . 'way up beyond Oodnadatta . . . out west of Alice Springs . . . in the Musgrave Ranges!' Within a year or two such journeys were possible. *Plus ça change!* Close to the immense walls of Ayers Rock, in those days well beyond the ends of roads, we discovered the eroded ruts of waggon wheels, made nearly three-quarters of a century earlier,[31] still plain among the low mulga scrub. Had a thousand years passed there would have been no visible change in the magnificent monolith.

Anyone travelling in that country on an unsurfaced road will leave his mark if he meets heavy rains, which is, however, fairly unlikely; in fact it is not uncommon for a year to pass with no more than a few millimetres or so, although my first excursion into the region of the great tors left deep impressions which will certainly still be visible. After driving all the way from Adelaide to Erldunda homestead, a distance of about 1500 kilometres, we received more than a year's average rainfall in a week.

Erldunda occupies 6500 square kilometres, and the homestead is 230 kilometres S.S.W. of Alice Springs. West of the station lies sand, spinifex, and mulga, with occasional claypans of all sizes, some 3 or 4 kilometres in diameter. Following what tracks we could, and often plunging over featureless country which promised better progress, in that most exceptional September, we were bogged time and time again, and covered only 120 kilometres in the first five days.

It was not always easy to appreciate the beauty and wonder of rain and lightning in the desert, of stormy clouds reflected between the water-washed mulga roots, but the sight was often superb. Frequently we were above our ankles in soupy mud, and daubed with bright red all over, shoving and digging, jacking, and cutting heavy wet branches to place beneath the wheels. At times, with only small arcs of the wheels visible, even the differentials ploughed long slimy furrows. The correct procedure, under such conditions, is to stop immediately the wheels lose their grip. Sometimes it is possible to back out, and choose a new route; otherwise it is essential to remove opposition by digging trenches at once, rather than waste fuel in burying the wheels still further. Our petrol consumption became alarmingly high, and, eventually, near the foot of the Liddle Hills, close to where the road to Ayers Rock was later graded, further progress became manifestly impossible until the ground became firmer.

No sooner had we erected tarpaulins and established camp than the sun started drying out the country. We spent two delightful days tramping over the Liddle Hills and the Wollera, reorganising our collections and imbibing much local wisdom from a famous old pioneer, William Liddle,[32] and from his sons, whose shack lay a few kilometres distant across a treacherous claypan area. Its normal access then was south from Middleton Ponds. Today it is the Angas Downs Station homestead, on the well-graded road that leads out to Ayers Rock and passes swiftly by the scenes of our heavy progress. The Rock is certainly a grand objective, but nothing is lost by savouring the quality of the surrounding country. I was glad, later on, when my old friend, Bill Harney, was appointed custodian of Ayers Rock; and yet, Bill Liddle would have been even more fitting, for Harney's territory was really further north, far away from this Luritja country in which Liddle had travelled courageously, pioneered fearlessly, and been absolutely accepted by the Aborigines whose blood was blended in his sons.

From time to time we met Luritja Aborigines, all of whom had contact either with some station or with one of the missions. There were, indeed, a few completely primitive tribes and nomadic families living 400 or 500 kilometres to our north-west near Lake Mackay—the Pintubi,[33] who, even a hundred years after John McDouall Stuart's crossing, had still made little contact with Europeans, or, for that matter even with cattle. There is a remarkable story of the absolute fear some of the contemporary Pintubi displayed at the sight of a rogue bullock which, in an unusual season of rain and lush parakeelia growth, strayed hundreds of kilometres into their Gibson Desert reaches.

The Luritja we met were fine men moving easily through their country, and seemingly impoverished only by the European rags they wore. Yet no one who has felt the chill of the desert at night, would doubt what a blessing these garments were to men who had slept almost naked by a flickering fire in a trench scooped in the sand. I often wished I could communicate with the Aborigines more directly than with the few toy English words they possessed, so that I could understand what thoughts their minds held behind shining and sometimes smouldering eyes.

A few days later we picked our way south and round the Wilbeah Range, a well-timbered ridge of sandstone hills. Spinifex-covered sand made firmer traction than the more clayey soil we had been crossing, and, from an occasional crest, we could now see Mt Conner 25 kilometres, a long scarp, hard cut against the south-west horizon.

As we approached, the mountain presented a superb sight, its unbroken northern rampart constantly changing colour with the movement of clouds. At one moment it lay evenly blue, like a distant tabular iceberg in a grey sea; in the next its sheer cliffs became alive with flaming red detail under a vertical shaft of sunlight. From the north-west, the vertical cliffs, appearing quite unscalable, are visible rising above the tall screes to a total height of 300 metres from the surrounding plain. Subsequent road-making has left Mt Conner sufficiently isolated to be the least visited of the great tors, while routes that then had no existence have encircled Ayers Rock and reached the domes of Mt Olga.

Towards evening the mountain was hidden behind a steep secondary scarp, and we camped out of sight of our goal. All desert travellers are familiar with what, at first, is a disconcerting phenomenon—the complete disappearance of a major objective behind aggressive belts of mulga or some small, persistent sandhills. The foot of our rocky scarp was followed for several kilometres, the route slowly ascending until it gave access to the vast shallow basin that surrounds Mt Conner. After such rains the whole country appeared beautifully fresh; several species of emu-bush[34] were in brilliant blossom. These shrubs all carry brightly coloured labiate flowers, ranging from crimson through several shades of red, with motley combinations, to pale mauve. They vie with the cassias for sheer display of colour, though the latter far excel them in perfume.

Floodwaters near Nhill,
Victoria, with a colourful
growth of the red floating
water weed *Azolla*

Top: Grass-trees near Gosse Bluff in the MacDonnell Ranges, Northern Territory.
Bottom: Mount Connor, 'a sculptured citadel towering above the colourful plain'

157

In the Centre, it is difficult to imagine the weather contrasts a month or so may provide. Next morning, as we skirted the last low cliffs and breasted the scarp, the cloudless skies were redolent of the southern spring.

Suddenly Mt Conner reappeared, its shadowed western face wreathed in rising mists. There stood what, for this season, was to be the apogee of our 2500-kilometre journey, a sculptured citadel towering above the colourful plain. The mountain is clearly stratified with bands of conglomerate sandstone, some exceedingly fine in texture, some containing rounded pebbles up to 10 or 12 centimetres in diameter. The strata are horizontal, uniformly hard and, at times, difficult to differentiate in detail. It would seem obviously part of an ancient sea-bed, a mesa that has resisted, through a great period of geological time, the forces which have lowered thousands of square kilometres surrounding it.

Already the summit of the high maroon cliffs was flaming in the direct sunlight. Gradually, as we drove cautiously over sharp rocks and between the spiky mulga, as we made our camp at the foot of the tremendous scree, as midday came . . . the whole mountain took the colour of the incredibly red earth.

The more one sees of the Centre, the more strangely it seems to contrast with other parts of the continent. The angular, exquisitely proportioned corkwood growing in the foreground, might have been transplanted straight from a Japanese woodcut; the shapely mulga, except for its colour, from an English bluebell wood. If the silver-grey of this acacia is strange, the bloodwood, a eucalypt, bears leaves as green as springtime English oak.

The western wall, beneath which we camped, is about 2 kilometres long. From the plain, the accumulated debris of fallen rock which surrounds the entire mountain rises, at a steadily increasing angle, to the base of the cliffs. Composed of jagged conglomerate blocks, ranging from 30 centimetres long to chunks weighing hundreds of tonnes, it provides a rough scramble for well over half the mountain's height. Above the scree, the cliffs from which it has fallen tower a further 120 metres, and are quite spectacular, being incut at the base in most places, and therefore very difficult to ascend. There is a sharp corner at the north-west leading round to an equally uncompromising face stretching approximately 5 kilometres before it swings away to the south. The disintegration of these metamorphosed sedimentary rocks is assisted by the plains of cleavage between ancient strata, and is more massive and more frequent than that of formations of granite, gneiss, and of other homogeneous rocks. The whole mountain is steadily falling away and, ultimately, will be a rounded hill; in the meantime the cliffs are steep and freshly faced by frequent rock-falls.

To follow along the base of the cliffs is an arduous journey; to encircle the tableland at any level below them is more than a long day's struggle. In several places they overhang by at least 15 metres, and this emphasises the huge unstable blocks of which the walls are composed, making them a truly awesome sight. Riven by huge fissures, often developing into considerable caverns, they possess mysterious depths, the exploration of which, even where access may be gained, would take several weeks. One of the most fascinating aspects is simply the contrast of the colours of rock and sky, both so unbelievably brilliant to eyes accustomed to higher latitudes.

The ovoid perimeter of the mountain stretches 15 kilometres; only in the south do the vertical walls give way to several rocky gorges. These are all obvious lines of ascent, and involve only mild climbing up the steep beds of dry ravines.

There was remarkably little water in rock pools in these gullies, even after such heavy rain. We could not locate a perennial spring mentioned by the Aborigines.[35] Ironwoods, eucalypts, and the beautiful white cypress-pine[36] find graceful root-hold in rock crevices of the winding chasm; the narcotic 'pituri,'[37] used as a chewing plug by the Aborigines, is also common, its lush green leaves very distinct against the cinnabar rock. It is interesting to find how carefully a people who do not plant crops pluck leaves from a plant without destroying its capacity to produce further bounty. Only on inaccessible ledges were unmutilated plants at all common; these could have been reached by euros had they been a favoured diet; we therefore presumed the harvesting had been entirely by humans.

At one point on the western cliffs a successful direct assault was made by some of my party using an orthodox rock-climbing technique. At many points the sandstone, although as hard as flint, is bedded loosely, and cannot be trusted to provide a safe footing. The reward of such an ascent lies in the exploration of numerous caves and aery ledges, most of which are virgin territory. Some of these are worn smooth by the passage through endless centuries of rock wallabies, bats, and mice. In many of the caves lie piles of petrified, pitch-like dung. In the largest recess we visited, a depth of 45 metres is reached, and the summit of the sloping bed rises to within 30 metres of the plateau above. The overhanging lip cannot be climbed without mechanical aid.

Except for a very slight slope southwards and a depression above the gorges, the tableland is quite flat. Several kinds of mulga clothe it with scrub about 3 metres high; a particularly merciless species of triodia also freely grows there.

Even exceeding the interest of the mountain itself are the tremendously wide views. These embrace, in any swing of the eyes, areas of 25 000 square kilometres, vast level tracts of plainland broken by no eminence nearer than Ayers Rock. It is probably the extreme flatness of the immense plain, with vegetation, graduated by distance from fair-sized trees to featureless blue stubble, faithfully tracing the phantom watercourses, that makes the curvature of the earth seem actually perceptible. It is very easy to imagine all the horizontal ranges—the Musgraves, Petermanns, or MacDonnells—as distant coastlines; The Rock and Olga, closer at hand as cliff-girt islands. Yet never was sea of water so variously coloured. From the red screes to the meeting of earth and sky the scene is flooded with washes of many subtle shades, slowly but constantly changing with shadows and sunlight. Far below, the large camp, with its taut white awnings, is a lonely ketch becalmed; the distant smokes from Aborigines' fires, black from spinifex fuel, are tramp steamers, perhaps notifying their existence in great arcs of vision reaching beyond our horizon, making port of Ernabella or Hermannsburg.

Nightfall in the Centre is noticeably swifter than in southern Australia. Mt Conner lies close to the 25° S. parallel, less than two degrees south of the Tropic of Capricorn. It is interesting to remark that the difference of latitude between Wilsons Promontory and Mt Conner considerably exceeds that between Iceland and the south of England.

The infinitely clear stars of the Centre, sweeping undimmed from rising to setting, are a sight to be long remembered. A sense of great well-being comes from seeing new lights within familiar constellations. It is, perhaps, that enhanced sense of vision, stimulated by unusual contours, unique colours, and almost infinite distance, that provides the richest memories of Mt Conner.

Although W. C. Gosse named Mt Conner, Ernest Giles was the first to pass closely, in 1874. He considered the summit inaccessible, and did not attempt it. His peace of mind was, however, somewhat troubled by knowledge that the nearest certain water lay in pools in the Finke, 300 kilometres away. He describes the country as 'perfect desert,' probably for the same reason. All life in this central country of 'The Dreaming' is conditioned by the

Facing page:
The colours of the Out-
back; Rainbow Valley in
the Northern Territory

seasons. My first visit to Mt Conner occurred when the desert was stirring after rain into incredible fecundity and beauty. The animals we saw, whether native or exotic, were sleek and fancy-free—able to roam as far as they liked over waxing pastures. How different is the state as I write, when prolonged drought is still taking terrible toll of herds which can no longer await the inevitable rains.[38]

The native animals of Central Australia are unobtrusive. As Finlayson demonstrated, there are a number of shy and chiefly nocturnal species—not all marsupials incidentally—which may be observed by the patient naturalist; especially if he is aided by the Aborigines' local knowledge.

All visitors are delighted by swift glimpses of great red kangaroos,[39] often moving in large mobs across the roads, the smaller but heavily built euro,[40] and perhaps, in the sandstone hills, the agile rock wallaby.[41] The progress of a mob of red kangaroos, at speed, is one of the loveliest compound movements that can be seen. The uneven leaps, varying according to the size and capability of the individual, create a wonderful wavelike pulsation running through the entire mob. Sometimes they stop and gaze, then, moving again in quite straight parallel lines, they recede to the distant horizon.

Isolated euros and rock wallabies were seen near Mt Conner, the latter often high up the cliffs, making their way down precipitous slopes with enviable ease.

Wherever one travels in the Centre there are lizards. Moving with a swiftness that defies the human eye, little geckos and skinks flash between the clumps of spinifex and across the rocks to sheltering crevices. It is no easy job to locate these smaller species at the base of the prickly triodia, and often long periods were spent in fruitless pursuit of some tantalising flash of mottled colour. The agamids, larger as a rule and lazier, bask motionless in the sun; they often courted death beneath our slow-rolling trucks. They include the famous horny dragons and the jew lizards. Their unprepossessing appearance—the dangerous-looking spines and aggressive armour—belies their nature; they are quite harmless and are usually easily handled. To the Aborigines, all lizards, especially the big monitors, or perenties, are good tucker; without them they would often spend hungry days.

A drawback to fast journeying is the impossibility of observing any birds smaller than emu or plain turkey unless, like the sulphur-crested cockatoos, they fly screaming beside the vehicles. Often a camp near the red mountains is presided over by eagles and hawks. The wedge-tailed eagle nests in the crags of Mt Conner and a pair was visible for much of our stay, wheeling around the brilliant rock or sky, while lower, hovering round the red rock faces may be seen the black kite and the ubiquitous peregrine. High above the waterholes of Ayers Rock are flocks of finches looking no bigger than flies.[42]

The attraction of Ayers Rock is irresistible. It is 1600 kilometres from Adelaide, and a quarter that distance from Alice Springs, but is accessible now by tourist buses speeding over bitumen roads, or it may be visited easily by air. Accommodation and camping facilities at Ayers Rock have been greatly extended through the years. Fortunately, the realisation that part of the essential nature of the Rock is its solitude, has moved tourist facilities much further from the monolith, allowing controlled access. Although the chains and painted lines are probably necessary to safeguard many who essay the climbing of Ayers Rock, it is hoped that the pigment at least will be replaced by stone cairns, and possibly a few fixed stones in between. Almost directly south-west of 'The Alice,' the surprising tor is about half-way between the George Gills Range and the Musgraves. The prevailing direction of all these mountain chains of central Australia is nearly east and west. Mt Conner, Ayers Rock, and Mt Olga—the Three Tors—are also lined up on

Top: A member of the gecko family at Ormiston Gorge, Northern Territory. *Centre:* A thorny devil *Moloch horridus* in the Gibson Desert. *Bottom:* Goannas are noted for their tendency to climb when disturbed

Top: Partridge pigeon *Petrophassa smithii* enjoys the tropical and savannah woodlands from the Kimberleys to north-western Queensland. *Centre:* Sulphur-crested cockatoo *Cacatua galerita*, widespread in the north, east, and south-eastern Australia. *Bottom:* Zebra finch *Peophilia guttata*, seen here at the base of Ayers Rock, Northern Territory

about the same bearing, with the Petermann and Rawlinson Ranges further west. From Mt Conner, on a clear day, the higher peaks of the Petermanns are horizoned at a distance of 250 kilometres; Mt Olga is just visible 120 kilometres away, almost directly beyond Ayers Rock. Just 250 kilometres from Mt Olga, in the same line, but accessible by a road through the Musgrave and Mann Ranges further south, is the Giles weather station, at the eastern end of the Rawlinsons. The so-called Gunbarrel Highway,[43] through the Gibson Desert, extending far into Western Australia, eventually reaches Wiluna and Meekatharra.

It is probable that safe access roads will eventually be available through all this country, and link up with roads in Western Australia. At present, this is not so; and many of the roads that do exist are still negotiable only by specialised vehicles. Much of the territory is classed as Aboriginal Reserve, and may not be entered without a permit from the proper authority. From north to south, the Central Australian Aboriginal Reserves stretch about 1000 kilometres from south of Halls Creek to the Nullarbor.

Even before roads were scored across the Inland, there were never any problems of path-finding, provided the traveller possessed the means of sustenance and locomotion. The only faith needed was that a compass course over a seeming eternity of red sand waves, bristled with mulga and spinifex, would eventually intersect a known traverse, or reveal a goal. Thus The Rock would crystallise from a tantalising phantom, visible only from isolated crests, to a vast and constant reality.

Its appearance is always unexpected. The eyes are turned from thousands of square kilometres of many-coloured plain to the sky-towering heights, hard and striated in extraordinary contrast. That this mass, twice the area of the central City of London and higher than its tallest buildings,[44] should rise without scree or foothills from the desert, is strange enough, without analysis. Any explanation of its metamorphosed conglomerate, fine and crystalline in texture, not resting on its original horizontal bedding, as at Conner and Olga, but tilted almost upright, must only add to its wonder.

For almost 10 kilometres, the scalloped cliffs meet the desert in an endless variety of incut caves and overbearing buttresses. In shaded clefts, between the vast recumbent limbs, lie three large pools of clear water, surrounded by luxuriant growth.[45] Some of the caves reveal wall paintings 'from the Old Race, to whom Oolra (Uluru) was always a place of awe, to which the wind gave a moaning voice between sunset and dawn.'[46]

The vast rock mass absorbs by day a good deal of solar heat which, being re-radiated at night, causes local air turbulence, updraughts in the evening, and quite powerful katabatic winds in the morning. The diurnal difference in temperature of the rock surface must frequently exceed 45°C, causing such surface expansion and contraction that flakes of rock are constantly being loosened. Attrition by friction and wind cause these plates to disintegrate before they reach the ground, so that the rock always seems to be solid, enduring, and immutable. More massive rock falls, since they require lines of weakness, and possibly the freezing of water which has seeped into them, must be extremely uncommon. The shape and homogeneous composition of the rock itself does not favour such processes; what fallen rock lies at its base is scarcely noticeable in the general scale of the monolith.

In many places it is possible to stand on a flat desert surface stretching unbroken for thousands of square kilometres, and to lean against an upright wall that towers skyward, seeming one of the barriers of the world, a veritable end of space. I remember finding myself repeating old childlike words . . . 'what lies on the other side of the end of all space?' How finite is the hard, high rock! Its very abruptness, the sudden adamant for air, makes you think of its depths, immensely still and quiet. If you creep far back into a

164

cave and chip away a fragment to reveal particles that may not have seen the sun since before the first living organisms were created on the planet, their colour may be dusty green, still awaiting complete oxidation.

Unvisited caverns without end exist high in the walls of Ayers Rock.[47] They are known only to the winds that surge up and down the red walls, eroding as surely as water, the hard arkose grit. The eye lingers fascinated at the edges of their shadowed depths, and in imagination you enter them in triumphant levitation, and stand solitarily where no one has ever stood before . . . where none will ever stand. Perhaps some could be reached by rappelling; such a venture might provide a new delight for mountaineers of the future.

One of the most curious features of Ayers Rock is a huge vertical slab of rock rising about 60 metres at the north-west corner. This is evidently part of a former shell that has otherwise disappeared completely. A space of something over a metre separates the pillar, for the greater part of its length, from the main wall. Exfoliation on such a vast scale might have been associated with cooling and contraction that took place after the period of metamorphosis that virtually re-fused the particles of much more ancient granitic mountains to form the present mass.

Although, superficially, the stone looks like red granite, with a marked crystalline texture, a close examination will reveal small pebbles that have not lost their water-worn form imparted by proterozoic streams. Geologists consider that Mt Conner, Ayers Rock, and Mt Olga are all derived from older mountains in the south, of which the Musgraves probably constitute a remnant, persisting from the time when an ocean washed their slopes and carried their grains and boulders to new beds.[48]

There are two normal routes of ascent; one, up a western buttress, follows a slope averaging not more than thirty degrees. Only the constant exposure of the long trudge could give any cause for unease during the climb to the summit. But because of the length alone, and the absence of respite, each loose flake of rock seems to warrant wariness. You look askance over your shoulder, down a vast, steep ramp 500 metres long, to the broad, bright landscape.

From a distance the vertical strata are clearly visible, however incomprehensible they may seem beside the sedate horizontal bands of Mt Conner or Mt Olga. However, when one reaches the top of the monolith, and sees them on edge they become great, rolling waves, wrinkling the hide of a tellurian. Deep in their crevices, in almost hidden, tussocked pools, water will lie for a long time—in one or two places for years. A few mulgas and a dead finish or two had found clefts also on the summit when last I wandered there. I hope they remain, for they were a part of the pristine wonder, and had been there since 'creation times.'[49]

I have wandered over the summit of The Rock from end to end by day and night. Once a starlit euphoria suffered a terrifying change when I found myself descending by a wrong spur that grew steeper and steeper until I suddenly realised that I was fast approaching the point at which gravity must triumph. In the dim starlight I had naturally taken precautions, leaving three white handkerchiefs under flakes to mark my line of descent. Now these had been retrieved, so there must obviously have been an unnoticed fork below them. My companions' campfire was out of sight beneath the bulge of the rock. I nearly spent the night against the sky.

Of the three strange monuments, my favourite is the Olga cluster, 30 kilometres from Ayers Rock, away to the west. Each of the domes is distinctive, but the group possesses a wonder that will evoke new comparisons for ever. Between the huge helmets are ravines where concentrated moisture from the impervious slopes allows luxuriant vegetation, even more vigorous than

This page and facing page: Ayers Rock, Northern Territory. Weather patterns and time of day produce varying effects of great beauty

that margining the pools of Ayers Rock. The walls of Olga are often quite smooth, yet they reveal their agglomeration of ancient water-worn boulders, much larger than anything at either of the other tors. It would seem that the siliceous cement combining them together is precisely as hard as the embedded stones.

The summits of many of the domes are accessible, but their ascent may be very much more difficult than that of Mt Conner or The Rock. The highest point may be reached by those who don't mind a rather featureless, steep scramble continuing for 450 metres. There are ample holds for both feet and hands, and, occasionally, a delightful little sentry-box cave where one may be an anchorite, withdrawn from any inclination to progress further up or down. On the summit is a cairn first built by William Mackinnon. People who climb Mt Olga often feel like conversing with their predecessors, some of whom have added their names to the record in the heap of stones on the top. The way down does seem steeper than the ascent, and from the brow the rock curves out of sight for 20 or 30 intimidating metres. But, at all times, the views are superb.[50]

The gorges and canyons of the ranges—the MacDonnells, the George Gills, the Harts, and innumerable other rocky walls, riven by narrow clefts and immense chasms—are spectacular and lovely places where high light is reflected in cast shadow so that walls untouched by the sun appear luminescent with warm colours. There may be sudden illumination, as in the famous Standley Chasm in the Chewings Range, about 50 kilometres out of 'The Alice,' when the sun slides into line, or more tranquil facetting that points trees and crags sometimes reflected in still pools as at Ormiston Gorge, Glen Helen, Palm Valley, or in Kings Canyon. In some of these glens the vegetation includes a famous species of palm and a cycad, that are probably residual from a period when the climate was lush and tropical.[51] Almost yearly the repertory of the ranges is revealed more extensively, and there will not be an end in centuries, for in the Northern Territory alone, the legendary country covers hundreds of thousands of square kilometres of the ancient ranges.

The isolation of certain natural features, such as Ayers Rock, seems an additional aggrandisement, for their lonely stature is emphasised by the emptiness of the surrounding air. There is one strange residual which, because it is high and separate, seems to speak of an entire vanished continent. It stands dominating the sandhills of the Finke River a few kilometres north of the South Australian border. James McDouall Stuart discovered this sandstone monolith, five times as high as it is broad, in 1860, and named it Chambers Pillar, after a patron. The Aborigines had long known it as Idracowra;[52] it is the remnant of old highlands disintegrated by an ancient sea. Twelve years after its discovery by Stuart, Ernest Giles wrote:[53]

The appearance of this feature, I should imagine, to be unique in Australia, and it is not likely that any future explorer will ever discover so singular a monument . . .

By this time we were close to the Pillar, and its outline was most imposing. Upon reaching it, I found it to be a columnar structure, standing upon a pedestal, which is perhaps eighty feet high, and composed of loose white sandstone, having vast numbers of large blocks loose and lying about in all directions. From the centre of the pedestal rises the pillar, composed also of the same kind of rock though at its top and for about twenty or thirty feet from the summit the colour of the stone is red. The column itself must be about 150 feet above the pedestal. There it stands (not indeed, quite alone, as there are other peculiar eminences near), a vast monument of the geological periods that must have elapsed since the mountain ridge of which it was formerly part was washed by the action of the ocean waves into mere sandhills at its feet . . . In a small orifice

168

or chamber of the Pillar I discovered an opossum asleep; it was the first I had seen in this part of the country . . .

We turned our backs upon this peculiar monument, and left it in its loneliness and its grandeur—'clothed in white (sandstone), mystic, wonderful.'[54]

Giles was at the beginning of the explorations which in the next five years were to take him through so much of the Dreamtime landscapes; today they are little changed, and you may follow confidently in the steps of those who discovered them to the vision of white men. It is no longer difficult to carry with you on your travels the published works of most of the explorers[55] and, in so doing, annul that 'great gap of time' in which fear and uncertainty have given way to safety and delight.

Another world lies to the north, much of Arnhem Land still remaining in detail virtually unexplored. Country that has been desiccated by millions of dry seasons, and dissected by as frequent monsoon rains, may produce regions where the imaginative will find ruined cities, places where weathered stones and steep defiles will seem the remnants of colossal artefacts. That, of course, is just what they were to the Aborigines . . . the mighty, immortal works of their giant spirit ancestors, imbued with majesty, awe-inspiring . . . the Dreamtime Landscapes. And often, when the great totemic beings had finished their struggles, they themselves were turned to stone, and must remain for ever.

[1] The red of the desert is caused by atmospheric oxidation, over very long periods, of the iron-bearing rocks—iron being the commonest metal, after aluminium, in the earth's crust, and oxygen, of course, being the commonest element. In arid climates less leaching takes place. The 'greenstone' brought up from deep auriferous basins in the Western Australian gneiss, at places such as Kalgoorlie and Norseman, is ferrous, but the process of roasting, necessary for the extraction of the gold, speeds up a similar process of oxidation, taking hours rather than thousands of years, and the treated concentrates are bright red.

[2] Sturt's mention of the Pole may have been inspired, perhaps, by thoughts of the ill-fated expedition of Sir John Franklin, also in 1845. Franklin had been a contemporary of Sturt's in Australia for several years, and had left Tasmania only two years before, in order to undertake further polar exploration.

[3] See note 17 on *The Red Centre* (H. H. Finlayson).

[4] *Acacia tetragonophylla, Atriplex vesicarium*, and *A. mummularia*, the salt-bushes, are nutritious moisture-hoarders. The Parakeelia (*Calandrinia balonensis*) is an ephemeral succulent that rapidly clothes much of the desert after rain.

[5] The Dreamtime: In the Aborigines' 'Dreamtime' lie the events of creation, in the past, present, and future. The myths of the Aborigines, frequently associated with landmarks such as conspicuous stones, caves, hills, waterholes, and other natural features, are the tribal history taking place in this Dreamtime. Elkin, *The Australian Aborigines* (Angus & Robertson, Sydney, 1938), chap. 8, writes: 'It is the eternal dreamtime and is manifested in the past through the heroes, in the present through the initiated (especially in sacred ceremonies) and it will be manifested in the future, provided that the links with it are not broken.'

[6] *Uluru*, with variants of spelling is Ayers Rock, or, more particularly, the waters in a summit cleft. *Katatjuta* is the area of Mt Olga. Many Aboriginal words were variously pronounced in different areas; when they were written phonetically by anthropologists, they tended to become crystallised in later writings. However, the early 'Arunta,' for instance, is now frequently given as 'Aranda.' Less explicably, perhaps, there is a good deal of variation in the legends of the Aborigines, as recorded by different travellers. During one visit to the Centre I discovered that some of the more sophisticated Aborigines were quite capable of inventing tales on the spot rather than disappointing an avid European.

[7] It is possible that the Aborigines arrived in Australia in time to see some of the great 'pre-historic' marsupials, in a much wetter, more lush continent. Prof. G. N. Blainey, in his *Triumph of the Nomads*, argues that, at least before white colonisation, the Aborigine lived as well, if not better, than their contemporaries in many other lands and circumstances. *Triumph of the Nomads* (Macmillan, 1975; Sun Books, 1976) by Geoffrey Blainey.

[8] The 1982 *Commonwealth Yearbook* reported 12 500 bores and wells in the Northern Territory, of which about half were for pastoral use. Leased and alienated land takes up 72%

Mount Olga comprises a group of some 30 monoliths west of Ayers Rock and south of Lake Amadeus in the Northern Territory. The highest rises almost 600 metres from the surrounding plains and the rocks are separated by narrow ravines. They have weathered to a dome shape and at certain times of day are a brilliant red colour

Top left: Kings Canyon is one of the beautiful untouched spots in the MacDonnell Ranges. *Top right:* Chambers Pillar dominates the sandhills of the Finke River. It is a sandstone monolith, rising some 30 metres above its base. *Bottom:* Palm Valley in central Australia is a unique restricted area of palm trees in the dry inland

of the Northern Territory's total area of approximately 1·35 million square kilometres. The average number of cattle grazed per square kilometre was less than two. Ground water, in Australia, is more important than surface water over about 60% of the country. In the 1980s about one-twentyfifth of Australia's average annual recharge of ground water was being used.

⁹ In the Alice Springs area, I have been told that, provided bores are at least 25 kilometres apart, the various herds of cattle may be localised.

¹⁰ *Triodia aristata*, not really a spinifex which is, correctly, a coastal sand-binding grass.

¹¹ Corkwood (*Hakea lorea*).

¹² Desert oak (*Casuarina decaisneana*).

¹³ Desert pea (*Clianthus speciosus*—the Sturt pea); emu-bush (*Eremophila* spp.)—there are several species, all with brightly coloured labiate flowers. Their popular name is derived from the fact that the Aborigines infused a stupefying poison from their bright, glabrous foliage, and used this to dope certain selected drinking places of their feathered quarry. (At least one species is dangerous for cattle.) There are many cassias (one of the important genera of the Leguminosae). The ghost gum is *E. papuana*; the ironwood, *Acacia estrophiolata*.

¹⁴ Phrase used by George Farwell.

¹⁵ Phrase used by H. H. Finlayson.

¹⁶ Alice Springs was named after the wife of Charles Heavitree Todd who was in charge of the construction of the Overland Telegraph Line between this station, just north of the MacDonnell Ranges, and Darwin.

¹⁷ *The Red Centre: Man and Beast in the Heart of Australia*, by H. H. Finlayson (Angus & Robertson, 1935) has been reprinted several times. It is still one of the best preparations for a visit to the Centre, although, of course, travel has become infinitely easier. Finlayson's expeditions, in the decade before the second World War, still favoured the camel as a means of transport, but had experimented with the car with notable success.

¹⁸ *Narrative of an Expedition into Central Australia*, by Captain Charles Sturt, F.L.S., F.R.G.S., in two volumes (London, 1849). A Facsimile Edition was issued in 1965 by the Libraries Board of South Australia.

¹⁹ The manuscript of Stuart's Journal, in the Mitchell Library, Sydney, is quoted by Prof. E. Scott: *A Short History of Australia* (Oxford, 1930). In this Stuart named Central Mount Stuart (as it is now generally known), Central Mount Sturt 'after my excellent and esteemed commander of the expedition in 1844 and 1845, Captain Sturt.' The published Journals of Stuart (edited by William Hardman, London, 1864) give the name Central Mount Stuart.

²⁰ From McKinlay's *Journal of Exploration* (1862?) Melbourne, Baillière, published in facsimile, 1962, by the Public Library of South Australia, Adelaide. The extract is from 15 June, and was, in fact, describing country in Queensland, just north of the S.A. border. It is interesting that, in 1965, a Melbourne Agricultural scientist suggested seriously that 'Australian farmers might one day be breeding kangaroos instead of sheep and cattle.' (*Geelong Advertiser*, 19/6/65).

²¹ Harry Lasseter perished in the Petermanns, while making an attempt to reach Mt Olga, in January 1931. The road from Mt Olga to Giles Weather Station passes the cave where Lasseter sheltered before making his last journey.

²² *Oodnadatta:* The Aboriginal name for the bloom of one of the mulgas. For so long a frontier town where strings of camels were mustered for journeys further north, with the extension of the railway, Oodnadatta lost something of its importance. Many of the camels were owned by Afghans. The train that travelled between Port Augusta and Alice Springs, before the re-routing of the new line from Tarcoola, was known affectionately as 'The Ghan'.

²³ See chap. 9, 'The Delectable Mountains.' The Dandenongs are southern outliers of The Great Divide in Victoria, visible from Melbourne, and constitute a favoured retreat not only for week-enders, but, increasingly for commuters working in the city.

²⁴ The best known of these was the Horn Expedition whose reports were published in four substantial volumes, in 1896, under the general editorship of Baldwin Spencer.

²⁵ *The Dead Heart of Australia: A Journey around Lake Eyre in the summer of 1901–1902*, by J. W. Gregory, F.R.S. (John Murray, London, 1909).

²⁶ *Australian Journey* (New Revised Edition), by Paul McGuire (Heinemann, London, 1942).

²⁷ Among the important novels appeared *Capricornia*, by Xavier Herbert (Angus & Robertson, Sydney, 1938, many times since reprinted). The artists who introduced the landscapes of the Inland included Rex Battarbee, who, discovering a talent for water-colour painting among the Aborigines of Hermannsburg Mission, greatly assisted their contribution also. Miss Violet Teague and William Rowell also visited the Centre and exhibited collections of striking landscapes. Hans Heysen's great field had been further south, in the Flinders Ranges.

Frank Clune's *Dig* and Ion L. Idriess' *Lasseter's Last Ride* are highly imaginative. Lasseter has become a legend, largely through Idriess' book which, however, is fundamentally fiction. However, gold does in some places fulfil Lasseter's Dream. The largest working gold-mine in Australia, at Telfer in the Paterson Range, 200 kilometres east of Nullagine and Marble Bar, showed rich surface gold in surface reefs bared by erosion.

[28] Charles P. Mountford, in *Brown Men and Red Sand* (Robertson & Mullens, Melbourne, 1948) states: 'The snake is a huge creature, many-coloured, with a mane, and often a beard; it is feared by the Aborigines because it attacks all strangers who approach the water in which it lives, usually calling with a deep, booming note. The rainbow-serpent is essentially the water element in nature, and is related to everything that the Aborigines associate with water, rainbows, pearl-shells, rivers, permanent springs, and rock-holes. The serpent, being afraid of the opposing natural element, fire, will always endeavour to escape its influence.'
(The late Charles Mountford did not associate the snake with the Devil's Marbles.)

[29] *More Australian Legendary Tales* (London, 1898), by K. Langloh Parker. The author is indebted to the selection of these tales made by Mrs H. Drake-Brockman, illustrated by Elizabeth Durack (Angus & Robertson, Sydney, 1953), a valuable volume containing about fifty legends and some useful appendices.

[30] Michael Terry is perhaps the best known of the early desert motorists. His expeditions, using both motor vehicles and camels, covered a great deal of territory between the Overland Telegraph Line and the goldfields of Western Australia. H. H. Finlayson, in *The Red Centre*, describes a journey he made with his brother, in 1934. Terry commenced motorized expeditions in the middle 1920s.
Camels and the Outback, by H. M. Barker (Pitman, Melbourne, 1964) contains, in addition to much unique material on camel transport, a valuable account of pioneering with motor-trucks in Western Australia, between Meekatharra and Marble Bar.

[31] W. C. Gosse first reached both Ayers Rock and Mt Olga in 1872, although the latter had been sighted by the indomitable Ernest Giles who named it, and was only prevented from reaching it by the treacherous 'Lake' Amadeus. It was a bitter blow to Giles to discover the tracks of Gosse's waggons a year later.

[32] There are numerous accurate references to W. H. ('Old Bill') Liddle, and his two half-European sons. in *I Saw a Strange Land*, by Arthur Groom (Angus & Robertson, Sydney, 1950). 'Liddle took up desert and plain country between the Basedow and Wollara Ranges, and brought his sheep across country from Oodnadatta. . . . Wool had to be camel-packed nearly three hundred miles to the Oodnadatta railhead . . . Up to 1947 Liddle had put down nineteen bore-holes without striking good water.'

[33] *The Lizard Eaters* (Cassell, 1964) by Douglas Lockwood is a sensitive account of a journey the author made in the company of a government patrol to the Gibson Desert. During this journey, it is said that contact was made with Pintubi Aborigines who had formerly never seen a white man.

[34] Emu-bush: The Eremophilas, especially *E. latrobei*. Six of the species of eremophila collected on this expedition had been named by Baron F. von Mueller, presumably from collections brought back by Ernest Giles. The Baron's keen sponsorship of Giles's expeditions was responsible for many of the German names bestowed on features in the Centre, including Mt Olga, and the Ehrenburg Ranges.

[35] Our own supplies of water were carried in 160-litre tanks, refilled at station tanks and bores, and where else occasion permitted. If water is potable, it is generally best to empty out tanks and refill them completely, rather than to mix waters from different sources.

[36] *Callitris columellaris*, one of the commoner members of the Australian *Pinaceae*, often called the Murray pine. Of three or four species favouring the Inland, *columellaris* is most common.

[37] Pituri: According to H. H. Finlayson, the term is not applied by the Aborigines to the species of *Nicotiana* which they use as a narcotic, though the term is common among the station people in the Centre. Finlayson states: 'It has evidently been derived from western Queensland, where, however, it is rightly applied to another plant, *Duboisia hopwoodi*.'

[38] In mid-August 1965, some useful rains fell in parts of the Centre for the first time in several years. The Melbourne *Age* reported that rains had saved the 'heart,' and that cattlemen, stock, and land had been 'reprieved.' Many tourist buses and private cars had to be abandoned, and the rescue of passengers effected with four-wheel-drive vehicles. 'This drought,' reported the *Age* correspondent in Alice Springs, 'cannot be called broken until there is more good rain within two months—then more and more.' That drought, in fact, persisted until 1968 and affected also much of eastern Australia. Severe drought affected one-third of the continent in 1972. Other serious drought years were 1976 and 1982–83.

[39] *Macropus rufus*.

[40] *Macropus robustus*.

[41] *Petrogale lateralis*.

[42] Perhaps the Diamond Sparrow, *Zonaeginthus guttata*.

[43] Len Beadell, who made the Gunbarrel and several other 'roads' in central Western

Australia, gives details of his epic route-making in his books, *Too Long in the Bush, Bush Bashers, Blast the Bush*, and others. The road connecting Mt Olga with Giles is often, but erroneously, called the Gunbarrel. The latest World Aeronautical Survey maps accurately name most of the still exiguous roads in the area of the Gibson Desert.

[44] Ayers Rock rises to 860 metres above sea-level; its height above the plain is 348 metres; and it has a perimeter of approximately 9 kilometres. C. D. Ollier and W. F. Tuddenham, in their article, *Inselbergs of Central Australia* (*Zeitschr. f. Geomorph.*, vol. 5, pp. 257–76), quoted by C. P. Mountford in his *Ayers Rock* (Angus & Robertson, 1965), say: 'The unity and isolation of the monolith is truly remarkable, but the lack of perspective on the plains country prevents appreciation of its true size. . . .' Incidentally, the Empire State Building in New York is 450 metres high, and the Chrysler Building, 319 metres—so that a cluster of New York sky-scrapers resembles fairly closely the general contour of Ayers Rock.

[45] Charles Mountford, in his excellent *Ayers Rock* (Angus & Robertson, Sydney, 1965), mentions eleven permanent or semi-permanent waterholes round Ayers Rock. The volume is a most valuable reference for all travellers to The Rock.

[46] From the author's description in *Walkabout*, January 1949; also quoted by Laseron in his *Face of Australia.*

[47] Almost all these caves; indeed, virtually every prominent feature of the entire rock mass, whether it be a hollow or protrusion, seems to have been the subject of an Aboriginal legend. In 'creation time,' according to myths recorded by Charles Mountford (*Ayers Rock,* previously cited), various totemic beings—poisonous snakes and pythons, hare wallabies and sleepy lizards—moulded the topography by their battles and their exploits.

[48] See 'The Three Tors' in C. F. Laseron's *The Face of Australia,* for a general account. A valuable scientific survey of Ayers Rock and Mt Olga, *Bornhardts developed in Sedimentary Rocks, Central Australia*, by C. R. Twidale and Jennifer A. Bourne, appeared in *The South Australian Geographer*, April 1978.

[49] Vandalism is not unknown even at Ayers Rock. The stupidity which prompted some early visitors to splash their initials in heavy paint over the drawings of the Aborigines might as thoughtlessly destroy a tree.

[50] The author made the second ascent of Mt Olga, in September 1948. An account (originally published in *Walkabout*, December 1949) was later reproduced in *Walkabout's Australia* (Ure Smith, Sydney, 1964).

An account of a more recent ascent, 'Conquering the Domes of Olga,' by A. E. Healy, appeared in *Walkabout*, June 1965.

[51] Respectively, *Livistona mariae* and *Macrozamia macdonnelli.*

[52] Or Etikaura (*Australian Encyclopaedia*, Grolier Society, Sydney).

[53] 23 August 1872. This was the year of the opening of the Overland Telegraph Line up which Giles travelled as far as his turning off point at the Finke River. Giles published: *The Journal of a Forgotten Expedition* (Adelaide, 1880), and *Australia Twice Traversed* (two vols., London, 1889), the latter covering the explorer's five major expeditions through the interior. Other Journals were published in 1873–5).

[54] 'Morte d'Arthur,' Tennyson's poem, subsequently incorporated in his 'Idylls of the King,' was first published in 1842. It is obvious that Giles must have been familiar with it. The Arthurian Legend poems were published contemporaneously with the exploration of Central Australia.

[55] The remarkable *Australiana Facsimile Editions*, the result of a courageous, but highly successful venture of the Libraries Board of South Australia, are indispensable to the historically minded traveller in Central Australia.

CHAPTER 8

Reefs, Cays, and Islands

Crescent upon his waves the cities gleam,
Blue mountains carry roads beyond his dream,
And where his seaway scarcely parried grief
Lie unconcealed the treasures of the Reef. . . .
                                        —*from* WIDE HOMELAND

A TRAVELLER SEEKING THE HIGHEST MOUNTAINS, the greatest rivers and waterfalls, or the widest deserts and lakes, would not find them in Australia. In considering Australia's physical attractions, a perceptive visitor might realise that it is in unique combinations of their simple elements, and in subtle qualities of form and colour, that they present a distinct and special character. All may discover, however, one immensity that is as intriguing, as beautiful, and as adventurous in its own way as any other region on earth — a great wall, its sections aggregating almost 2500 kilometres, that divides the coastal waters of Queensland from those of the deep Pacific. It was discovered quite suddenly by Captain James Cook in 1770, after he had sailed more than 1600 kilometres north from Botany Bay.

Following the coast, charting and naming many of the features which today are known to countless thousands, he was oblivious of its existence as a continuous barrier until he reached the latitude of our present Cairns. Here the reef is closer to the coast than anywhere further south.

> Hitherto we had safely navigated this dangerous coast, where the sea in all parts conceals shoals that suddenly project from the shore, and rocks that rise abruptly like a pyramid from the bottom, for an extent of two and twenty degrees of latitude, more than one thousand three hundred miles. . . .

he wrote, of Sunday, 10 June 1770. In the evening, he decided 'to stretch off all night' and 'see whether any island lay in the offing,' perhaps one of those said to have been discovered by de Quiros.

> We had the advantage of a fine breeze, and a clear moonlight night, and in standing off from six till near nine o'clock, we deepened our water from fourteen to twenty-one fathom, but while we were at supper it suddenly shoaled, and we fell into twelve, ten, and eight fathom, within the space of a few minutes; I immediately ordered everybody to their station, and all was ready to put about and come to an anchor, but meeting at the next cast of the lead with deep water again, we concluded that we had gone over the tail of the shoals which we had seen at sunset, and that all danger was past: before ten, we had twenty and one and twenty fathom, and this depth continuing, the gentlemen left the deck in great tranquility, and went to bed; but a few minutes before eleven, the water shallowed at once from twenty to seventeen fathom, and before the lead could be cast again, the ship struck, and remained immovable, except by the heaving of the surge, that beat her against the crags of the rock upon which she lay. In a

few moments every body was upon the deck, with countenances which sufficiently expressed the horrors of our situation. We had stood off the shore three hours and a half, with a pleasant breeze, and therefore knew that we could not be very near it, and we had too much reason to conclude that we were upon a rock of coral, which is more fatal than any other, because the points of it are sharp, and every part of the surface so rough as to grind away whatever is rubbed against it, even with the gentlest motion.[1]

This mention of coral is, I think, the first in Cook's description of Australia, although, of course, he had been wary of shoal waters and breakers as far south as the latitude of Cape Byron and that 'remarkable sharp peaked mountain' which he had named Mt Warning for the benefit of future mariners.

The terrible predicament of the *Endeavour* and all her company is conveyed most graphically by Cook's account. Events seemed hopeless until Mr Midshipman Monkhouse's strategem of fothering the leak, by passing a sail thickened with wool, oakum, and animal dung round the outside of the hull, was successful.[2] The inrush of water was stemmed, the pumps could easily deal with what still entered, and, eventually, the vessel could be careened ashore (near the present Cooktown), and repaired. Cook had written:

> We well knew that our boats were not capable of carrying us all on shore, and that when the dreadful crisis would arrive, as all command and subordination would be at an end, a contest for preference would probably ensue, that would increase the horrors even of shipwreck, and terminate in the destruction of us all by the hands of each other. . . .

The course of history seems to have been assured by two factors other than the immense efforts of the ship's company in jettisoning and pumping. One was the successful fothering; the other was the partial sealing of the rent in the ship's bottom by the penetrating coral, some of which remained embedded when the vessel was warped off the reef.

Today, in the Great Barrier Reef, Australia possesses a specialised physical attraction unrivalled elsewhere in the world, and a region of inexhaustible beauty, diversity, and romance. Here are desert islands and blue lagoons, coral gardens in water that seems more transparent than air, and lights and colours so intense that everyone who visits these places has some feeling of heightened well-being, as though perception through all the senses were miraculously acute. Like those of Australia's snowfields, the facilities for tourists range from little more than essential shelter to hotels providing for the most sophisticated delights. On some of the reef islands nightfall may be reminiscent of Hawaiian dusks, with little less glitter for the tourist. There may be firelight and barbecues; grass-skirts, dancing, and soft music; flood-lit swimming pools, and a general atmosphere of Cannes or Hollywood. Glass-bottomed boats and underwater aquaria permit wonderful observation of the creatures of the reef and, wherever there is a convenient area of coral exposed at low water, its attractions usually take precedence over anything that has been imported.

Nowadays, on the reef, as in the mountains, it is easy to use energy to its best advantage and retain sufficient for the gaudy night; for those who desire expensive fun, it is readily available. Perhaps it should be stressed that the converse is also true. There are still some hundreds of uninhabited islands within the Great Barrier Reef where the intrepid may find conditions unchanged since Lieutenant James Cook first mentioned the word 'coral'— 'more fatal than any other' rock.

176

Top: The harbour at Cooktown, northern Queensland. The *Endeavour* was repaired here in 1770 after striking a coral reef. *Bottom:* A coral atoll, with typical circular reef enclosing a lagoon, in the Coral Sea remote from the Great Barrier Reef

'No need for mescalin here!' one of my companions once remarked as he trod carefully over the exposed reef at Heron Island. It was true. There is a special delight for all the senses in relating colour with texture—soft pink, and violet shadow, for instance, of some staghorn coral, with the surprising brittle hardness of its branching form—and both with the smell and sounds of the sea. I am reminded of the exquisite and extravagant later vaulting of the Tudor period, where men had made pendant stone seem light as air. In the coral garden, nature provides similar sensory surprises. Fronds that look as though they should yield gently and be parted by the least intention of the limpid water are refractory. Brilliant fish seem to dart weightless through air, but, as though still further to intrigue the senses, some of the most lovely float tranquilly, striped and winged like butterflies.

Living corals display a spectrum range of bright and subtle colours which, as evanescent as the life of the individual polyps, soon disappear when a colony and its ancestral skeleton are lifted from the warm wash of the tropical seas. Occasionally one still sees skeletal corals dyed brilliantly to simulate the various species as they appear underwater, but they must lack the characteristic living texture, and, however skilfully the colours are blended, they are bizarre rather than beautiful. The best way of seeing coral is through still, clear water, often from a glass-bottomed boat. The general effect may be greatly heightened by the revealed mantle of an open clam, intensely bright, or by a shoal of coral fish, or by brittle stars, sea-stars, and bêche-de-mer—all possessing deeper hues than the coral itself.

A curious but delightful impression that an excursion over a reef flat at low tide may give is of a gargantuan progress through a land of strange arboreal growth, set with calm, sky-reflecting lakes; although in my experience, this only happens under certain conditions of side-lighting, and when the horizon is unbroken by any near-by land to destroy the illusion.

The clearest, driest months in the Capricornian tropics correspond with the southern winter; the rainy season with the hottest months of the south. Much as I dislike some aspects of the summer monsoons on the mainland, to the islands within the Barrier Reef, they bring warm, pearly calms, and strange shadowless vision often followed by clear, lotus-eating weather. As E. J. Banfield, the observant beachcomber of Dunk Island once wrote, 'warm as the rains are, they bring to the air coolness and refreshment. Clear, calm, bright days, days of even and not high temperature, and of pure delight, dovetail with the hot and steamy ones.' The same great character, whose twenty-five years of residence never palled, went on to say:

> The prolificacy of vegetation is a perpetual marvel; the loveliness of the land, the ineffable purity of the sky, the glorious tints of the sea—green and gold at sunrise, silvery blue at noon, purple, pink and lilac during the all too brief twilight, a perpetual feast.[3]

Sensations of well-being are not communicated only through the visual sense; even our feet, that day on Heron, protected as they were in strong shoes, on the coral, nevertheless, felt the old prehensile grip that the toes of civilised man seem too seldom to experience. Incidentally, it is as well to wear strong footwear on reef rambles. Quite apart from the lacerating coral, there is always the danger of the odd stone-fish, the seeming malice of this Eden, whose spines can inflict deadly wounds.[4] A few days of excursioning over coral are usually sufficient to put shoes on their last legs!

It is probable that the brilliant sunshine on white coral sand, composed of crushed coral and shell, and the skeletons of minute foraminifera,[5] causes a maximum contraction of the iris and, consequently, excellent definition and depth of focus, particularly for eyes that have lost their youthful resiliency.

178

Curiously perhaps, the only experience I have had comparable to that of exploring a coral reef at low tide has been in Antarctica, walking warily over sea ice with the long summer had eroded into a field of encrusted crystals. This sensuous therapy, caused by unexpected associations making the ethereal most substantial and showing living forms in their utmost variety— blue sea-stars, butterfly cod, and banded perch, mushroom, brain, and honeycomb corals, fish that walk,[6] and pandanus trees that seem to have legs, is capable of arousing or restoring a real zest for living. The mescalin-eaters of South America are said to enter a strange ecstasy and to discover new significances in colour and form. 'No need for mescalin' was as succinct a description of a late winter's day on the reef-flat at Heron Island as could have been given.

The Great Barrier Reef extends for well over 2000 kilometres along the north-east coast of Australia, between the Tropic of Capricorn and the great island of New Guinea. From any port between Bundaberg and Cooktown and, less conveniently, for 800 kilometres or so to the north of where Captain Cook repaired his vessel at the mouth of the Endeavour River, you may embark for coral islands, barren or vegetated, or for the reef itself. This sparsely breached wall bounding the south-west Pacific in its Australian sector, ranges between 300 kilometres and about 80 kilometres from the Queensland coast, and varies greatly in width. In some regions the complex of reefs occupies a breadth of more than 150 kilometres; in others it may narrow to 15 or 20 kilometres. Cook quite aptly named the area north of our present Cairns the Labyrinth. As a whole, the Great Barrier Reef has been accurately described as the largest structure resulting from the activity of living creatures in the world and often been compared with the Great Wall of China which, however, is longer, but much less massive. Within the reef, over an area of about 20 000 square kilometres, corresponding to that of the continental shelf in these parts, the sea is relatively shallow, mainly much less than 150 metres, compared with that beyond, where it plunges to depths of a kilometre or more. Inside the reef, also, as on the night of Cook's misadventure, the sea may be very calm, for the reefs interrupt the great rollers of the Pacific which, further south, provide such excellent surfing. A number of navigable passages through the reefs are now well charted; some—Whitsunday, Trinity, and Cook's—commemorate the discoverer of our east coast. The Flinders Passage remembers a coastal explorer who was in many respects his equal.

Along the Queensland coast, the tidal range varies between about 2 metres and, in Broad Sound (between Rockhampton and Mackay), more than 6 metres[7]. All excursions over reef flats must, of course, be carefully timed; those to the outer reef will be planned so that arrival at the reef area may coincide with the last of the ebb. Naturally, the most profitable expeditions, when the coral is most exposed, coincide with seasonally low tides. However, for cruises to the outer reef, the ebb of the spring tides normally occurring twice a month at the times of the new and full moon, is generally propitious in good weather. On most calm days, short excursions may be taken to island reef flats. Their emergence at the ebb is always a fascinating sight. The consultation of tide tables, available in all capital cities, is worth while in planning a visit to the Great Barrier Reef, especially if extensive cruising is envisaged.[8]

If there is much delight in the objective vision and sensory experience of reefs and cays, it is matched by the intriguing knowledge that coral consists of accumulations of the limey secretion of numberless minute polyps—tiny, flower-like, 'tentacled' creatures, not unlike miniature sea anemones.[9] Each coral polyp possesses an external 'skeleton' in the form of a minute container—in several species, a cup with radial partitioning walls from which

179

Facing page: Snorkelling on the reef edge. Great Barrier Reef. *This page top:* Reef fish feeding; this species always swims in pairs. *Bottom:* Fish observed from the glass underwater observatory at Green Island, off Cairns, Queensland

the creature may extend its tiny waving arms and entrap the still smaller animals that are its food. Most corals are mainly active at night, and, seen by torchlight, may have an unexpected appearance, acquiring a colour and texture different from that seen by daylight in the underwater surface of the coral aggregate.

Corals multiply by binary division, or budding, as well as by egg. Each animal separates into two branches of itself and each becomes entire. Such immortality of stock, under favourable conditions, may cause a very rapid increase of population. Serventy quotes the growth of a colony of 25 000 polyps in 1000 days. Presumably this colony, formed on an anchor chain, was established by a floating individual resulting from a fertilised egg produced sexually, but the subsequent growth would have been by binary division, which must, in this case, have been completed, on the average, once in about sixty days.

The characteristic form of the branched corals is attained as individual polyps divide, and new cups are secreted either as on an expanding surface, which might be likened to the trunk of a growing tree, or as branches developing from it. Obviously, in order for a surface to be expanded outwards (as from a cylinder), the cell floors must be sealed off, and new skeletons secreted upon this foundation which, below the living surface, is then virtually cellular limestone. Many reef-forming corals[10] do not branch, but continue in colonies growing outwards from a bounding surface in specific patterns.

Some of the brilliant colour of the underwater coral gardens is contributed by algae and colonies of minute plants which, of course, are essential to the cycle of life, marine no less than terrestrial. We have noted that when coral formations are removed from reefs, the polyps, naturally, soon die. The specimens of coral, now no longer so common as collectors' pieces under glass domes, are the beautiful aggregations of cellular skeletons composed principally of calcium carbonate. Such limestone, metamorphosed by pressure, provided the genesis of marble and alabaster now quarried from some ancient sea-beds.

Reef-building corals, requiring water of temperature never falling below that of the warmer latitudes (about 20°C), and light not less than that penetrating to depths of about 50 metres,[11] provide evidence of apparently immense changes in world sea-levels. Charles Darwin supported the theory that the existence of reefs in deep water could only be explained by the assumption that their foundations were laid when the sea-floor was close to the surface. The recent depthing of coral formations, both by drilling and by seismic sounding, has revealed how immense the changes must have been. It would seem certain that the melting of the Pleistocene ice-caps could have caused only a fraction of the increase.[12]

Because corals flourish in shallow water, we would expect to find them surrounding tropical islands and following coasts where conditions are favourable. Such fringing reefs indeed surround some of our most beautiful continental islands which before being isolated by the sea were mainland hills. As the Great Barrier Reef closely follows the edge of the continental shelf stretching eastwards into the Pacific, its foundations are presumed to have been laid when the Australian coast extended to seas shallower by at least the present depth of the reefs and to somewhere near their present position.[13]

Australia's true coral islands lie on or within the Great Barrier Reef. None rises much above high tide, for they result from the accumulations of coral debris that, by being heaped up by storms and thus remaining a little above the sea, have gradually increased their elevation. This increase was furthered by the advent of vegetation, which provided a base for added deposition by wind and water. Some cays still possess little vegetation—a few coarse grasses and creepers; others possess mangroves, casuarinas, pisonia trees and pandanus palms, figs, and numerous shrubs. The majority of the coconut palms now present on islands within the reef were introduced by man.[14]

Coral atolls, as distinct from cays, are typically rounded reefs, more or less vegetated, enclosing a lagoon. These probably originated in a reef fringing an island that became submerged, leaving only the ring of coral to grow upwards towards the surface and to indicate the former position of the island. Such formations occur in the deeper water beyond the reef proper, but are quite familiar to plane travellers crossing the Coral Sea.

From the air you also get a good view of the outer edge of the Great Barrier Reef, generally marked by white breakers—a brilliantly high-lit edge to regions of green and violet pools in the coral. Perhaps nowhere else in the world is there such gradation of colour as may be seen from above the Coral Sea. On the rare days when a visit by boat to the outer barrier is completely successful, one may peer down between coral boulders and 'nigger-heads' to abysmal depths of water pulsing from the ocean's heart. In contrast to its lateral regions, the summit of the reef wall, over which the ocean washes into the inner channels, is frequently hard and featureless, like a road. I hope, some day, to land on the outer reef by helicopter, just when conditions are perfect, and to spend as much time as possible hovering along its outer edge.

A group of typical coral islands, the Capricorns, of which I have already mentioned Heron, lies about 80 kilometres offshore from Gladstone. They are all low cays with reef foundations, and practically no soil. Their main natural vegetation is the vivid green pisonia tree with its vast, brittle trunks and massive branches, and the fascinating pandanus palms, or breadfruit,[15] whose multiple roots impede human progress, but provide excellent sanctuary for immense numbers of wedge-tailed shearwaters (muttonbirds) and terns. The muttonbirds' burrows honeycomb the ground in the pisonia jungles. During summer days, the birds are far away over the ocean, feeding in great rafts, but, after dusk, they return and, from a darkening sky, fairly hurtle themselves at their nesting areas in the soft, undermined sand.

On one memorable occasion, I inadvertently pitched a tent over a burrow, but I discovered next morning that this was no impediment to the rightful owner of the claim. He must have found his burrow while I sat at the embers of my fire listening to the incredible cacophony of thousands of squawking birds settling in for the night. Next morning, I was conscious of convulsive but determined movements beneath my sleeping bag. With apparent unconcern, the bird worked his way from under me, eyed me with disdain, purposefully squeezed under the brailing, and joined the energetic and vocal predawn exodus. Muttonbirds of two or three species inhabit innumerable Australian islands—anywhere from the Abrolhos Islands of the west, by way of some of my favourites in the Recherche Archipelago and in Bass Strait, right up to the Queensland coast. On many small cays, the terns in their breeding season, leave no roost unoccupied over hectares of land and tussock. Michaelmas Cay, about 25 kilometres from Cairns, not far from Green Island, is one of these; it is still sparsely vegetated, but, in season, it has an immense population of terns.

These 'sea-swallows'—the snowy caspians, of almost universal distribution, black-capped and red of beak; the crested and roseate species; the black-naped; the sooties, and the dusky noddies—are fairly common on the nesting islands of the Reef. Gulls, the Silver and the Pacific; two species of eagle, and the ubiquitous osprey; herons; egrets; both the well-known oyster catchers; frigate-birds and gannets—all add interest for the numerous bird-lovers who visit the islands of the Great Barrier Reef every year.

There is little wonder that the popular and scientific literature of the Great Barrier Reef yearly grows more extensive, for the marine fauna

183

184

Facing page top: Michaelmas Cay, well-known bird sanctuary in the Great Barrier Reef, off Cairns, Queensland. *Bottom left:* Juvenile sooty terns *Sterna fuscata* at breeding grounds. *Centre:* Sooty terns in flights. *This page top:* Green Island, off Cairns, is one of the most popular coral cays for visitors to the Great Barrier Reef. *Bottom right:* Another view of Michaelmas Reef on the outer edge of the Great Barrier Reef

185

includes no less than 350 species of coral, 4000 molluscs, and 1200 species of fish. About 80 species of birds are commonly sighted. The land flora of the cays and atolls is not extensive, but marine algae, in vast quantities, augment the corals as reef-builders, and provide characteristic colour. The high islands—such as Hinchinbrook and Dunk—carry vegetation as rich as that of the contiguous tropical mainland. From any of the ports, between Rock-hampton or Gladstone in the south, to Cairns in the north, there is access to coral islands. Green Island and Heron Island, 1500 kilometres apart, and numberless islands in between, reveal a unique marine world of difference.

Among Europeans, even among most Australians, mention of coral islands is apt to arouse romantic visions that neither time nor even experience ever quite efface. For they enter freely into the exciting storybooks of children, along with their blue lagoons, tempests, treasures, and tribulations, and miraculous salvation among the breadfruit and coconut palms. Even the Swiss Family Robinson 'had determined to emigrate to a newly discovered region in the Southern Ocean, which has since been named Australia.' Defoe's immortal *Robinson Crusoe*, of course, might have been a boyhood inspiration for James Cook, apprenticed to a village haberdasher. For most Australians today, a little of R. L. Stevenson and Herman Melville always lingers, with later overtones, perhaps of Conrad, or Gauguin, Stacpoole, or Rupert Brooke; or of the journals of the explorers, Cook, Flinders, and Blight. Yet there is a wonderful freshness about the Reef, compounded of sky and air, as well as sea, that seems to speak of the dawn of time, before cities and roads were imagined. There is a special joy in the low islands that have escaped from the heaving sea; where the blowing of the calving whale is blended with the sweep of birds; where the mermaid dungong hauls out to bear its young,[16] or the turtle to lay its eggs. In recent years, commencing with the contemplative and literary works of E. J. Banfield, and the treatises of such scientific writers as Yonge, Roughley, Dakin, and Bennett, many authoritative books concerning all these wonders have emerged, so that there is now little difficulty in making adequate preparation for a visit to the Reef, or in finding sufficient memories to stir the imagination.[17]

When I first watched a big green turtle scuffling slowly and purposefully up the beach I thought of Lewis Carroll; but very soon I was lost in the contemplation of an age-old behaviour pattern, in which actions as definite as the flipper track left in the sand, were performed as deftly and as confidently as they had been since before an Adam arose burdened and blessed with deductive thought. Perhaps only man may consciously interpret the impressions that lead to the smoothed-over repository where the female turtle has buried her hundred eggs in the soft sand. Time is not old enough to have evolved a protection from man, so late an interloper on the beaches, who can not only read the language of the turtle's marks in the inanimate sands, but, alone among her enemies, can conquer all her defences—by turning her helpless upon her back. Several creatures may rob the solar incubating cache of the turtle. Even successfully sun-hatched turtlets probably have only one chance in fifty of surviving the attacks of birds and crabs in their first hours of light; and, of course, further predators wait beyond the little waves that run up to embrace them.

At mating times, the adult turtles, floating in pairs, are easily caught by skilled and purposeful boatmen and, certainly on *terra firma*, de Rougemont's tales of turtle rides can be enacted and enlivened as opportunity and skill permit. Providing the essential primordial note among the larger creatures of these parts, the turtle, like Bernard O'Dowd's Australia itself, may seem a 'last sea-thing dredged by sailor Time from Space.'

Much as I have benefited by investing time on cays and atolls, among the pisonias and pandanus trees, or at low tide on their wide, fringing reefs, my

186

greater pleasure has been in the continental islands such as Dunk[18] and Hinchinbrook, or in the islands of the Cumberland Group, off Bowen, of which Whitsunday, Pentecost, Hook, and the Molles are best known. These islands, which often consist of high granite uplands, clothed with a rich tropical flora, are dissected by clear permanent streams entering the sea in sequestered coves where beaches of true sand are often backed by mangrove flats teeming with life and interest.

There is much pleasure in planning any kind of excursion: reading what may be available, gathering together equipment and maps, considering possibilities. Some of the islands of the Queensland coast may today be visited and enjoyed with a minimum of preparation—virtually everything being provided for the enjoyment of scenery and, more or less, the sophisticated social pleasures which many believe should be concomitant. From a travel agent in any of the cities one may obtain a planned itinerary and a luggage manifest that will satisfy every demand of custom and convention. But, for all time, I imagine, there will be desert islands for the adventurous, shores to be approached with that element of uncertainty which, whatever else it might contain, is pregnant with a special delight.

Such journeying is always memorable, for it is accompanied by an alert and confident mind that has been briefed by adequate preparation. Of my island expeditions, though many have been more difficult, none is more memorable than that which included my first visit to Hinchinbrook with a small party of students from three states. A reconnaissance of Hinchinbrook was included in a wider itinerary; in fact we discovered that the island could have sustained our interest and energies for more than the whole period given to the north.

For months we have circulated equipment lists, maps and plans, notes and queries . . . just as though we were embarking on a major voyage of discovery; which is the best way in any such venture. To plan before packing, to try the bundle and discard the unnecessary, to make the fullest trial imagination can offer, and then to repack; ultimately to join up with one's team, its nucleus tested in previous encounters; that is as much part of the adventure as anything that follows. So was the prelude. Then we tossed down our gear from the jetty into the well of our launch, and in due course came in sight of our destination.[19]

There, mounting before us in royal blue towers, was the map translated into reality: an island hardly known except from sea-borne vision, its remote heights untrodden, its vast Eden-fresh crags and valleys open only to the elements. For every thousand who glimpse Hinchinbrook's fantastic mountains, not one sets foot on its scalloped sands, and even those who test curling surf seldom penetrate its jungle defences. The green spurs soar directly from the sea to ramparts of granite 1000 or 1250 metres above. They spike the clouds, silver and majestic when the air is calm; or when it is stormy, torn by the wind that comes rushing down the ravines; sometimes drooping sullenly almost to the waves, and remaining clutched by the jungle for days.

Hinchinbrook Island is Australia's Skye, about the same size and no less rugged, but clothed dramatically in viridian and gamboge, uninhabited but alive with tropical scents, surrounded by coral seas, and trailing exotic orchids instead of boreal heather. Like Skye, it loses no grandeur by its proximity to a main coast. The deep Hinchinbrook Passage, one of the world's loveliest waterways,[20] fills the great drowned valley that once may have borne the Herbert River, and now separates the island's peaks from its sister summits of the Cardwell Range. The island is gazetted as a national reserve.

Astern lay the harbour of Dungeness, the sugar port of Lucinda, and the exciting colour and prodigality of the canefields. We had long since left Brisbane, and the even more distant southern cities, where latitude still

Facing page top: For all their popularity, Dunk Island's beautiful beaches remain unspoilt havens, backed by dense tropical rainforest. *Bottom:* Mangroves on the west coast of Fraser Island, off the south-east coast of Queensland. *This page top:* Small blue crabs scuttling over the beaches of Fraser Island. *Centre:* Australia has a number of species of turtles, the marine forms of the Order Testudines. *Bottom:* Cane toad on Fraser Island. Many such toads frequent the sugar plantations of Queensland and in wet weather are common in the tropical north

ordained winter. Abeam were sunlit leaping seas and an air of pristine adventure. We were not alone on the timeless waves. On our starboard bow, just about two centuries away, rolled the converted collier *Endeavour*, with Lieutenant James Cook, eager-eyed, and without premonition that the dangerous reefs were narrowing before him. He named the precipitous granite of Hillock Point for which our course was set . . . and sailed on to near-disaster and immortality. Trailing the *Endeavour*, at a cable length of fifty years, rode Captain Philip King's cutter, *Mermaid*. Historically, of course, it was in the dawn of 8 June 1770, that Cook commemorated his patron, the First Lord of the Admiralty, George Montagu Dunk, First Earl Sandwich of Hinchinbrook,[21] by naming a cape which he supposed part of the mainland; and in June 1818, that King made an island of Cook's 'high and craggy' land.

There is a brief period between embarkation and a chosen landfall when action ceases. Every thought and thing superfluous to the venture has been discarded; the plan and the equipment, the provender and the men, all are compacted in one small hull. There is a perfect break between past and future. Everything is crystallised in an eager party, a dancing sea, gleaming beaches, and dark mountain peaks. There, surely, in Zoe Bay, backed by mangroves sweeping round to the little waterfall. It is oddly familiar, for description by previous visitors becomes illuminated, stereoscopic, and the brown map-contours leap into place on verdant ridges and granite walls. In the safety of 9 metres our launch coasts northward towards Agnes Island.

Now, momentarily, the skyline changes. The gleaming shoulders of Mt Straloch twist astern and Diamantina's immense square crown is clearly visible. Then, through a wind-gap behind Hillock Point, emerges a dramatic and beautiful mountain profile, that of The Thumb, a vertical colossus thrusting from the jungle bare cliffs almost 1000 metres above the sea, and scarcely screening the grandeur of aloof Bowen, a summit of the island. There is both mystery and fascination in those impressive tops of an island reluctant to make any way easy.

The high hills parade the background, slowly gyrating to our coasting so that spurs become foreshortened and lose promise as routes to the peaks, and appear unscalable. Everything is relative to distance and angle of vision; fine cracks in the rock faces are mighty fissures; soft green moss is a vine-meshed torment. Our camp must be sheltered if possible, and our beaching protected from the south-easters; fuel may be desirable, but fresh water is essential, and every consideration is bracketed with the thought of access to the granite ridges we hope to climb. Here are the little white coves at the south end of Ramsay Bay, clean sand between the red, lichened headlands. A green-grey mist becomes a stand of she-oaks quivering above the sun-drenched sand. Why should there be surprise that the charts are faithful? There is the veritable valley which up to this moment has been a blue line on a paper sheet; if it carries a stream of any colour our plan of campaign finds support. We sound our way into a metre of limpid water sheltered by a knuckle of creviced granite, and let go the kedge, then launch a dinghy and row to the beach across a low swell and lazy breakers.

Unforgettable are the moments of first-footing a sunlit shore where the bright shells lie undisturbed except by the waves, where the ancient cycles of season and life still preserve the finely ordered balance of the centuries. Our predecessors had left no trace, and we thrust our way inland from virgin sands in search of water.

A large brackish lagoon connected to the sea by a high-tide channel lay behind the casuarinas, and reflected the vivid green of its mangroved margins like a bar between real and mirrored mountains. Skirting this along a granite rib, we lost the sea and entered the gloom of the mangrove flats, pervaded by

190

an air of strange, rustling watchfulness not completely accounted for by the more obvious life of primordial mud-skippers,[22] scuttling crabs, and the few nervous birds. Beside a tall breadfruit aglow with golden knotted fruit, the stream emerged from the jungle and filtered itself away among the mangrove claws; not much flow, but fresh and clear in idle pools between boulders. With driftwood in plenty washed high over the spit, now carpeted with she-oak needles, the reality of the site for a main camp exceeded the expectations study of the map contours had given us. We made our way back to the sea, warily conscious in places of the green tree-ant hordes;[23] mosquitoes and sandflies would probably also be voracious.

Hot work in shallow water soon laid packs and gear above the wash of the returning tide. Marooned in our 'land of heart's desire' we squatted on the burning beach and waved our boatman away. There were plenty of tasks, but everyone bent to them with enthusiasm while the wonder and beauty and the sunshine wove a new pattern for us all. The party had been arranged in three groups with independent fires and food supplies. There was one central expedition tent which might serve as additional shelter, medical tent, etc. We all had mosquito nets and copious supplies of insect repellent. What fun there is in arranging a camp in fair weather! You lay out your gear like children at play, all sparse and orderly, and smile at skies that will always be innocent. The mood passes; but even if the storm should come and the she-oaks creak, though your home be on sand, it will rest secure.

Had I been less ambitious in our overall itinerary, we might have remained lotus-eating for weeks on the beaches and in the valleys, strolling along the sands with cowries, corals, and the miraculous beaded excavations of crabs to quicken interest. Or, for those who so desired, there might have been fishing and the gathering of succulent oysters. Exquisite trailing orchids (*Dendrobium* spp.), cream and scented, or little leopard heads with long ears, ran up the sides of streams and even overhung the salt sea spray; hibiscus flowers, yellow as the sun, floated down and turned slowly crimson among the saffron pea-flowers of a creeping succulent.[24] In the next cove there were coconut palms heavy with fruit.

Green tree-ants were the most obvious form of insect life. Bodies translucent like chrysoprase, golden-eyed and fanatically industrious, streaming their arboreal highways, fashioning their leaf nests in concerted rows, straining on stilted legs, and extruding fine white silk, these fragile ants appear completely preoccupied with their labours until one looks closely and notices two in ten immobile, staring steadily back with quiet ferocity . . . or so it seems, even to the most dispassionate observer. Brush the tree, or have the misfortune to disturb it in passing below, and anything up to 500 will swarm all over you. Later, by an obvious procedure, you may calculate their effective numbers more precisely.

The early evening often brings swarms of mosquitoes and tiny sandflies to a low level camp . . . but Hinchinbrook is considered free of malaria, dengue, and scrub typhus. Only their obliging hosts are present, but, against these, there are numerous protective and combative methods concerning which local advice is generally copious and sound.

On Hinchinbrook at times, unlike on the lower islands, there is a curious paucity of birds, apart from a few terns wheeling the surf, a hawk circling the crags. High in the air white cockatoos fly singly with raucous cries, and king-fishers are glimpsed flashing the mangrove lagoons. The jungle is often submerged in silence, a hush that companions the deep green light and the malignant lawyer vines. Other animal life is also unobtrusive, nocturnal, and difficult to observe, yet one is often conscious of endless quiet rustlings in the vegetation, and morning reveals fresh marsupial tracks in the sand. In the olive depths of the tidal pools, and in most of the creeks flowing into the

Top: Kumboola Island and Timana Island, as seen from Mount Koo-ta-loo, Dunk Island, Queensland. *Bottom:* The royal blue heights of Hinchinbrook Island, northern Queensland

Channel may lurk great and small crocodiles, cold, repulsive, sharing the flooding tide with cruising sharks that match their malice. The powerful pythons, or carpet snakes, usually coiled in a watchful slumber in the tree-tops are not sinister. They are lazy, gaily-patterned guardians in this Eden, sliding luxuriously in the high dappled shadow. Their cousins of the earth are as common, and some are venomous, but they are among the shyest of living creatures, and, fortunately, are usually only glimpsed in flight.[25]

A fine, clear night possesses a restless tropical energy. The stars pulsate; the sea glows, and the lagoons are threshed by large shoals of mullet. To stand behind a powerful torch-beam is to witness a scene reminiscent of the dawn of life in dark primordial seas: the fish leap in a hundred silver arcs and trouble the face of the waters. Imagination marks a pterodactyl skimming the purposeful inrush of the ocean.

The lure of the peaks gave us little time for beachcombing and idleness. The morning after the landing we were all astir at first light and packing our rucksacks for an inland expedition. An obvious spur leading south and west rose fairly steadily to the heights. At length the last water-bottle was stoppered and the party gathered on a granite rib where king-tides and storms had deposited myriads of pumice fragments, lightest and most enduring of flotsam, from some faraway volcano. There was an informal briefing—and we were away in single file through the brush. The mangroves gave way to stately paperbarks with splendid white trunks and emerald pendent foliage; higher came a profusion of tea-tree, she-oaks, eucalypts, and banksias knitted together by wiregrass and sarsaparilla.

To our surprise, the spur, initially, provided little difficulty, only packed trees, thickets, and wiregrass; and by midday we had gained about 300 metres and a beautiful ferny pool in a small ravine. Below the sedges and bog-rush lay a green shade of maiden-hair and club-moss, coral ferns and sundews. It was a welcome lunching halt with superb views of the coast.

A small plateau, bright with the starry foliage and cream pin-cushions of a borya[26] and crowned with skull-like granite monoliths, led by a narrow col to the flank of the main island ridge already revealing naked rock. The weather was too still and sunny for the tussle, and, as the afternoon wore on, our progress became slow. The cool aerial depths leapt to the sea and were spiritual refreshment for our bodies steamed with the effort of thrusting upward, hands clutching sticks sprouting from the furrowed hide of a tellurian. At last his mighty spine, 250 metres or more above, rose without easy compromise. For a while we found no way up but traversed slowly in a south-easterly direction on a rising niche at the foot of the cliffs.

It became evident that this was an unusually dry period and that we might find no water on the mountain, and therefore our quart-pots, replenished at the lunch-halt, were already tantalising but, for the time, forbidden. Every cleft was now being minutely examined, but the plunging granite held little moisture. With even a trickle we might have camped and taken the ascent of the crags refreshed by a night's rest; however, time requires quenching, and it was decided to ascend the ridge that night if possible.

At the point where the natural terrace dropped away below a wall, there rose most conveniently a 'chimney,' scarcely 4 metres high, which evidently led to more broken rock. It is extraordinary how these chinks occur in most mountains' armour. In perfect security we wedged our way upward, backs to the wall and feet pressed in opposition. Unfortunately the insentient packs required roping and, unlike the men, made no effort to counter gravity. The chimney relaxed to a narrow shelf leading to a wall well supplied with rock and tree holds, a total distance of 15 or 16 metres. A system of movement was soon organised, but a full hour passed before the whole party of twelve had surmounted the obstacle, by which time night was rushing up over the

Overleaf: View across Hinchinbrook Channel to Hinchinbrook Island from the Cardwell Range, near Ingham, Queensland

South Pacific. However, by the time the last man had edged along the shelf and swung a simian silhouette up the wall, the van had slashed a pretty furrow to the summit ridge still almost 200 metres above. The trail subsequently inspected by daylight did credit to the lads who had broken it; though it was steep, and in places, exposed, there was certainly no more satisfactory way up.

By stealing time we had conserved water but, on the ridge, nevertheless, we pooled all water-bottles. Exactly 13 litres of water constituted our licence to remain on the premises. For about an hour there were muttered imprecations as we struggled among harsh dwarf banksia and brittle tantoon[27] in efforts to light fires and find coverts. When success came, we fed well, swallowed salt tablets[28] and drank sparingly, generally of black coffee.

There was utter bliss in lying at rest, lightly draped under tired stars, with the countless cheepings of some insect creatures sounding like high-pitched fairy bells, and the slow-moving air, heavy with the scent of boronia, drifting up our dark wall. The misted stars' promise of rain would not be fulfilled before dawn, and probably not for twenty-four hours. The fires, of brushwood, soon flickered to ash and the night wrapped us in sleep more than 600 metres above the indolent Pacific. Some time later, I remember, I awoke momentarily to the indescribable peace of solitude in high places, then, as I lay back in half-sleep, there came a curiously tranquil illusion. The little bells still sounded merrily, but they were of the stellar heights, the audible twinkling of stars.

In the early afternoon of next day, the party having traversed the main ridge of the island for some distance, often on rock that gave a clear view of the island, I decided upon a descent before shortage of water robbed the excursion of pleasure. The sight of a tree-ferned gully dropping below the main Bowen-Thumb col, with the 'downward smoke' of a slender cascade billowing into an iridescent cloud over the jungle, cried for wings. Without them, we found insecure resting places, and tried to swallow food. But the almonds were like chalk, the raisins stuck in our throats, and we possessed insufficient saliva to dissolve barley sugar. At least on one wave-length we were completely happy, for we knew our discomfort was limited to a few hours at most.

A veil of cloud lessened the burning of the sun as we retraced a long steep path to our morning's camp where 5 litres of water made a magnet for human flesh. We continued the descent and, with scarcely sufficient daylight, we eventually dropped the last pack over the familiar chimney and moved wearily down the main spur. In the dusk we regained our ferny pool. With salt and water a transformation rapidly took place, and we sang in the firelight.

By way of the main southern stream, a string of clear pools threaded by foam, we reached the mangroves in the morning, lingering to bathe and bask on sun-warmed slabs. The remainder of the day dribbled away in unorganised delights. At night there was much to do sorting out plant specimens and other records. At about ten o'clock the rain started, a real command performance, and a new roaring note sounded from the sea just down the sand-slopes beyond the she-oaks.

The island brooded when the light came, with nothing visible above a cloak of rain-clouds a hundred or so metres up the spurs. Every now and then they shook out prolonged showers in answer to the sea-winds, but most of the time, there was just determined drizzle, softening all edges of rock and the white-caps over the sea. For contrast with our ridge ascent, we decided to travel as far as possible up the large northern stream.

Our way led up a valley of gigantic boulders piled in utter confusion through the jungle. If the stream offered good progress we had hopes that the northern end of Mt Bowen might later be approached by this means. It was hard work, clambering over these rocks, many of them as large as cottages, rounded by an eternity of floods and weather. It would have been impossible to make any progress at all except on foot. Every limb and muscle was used, and when the rain saturated the brown and green slime on the granite, we used the seats of our trousers for additional friction, and became coated all over with algae. Although we worked upstream for four hours, past honey-scented orchids, fallen blossoms of the crimson eugenia,[29] and deep pools suspending fish with white-ringed eyes, we didn't get far, and returned at dusk quite sure that the valleys did not hold the way to the high ridges.

We remembered our thirst on the mountain. Now all the clefts would be foaming, the rock-faces shining and cold, and every small hollow in the summit rock filled to capacity.

Revisiting the streaming summit crags, and exulting in the varied struggle, we made the most of three stormy days. Then the island shook off his defences and revealed unsullied peaks, but not until we had lugged all our gear to the next cove in anticipation of the return of our launch for embarkation, and for the next stages of our island exploration.[30]

Our cruise in the Hinchinbrook Channel was perfect. The island rose from brilliant mangroves, their roots laced in a strange ecstasy doubled in the still water, through sun-struck jungle to the ethereal heights. Clouds accentuated their altitude; every detail of the moteless scene was reflected in the glassy channel from which long placid arms reached into the foothills and provided unexpected entries to delightful seclusion. The sense of wonder was always present; as though one had stolen upon some ideal experiment of creation, an almost unbelievable beauty.

Our final climbing offered fine rewards. We landed at Mulligan Bay, and this time the only impediment was the tough jungle foreground to the upper slopes. Swamp and lawyer vines held us back; it seemed impossible that the foreshortened slash of verdure visible from the sea could entail such toil. It was easy again to imagine that Hinchinbrook resented intrusion, but eventually, we rose above the festooned brush, and pressed on up steep cliffs and through the dense press of dwarf she-oak, banksia, and tangled grass to the huge split monolith of Diamantina (976 metres). Below us, south, west, and north, lay the whole fantastic pattern of the Channel passages, reflecting the pale afternoon sky.

[1] This and the previous quotation are from *Lieutenant Cook's Voyage Round the World* (London, 1773): chap. 5, from his (Cook's) journal entry for Sunday, 10 June 1770.

[2] In the author's experience, a similar method was used in the Antarctic, following the holing, on 16 January 1959, of the expedition vessel, *Thala Dan*, when she struck a submerged peak of granite in uncharted waters near the Australian research station of Davis.

[3] *Confessions of a Beachcomber* (T. Fisher Unwin, London and Leipsic, 1908): chap. 2.

[4] Stone-fish: *Synanceia* species, the specific names given being *horrida* and *trachynia*. This small, inconspicuous fish possesses a number of erectile venomous spines. It is very seldom that it has caused trouble, although it is not uncommon. Usually remains hidden in inaccessible crevices.

[5] Foraminifera: Minute marine creatures secreting limey or siliceous skeletons which are often symmetrical and of great beauty. Fossil foraminifera of various species are common in some very ancient strata which they help to date.

[6] The amphibious fishes, known as 'mudskippers' or 'gobies', frequent mangrove flats and leave the water to seek food over the mudflats. Their fins are modified to assist their

The blue hills of Hinchinbrook Island, Queensland. Such 'continental' islands frequently have fringing reefs of coral, as here and on Dunk Island

Top: Magnificent views of the islands surrounding Dunk Island can be seen from the top of Mount Koo-ta-loo. *Bottom:* Paperbarks *Melaleuca* sp., on the west coast of Fraser Island

movements out of water. The commonest species (*Periophthalmus koelreuteri*) may be up to 10 centimetres long.

[7] Nautical measurements are now commonly metricated: e.g. the 'fathom' (6 feet, or 1·8288 metre), and the 'nautical mile' (1852 metres), originally defined as one minute of latitude.

[8] *The Tides of Australia*: an excellent, compendious treatment of this subject, by Professor Sir Robert Chapman, is available in the Official Year Book of the Commonwealth of Australia, no. 31 (1938).

[9] In one of the several excellent little volumes on the subject, Vincent Serventy's *Australia's Great Barrier Reef* (Georgian House, Melbourne, 1955), the following note is given: 'The origin of the name polyp is interesting. It comes from the French *poulpe* which is octopus . . . meaning many feet. Some early naturalist decided that the tentacles that surround the mouth of the stinging animals look like the tentacles of an octopus . . .' The sea anemone, a flower-like animal easily seen attached to rocks in tidal pools, is very like a greatly magnified coral polyp removed from its limey cup.

[10] Such as *Goniastrea*. The growth of the different species of coral may be considered mathematical. If the colony continues to flourish, in the presence of bountiful food supplies and propitious temperatures and other physical factors, though its form may vary in detail, its overall pattern will be precise. It is an interesting exercise to relate the branched forms of staghorn corals, for instance, to the binary division of crowded polyps for which lateral expansion is impossible.

[11] Light energy is essential for the growth of plant life. This means that certain animal minutiae are confined to the surface regions.

[12] In the Pacific atoll of Bikini, prior to the testing of atomic bombs in the Pacific, seismic sounding revealed accumulations of material, thought to be coralline, reaching through more than 2000 metres to the basic rock. Actual bores penetrated limey material to depths of more than 600 metres. Australian borings in the Barrier Reef area have gone down to between 200 and 300 metres.

[13] The origin of the continental shelf, surrounding Australia and including large areas of the Great Australian Bight, the Timor and Arafura Seas, and all of the Gulf of Carpentaria, is not fully understood. It makes a single land mass of vast extent, narrowly separated from the southern extensions of Asia. That the sea has also extended far to the west is evidenced by limestones, containing recognisable coral structure, in areas ranging from Tasmania to Queensland. Some very early corals, considered to be Silurian, are visible typically in the district of Yass, a few kilometres north of Canberra.

[14] See *A Coral Reef Handbook* (The Great Barrier Reef Committee, 1978) for comprehensive lists of flora and fauna.

[15] Breadfruit: This term has been applied to the fleshy, compound fruits of several tropical trees. That most famous in the history and literature of the South Sea Islands is *Artocarpus incisa*. However, the Nicobar breadfruit tree is one of the Pandanaceae, not unlike that of the Barrier Reef Islands whose fruits were made into 'bread' by the natives. The Barrier Reef pandanus is also called the Screw Pine, from the helical arrangement of the leaves.

[16] Mr L. Macmillan's account of the calving of the dugong, quoted by Serventy (note 9, ibid.), makes it clear that, like the seals, the dugong is dependent on land as its birth element. Many sea mammals probably possessed land ancestors.

[17] Twenty scientists contribute to *A Coral Reef Handbook* (Great Barrier Reef Committee, Brisbane, 1978). *The Great Barrier Reef*, by Isobel Bennett (Lansdowne Press, Melbourne, 1971) and *Corals of the Great Barrier Reef* by W. Deas and S. Domm (1976) are but two of many contemporary works. The Handbook contains an exhaustive bibliography.

[18] Dunk Island, now the scene of excellent tourist facilities, will always commemorate Edmund Banfield, the Beachcomber, and Bertha, his wife. Although now out-of-print, and not always easy to come by, Banfield's *Confessions of a Beachcomber*, and his *My Tropic Isle*, must certainly be republished.

[19] Much of what follows is taken from my original account, published in *Walkabout*, in April 1953.

[20] Prof. W. J. Dakin, in *Great Barrier Reef* (Ure Smith in association with The Australian National Travel Association) quotes the famous Prof. Wood Jones (see chap. 1, note 25).

[21] Dunk's title is also remembered in the name of the common sandwich which he is said to have invented as a means of sustenance during his long sessions at the gaming tables.

[22] Mudskipper: The tree-climbing, or walking fish of the mangroves (*Periophthalmus argentilmeatus*) scuttles over water and mud at low tide, and spends long periods clinging to mangroves and other roots almost clear of the water. It uses fins and tail for propulsion. A special gill-structure enables it to breathe air direct.

[23] Green tree-ants: From Captain Cook's Journal, Wednesday, 23 May 1770: 'We found several bogs, and swamps of fresh water, upon which, and by the sides of the lagoon, grows

the true mangrove, such as is found in the West Indies, and the first of the kind that we have met with. In the branches of these mangroves there were many nests of a remarkable kind of ant, that was as green as grass: when the branches were disturbed they came out in great numbers, and punished the offender by a much sharper bite than ever we had felt from the same kind of animal before . . .'

[24] *Vigna lutea.*

[25] The great majority of cases of snake-bite in Australia have occurred when snakes have been molested. Only once has the author experienced aggression in a snake (a tiger, in Tasmania), and this was easily countered.

[26] Borya: *B. septentrionalis*—the Queensland Pincushion Lily.

[27] Tantoon: *Leptospermum flavescens.*

[28] Currently there is considerable prejudice against salt, but I have known severe dehydration and cramp to be rapidly relieved by an intake of salt, when water alone seemed inefficacious—J.M.B.

[29] Eugenia: *E. wilsonii.*

[30] Two launches were hired for Hinchinbrook operations, the *Moana* (J. C. Taylor, Orpheus Island) and, later, the *Warrawilla* (F. J. Waring, Lucinda).

CHAPTER 9

The Delectable Mountains

Recurring youth through sun and rain returns
To gusty mountain tops where spectres were
For those who came in exile to our shores,
Through urgent distance, tranquilly discerns
The endless spurs of tawny timbered ranges,
And all the bush-clad haunts in youth familiar,
The roads and ways our fathers learnt before us. . . .
                                    —from WIDE HOMELAND

WHEN I WAS A SMALL BOY IN MURRUMBEENA, I often looked out over the springtime paddocks to a high, far, magical range of hills. They were exquisitely blue, infinitely distant, and could be visited as effortlessly as I could dream. They were the Dandenongs, my delectable mountains . . . the foothills to all the ranges I have ever climbed. I began to suspect that there was a generic delight in sun-warmed distance when, across Port Phillip Bay from Mt Eliza, I beheld the You Yangs, and further away, Mt Macedon and other hills that were hard to separate from the sky. I shall never finish exploring all those high, youthful mountains; and they have never lost their charm. The Dandenongs still possess fern gullies where you may enter a deep-green, magical world that seems never to have been trodden, where the air is filled with exciting, primitive smells, and the call of the lyrebird is an invitation to live an eternity in the moment. If a man is perfectly fit, and he

Left: Glasshouse Mountains, southern Queensland. These mountains are the eroded cores of volcanic uplift. *Facing page:* Limestone Hills at Chillagoe on the Atherton Tableland, west of Cairns. The sharp fluted rocks are characteristic of the weathering of limestone, formed as part of an ancient sea-bed

has no hungers, he may forget his body; but to be disembodied and timeless is a nirvana existing in all the delectable mountains.

Rest your eyes on the Sylvan Lake from the big bend below Kalorama, with the light in the shining red and olive tree tops, or from the top of the mountain look through miles of air between Ringwood and the Lysterfields Hills to the spires of Melbourne and to the broad Bay; you may know what I mean. Stand on top of Flinders Peak in the You Yangs and command those green or tawny paddocks to Corio Bay, sharing your moment with an ecstatic magpie or quizzical blue wren, and then saunter slowly along the ridge of old plutonic tors. There every gum and hanging rock may be a friend of years, yet you will always find, between the zenith and your feet, something new and strange.

As the years passed I discovered that there were delectable mountains in many parts of Australia: few too hard to climb, and yet plenty with problem faces or isolated towers and *gendarmes* if you wanted that sort of thing; none very high but many crowning panoramas so extensive as to reveal territory for a lifetime. Think of the wild green and purple wilderness of the Warrumbungles, for instance, where dozens of old volcanic cores survive as fantastic obelisks and pinnacles after every sign of the ancient cones through which they rose has long since disappeared.

Keen bushwalkers have for many years been exploring the whole fascinating region of the Nandewar and Warrumbungles, where the Castlereagh and other tributaries of the Darling rise and have a perennial life among those mountains and scrubs west of Tamworth. This area of New South Wales shares a good deal of geological history with south-eastern Queensland where similar abrupt reminders of ancient volcanoes are apparent in the famous Glass House Mountains which Captain Cook saw from the sea and named in 1770.[1]

Perhaps such country has three phases: the first, when it is strange and distant and scarcely explored; the second, the period of the active, well-equipped bushwalker who knows what he's doing even if sometimes not quite certain where he is; and the last, that of a delightful familiarity that makes well-loved haunts of hitherto unknown places. In Europe, very many regions are in the last category, and, lacking thereby no respect, are none the worse for being in it. They have accumulated historical and literary associations, and their challenge and beauty have both been amazingly preserved. For with mountains, familiarity breeds no contempt, only a love that to some who cannot share it must seem quite irrational.

Fortunately, though, for the spirit of man, there is everywhere heard the plea: for mankind, now and always, keep inviolate these mountain glories, this flowering wilderness, that great wild river . . . lest we destroy an irretrievable heritage, of which we are part. The conservationists will not always succeed; they may be as prejudiced as the developers who also may contribute to human fulfilment. Conservation and development must be held in proper balance; only so may the biosphere and the benesphere be consilient.

Although Australia has not one active volcano, and is the most quiescent continent from a seismic point of view, there is much evidence of recent vulcanism both in North Queensland and in western Victoria, where one of the largest lava plains in the world extends from the longitude of Melbourne almost to the South Australian border; and, of course, in the Mt Gambier district there is abundant evidence of similar but less extensive activity.

Mt Gambier is probably the best known of all the old southern volcanoes, yet so green and tranquil is the scene today that sulphurous vents and fumeroles, and craters showering ashes over the lifeless, smoking plain to which streams of incandescent lava slowly descend are difficult to imagine. The huge crater with its grassy rim rising some 150 metres above the wonderfully rich farmlands and their thriving city, holds four sheltered lakes. You could spend a contemplative week wandering through the pleasant plantations and round the waters of the largest depression, which is accessible by a good road. Most famous is the steep-sided Blue Lake, more than 60 metres deep, which preserves the level of the sub-artesian basin reaching well beyond the Victorian State border and so appears quite unaffected by the continuous withdrawal of water supplying the city below the scoria slopes. In clear weather the deep water seems almost unbelievably blue. A few kilometres south of Mt Gambier is the deep open crater of Mt Schank, its stratified walls showing clearly the innumerable depositions of ash. Mt Gambier is memorable for its quiet undulating slopes, its wonderful lakes, and its general atmosphere of well-ordered peace. Schank, and several of the extinct volcanoes of western Victoria, are lonelier, wind-swept places with their origins more apparent. As such they are immensely impressive, especially when unweathered scoria, buckled lava, and layered beds of tuff are visible evidence of their relatively recent activity.

Always when I travel through the Western District of Victoria, I am struck by the number and distinctive outlines of the old volcanoes. When the weather is calm and sunny I find them irresistible and their magic has often made me 'a borrower of the night.'

Over the extensive plain of lava and tuff, with its striking cones, other highlands are visible as one moves west. Those to the south, the Otways, carry not only some of the tallest eucalypt forest in the State, but magnificent fern gullies and streams that have cut deep coastal gorges through the old Jurassic sandstones. Not far along the Great Ocean Road beyond Lorne, one of the justly famous surfing resorts of the south-west coast, the She-oak River has carved out a ravine down which the stream tumbles in a series of falls and cascades.

At one point, scarcely a kilometre from the sea, are the Swallow Caves where, every few years, I have camped since boyhood, returning from places far away, with a particular rhythmic delight, to the roar of the waterfall, and to the fascinating firelit and shadowed honeycombed wall where the swallows nest. Almost spherical nodules have formed in the ancient sandstone, but the cementing solutions percolating the material between them is often so hard that the softer aggregates may be eroded away, mainly by wind, leaving the characteristic intaglio patterns. There are dozens of quiet haunts round the Otway coast—Apollo Bay, Johanna, and Glenaire, for instance—whence you may follow leaping trout streams up into the country of tall timber and shady beech forest, or exult with the great southern rollers tumbling on the broad beaches. It was Rudyard Kipling who caught something of the quality of this coast:

> Buy my English posies!
>   You that will not turn—
> Buy my hot-wood clematis,
>   Buy a frond o' fern
> Gather'd where the Erskine leaps
>   Down the road to Lorne—
> Buy my Christmas creeper
>   And I'll say where you were born!
>
> West away from Melbourne dust holidays begin—
> They that mock at Paradise woo at Cora Lynn—
> Through the great South Otway gums sings the
>   great South Main—
> Take the flower and turn the hour, and kiss your
>   love again![2]

Top: Unusual nodules, locally known as 'cannonballs', are eroded from the Jurassic sandstone along the south coast of Victoria in several places. *Bottom:* The Swallow Cave on the Sheoak River near Lorne on the south coast of Victoria—a favourite camping place for Aborigines in the past and hikers and holiday makers in the present

Twilight at Mount
Elephant on the plains of
the Western District of
Victoria

In the central south-west of Victoria are the Grampians, the triple range of rugged sandstone mountains which seem to place a colophon at the very end of the Great Dividing Range. On a small scale physical map of Australia, follow down the Eastern Highlands from Queensland. All the way from Cape York, for many thousands of kilometres, there are ranges within a short distance of the coast . . . including the delectable mountains of all the towns between Brisbane and Melbourne. There, out behind the Queensland capital, you will find the Darling Downs, the fascinating uplands such as Lamington, with its tropical rainforest scrubs, running down into the New England Range, the Warrumbungles, and the Blue Mountains, which Sydney people will swear are as beautiful as any other in the continent. Continuing in an unbroken line in spite of all its spurs and foothills, the divide leads into the Snowy Mountains—Mt Kosciusko, highest in Australia[3]—and all the huge complex of the Australian Alps where hundreds of square kilometres of dazzling snowfields give way to a summer season as bright with wildflowers.

The watershed of the Murray Valley and all the southern rivers of Gippsland, Port Phillip, and the Western District, moves on quietly westward; then, with a final grand statement as definite and distinctive as anything in Australia, all mountains make way for the coastal plains of the broad Murray Basin. A few hundred kilometres to the north-west, then, rise the pleasant Lofties, and the rugged, colourful Flinders Ranges; the next southern mountains are those of Western Australia—the Darling Range, with its fine timber, wildflower gardens unrivalled by most other mountains in Australia, its historic and beautiful waters,[4] and nationally famous limestone caves.

It was almost fifty years after the first settlements in Australia that Surveyor-General Major T. L. Mitchell made his journey through Australia Felix, and first sighted the Grampians. He is one of the most loquacious of the explorers, but, even making some allowance for the enthusiasm of discovery of mountains which are praised so highly in modern tourist folders, what he says of the region might be quoted:

Sir Thomas Livingstone Mitchell, surveyor and explorer, was better known as Major Mitchell. He was Surveyor-General of New South Wales 1828–55

> From a high forest-hill, about a mile east of our route, I first obtained a complete view of a noble range of mountains, rising in the south to a stupendous height, and presenting as bold and picturesque an outline as ever painter imagined. The highest and most eastern summit was hid in the clouds, although the evening was serene.[5]

'We had discovered,' he wrote two days later, on 13 July 1836, 'a country ready for the immediate reception of civilized man; and destined perhaps to become eventually a portion of a great empire. . . . Of this Eden I was the first European to explore its mountains and streams. . . . The lofty mountain range . . . was now before us, but still distant between thirty and forty miles.' Mitchell decided to make an excursion on horseback to the high eastern summit, leaving the main party to prepare a route for the bullock waggons over the undulations of northward flowing streams. He crossed several headwater streams of the Wimmera, all in flood. Eventually, in icy weather, Mitchell and his party

> . . . reached the highest point, and found that it consisted of naked sandstone. The top block was encrusted with icicles . . . All around us was hidden in mist. It was now within half an hour of sunset, but the ascent had cost so much trouble, and the country, this summit commanded, was so interesting to us, that I was unwilling to descend without trying, whether it might not be clear of clouds at sunrise. We had not come prepared in any way to pass the night on such a wild and desolate spot, for we had neither clothing, nor food, nor was there any shelter; but I was willing to suffer any privations for the object of our ascent.

Facing page top left: Waterfall at Morialta in the Mount Lofty Ranges, South Australia. *Top right:* Castle Rocks in the Grampians, Victoria, as seen from the Goat Track, Victoria Range. *Bottom:* Barnett Gorge in the Kimberleys, north-west Western Australia

Anyone who has been cragfast on a mountain will feel for Mitchell and his companions through that dark night of sleet (14 July 1836). Dawn brought some view of the country ahead. Considering the circumstances, it is remarkable how many plants Mitchell collected; they included his famous 'new species of eucalyptus with short broad viscid leaves' named *Eucalyptus alpina.*[6]

As thousands of visitors now annually testify, Mitchell's 'noble range of mountains' is one of Australia's finest wildflower regions, containing about 800 known species,[7] including some that are unique to it. Grevilleas and hakeas, boronia and guineaflowers, many different heaths, with the whole range of colours from white to deep red, and the lovely heath-myrtles or thryptomenes are among the more obvious flowering shrubs; but wherever there is a more open patch of springtime grass, there are clustered rice-flowers, fan-flowers, sun-dews, and many terrestrial orchids. The frosty summit, ascended by Mitchell, he named Mt William:[8]

> . . . I ventured to connect this summit with the name of the sovereign in whose reign the extensive, valuable, and interesting region below was first explored; and, I confess, it was not without some pride, as a Briton, that I, 'more majorum,' gave the name of the Grampians, to these extreme summits of the southern hemisphere.

Far more extensive than many visitors to the celebrated Halls Gap district ever realise, the Grampians form a complex north-south pattern of ranges from a few kilometres south of Horsham all the way down to Dunkeld, spreading broadly between the 142nd and 143rd eastern meridians, south of the 37th parallel. It is probable that the whole massif once projected as a promontory into the sea, that the immense cliffs were partly shaped by marine erosion when the valley of the Lower Murray Basin was occupied by a Tertiary gulf whose fossiliferous sediments are found in the Mallee, and which are cross-sectioned in a few residual fragments uplifted upon the old Cambrian rocks of the Mt Lofty Ranges of South Australia.[9]

Originally the Grampians rocks were laid down in the Carboniferous period hundreds of millions of years ago. Subsequent disturbances tilted these ancient sediments so that the remnants as seen today are sloping westward with abrupt scarps, often perpendicular to the original bedding, forming walls to the valleys now bearing the headwaters of the Wannon, Glenelg, and Wimmera Rivers.

Nowhere among the easily accessible mountains of Australia are there such defiles and gorges as in the Blue Mountains of New South Wales and in the Victorian Grampians. Both have resulted from the unceasing action of water in carving deep gorges in up-raised sandstones, themselves the water-deposited detritus of older igneous rocks of the earth's primal crust. Characteristic of such erosion are the deep, vertical-sided canyons and the curious weathering of isolated residual pillars of layered rock. Frequently harder strata project from wall faces forming silhouettes that stir the imagination; for the intrepid, there are all sorts of overhanging balconies and 'nerve tests'; and for the contemplative, the endless challenge of trying to match vision with knowledge.

In the Grampians, the well-known and well-named Wonderland Range is an excellent area to commence one's explorations. As a youth I first trod the worn paths of the Grand Canyon completely enthralled; every named rock found me acquiescent, and, even today, I cannot hear of Silent Street or of the Towers of Time without recalling my enchantment. It was a very dry season, I remember, and some of the streams were very low, but there were wonderful secluded sunbaked potholes reflecting the sky. One could disturb their reflections and feel the spherical grinding stones; and everything not

210

only seemed, but was wonderful. Since then I have wandered periodically all over the Grampians, and I know that no one could ever exhaust the interest of the huge dissected walls that may glow as in firelight, or stand remote and cold as ice; or of the many caves where the Aborigines marked up their scores and left the pattern of their capable hands outlined by blown ochre; or the delight of densely vegetated spurs and valleys so complex that there will be parts of them untrodden for the rest of time.

In the heart of the Grampians, between the Serra and the Victoria Ranges are large, rather mysterious swamplands and occasional islands of higher ground which, in some seasons, make quite wonderful camping grounds, and at others require a mosquito net and copious supplies of insect repellent. Such is Phillips' Island, by the White Bull Swamp,[10] where we have often sat round huge campfires, singing under the stars, or planning the morrow's excursions. Such is that along the Moora Track, for instance, with a turn-off into dense scrub and a long untracked ridge for most of the way to lonely Tower Hill, in the Valley of Mystery. If you should go that way, you will find that a small chock-stone in a crack, properly used, helps solve the attractive little problem of ascending to the topmost rocks.

There are numerous reservoirs and man-made lakes in the Grampians area; rivers have been turned, and channels run back into the thirsty Wimmera,[11] but still Major Mitchell's Lake Lonsdale is visible, especially after the kind of weather the explorer experienced on Mt William. His mountain is precisely as he left it; much of the area, in fact, is untracked to this day, and there are monuments as fine as those that have become so familiar on the 20-kilometre circuit between Halls Creek and the Silverband Valley.

It would be impossible to know or even to attempt to list all the bush-clad uplands within reach of our Australian cities. Each one has its favoured resorts, anything from an hour to a long day away from the suburban streets. Bush and beach are alternatives that offer themselves to all the dwellers of our seaside capitals who are so accustomed to the freedom of the primordial forests and scrubs and the long, wide sands where so effortlessly they may find picnic and camping places that they perhaps take too much for granted. Sometimes there is as much refreshment as amusement in reading the older accounts, when the Australian world, having become secure after seventy years, was yet incredibly vast and new:

> Many, at holiday times, form pic-nic parties. They leave the city early in the morning in a cart or chaise, retire to some mountain gully, perhaps twenty miles from Melbourne; and there, by the side of a rippling creek, where the laughing jacquars wakes the wilderness with his wild ha, ha! and the glistening plumage of chattering, many coloured parrots sparkles in the sun like precious stones. . . . They sit among these mountain wilds, without fear from man or beast, and surrounded by all the grandeur, the awful sublimity of uncultivated nature, to breathe the pure invigorating air that has never been contaminated by plague, cholera, or pestilence; and listen to the thousand wild harmonies . . . all so new, so wild, so curious, that you may fancy yourself in a land of sprites and fairies!
>
> And then the journey home by moonlight, among those mountain gullies, is most imposing, awakening, as it does, all the feelings of awe and devotion experienced on visiting a cathedral, or the ruins of an old castle; the bright moon lighting up the perpendicular rocky mass on one side, gives it the appearance of a mighty battlement touching the sky . . .[12]

It would be interesting to know precisely which mountain gullies so close to Melbourne the author had in mind; but the passage might have been

Facing page and this page:
The Grampians, Victoria

Facing page top: Sunset over Mount William. This mountain was climbed by Major Mitchell when he trekked through Australia Felix. *Bottom left:* View from the edge of the Wonderland Range, looking down on Halls Gap. *Bottom right:* Tower Hill; this crag may be scaled by tyro rock climbers. *This page top:* The Grand Canyon of the Grampians, one of many natural wonders in the area. *Bottom:* The Balcony, also called the Jaws of Death; the formation is near Mount Victory and Reed's Lookout, and the view is across the Victoria Valley

written by a romantic of almost any of the blue ranges that townspeople glimpse on their horizons, whether they are Brisbane's D'Aguilars or Conondales, Sydney's Blue Mountains, Canberra's Brindabellas, Melbourne's Warburtons, the Mount Lofties of Adelaide, the Darling Range behind Perth, or, of course, Hobart's Wellington, from which hundreds of other mountains may be seen. All have their foothills, and all contain wilderness; from any of them, you may glimpse further allurements, an intriguing tower far away in a sun-haze, a gleaming snowfield, or a series of receding crumpled ridges and valleys so deep blue and lonely that you fancy they must all be quite untrodden.

Certainly many parts of the Flinders Ranges of South Australia have emerged from the slightly intimidating realms of the explorers and become as secure as they are intriguing—always provided that the rules are respected and that the boundaries of knowledge and experience are not stretched unduly. It is still possible to stray too far from food and water almost anywhere in the bush; to become lost. Anyway, without the basic abilities to carry a water-bottle and a little food, to light a fire, to wear the right clothing, to follow a compass course, and if necessary, to take or contrive the right kind of shelter, delight is only a fraction of what it might be. The need for self-reliance in the bush is not the least of its values; only he who is prepared, informed, and confident, earns the right to deviate from the beaten track or discover what lies beyond it.

For austere rock-forms, superb colour, monumental trees, and the typical golden light of the Inland, there are few places to compare with the Flinders Ranges. They continue for another 350 kilometres the formation of the Mt Lofty Ranges, as a horst of Cambrian metamorphic rocks, tilted variously but often very steeply, and revealing in their domes and pounds the evidence of immense tectonic forces. Often the hard profiles of the strata are completely harsh and bare, pointing to a cloudless sky, any shade of cinnabar, chrome, or even cerise in the sunlight, but deeply blue, black, and violet in the shadow. The hardy cypress-pine clothes the uplands as far as trees will grow, wherever it can find support to the tops, but the old gums which Sir Hans Heysen has immortalised and made the pride of Australians everywhere occur in the valleys and gorges where the sparse rains are concentrated, and water lies for long periods in bright reflecting pools. For Heysen the Flinders Ranges opened up a new world. He wrote: 'The great Red Gums in the creek-beds of the Flinders fill me with wonder; their feeling of strength of limb, of vigour and life, suggest the very spirit of endurance. They fascinate me as do the bare bones of the ranges.'[13]

It was Matthew Flinders and his party who, penetrating Spencer Gulf with the hope that it might lead northwards to the 'Gulph of Carpentaria,' first sighted the 'chain of rugged mountains' which was rightly named for him, though not until a quarter of a century after his death. While Flinders was exploring the disappointing shallows at the head of the gulf, his famous botanist, Robert Brown, and the excellent topographical artist, William Westall, with some companions, essayed to reach a 'remarkable peak' noted by Flinders. They had a hard time of it, having grossly underestimated the distance because of the clear air and, suffering from thirst and fatigue, only regained the *Investigator* after two days' travel.[14] Actually they had ascended a ridge that diverges from the main system, and were unaware of the extent of the Flinders Ranges. Unlike Thomas Mitchell in the Grampians, the climbers did not wait for dawn before commencing the retreat; at the sunset hour when they reached the summit, they caught no gleam of the higher peaks to their east, across the Willochra Plain. The extent of the system began to be realised after Edward John Eyre made his journeys along the 'stepping stone to the interior'—the Flinders Ranges, with their hope of

214

water—to the salt wilderness that is named Lake Eyre. As a natural line of entry into the centre of Australia, little could contrast more with the visionary river that never materialised.

It was over this desolate tract, beyond Eyre's Termination Hill, over the sharp purple peaks near Mt Painter, and the huge glistening plains of salt that are Lake Torrens and Lake Frome, that I flew, in 1950, in a small aircraft to observe the extraordinary phenomenon of a flooded Lake Eyre, putting down on well-baked salt-pans between the immense depression[15] and Lake Gregory, beyond the reach of the floods that rolled down from Queensland. From the air you could not have imagined barer, less fertile desert—its only attractions were colour and form—but, once on the ground, you could wander through a resurrection of daisies and all sorts of delightful ephemerals that a reasonable season had ordained.

Following the explorers, as ever, came the graziers, and they too were pioneers in their own way. Some of their discoveries, such as that the various saltbushes could provide excellent nutriment for stock, first began to change the whole conception of pastoral possibilities in the foothills of the ranges north of the head of the gulf, not only on the side of Lake Torrens, but along the vagrant streams that sometimes flow into Lake Frome.[16] Some of the great inland explorers, including John McDouall Stuart, called on the early pastoralists, and were grateful for their succour. Country was even taken up out by Lake Callabonna, where the complete skeleton of the giant marsupial, Diprotodon, was discovered, a relic of Pleistocene times when many giants roamed the fertile freshwater lakelands of the interior. Most present marsupials possessed gigantic relations in that voluminous period; the kangaroos had *Palorchestes*, parading at 3 metres, and the wombat, the lumbering *Phascolonus*.

Many of the first pastoralists were eventually eaten out of their holdings by the advance of the great Australian rabbit plague which the second half of the twentieth century might conceivably have brought under control. Naturally, the land settlers were most interested in any fertile plains country; it remained for prospectors and miners to penetrate the ranges up by way of Arkaba and Wilpena to the copper deposits of Blinman. Finally there came the last wave of all, the gap-fillers and scientists, professional and amateur who, well equipped with modern vehicles, and from the springboards of well-founded bases, have in recent times cleared up most of the remaining mysteries of the Flinders Ranges.[17]

On a short list of all outstanding natural features throughout Australia, the famous Wilpena Pound, south of St Marys Peak, would find a place. Less than 160 kilometres from the Mt Brown, observed and named by Flinders, the Pound, an extraordinary elevated depression, waited inside its raised rocky walls for another fifty years before it was discovered.[18]

From the head of Spencer Gulf, at Port Augusta, roads fork. The western branch, which wasn't much more than a track when I first travelled it, is now a well-graded main road leading up to the Woomera Rocket Range, then on to Kingoonya; it ultimately finds a route via Coober Pedy's opal fields to Alice Springs. The other branch drives through the Pichi-Richi Pass north and west of Mt Brown to Quorn and Hawker, where it divides, and between the arms which are joined for the first time about 100 kilometres further north, between Blinman and Parachilna, is some of the finest scenery of the ranges, including the celebrated Wilpena Pound.

It is little wonder that the curious basin remained so long undiscovered. North of the impressive Arkaba Hills, the road passes lower land clothed with pines and casuarinas before settling again into a characteristic valley at the base of colourful tiers which are the strata of rocks obviously dipping westward. A gorge, usually containing some water, leads from the Wilpena

The Flinders Ranges, South Australia. *Top:* Looking towards the A.B.C. Range and Wilpena Pound from Bunyeroo Valley; the view in spring. *Bottom left and right:* The northern Flinders Ranges are typified by rough quartzite ridges and valleys, mostly arid

The Flinders Ranges. *Top left:* Approaching St Mary Peak, the highest peak of the walls surrounding the famous Wilpena Pound. *Top right:* Walking in the Gammon Ranges in the northern Flinders. *Bottom:* Mount Rowe in the northern Flinders

217

junction directly up through a conspicuous gap into these hills, when it is discovered that a similar formation a few kilometres away to the west dips back in the opposite direction. In fact the two sides curve round to meet at Rawnsley's Bluff and, in the north-west, sufficiently high scrubby land gives the appearance of completely enclosing the elevated valley. The curved floor, conforming to the dip apparently caused by pressure from all sides, is quite densely wooded in places with eucalypts, cypress-pines, and wattles, except where natural grassy clearings accentuate the park-like landscape. From these clearings, especially, the high scarp, most of whose eminences have been named, is visible in all directions. It is possible to conjecture something of the ancient topography before the folded strata were eroded to continuous tiers, marking the springing of domes that time has completely destroyed.

Like the Grampians and the Blue Mountains, the Flinders Ranges are known by relatively small localised areas that are being increasingly well served by tracks and roads. Each year the keen bushwalkers of Adelaide improve the maps and give new place names where they cannot find old; and they help also to bring into the fold of the delectables, routes which so recently were trodden for the first time. They will be able to continue their good work for some generations.

I shall not attempt to write very fully of the Blue Mountains, for of them there has been more published description both in words and photographs than of any other Australian mountains. Could there be anywhere in the world such astonishing reversal of sentiment as has occurred since the first settlers at Port Jackson discovered that they were prevented from entering the continent at large by 'a confused and barren assemblage of mountains with impassible chasms between.' Governor King, author of this description, went on to say that an endeavour to penetrate such a terrible barrier 'would be as chimerical as useless.' Numerous attempts had been made by well-equipped parties and individuals, fired by the challenge of the forbidding wall, bringing to the contest not only energy and determination, but even grappling-irons and rope-ladders.

> To the early inhabitants, the distant mountains, wrapped in an atmosphere of perpetual purple, were a region of mystery, to many a gateway of hope; to some they proved a lure to delusion and death. There were so blue, and so soft to the distant view, that a superstition sprang up that delectable lands lay on the farther side of them; so that Governor King, after some had perished, had to issue an order denouncing the story as being 'wicked as it is false, and calculated to bring the believers in it to destruction.'[19]

A quarter of a century after the arrival of the First Fleet in Sydney Cove, the ridge approach which is still used was discovered by Blaxland, Lawson, and Wentworth, and their discoveries were followed up successfully by George Evans and John Oxley.

Today there is, formally constituted, the 'Blue Mountains City Council'—with twenty-two townships within the area of its jurisdiction. Extraordinarily, there are still only two roads in 250 kilometres rising from the coast and converging on Bathurst,[20] the first of the inland cities; but, more surprising, the uncompromising ravines and precipices, completely unchanged since they urged King to issue his stern warning, are visited annually by hundreds of thousands of tourists.

Almost beyond imagination is the erosion that has carried away many cubic kilometres of the old sandstone tableland and sculpted the breathtaking declivities and precipices of the Blue Mountains. On granites and other bedrock, including some very ancient quartzites (themselves the

218

remnants of older mountains) the material of the Blue Mountains began to be laid as sediments under Permian gulfs probably something over 200 million years ago, but the greatest thickness of depositions, first the coal measures; then the Narrabeen Series of sandstones, shales, and conglomerates; and finally, the Hawkesbury and Wianamatta sandstones, were laid in the great swamps and lakes which persisted up to the close of the Triassic period. The elevation of these strata, with thicknesses aggregating up to 600 or more metres, occurred in the late Tertiary Period, first, probably, as a more or less horizontal plateau. Under crustal pressure they were then tilted as the eastern slope of a mighty fold falling away into the depths of the Tasman Sea.

During the original elevation, the valleys of the eastern rivers were commenced, but the subsequent dipping enormously accelerated the process which, of course, continues to this day. The rugged honey-coloured cliffs forming the Heads of Port Jackson, past which Cook sailed without realising their hidden depths, are of formation similar to that of the tremendous walls of the Blue Mountains.

No one, considering the stupendous quantities of silt that have been removed from the old sandstones, and carried down to flood plains or out to sea, would expect the earth's crust to be stable. Changes in its regional burdens must be compensated by elevation or depression of land masses. These may be so slight and constant as to be imponderable by any human time scales; occasionally, they are more abrupt, as the earth settles, and a tremor is felt in our ephemeral cities.

Rachel Henning, whose letters[21] have recently been published, made a journey over the Blue Mountains to Bathurst in 1856, returned to England, and, five years later, again crossed the mountains. Her opinions are decisive; she greatly disliked the first journey, and almost everything she saw. On the second occasion, she saw most things through different eyes. A brief extract from one of the earlier letters reads:

> It seems absurd to talk of dreading a journey of about 120 miles, which in England we should do in about four hours, but it really is no trifle here. We take three days about it, the roads are so bad that we get nearly shaken to pieces, and the inns at which we have to stop are in general so swarming with insects of all description that sleep is nearly out of the question . . .
>
> I cannot say I admire the 'city' of Bathurst. It stands in the midst of the Bathurst Plains without a tree or shrub near it.
>
> The background of the whole scene is the best part of it, as it consists (on two sides) of the beautiful 'Blue Mountains.' They are clothed with bush to their very summits and make a beautiful contrast to the weary plains . . . the scenery was magnificent . . . it really is very fine for Australia.

Her best opinions are confirmed five years later, and Bathurst certainly seems to have improved:

> I wish I could give you the least idea of the beauty of the scenery here. It was a lovely morning, and we wound along one side of the hill with a deep ravine on our right . . . I had forgotten how magnificent those Blue Mountains were . . .
>
> Bathurst agrees with both Amy and Mr Sloman, I think. The climate is more like England than Australia; just now, for instance, it is like our very best autumn weather. There was a sharp white frost this morning, and it was quite cold enough to make fires very comfortable; then it came out into the most splendid day, clear sunshine, no wind and such a cloudless sky.

Once the summit of the old plateau had been attained, and satisfactory routes discovered down into the promised lands of the Lachlan and Macquarie,

Left: Curious patterns of erosion on the cliffs of southern New South Wales near Tathra. Evidently the solutions penetrating the rock have formed a harder substance than the main body of sandstone, and are left upraised as the softer material is eroded by wind and wave. *Facing page top and bottom:* The Blue Mountains, New South Wales, near Govetts Leap

220

and, with unremitting, terrible toil—under such pressure that convicts might not sing as they sweated, either in or out of their chain-gangs—a safe road had been constructed, men might pause and behold their conquest in a new and wonderful light. It was almost as though a fearful monster of the darkness had been caged, and might now be safely observed behind bars, purring in the sun. Its terrible impotence was the more fascinating; the colours of its skin, and the superb rippling of its muscles, could be appreciated for the first time. The observation platforms grew and prospered . . . the towns and cities of the Blue Mountains built on the vestigial tableland, Katoomba and Leura, Blackheath and Wentworth Falls and Mt Victoria, and the rest. From any of these you may turn your back on a comfortable hotel, or other of the amenities that may be bought for money, and come to the end of your secure tether, beyond which you may travel only with your imagination,[22] and with the eagle, soar out over the chasms of blue air, skimming those incredible cliffs that reveal a vertical time scale dipping back a hundred thousand times as far as man's recorded history.

Like all rock faces, those of the Blue Mountains vary as much in colour as in form, though there is a general vertical quality in the latter that results from the undercutting, by weather and water, of the softer, basic strata, and from the collapse of the overhangs. Always there are the nearly horizontal striae, catching light and seeking shadow and giving a rough woven texture; but pinnacles and turrets may be gilt or blue, rose or apricot, black and violet-shadowed; and distance produces quite other-worldly opalescence through which walls across broad, blue valleys are as fantastic as clouds at sunset. And there are the falls of water like channelled cloud, infinitely tranquil at a distance, but rather too free and frightening close at hand as they roar into space. When the great valleys such as those of the Grose, the Jamieson, and the Megalong are flooded with mist, which seems substantial, it is as though Darwin's vision of massive coastal erosion was fulfilled,[23] and the great ocean were being brimmed by the plunging cataracts. Not even the City of the Blue Mountains can subdue the grandeur of Govetts Leap or Echo Point.

There are any number of good tracks tracing the crags along their upper edge and descending at convenient places to the depths; it is easily possible to get away from iron railings and ordered ways, and to sense the desolation of the Blue Mountains, and the challenge they offered the first-footers, glancing fearfully behind them at the pursuing trees.

If the Blue Mountains are unique in their way, the nearby Jenolan Caves surpass many similar tenebrose glories. Being something of a troglodyte, I have always been at home in caves. I suppose travelling in caves is a sort of inverse mountaineering, and, though not as often as I have essayed wall and buttress, I have very often traversed stalactited drip-filled silence, even, occasionally, beyond what I have always considered most unpleasant—a syphon necessitating a passage through Stygian water. There is no need to describe the splendours within and beyond the Grand Arch; there is a generic quality in stalactites and stalagmites, shaped like shawls and columns, cascades and minarets; and a constancy in their glistening surfaces. There is infinite scope for vision and make-believe, and some of the effigies of the imagination can bear transitions in topicality and reflect the passing parade of generations of men. For the solutions impregnated with the limey substance of the Silurian coral reefs drip slowly, and so minute is the solid substance deposited that 1 centimetre may represent a thousand years. My own pre-dilection is for the lonelier caves of which there are many still to be explored in almost all the States of Australia, but I have seen nothing to rival the grottoes of the Jenolan Valley, less than 80 kilometres from Katoomba, the Buchan Caves of Gippsland, and those of Yanchep, not far from Perth.

I have left till last the Australian Alps, which for me, and many, hold glories as great as any mountains in the land.[24] Again there are generic qualities in our snowfields wherever they are, from Kosciusko north to the Brindabella, and south to Tasmania's Mt Mawson in the Mt Field National Park. Generally for three months of the year, July to September, but very often until well into October, there are snowy summits through 800 kilometres of latitude, with a gap, of necessity, for Bass Strait. Over hundreds of square kilometres of the Eastern Highlands, around the 1400-metre contour is the typical snow-gum vegetation—low stalwart eucalypts, clean-limbed, yet twisted, white with wonderful polished daubs of colour, as though lacquered red, green, or yellow. Well below this belt, into the territory of the big gums and stringybarks, the snow often extends in the depths of winter, and, of course, it lies deeply above the tree-line on the high plains and open tops of the Snowy Mountains, rising above 2100 metres, and on the complex remnants of the tableland well down into South Gippsland.

To discuss so vast a region geologically is not easy. On many summits—Kosciusko, Buffalo, Bogong, and the Baw Baws, for instance—erosion has revealed the uplifted granites; other tops retain their Ordovician metamorphic rocks, and some, like parts of the Blue Mountains, show ancient basalts that probably flowed over the sediments before the lands were elevated. The Snowy Mountains, in the Kosciusko region, like the dolerite highlands of Tasmania, show clear signs of glaciation.

Generally, especially when seen from the air, the Australian Alps are not alpine in the sense of being young, abrupt, recently eroded fold mountains. Their general appearance is one of gentle whale-backs and rounded remnants, representing forms much more ancient. In fact, however, their formation is due entirely to erosion, uplift, warping, and vulcanism of an ancient Cretaceous peneplain from which any earlier mountains had completely vanished. The granites, generally speaking, resisted erosion and became the plateaux—such as those of Buffalo and Baw Baw—while much of the intervening softer rock was disintegrated and removed by stream action, unless, as in the case of the Bogong High Plains and the Warburton Ranges, it was protected by lava flows of various periods.[25]

Anyone who has travelled over the alps on foot or horseback (or jeep) in the summer, or by ski in winter, knows that although the tops of the main ridges are seldom steep and angular, the side spurs, walls, and gullies, inconspicuous from a distance, may drop away at angles as steep as the climbing ridges of Everest. The west faces of Kosciusko and Townsend, for instance, a region that has only become familiar to numbers of people[26] since the whole area became the province of the Snowy Mountains Authority,[27] fall almost continuously to the Geehi more than 1500 metres below. The isolated massif of Mt Buffalo is quite steep on several sides; Mt Feathertop plunges from its cornice at an airy angle; and the Howqua ski-runs from the summit of Buller, and several on Bogong—in fact, some slopes on all the famous winter resort mountains—provide scope for the most expert skier.

For tens of thousands who take delight in the sport of skiing on downhill courses, the fastest, most graceful sport on earth, where absolute control carries an exaltation that might be shared by a wheeling albatross—and, alas, not by the author—there are too many centres and resorts to be listed here. They have names that call to mind great days in good company . . . some that go back a long way, like Hotham, Buffalo, Kiandra, and Charlotte Pass; some that have recently highlighted old names; and others that although quite new, are already established and popular, with increasing numbers of chair-lifts and ski-tows, expert instruction, and delightful accommodation. Information about snow conditions, centres, and resorts, and general access is readily available throughout the season. The extension of roads has

Facing page: First winter
snows on Mount
Feathertop near Bright,
Victoria

increased the safe areas for the ski-tourer so considerably that a well-balanced party which has proficiency on ski, and has taken enough trouble with other equipment, may travel safely to any mountain destination in winter.

It is very strange looking back through the years . . . to the night a friend and I were caught out by darkness and blizzard on the Bon Accord Spur, for instance, and spent the hours until dawn tied to a tree . . . or that other night on the same journey when, after searching for a long time, we found, by a pale moon, the top of the chimney of the old Blowhard Hut, and, having tossed down as much brittle dry snow gum as we could find, went down it to much needed shelter. In the July of the year I turned seventeen, I remember, I decided to walk with my pack all the way from my suburban home at Murrumbeena . . . until I came to a snow-covered mountain. It turned out to be Torbreck, and for the last four days I saw no one.

For a number of years I have visited Mt Buller, which in many ways is typical of the resorts that carry not only large public chalets, but anything from a dozen or so, to a hundred or more, ski-club lodges. These alpine villages are already a feature of all our snow mountains. When the light fades on the slopes and the crust becomes icy, the lights twinkle out invitingly from the gaily curtained windows behind which new energy and happiness extend the day . . . and perhaps often carry it further than was intended. Lanterns lead wanderers along the well-pressed frozen tracks and a zestful community spirit seems to pervade the night. And when a blizzard of snow blows up, all the safe happiness is accentuated. I recall early experiences on Buller, when there was a small chalet down near the present parking site, and a diminutive hut, belonging to the youthful Victorian Ski Club, some way down a spur below the summit . . . and nothing else except the long virgin ridge of the mountain.

After a long drive in my old 'A' Model Ford, sometimes with the assistance of a draught horse to get us through the bogs on the road, we usually found a camp at Christensen's Mill. Early the morning after, it was customary for us to climb up a steep spur directly to the hut, making as much vertical progress as horizontal. We lugged great packs, into which we had stuffed a week's supplies, and, clinging to the scrub, sweating, and cursing our shouldered skis, we eventually got through the tall timber and came on the more open snow gum, and the tiny shelter. Always, in the Australian bush, as one approaches the snow-line, there are intermittent patches of snow patterned by the vegetation. On the Buller spur, these quickly coalesced and formed continuous snow cover, and our enthusiasm mounted. The snow was often metres deep long before we got to the hut, but we floundered exultantly, and ultimately rose out of our packs like released spirits, and were off up the final glittering slopes to that distinctive corniced summit from which, after surveying a magical world stretching in every direction—and generally all our own—we always took that first beautiful slope as straight as we dared.

Once, I remember, a friend and I battled along the whole length of the ridge in a furious blizzard that blotted out the world and made our elements a combined fear and grey fury, and sometimes laid us prone. One of the party had become ill just at the bottom of the spur, and we had taken him along to the old chalet, promising the others to ski across and meet them, and show them where the hut lay. From the moment we started the combined operation, the weather worsened. I'll never forget how completely iced we were as we made down the ridge to a still deserted hut. We kept a candle burning for the others in case they should not have turned back, but they had a responsible leader, and joined us next day when the storm had abated.

And there was that night on the Gable End of Mt Wellington in East Gippsland, when we were making one of the first winter ascents to the

225

Facing page top: Mist in the Myrtleford valley, Victoria, as seen from Mount Buffalo National Park. *Bottom:* Mount Bogong with first winter snows. *This page top:* Main ski-ing area on Mount Buller. *Bottom left:* A blanket of snow on Mount Buller. *Bottom right:* An ancient gum on the shore of Lake Tarli Karng, East Gippsland. Tarli Karng is Victoria's famous mountain tarn

plateau. I had a couple of pack horses to help us as far as the snow-line but its margins came down to meet us, in a thick night that developed from a sudden swirling dusk; we learnt a lot from this experience. It was as a result of such experiences that, years later, I designed a series of special tents, the pattern of one ultimately becoming standard light-weight shelter in the Australian Antarctic. But I never knew any days such as these that were not ultimately rewarding. What joy we had up on Spion Kop, with the whole of the Bennison and Snowy Plains untrodden before us, and the descent into a springtime Tarli Karng, where we bathed in the still lake, even then scarcely visited.

I had begun writing *Australia: World of Difference* while I was fulfilling an old ambition—to put tents on the very summit of Mt Stirling that looks across the Delatite to Buller. This time we hauled all our gear up on a Nansen Sledge, pulling in the traces from the King Saddle. We finished piling snow on all the tent aprons and over the guy anchorages just as the lights began to wink from the Buller Alpine Village. We scarcely saw them again for a whole week, by which time our tents were half buried, but secure, and, in an enormous igloo, we had made our own community centre for cooking and laughter. It hadn't been good weather for skiing, but we had revelled in our capacity to match the strength of weather and ice which, as the old Eskimo proverb has it, 'are kings.'

In summer, when the high plains and ridges are still in spring, starred with snow-daisies, gilded with feathery kunzea, and sweet with pale violets, you may still find sheltered snow drifts. There is much to be said for travelling over the delectable mountains in summer and winter, camping in both seasons, and enjoying the contrast between them. 'They came,' wrote John Bunyan, about three hundred years ago, 'to the Delectable Mountains . . .'

[1] *Cook's Voyages*: Thursday, 17 May 1770: 'These hills lie but a little way inland, and not far from each other: they are remarkable for the singular form of their elevation, which very much resembles a glass-house, and for which reason I called them the Glass Houses . . .'

[2] 'The Flowers,' by Rudyard Kipling (Methuen). 'Melbourne dust' is long since a thing of the past—when a great many roads were unsealed.

[3] Kosciusko: See chap. 12, note 30.

[4] Serpentine Dam, Canning Dam, and Mundaring Weir conserve the waters of the Darling Range. The Mundaring Weir, completed in 1902, about 50 kilometres from Perth, is the source of the goldfields water supply—pumped through a vital pipeline, nearly 500 kilometres in length.

[5] From Vol. 2: *Three Expeditions into the Interior of Eastern Australia, with Descriptions of the Recently Explored Region of Australia Felix, and of the Present Colony of New South Wales*, by Major T. L. Mitchell, F.G.S. & M.R.G.S., Surveyor-General (Second Edition: T. & W. Boone, London, 1839). The above quotation and those following are from the Facsimile Edition (no. 18), reproduced by the Libraries Board of South Australia, 1965.

[6] *Eucalyptus alpina* is not found outside the Grampians. The snow-gum of the Australian Alps, *E. niphophila*, has a wide distribution.

[7] J. R. D'Alton, in his *Moora Savage*, says: 'The rugged nature of the mountains causes a great range of micro-climates that preserve remnants of those (past) ages in a living museum of over 1000 known species. Some other estimates are more conservative.'

[8] Mt William, 1168 metres.

[9] The formation of the Grampians is discussed by Prof. E. S. Hills in his *The Physiography of Victoria* (Whitcombe & Tombs Pty Ltd, Melbourne and Sydney, 1940). The subject is interestingly treated also in Charles F. Laseron's *The Fact of Australia*, and in his *Ancient Australia*, previously cited.

[10] A large white wild bull, known as the Moora Savage (see note 7), once dominated other wild cattle, and was very aggressive towards anyone who approached him.

228

[11] From the Rocklands reservoir, on the headwaters of the Glenelg, a channel runs north to augment the Wimmera-Mallee stock and domestic water supply. For the first time in Australia, the waters of a river normally flowing to the coast were diverted to the Inland.

[12] *Australia as it is*, by F. Lancelott (Colburn & Co., London, 1852).

[13] Quoted by Hans Mincham, in his *The Story of the Flinders Ranges* (Rigby, Adelaide, 1964).

[14] See chap. 1, note 17.

[15] Lake Eyre is depressed about 12 metres below sea-level.

[16] Lake Frome: This lake is part of a much larger ancestral lake that included Lake Eyre—all formed when the land rising in the south prevented the outflow of the original Finke River which in Pliocene times, before the Flinders and Mt Lofty Ranges had been elevated, was possibly the kind of river the explorers were always seeking.

[17] In recent years the work of Warren Bonython, of Adelaide, in the northern Flinders Ranges—such as the Gammons—and in Lake Eyre itself has achieved some interesting results. He has been accompanied by several parties of observers. See *Walking the Flinders Ranges* by C. Warren Bonython (Rigby, 1971).

[18] E. J. Eyre must have seen the Pound Range. According to Mincham's account, William Chace examined the Pound in 1850. In 1851, C. N. Bagot described himself as the discoverer of the Pound.

[19] Ernest Scott, in *A Short History of Australia*, previously cited. The words of Governor Philip Gidley King (1800–1806) are quoted from the same source.

[20] Bathurst, founded 1815. Governor Macquarie used convict labour to build the road.

[21] *The Letters of Rachel Henning*, edited by David Adams (Sirius Books, Angus & Robertson, 1963). First published in the *Bulletin*, 1951–52.

[22] In fact, of course, the chance of flying in a small plane may be realised; and there is an aerial cable-way convenient to the golf-links which allows you superb birdseye views.

[23] In 1836 Charles Darwin visited the Blue Mountains; he thought: 'To attribute these hollows to the present alluvial action would be preposterous.' Laseron suggests that Darwin regarded the great valleys as originally bays created by the sea; he was, of course, proved incorrect.

[24] *The Alps at the Crossroads*, by Dick Johnson (Victorian National Parks Association, 1974) is a fine compendium, summarising the history of the Victorian Alps, the dangers that threaten them, and the vital importance of their preservation. The Victorian National Parks Association, and the Australian Conservation Foundation, and other such organisations have greatly influenced both public opinion and government policy towards adequate permanent reservations.

[25] *The Physiography of Victoria*, by E. Sherbon Hills, already cited, provides a clear description of the dissection of the former peneplain, with diagrams.

[26] *Australia's Alps*, by Elyne Mitchell, is indispensable, not only as a guide to the western slopes of Kosciusko, but as a sensitive description of the alps in general.

[27] Any consequential discussion of the work of the Snowy Mountains Authority—and of the Victorian S.E.C. Kiewa Project—are outside the scope of this book. In themselves they would require volumes.

Thousands are beginning to appreciate the opening up of the high snow mountains and to discover places which, for a century, had been so inaccessible as to be rarely visited. The gigantic project of the Snowy Mountains Authority, completed in 1972, to control and divert the snow-fed streams of the Australian Alps for both irrigation and the generation of electric power, is now producing impressive contributions to each. New villages have come into being, and hundreds of kilometres of splendid alpine roads serve all their purposes. Two major aspects of the work are: the diversion of the upper Snowy River to the Murray, and, secondly, of the Eucumbene, Tooma, and Murrumbidgee Rivers to the Tumut.

There are sixteen dams, seven power stations, 80 kilometres of aqueducts, and 145 kilometres of tunnels passing deep below the gleaming snowfields. The aggregate capacity of the Snowy Mountains power stations is 3740 megawatts. Below the generators about 1 150 000 megalitres of water are used to augment irrigation of the Murray and Murrumbidgee systems.

The Kiewa Hydroelectric Project, producing about 200 megawatts, has likewise incidentally caused much of the Victoria Alps to be developed, so that access and facilities are available for several once remote areas.

CHAPTER 10

Kangaroo and Kookaburra

Perhaps rare Myrmecobius, of many teeth
(The banded eater of the western ants!)
Shall steal again from his outraged retreats
To boast his true Jurassic ancestry—
Or wolf-like Thylacine, the fleetest limbs
Of green Tasmania, advance to prove
That modern times are not too much for him!

—from WIDE HOMELAND

OF WHAT DOES A TRAVELLER SPEAK WHEN, in congenial company far away, he is questioned about his homeland? What are the persistent memories to the source of which he wants most to return? From whichever Birmingham he may come—Warwickshire, Alabama, Michigan, or New Zealand—he will hold to certain irreplaceable values; whether his childhood was spent in England or New England, South Wales or New South Wales, he will be prejudiced. How much poorer he would be if he were not! Only by discovering a man's predilections may you begin to know him; the more you consider them, the more you will understand his country, for all knowledge and all opinion is centred in man. Ultimately you may understand his bias and even share his affections, but you will not lose your own.

There are, for everyone, environments that are too complex for simple description: smells, for instance, peculiar to every latitude, and as particular as the smell of rain-washed vegetation or of wet earth; the smells of summer, too, which are as different in the Cotswolds and the Dandenongs as oaks are from eucalypts. The quality of sunshine is varied: heavy and golden, or silver and clear; and in different parallels its cast shadow may softly intensify local hues, or lie in pools of exotic colour. Even the starlight changes . . . as much as the common constellations of the hemispheres. Dawn choruses of birds blend different notes for that region of sensitivity between the timeless depths of sleep and the morning awareness, even though 'the cock's shrill clarion' may link them all. And the other voices of the morning world, of fellow travellers in streets and trains, of streets and trains themselves, all the sounds of stirring in countryside and cities . . . are part of the air that makes a native of any place feel at home there. The exile will recall these when some familiar nuance touches him: they surrounded his memories of what he may try to describe.

Only on high mountains when the air is still, and sometimes on lifeless plains of ice or sand, is there absolute silence; all other absence of noise is but quietness, and it differs extremely in quality, compounding innumerable minute whispers and impacts, the droning and the splashing and the creaking, the humming of living creatures and machines, a vibrancy that changes with place as surely as vegetation, as birdsongs, and as people's voices. One of my most persistent childhood memories in Australia is auditory: of lucerne pods

Facing page: Musk lorikeet *Glossopsitta porphyrocephala*; this member of the parrot family feeds on honey and also flowers and fruit

230

crackling in the sun, scattering their shining black seeds over the dry earth. Occasionally, in Europe or America, I have traced a sudden sense of familiarity, of integration, to the ejaculations of a local pea or vetch, or of the vigorous gorse.

'Tell us about Australia!' I have often been urged . . . English children under the chestnuts . . . Russian explorers in Antarctica . . . 'What is it that you miss most?' The wandering years always gave me the same answer . . . the carolling of magpies, the quality of golden sunshine falling and re-radiated from a granite headland above slow breakers combing in from the Southern Ocean, and the Southern Cross! Like other expatriate Australians, I burnt gum leaves, and recalled the extraordinary freedom of the scented bush; of the hot, wide beaches; even of the 'back paddock' at Murrumbeena which, in the whole history of the world, had never been built upon. There was a big gum tree there round which, in the summer evenings when it was becoming a little too dark to play, swarms of brown, iridescent beetles whirled; where the magpies often warbled away deliciously even long after we had squeezed through the gap in the paling fence back into our place. Our place! More often in the mornings than in the dusk, the kookaburras came to that tree, and their laughter was the most exuberant sound on earth. We considered the early settlers very odd in finding their robust mirth frightening and horrifying, for at that time we had never considered the bush inhospitable, nor any of its creatures capable of mocking a lost or homesick migrant.

'One of the largest kingfishers in the world,' I might tell my audience, 'lives in Australia. He's a brown and buff bird—oh, about as big as a crow—flecked with bluish-white when you see him close up, with a head almost as big as his body, a long tail checked with rust, and a great, powerful bill with which he laughs so loudly and raucously that he may be heard a kilometre away!' And my mind is suddenly full of visions and attributes of the old kookaburra, our familiar laughing jackass,[1] a true Australian bird of dawning, and of sunset. Although he does not reserve his happiness for fine weather, he obviously likes the sun. In the noontime he may betray his presence by a sleepy chuckle or two, and, suddenly alert, swoop swiftly down from a tall tree to regard you intently from a stump. But, when the sun is low, and the branches flushed, in many parts of eastern and southern Australia, a pair of kookaburras will find perches above you, or, even if you are within the rumble of a city, at the bottom of the garden.

Their laughter is a duet, a low rapid rattle of encouragement from one leading to a full-throated paeon of mirth from the other. Then they both throw back their heads in a kind of ecstasy and create a unique vernacular, ribald and gloating, seemingly effortless, increasing in volume, changing pitch, ebbing, flooding the dusk or the dawn with triumphant peals of sound. Very often, in the distance, other birds join the chorus until the edge of the day possesses a wonderful animation that one might fancy follows the low sunlight right across Australia.

Traditionally the kookaburra is respected as a snake-killer, but, although he has been observed with young snakes, his more familiar diet includes lizards, frogs, mice, and fish. He is a cheeky bird and will often swoop down and seize some other bird's quarry. One naturalist,[2] recording his observation of a pair of kookaburras feeding tiger-snakes to their young, wrote: 'The young jacks, on receiving a snake, gave it a preliminary bashing on a stone, and then proceeded to swallow it, head first, getting so much down at a time as their stomachs could accommodate, the remainder following by degrees until the whole thing disappeared. In this way they disposed of snakes up to eighteen inches in length.'

More than sixty years ago, Dr Frank Tate[3] praised the kookaburra:

232

Marcus Clarke wrote of the Laughing Jackasses as bursting into 'horrible peals of semi-human laughter.' But then Marcus Clarke was English-bred, and did not come to Australia till he was eighteen years old. It makes all the difference in our appreciation of bird or tree or flower to have known it as a child. I venture to think no latter-day Australian who has grown up with our Kookaburra can have any but the kindliest of feelings for this feathered comedian. For myself, I confess that I find his laughter infectious, and innumerable times he has provoked me into an outburst as hearty and as mirthful as his own.

The bright-eyed kookaburras with their feathers fluffed out, sometimes seeming almost crested, certainly look cheerful, cocking their generous bills, dark above, blending with buff breasts below. They are comical fellows, much too well loved throughout Australia in these days ever to need to be fearful of man. In many districts they are quite tame, and will keep an appointment for scraps, establishing a daily routine which is most rewarding for all concerned. And what payment they make! There is always the discussion first, a low muttered colloquy, some clicking of bills, a little chuckling as though they are mightily content with the affairs of the day, then, no longer able to contain themselves, they burst into unrestrained hilarity, first one, then another, then all the rest. And more sweep over to the edge of the clearing, and still others are far away conducting their own session. They rollick and subside, fall to silence; and then, just when you think the performance is at an end, once again the infection of mirth spreads through the warm tree-tops, and there is more uncontrollable laughter.

May generations of kookaburras inhabit Australia to 'the last syllable of recorded time,' and never lack sufficient secret hollows for their clutches of pearly white eggs. It amuses us now, that the older travellers adopted such a superior note when writing of the Antipodes. Although Anthony Trollope,[4] a century ago, was able genuinely to appreciate some aspects of Australia, one of his passages might serve to show how greatly opinion has changed—and, at the same time, introduce two other birds that no Australian would trade for nightingale or thrush:

> The sounds from the birds too are very different from those of English birds,—much less melodious, but clearer, louder, and more continuous, and sometimes very melancholy. That of the laughing jackass—an ugly, healthy, ubiquitous brute of a bird—is the most common. I have heard it much abused, but I learned to like it, and to feel that there was something friendly and familiar about the animal. Its proper name is the gigantic kingfisher. It is also called the settler's clock;—and by the aboriginals, gogobera, that being to the black man's ear the sound of the animal's voice. The bell-bird and the magpie are also to be heard—the latter in some parts of Australia very continuously. The magpie is in no respect akin to the bird which stole the cardinal's ring. It is much larger and has a loud clear note, which was to my ear full of melancholy.

The melancholy that was sincerely felt by the first Europeans in Australia when they heard the melodies of the magpie[5] is not inexplicable, and yet I cannot recall anyone of my generation ever sharing it. To me the song of the European nightingale, one of the loveliest birdsongs in the world, is redolent of almost infinite sadness. Year after year I heard the nightingales in those luminous dusks of the early English summer, and always, while I compared the nightingale's quality of tone with that of the Australian magpie, almost all the emotions aroused by one were in complete contrast to those inspired by the other. The great John Gould,[6] whose *Birds of Australia*, in seven volumes, is one of the supreme ornithological works of the world, wrote: 'To describe the note of this bird is beyond the power of my pen,' and another naturalist, Alfred Wallace, considered its 'wonderfully modulated whistle . . . unequalled

Facing page: Australia's well-known Kookaburra *Dacelo gigas* is a member of the Kingfisher family. *This page top:* The Blue-winged kookaburra *Dacelo leachii* is distributed across the north of Australia and has a harsh scream rather than the raucous laughter of the common Kookaburra. *Bottom:* The Australian magpie *Gymnorhina hypoleuca*, white-backed variety; the carolling of magpies is one of the most Australian of all sounds in the bush

among European birds.' Gradually 'bird-watching' has become as popular in Australia as in Britain, and many excellent well-illustrated books today make identification easy, and provide concise notes on species.[7]

Certainly the literary associations of the nightingale include much that is poignant: the hopeless yearning of Keats, the serenades of Shelley; there is sadness in both poets' search for immutability. The melancholy of the early settlers was compounded of everything unfamiliar with those very scenes and sounds that in some way fed their nostalgia. Thus, the unforgettable fluting of the magpie, the exquisite overflowing of sound, especially in the most sensitive hours at the beginning or end of day, touched the same expatriate chords which for the Australian in Europe are plucked by the song of the nightingale.

The two songs, in themselves, are as different as their settings and circumstances. The ecstasy of the magpie seems to express a fullness of heart even at midday. It has some rivals such as the song of the butcherbird,[8] but for many it is the truest, clearest song of the parklands and open forest, for which the notes of all lesser birds form a soft, harmonious orchestration. It is associated in some seasons with the full, clear sunshine, though for all the year except a long wintertime, it is most glorious early and late. Shakespeare has it:

> The nightingale, if she should sing by day,
> When every goose is cackling, would be thought
> No better a musician than the wren.
> How many things by season season'd are
> To their right praise and true perfection!

This is probably the truth of the matter. But Dan Chaucer also might have been writing of the magpie for, at times, even the long day cannot contain his enthusiasm . . . Throughout the night he warbles softly, clearly under the stars,

> And smale fowles maken melodye,
> That slepen al the nyght with open eye, —

The distinctive black and white plumage of the magpie is as clearly defined as his behaviour patterns. Strict territorial rights[9] are claimed by the birds, and, if necessary, defended against all avian intruders. I have often seen a pair of magpies, with a capacity of swifter manoeuvre, harrying even a great wedge-tailed eagle whose slow wheelings passed too close to their rough, twiggy nest. In the spring breeding season when they are most aggressive, they swoop down fearlessly on all passers-by, and, although they seldom inflict any damage, the sharp, straight bill and the rush of wings are close enough to be intimidating. Anyone energetic and simian enough to attempt an assault on the high, strategically placed nest, is likely to be attacked continuously.

Many of the aspects of Australia that troubled our ancestors would not be noticed by them today. There are any number of contemporary Australians who dislike rural life and are less capable of 'roughing it' than almost any of the first settlers. Apart from an annual holiday at one of the fashionable surfing beaches or, perhaps, at a well-equipped, even luxurious skiing lodge in the Australian Alps, they spend all their lives in the cities and suburbs. There need be no discomfort in modern travel: one may fly anywhere, or choose a route for a caravan tour where nothing that money can buy will be denied. The great majority of new settlers enter into a suburban environment and discover, on the whole, that cities may have a good deal in common anywhere in the world.

236

It wasn't until I had lived in England for some years that I realised quite what an astonishing range of fruits had flourished in my childhood garden in the suburbs of Melbourne. They included limes and lemons, apricots and peaches, apples and pears, quinces, plums and nectarines, grapes, raspberries, gooseberries, strawberries, and tomatoes. I missed this mellow fruitfulness, though perhaps had I lived in lower latitudes as a child, I should have found the contrast even greater, for there are plenty of suburban blocks in northern Australia where papaws, oranges, bananas, mangoes, pineapples, avocado pears, and macadamia nuts are swapped between neighbours. Of all the fruits I have mentioned, I think only the last occurred in Australia when the *Endeavour* visited our eastern coast.

Yet, in Europe, more than I ever missed any material delights—for these were always matched by compensations—I missed the familiar constellations of the southern skies. Cassiopeia and the Great Bear were magnificent, and it was most convenient having a ready-made pole-star. But who could ever compare these with that tremendous sweep of the Milky Way which by-passes the southern pole—and includes the Cross, the Pointers, Canopus and Argus of Carina, Antares of the Scorpion, Sirius of Canis Major, and even the brilliant clusters of Sagittarius? Experience brings the answer: all those who have watched the northern stars cross the windows of childhood; anyone, almost, born north of the Tropic of Cancer! The stars are part of our world of difference. Often I look at the Cross and the Pointers, and think of that immense oceanic emptiness that lies darkly and for ever beneath them as they follow Magellan's Clouds round the coast of Antarctica. The more brilliant stars of the south even penetrate to our city pavements.

After a digression on stars . . . or on anything from the Sydney Opera House to Ayers Rock—the discussion most often returns to natural history. Everyone seems to have heard of the lyrebird. I have wondered sometimes at such a felicitous confluence of the streams of avian evolution. *Menura novaehollandiae* is not only a siren with a lovely voice, with a capacity for imitation that enriches even the sweetest source material, but a bird of distinction and beautiful plumage, of superb form and subtle colour. To hear this bird's exquisite song and almost incredible mimicry issuing from a misty forest is a memorable and disturbing experience, an anodyne to the over-business of the world. There seems no reason why a voice so melodious should exist in the sodden bush, in the pungent atmosphere of fungi and rotting leaf-mould, the green twilight of arching tree-ferns.

When you visit the haunt of lyrebirds in the dank winter and early spring—they are confined to the eastern ranges from Victoria to southern Queensland[10]—you may hear the 'whirring, snapping sounds'[11] that precede the display. First, very often, there are some rich, contralto, yet piercingly clear notes, related from the start, separate and yet continuous, so earnest as to reduce the whole surrounding bush to silence. To describe their quality would require inexistent comparisons, but what follows may be an imitation of all the innumerable songs of the bush, often with added grace-notes and new arrangements, or wonderful blendings that would have seemed beyond any vocal possibility. Swiftly the lyrebird passes through his repertoire, but by no means limits his numbers to those splendours borrowed from other great singers who might almost rival that clear ringing voice—the rich notes, for instance, of currawongs and butcherbirds. He takes up the song of the little birds; he may easily imitate a thrush, he may call to the bellbirds, and even show off his virtuosity to the carolling magpies. It always seems to me that there is an added resonance in the reproduction when the lyrebird pretends to his singing peers—and none can match his fervour and vitality; often he magnifies the sounds of the small, twittering thornbill or cheerful whiteface, and a special *tour de force* is the call of the whipbird. Some

Top: Australian magpie *Gymnorhina hypoleuca.* *Bottom:* Grey currawongs *Strepera versicolor* are members of the same family as butcherbirds and magpies, and are actually the largest members of the family. *Facing page top:* Superb lyrebird *Menura superba* belongs to a family unique to Australia with only two species; this specimen was photographed in the well-known Sherbrook Forest, east of Melbourne. *Bottom:* Female grey butcherbird *Cracticus torquatus* with young at nest

observers of the wily singer of the fern-glade aver that he can just as easily simulate the barking of a dog, the whirr of the circular-saw and all the sounds of the logging camp, the laughter of the kookaburra, the screech of the cockatoo, or even the splash of running water.

The lyrebird is more easily heard than seen, but sufficient patience in a haunt where lyrebirds have become somewhat used to man—like Sherbrooke Forest, in the Dandenong Ranges, east of Melbourne—will reveal the master musician as a warm, mottled brown and grey pheasant of a bird with a high, sagacious-looking head, an eye as shining as Andrew Marvell's 'hatching throstle's,' very powerful legs and feet, and a trailing tail of most unusual feathers extending the length of the bird by 50 or 60 centimetres. The male possesses two broad marginal feathers in the tail that may be erected momentarily in the shape of a lyre, but, when spread in display, are usually held like a cross-bow, almost horizontally. They are transparent as though notched at intervals of 2 or 3 centimetres, and between them, extending on either side, are spread a dozen ethereal filaments in a delicate veil-like fan, backed by two very long thin plumes like the antennae of a huge moth.

In the ceremonial generally associated with the melodious mating period of early winter, the tail feathers are lifted right over the body until they lie horizontally, or even downward-dipping, over the head. From the front, the body is almost hidden beneath the spread of the tail feathers. The bright undersides, white and tan, appearing serrated, with black tips and pale grey filamentaries are now fully revealed, when previously their upper sides, trailing, were almost invisible against the forest floor. But nothing is static in this performance. Soon the whole bird quivers to his singing, either pacing his specially prepared 'dancing mound' or, with tail in repose, perched on a branch of hazel or sassafras.

Most of the Australian birds that build mounds, such as the brush turkey and mallee fowl, use this structure as a natural incubator in which the large eggs are hatched by the heat of decomposing vegetation.[12] The lyrebird, however, makes a number of small, raised platforms in clearings where he may display and sing to his bride without the indignity of becoming entangled in the undergrowth; that is their whole purpose. Between the extravagant, proud exhibitions of melody and prowess, the birds engage in a farandole courtship, energetic and coy, with the female ecstatically setting the pace and the male pursuing her up trees and through glades until, after the stimulation of the chase, again he pleads in full voice that he is monarch of the bush and that fine feathers also make fine birds.[13]

The female probably sings almost as sweetly as the male, but she devotes much of her energy to building a safe nest, often high off the ground, especially in places where there are men. In that she performs all the family chores without assistance, she is the sailor's wife among the birds. Her tail is more substantial than that of her roving husband, with none of the ethereal filamentaries, but sixteen long, proper feathers. The great John Gould considered the lyrebird quite the most appropriate bird emblem for Australia. Dr John Latham,[14] writing of the lyrebird one hundred and fifty years ago, said:

> I do not find that it has been yet attempted whether this bird will bear confinement; but if the trial should turn out successful it would be a fine acquisition to our menageries . . . This hint has, we believe, never been acted upon; the lyrebird has not as yet been conveyed alive to England, which, were it a truly *gallinaceous* bird, would be no very difficult task to accomplish. The emu lives and breeds in our parks and menageries . . . but, from some cause or other, the lyrebird . . . has yet to be made the subject of trial.

It is interesting to realise that attempts to breed this strange and lovely bird

Facing page top left: Crimson rosella *Platycercus elegans*, found along the south-eastern and eastern coastal areas; rosellas are a genus of parrots found only in Australia. *Top right:* Mulga parrot *Psephotus varius* is common and widespread south of the tropics. *Bottom:* Rainbow lorikeet *Trichoglossus haematodus*, common in eastern coastal areas where they frequent nectar-bearing trees and bushes and screech noisily

240

in captivity have since been successful, though efforts have been not so much to make it 'an acquisition to our menageries,' but to ensure that the species is placed beyond danger of extinction.[15]

It is not only the strange and exotic-seeming birds that appeal to visitors, but some of families that are of wide geographical distribution. An Australian once asked a visitor from England,[16] 'What has impressed you most in Melbourne?'

'Well,' he said, 'I hope you won't laugh—I'm sure you won't laugh—when I say that what has most appealed to me is not your streets or your buildings, but those beautiful little blue wrens that I have seen in several of your gardens.'

For 150 years before Captain Cook's visit to eastern Australia, the Dutchmen, blown off course while following Brouwer's route[17] due east of the Cape of Good Hope bound for the Isles of Spice, made various random landfalls of the arid coast of New Holland. Some vessels were lost without record; others left sparse accounts of an inhospitable coast. Dirk Hartog, in *Eendracht*, reached Shark's Bay, and nailed to a tree there his famous plate recording his arrival (25 October 1616). Vlamingh found the plate eighty years later under not dissimilar circumstances, but he also named the Swan River, because he found there *een soorte van swarte swanen*. This was indeed a *rara avis*.[18] Captain Cook did not identify such an anomalous creature on his first visit to the east coast; however, his description of the great pelican is memorable:[19]

> The woods, as I have before observed, abound with birds of exquisite beauty, particularly of the parrot kind; we found also crows here, exactly the same with those in England. About the head of the harbour, where there are large flats of sand and mud, there is great plenty of water-fowl, most of which were altogether unknown to us: one of the most remarkable was black and white, much larger than a swan, and in shape somewhat resembling a pelican.

However, when the First Fleet arrived in the same season eighteen years later, men had begun to believe their eyes and, in fact, to realise that in the Antipodes, even such an impossibility as the black swan might exist:[20]

> . . . On this lake they first observed a black swan, which species though proverbially rare in other parts of the world, is here by no means uncommon, being found on most of the lakes. This was a very noble bird, larger than the common swan, and equally beautiful in form. On being shot at, it rose and discovered that its wings were edged with white; the bill was tinged with red.

If the poetry that exists in the blacks' wild legends, in the names of the kookaburra, bilinga, the magpie, and koorawarri,[21] the black swan, were laid aside for a while during the objective description of the strange and paradoxical creatures of New South Wales, it was not for very long. To accurate delineation was added affection. We have a lovable record of truth combined with feeling in Paterson's poem on the black swans:[22]

> As I lie at rest on a patch of clover
>   In the Western Park when the day is done,
> I watch as the wild black swans fly over
>   With their phalanx turned to the sinking sun;
> And I hear the clang of their leader crying
> To a lagging mate in the rearward flying,
> And they fade away in the darkness dying,
>   Where the stars are mustering one by one.

One of the oddest inversions the first European Australians discovered, apart from the fact that the sun lay in the north at noon, that some of the constellations such as Orion were turned upside down, and that Christmas came in midsummer, was that the cuckoo became a night bird in this land of paradoxes and contradictions. Nor was the bird of darkness, that echoed so persistently the settlers' nostalgia for the soft lights of the English spring, really a cuckoo at all, but the boobook owl.[23] Another night bird, the tawny frogmouth, often seems to accompany the boobook. His sound is low, penetrating, and stertorous. Because he may still be visible in the morning light, a strange form simulating a broken branch, he is often called mopoke, though the name is onomatopoeic from the call of the boobook.

There is a world of interest in Australian birds, from the great strutting emu, primitive runner of the plains, to the minute fairy wrens and finches, jewel-like in colour, as pretty and perky as any English jenny-wren or robin. Australia is extraordinarily rich in brilliant parrots and cockatoos which find plenty in the innumerable seeds, roots, and pods, galls and capsules, that to man are mostly inedible. As I have said elsewhere, Australia's original ecology held no special place for man who, in order to live, found he had to match the speed of, and find ways of deceiving, the shy, fleet marsupials; to dig in the earth for witchetty grubs and yams, or, in certain tribal areas, follow the bogong moth, congregate for the rich harvest of the bunya pines, or forage for shellfish. In order to live like his brother animals, he learnt to imitate them, and to propitiate certain totemic ancestors so that, even in the hardest times, their sacred progeny should never be totally exterminated. The historian, Geoffrey Blainey, in his *Triumph of the Nomads*, argues that many Aborigines were so well adapted to their diet that they were probably better nourished than many peasants in medieval Europe.

An account of Australia must mention the marsupials and the monotremes, though any single genus might provide material for a lifetime of study. It must have been an amazing experience for European man suddenly to begin his acquaintance with them in the seventeenth and eighteenth centuries just when the age of medieval credence in fairies and monsters, dragons, and even in anthropophagi was coming to an end.

Francis Pelsart, whose vessel *Batavia*, was wrecked near the Abrolhos[24] in 1629, was the first to carry back to Europe an account of the kangaroo. His records[25] show that although he was in error in supposing that marsupials were actually born in the pouch,[26] he was nevertheless a careful observer.

> Below the belly the female carries a pouch, into which you may put your hand; inside this pouch are her nipples, and we have found that the young ones grow up in this pouch with the nipples in their mouths. We have seen some young ones lying there, which are only the size of a bean, though at the same time perfectly proportioned, so that it seems certain that they grow there out of the nipples of the mammae, from which they draw their food, until they are grown up and able to walk. Still, they keep creeping into the pouch, even when they have become very large, and the dam runs off with them when they are hunted.

It was 160 years later that Phillip's First Fleet arrived on the other side of the continent. The description of the kangaroo in Phillip's *Voyage to Botany Bay* is perhaps more tentative, but it enlarges the bestiary of the *marsupialia* to include many more creatures ranging from those weighing as much as a man to some no larger than the familiar rodents:

> The kanguroo, though it resembles the jerboa in the peculiarity of using only the hinder legs in progression, does not belong to that genus. The pouch of the female, in which the young are nursed, is thought to connect it rather with the opossum tribe. This extraordinary formation, hitherto esteemed

Top left: Tawny frogmouth *Podargus strigoides*, noted for their ability to remain motionless and appear to be a branch. *Top right:* Pink cockatoo *Cacatua leadbeateri*, juvenile; better known as the Major Mitchell cockatoo. *Bottom:* Male variegated fairy-wren *Malurus lamberti*; the wrens are the 'pretty' small birds of the Australian bush

Centre: Black swan *Cygnus atratus*, with young. *Bottom left:* Emu *Dromaius novaehollandiae*, chicks; Australia's flightless bird, it can attain speeds of 50 km/h. *Top right:* Male red-capped robin *Petroica goodenovii*; Australian robins belong to the Muscicapidae family. *Bottom right:* Adult Emu

peculiar to that one genus, seems, however, in New Holland not to be sufficiently characteristic: it has been found both in the rat and the squirrel kind. The largest kanguroo which has yet been shot weighed about one hundred and forty pounds.

Soon afterwards, saying much less in the most extravagant terms, a handbill was issued advertising the public exhibition of an unfortunate kangaroo in London. This is preserved in the Mitchell Library, Sydney. The 'wonderful kanguroo from Botany Bay' was at the time, 'the only one ever brought alive to Europe.' For twelve hours daily it might be gaped at, at the Lyceum in the Strand, by anyone who subscribed the necessary shilling admittance:

> This amazing, beautiful, and tame Animal, is about 5 feet in Height, of a Fawn Colour, and distinguishes itself in Shape, Make, and true Symmetry of Parts, *different from all other* Quadrupeds. Its Swiftness, when pursued, is superior to the Greyhound; to enumerate its extraordinary Qualities would far exceed the common Limits of a Public Notice. Let it suffice to observe, that the Public in general are pleased, and bestow their Plaudits; the Ingenious are delighted; the Virtuoso, and Connoisseur, are taught to admire! impressing the beholder with Wonder and Astonishment, at the Sight of this unparalleled Animal from the Southern Hemisphere, that almost surpasses Belief; therefore Ocular Demonstration will exceed all that Words can describe, or Pencil delineate.

The kangaroo family—the Macropodidae[27]—contains several sub-families and many genera, with species ranging in size from that of a rat to those old 'boomers,' among the greys and foresters[28] which, standing erect, may be taller than a man, and weigh up to 76 kilograms. All are herbivorous, and members of the clan once ranged the entire continent. Some of the species were narrowly differentiated and it is feared that a few of them are now extinct. Kangaroos, wallabies, wallaroos, euros, potoroos—grey, black, and rufus, large or small—are most characteristic of the Australian fauna. Some of the smaller rat-kangaroos, doubtless by the necessities of 'parallel evolution,'[29] possess bright, rodent-like heads, pointed snouts, and small round ears. Generally speaking, as the sizes of the genera increase towards the kangaroos and wallaroos, the heads become longer, mild, and more deer-like, with an appearance of aloof yet benign sagacity, and with long, alert ears pricked forward sensitively.

The habit of all the 'great-foots' of using the front limbs only when moving slowly and tranquilly, grazing undisturbed, but leaping on the strongly developed rear legs, and at all times using the heavy tail for balance, is common to all members of the family and, indeed, characterises some of the little insectivorous marsupial mice of the family Dasyuridae,[30] and some of the bandicoots.[31]

When kangaroos take to flight, the verb describes their progress more literally than when it is used of any other terrestrial animals.[32] The immense tail is stretched back and curved slightly upward to balance the extended forequarters of the animal; the head is held proudly back as though by an invisible curb, and the 'hands' bent back as though for further streamlining. But the great thighs are prodigious in their activity. They reach forward beyond the vertical, completely parallel, with the long toes straining to out-distance the animal's head; the tail is raised. The immensely strong black claws strike the earth, bite in with a grip like hooks of steel. Then, like a missile from the Roman ballista, the body is launched forward in a rising parabolic curve which the lowering tail precisely follows, until the hind feet, still parallel, are far behind the tensed grey buttocks; and then they too leave the ground.

246

During the trajectory, which may rise as high as a man and exceed 8 metres in length, the hind feet are once more thrust forward for the landing, and the strange and graceful movements are repeated. The arc of thigh movement with the feet in line may exceed 120 degrees. When loping slowly, with the assistance of the 'hands'—which, incidentally, are prehensile and are often used for lifting tufts of herbage to the mouth—the hind feet are passed forward through them, while the balance is preserved by the tail taking the animal's weight. Advancing somewhat more rapidly, the same sequence of movements occurs, and the tail may thump the ground heavily, giving a characteristic booming sound. At speed the tail is used only for aerial balance, though it may just touch the ground at the moment of take-off.

Much has been written of the kangaroo at bay, and there can be not the least doubt that an 'old man' driven into a corner or to a desperate stance in a stream or waterhole may use his terrible nails on man or dog. Fights to the death between the bucks have also been graphically reported. The use of all talons simultaneously, the animal virtually lying back on his tail, can turn an old boomer into one of the most formidably armed creatures alive.[33] Could there be any contrast greater in the animal kingdom than that between a gentle doe, a picture of mother love and solicitude, with an overgrown joey peeping from her expanded pouch . . . and a furious buck, terrified and glaring, ready to eviscerate his opponent and capable of doing it?

D. H. Lawrence did not stay long in Australia, but he contemplated the bush with as perceptive a vision, and as accurate a power of description, as a trained naturalist. He never attained to much nomenclature but he defined the land and its creatures better than most word-wise taxonomists. Of the kangaroo he wrote:

> Her sensitive, long, pure-bred face.
> Her full antipodal eyes, so dark,
> So big and quiet and remote, having watched so
>   many empty dawns in silent Australia.

If the kangaroo excited the interest of the Old World, from a scientific point of view nothing could have been more dumbfounding than the discovery of the duck-billed platypus and of the echidna which seemed the ultimate paradoxes of the animal kingdom. There are innumerable early descriptions in which the wonders of these unique mammals, the monotremes,[34] were expounded, but the greatest wonder of all was reserved for almost another century—that the platypus laid eggs![35]

In 1832, when the more popular accounts were in full flood, and by which time the sceptics who had believed that the platypus was some strange freak or imposition produced by oriental taxidermists were at last convinced, the following statements appeared:[36]

> Two very curious animals exist, which though neither properly quadruped, bird, nor reptile, respectively combine, to a certain degree, some portion of the nature of all . . . The zoologists were much puzzled in allotting them a place in their respective systems, and they have been variously classed and named by the English and French naturalists.
>
> One of them, with reference to its combination of the porcupine and the bird, was named by Sir Everard Home[37] the Porcupine Ornithorhynchus, but the French naturalists did not agree on this point . . . the Baron Cuvier[38] established a distinct genus, which he named Echidna. . . .
>
> The name of the second . . . has also been a matter of difference.
>
> Dr Shaw was also the first describer of this animal; he named it the Duck-billed Platypus; but Sir Joseph Banks having shortly after sent a specimen to Blumenbach, that eminent physiologist preferred the name *Ornithorhyncus* for the newly discovered creature. . . .

Top left: Grey kangaroo *Macropus major*, distributed through most of Australia. *Bottom left:* Kangaroos in the late afternoon in open country at Zumsteins on the north-western side of the Grampians. *Top centre:* Potoroo *Potorous tridactylus*; once common in south-eastern coastal areas but now rare

248

Wallaby, near Wineglass
Bay on the east coast of
Tasmania

'Of all the mammalia yet known,' says Dr Shaw, 'this seems the most extraordinary in its conformation, exhibiting the perfect resemblance of the beak of a duck engrafted on the head of a quadruped.

'So accurate is the similitude, that, at first view, it naturally excites the idea of some deceptive preparation by artificial means, the very manner of opening, and other particulars of the beak of the duck, presenting themselves to the view . . .'

It must have been stimulating to read such descriptions while controversy still raged; perhaps, now, too much is taken for granted in Australia's world of difference. Although there is still scepticism among the old bushmen concerning the birth of marsupials, it has been a proven fact for about a century and a half[39] that, unaided, the minute embryonic kangaroo finds its way to the pouch after birth, yet Pelsart's belief that the young were born there *in situ* is still often encountered in discussions with men of the Outback.

Perhaps because the spiny anteater[40] superficially resembled the old world rodent known as porcupine he has excited less lay interest than the platypus. Yet this immensely powerful living fossil whose spines, capacity for hibernation, and extraordinary burrowing powers have preserved him against many enemies including the Tasmanian wolf—and the Aborigines—is scientifically quite as remarkable. As in the platypus, the male is equipped with poison spurs and glands on the hind legs. The use of these, however, is not clear; they are not attributes which link him with his undoubted reptilean ancestors, but they may be vestigial from a less spiny creature that required them more urgently for protection. Mother echidna lays eggs, but actually transfers these to her pouch where they are hatched and, presumably until their prickly presence becomes too uncomfortable, nourished with milk. From the powerful snout, which may be used to probe even hard earth, a long sensitive tongue emerges to capture ants that form his principal diet.

Today there is a very considerable literature of the Australian fauna, and although the kangaroo, the lyrebird, the koala, the platypus, and all the rest cause wonder, some Australians have a rather proprietary taken-for-granted attitude towards them. With considerable pride, they will escort overseas visitors to a wildlife sanctuary, without fully realising how rare their display really is. Koalas, rigidly protected, have increased in numbers since the period when indefensible open slaughter for their fur was permitted; but they are still unique, solitary within their family,[41] and, although they may range from Victoria to Queensland, theirs is so specialised an existence that the advance of settlement always appears inimical to their status.

Observation was often very acute in the early days, as is borne out by a description of the koala published in the London *Saturday Magazine* on the last day of 1836:

> They have four hands, having naked palms, which are armed with crooked pointed nails, exceedingly sharp and rather long. They are covered with fur of a bluish-gray colour, very thick, and extremely soft. It is darker on the back, and paler under the throat and belly, but slightly tinged with reddish-brown about the rump. The nose is somewhat elongated, and appears as if it were tipped with black leather. The ears are almost concealed . . . The mouth is small and they have no tail.

The koala's expression always reminds me of that of a Byzantine madonna, or of some dowager duchess . . . rather bored, well fed and well bred, immensely superior, and extremely intolerant. I can visit both him and the platypus at any weekend. When the day is ending, the latter often riffles a curved wake across a still pool in the Moorabool River, not far from my home in Geelong, and, in imagination, I have pursued him into his clever bankside burrow which is normally well above water-level. I never really considered his bill so extremely duck-like, but this sensitive plastic organ is the feature you would least expect to find in any furred animal alive. Only a trifle less expected are the sharp claws and the webbed feet.

There is less chance of seeing a platypus during the bright day than at dawn and sunset when he is most active in the streams, submerging in search of the worms, larvae, and other water-life, but surfacing to breathe and masticate. Most of his time is spent in subterranean galleries that are excavated with the powerful forepaws. Very many years of patient observation and research by naturalists[42] aver that the female platypus makes a special breeding burrow that may extend for several metres. Ultimately she seals this off with a series of earthen plugs set at intervals, and retires to a nest of leaves or twigs where one or two leathern, white, reptilean-like eggs are laid. Until they are hatched, for a period of a fortnight, the mother remains with them. Although she possesses a sort of pouch, it is not adapted for the aquatic carrying of the young which are fed from the rudimentary mammary glands, described by Troughton as 'enlarged pores.'

Numerous koalas live up in the Brisbane Ranges, also not far from my home; they were introduced there some years ago and appear to be thriving in small numbers. They are also well established in several fauna reserves where they have become the firmest favourites of visitors, especially on account of their habit, shared by some of the possums, of carrying their young firmly clinging to their backs. Locating koalas in their wild state is a matter of practice. I have found that a constantly roving eye against the light in the treetops will generally reveal a characteristic bulky silhouette fairly soon if koalas are present in reasonable numbers.

I am sure that another nature lover might make a different selection of Australian animals for his conversational bestiary; perhaps including the stolid old wombat or the energetic quoll, and the multitude of the tree-dwelling possums that range from dainty honey-eating pygmies smaller than squirrels, to the ring-tails, and the large brush-tails that have been described as arboreal foxes—although the latter are all either insectivorous or vegetarian in diet.

The rare, perhaps extinct, Tasmanian wolf,[43] which I have only seen alive once, and for which I have since searched unsuccessfully, is a fascinating subject of study, although we may now be for ever entirely dependent for our knowledge of him upon the sparse literature which, unfortunately, includes no complete record of his life history. Thylacine, as the heavy, carnivorous 'tiger,' 'hyena,' or 'wolf' is most aptly and scientifically called is a vertically striped marsupial, with the typical apparent continuation of the body into the tail, and hind legs by far the more powerfully developed. In early days some of the reports credited him with a bounding movement in which his front legs scarcely touched the ground; such action is considered improbable. His normal gait is slow and powerful. Although the largest Thylacine may have measured almost 2 metres from tail to muzzle, and although his jaws could open more widely than those of any dog or wolf, there is no record, I think, of his attacking man. Rather the striped phantom was shy of civilisation which harried him mercilessly, offering bounties for his scalp, and shooting him on sight.

It is a bitter commentary on our colonisation that our haste to clear and tame the country, and introduce our crops and herds, however necessary in themselves, should have been so heedless, and that our legislature was so slow in protecting a unique heritage from the greed, cruelty, and thoughtlessness of little men. Open seasons still exist for kangaroo and dingo. The dingo is always the outlaw who, of course, has profited immensely by the introduction of sheep and poultry. He has expanded his population accordingly, and the destruction of many thousands of dingoes and kangaroos

Top: Koala feeding on gum leaves. Although called a bear, the koala is actually a marsupial.
Bottom: Common wombat *Vombatus ursinus*; this is a burrowing marsupial of the south-eastern and Tasmanian forests

Top: A rare shot of a platypus *Ornithorhynchus anatinus* in its native haunts; photographed in the Barwon River, Victoria. *Centre:* Leadbeater's Possum *Gymnobelideus leadbeateri*, an inhabitant of the dense forests of south-eastern Victoria. *Bottom:* Echidna *Tachyglossus aculeatus* searching for food; this monotreme is better known as the Spiny Ant-eater

annually is essential to the pastoral industry. The kangaroo has probably benefited both by pasture improvement and the provision of waterholes,[44] and, again, control measures are essential if grasslands are to support capacity herds. The kind of thing we must try to avoid is indiscriminate destruction, the 'shooting at anything that moves' that occurred too often when troops were stationed in one of our finest national parks during the last war.

Although the uniqueness of Australian animals is not confined to the larger and more conspicuous creatures, it is worth remembering that, with the exception of our true dog, *Canis dingo*, and a number of rodents, bats, and flying foxes, our whole mammalian fauna is composed of monotremes and marsupials. The monotremes are completely unknown outside Australia and New Guinea, and, what is as remarkable, have apparently not existed in other parts of the world at any time during a period of more than 50 million years.[45] Because the marsupials have remained undisturbed and in isolation in the Australian region for immense periods of time, without competition from other orders, they have achieved specialised adaptations showing remarkable parallelism with that of the higher mammals.[46]

When I was visiting an old friend in Pennsylvania recently and discussing the Australian fauna, our conversation turned to entirely different aspects of the subject. I found that he wanted most to hear more about two much more lowly creatures . . . the giant earthworms of Victoria and Queensland, and the termites of the north. I realised then that, apart from seeing a few giant earthworms in the Warragul District of Gippsland—I happened to teach in a school not far away—and being taken in wet weather hoping to hear them squelch and groan as they contracted in their moist excavations, I knew next to nothing about these largest of all the annelids. In fact, the interesting observations of my friend, David Fleay, both in Gippsland, and later at Burleigh,[47] constituted my only real knowledge of the Megascolicidae. To me they looked very like ordinary earthworms magnified to a metre or more long, but somehow, because of their size and flesh colour curiously repulsive. I knew that they lubricated their 'burrows' with jets of fluid, and that with slight provocation, they tended to disintegrate into several pieces. Like common or garden earthworms they ingested soil and humus and presumably extracted nutriment. I understood that the creature bred by slipping backwards out of a cylindrical cocoon in which it had secreted eggs (very much in the manner of the common earthworm), but that, unlike the smaller domestic varieties it did not leave casts as evidence of its wonderful soil-making capacities.[48] I determined then and there to make a study of the giant earthworms soon after I returned . . . but that is still for the future.

It is natural to think of termites when one considers the movement of soil by earthworms, for the former build immense mounds sometimes weighing tonnes, every particle of which has been salivated.

Why should a certain kind of order, occurring in nature below the level of man, seem so wonderful? Find a water-worn stone reminiscent of any artefact, a fragment of driftwood like a dancing maenad, or a hill resembling a recumbent giant, and, instantly, there is gratification and conceit for the human mind, as though its authority came direct from some Ancient of days. Something of this primitive pleasure and recognition holds whoever looks on the magnetic anthills of northern Australia; each great wedge stands fairly aligned to the meridian, so that the neighbourly shadows broaden together as the sun passes into the afternoon.

My last clear memory of them was when we were losing altitude preparatory to landing in Darwin. A group of perhaps twenty of these hills was visible, orange-sided in the late sunlight, with lengthening north-eastern shadows forming a pattern, even from 1000 metres, that any man might have believed, wrongly, was artificial.

254

'. . . knew a bloke, during the war, who steered by those anthills,' my companion volunteered. 'Reckoned he could never get lost in Arnhem Land so long as he picked up a few of those tombstones!' Magnetic anthills are also common in flat swampy areas on the Cape York Peninsula.

I can think of only two species of animals that fabricate and precisely orientate their homes to take advantage of the sun's movement: man, a tyro at the game, and one of his most primitive earth-sharers, the lowly insect called 'meridionalis.' How could the tall grey 'anthills' of our tropical north fail to fascinate and intrigue, when their serrated wedge-like forms point north and south, casting little or no shade in the Capricornian noon, but sending broad swathes of shadow west in the morning, and east in the afternoon?

Now meridionalis is a termite, a member of the numerous Isoptera, an order of insects that feed on dead vegetable matter, especially wood, and are so anxious to avoid light and arid air that, if they cannot excavate tunnels in the earth to reach their food, they will construct, overnight, long tubes of mud cement across the exposed surface of an obstacle. Even concrete piles are thus not proof against some termite species; constant vigilance is required to prevent their conduits reaching to floor joists and timbers.

There is a monumental quality in the so-called 'magnetic' anthills of the north; one area, only a few kilometres south of Darwin, was once known, in fact, as Cemetery Plains—the hills looked so much like numerous headstones, up to 4 metres high, 3 metres long, and 1 or 2 metres broad at the base.

Blind instinct, working through the highly developed social organisation of the colonies of this termite,[49] raises their galleried mounds so that they receive the maximum possible warmth when the sun is low on the horizon, and the minimum when it is at the meridian. No other placement of a termitarium could provide a more even heating throughout the day. Other explanations advanced have included theories of the influence of prevailing winds and rains, but, as the nests of other species are not cuneate, but rounded, sculptured to resemble family groups by Henry Moore, this theory seems a much less probable explanation than that of orientation for temperature control. Some observers state that there is a daily movement of termites within the galleries, corresponding to an evident urge to keep warm.

Only in their complex organisation do the termites resemble the ants; like the ants they have queens, winged males, and sterile 'castes' of specialised function. The termitarium comprises several chambers at different levels. Some contain stores of food—fine mulches of grass and other vegetable substance; usually the 'royal chamber,' where a queen with vastly distended abdomen lays literally tens of thousands of eggs, is in the base of the structure. The nursery is at a higher level. In the nests of some species, however, the queens move freely within the whole mound. Unlike the true ants, these so-called white ants, lacking pigmentation, are soft-bodied, thick-waisted, and highly susceptible to fatal desiccation.

The powerful biting jaws of the foraging workers are completely efficient. Though their owners must subsist within a narrow range of high humidities and darkness, they are efficient workers, and may reduce a solid beam of wood to a thin, hollow shell, that outwardly shows little visible change. Digestion of the masticated pulp is aided by minute organisms within the insects' food tracts, protozoa providing a cellulose-digesting enzyme. Every milligram of cement forming their edifices has been salivated.

Alfred Searcy, a customs official well known at Darwin towards the end of last century, in his lively account, *In Australian Tropics*, writes of rolls of sheet lead being completely perforated by termites seeking a short cut to the pine wood core in which the lead was rolled. The same author, with less serious intent however, tells of a stockman, lying in a drunken stupor at Pine

Left: Termite mounds, near the tip of Cape York Peninsula, Queensland. *Facing page, top left:* Alpine grasshopper *Praxibulus* sp. with several red ticks, from the mountains of south-eastern Australia. *Top right:* One of the many Australian species of dragonflies, of the Order Odonata. *Centre left:* Wolf spider *Lycosa* sp. in its burrow, waiting for passing prey. *Bottom:* There are two Australian species of crocodiles and both are now totally protected. This is Johnstone's crocodile *Crocodilus johnstoni*, also known as the freshwater crocodile

Creek, being overwhelmed by thousands of swarming ants, all apparently intent on burying him alive. The truly wonderful will never lack miraculous embroidery among the generations of de Rougemont!

Incubated from the scores of thousands of eggs laid by a queen, once a year there is a vast exodus of young winged adults, both male and female. It is said that this always takes place at night, in drizzling rain. Relatively few insects survive the predators for which they are part of existence; but those that do, pair, lose their wings for life, and become the founders of potential ancient monuments, the strange gnomons of the north.

On Friday, 22 June 1770, and on the day following, shortly after *Endeavour* had been careened safely after her near shipwreck on the Great Barrier Reef, Captain Cook wrote:

> . . . some of the people were sent on the other side of the water to shoot pigeons for the sick, who at their return reported that they had seen an animal as large as a greyhound, of a slender make, a mouse colour, and extremely swift; they discovered also many Indian houses, and a fine stream of fresh water.
>
> . . . This day (23rd) almost every body has seen the animal which the pigeon-shooters had brought an account of the day before; and one of the seamen, who had been rambling in the woods, told us at his return that he verily believed he had seen the devil; we naturally enquired in what form he had appeared, and his answer was in so singular a stile that I shall set down his own words; 'He was, says John, as large as a one gallon keg, and very like it; he had horns and wings, yet he crept so slowly through the grass, that if I had not been afeard I might have touched him.' This formidable apparation we afterwards discovered to have been a batt. . . .

Cook himself gives a good description of the kangaroo; and on the 29th one of his midshipmen 'reported he had seen a wolf, exactly like those which he had been used to see in his own country' (America). On 3 July, 'an allegator was seen to swim about the ship for some time.' The Australian bestiary was under way. For two centuries there have been observations, descriptions, appraisals ranging from the purest imagination to the most scientific disquisition; yet still, in the words of the Rev. T. F. Palmer,[50] in a letter written from enforced exile in New South Wales, in 1794:

> To a philosophic mind, this is a land of wonder and delight. To him it is a new creation; the beasts, the fish, the birds, the reptiles, the plants, the trees, the flowers are all new—so beautiful and grotesque that no naturalist would believe the most faithful drawings . . .

[1] The kookaburra (*Dacelo gigas*) has many names including laughing jackass and bushman's clock. The Australian region is particularly rich in kingfishers, but the terrestrial members of the family number two.

[2] T. P. Bellchambers (*A Nature Lover's Notebook*); quoted by Charles Barrett in *Australian Bird Life* (Oxford, 1945).

[3] Dr Frank Tate, for many years Director of Education in Victoria. The quoted passage is from the introduction for J. A. Leach's *An Australian Bird Book* (Whitcombe and Tombs Limited, Melbourne, 1926).

[4] Anthony Trollope, *Australia and New Zealand*, two vols. 1872. One of the most sensitive contemporary descriptions of kookaburras appears in Eleanor Dark's *Lantana Lane* (Wm Collins, Sons & Co., London, 1959).

[5] There are in fact three well-known Australian magpies, the white-backed (*Gymnorhina hypoleuca*) of southern Victoria, South Australia, and the Centre; the black-backed

(*G. tibicen*), common in eastern Australia, except in the territory of the other species; and the western magpie (*G. dorsalis*) found in south-western Australia.

[6] John Gould, born Lyme, Dorsetshire, in 1804, having established his reputation by producing great folios of studies of Himalayan and South American birds, travelled to Australia to work on his *magnum opus*, published 1840–48. He also described the mammals.

[7] Both quotations are cited in Leach's *An Australian Bird Book*. Some of the available guides are: Robin Hill's *Australian Birds* (Nelson, 1967); *A Field Guide to Australian Birds*, in two vols., by Peter Slater and his team [Rigby, 1970]; *The Complete Book of Australian Birds* [Reader's Digest, 1976], and Graham Pizzey's *Field Guide* in one vol., illustrated by Roy Doyle [W. Collins, Sydney, 1980].

[8] The butcherbird: There are several species of the genus *Cracticus* (Gk. *cracticos*, loud-voiced). The grey butcherbird (*C. torquatus*), common all over Australia except in the far north, produces one of the most melodious of all bird songs.

[9] From *Birds of Western Australia*, by D. L. Serventy and H. M. Whittell (Paterson Brokensha Pty Ltd, Perth): '. . . instead of *pairs* of birds defending territory, as is normally the case, *groups* of magpies form the territorial units. The group consists of six to twenty individuals. . . . The birds are permanently resident on their territory and every bird, both male and female, adult and immature, participates in its defence, the adult males being the most aggressive.'

[10] A second species, *M. alberti*, also inhabits northern N.S.W. and southern Queensland.

[11] *The Lyrebirds of Sherbrooke* (Georgian House, 1951), by L. H. Smith. This author and all naturalists also pay tribute to the works of R. T. Littlejohns, including *Lyrebirds Calling from Australia* (Robertson & Mullens, Melbourne, 1943).

[12] The young of the mound-builders are born fully fledged, able to fend for themselves from birth. These birds—brush turkey (*Alectura lathami*), mallee fowl (*Leipoa ocellata*), and scrub fowl (*Megapodius reinwardt*)—have been accredited with having retained some of the reptilean egg-laying characteristics. Turtles and many lizards and snakes cache their eggs and are not present to assist the young.

[13] Dr Len Smith (see note 11) describes in some detail the energy of a lyrebird mating. See also L. H. Smith, *The Lyrebird*, 1968.

[14] Dr John Latham (1740–1837), an English ornithologist, published an important work on Australian birds as early as 1801.

[15] At the Colin McKenzie Sanctuary, Healesville, Victoria, a lyrebird egg was first laid in July 1965 by a bird in captivity. The large lyrebird aviary in the sanctuary simulates as exactly as possible the natural conditions in which the birds thrive. The lyrebird has now been bred at several such sanctuaries.

[16] The incident is recounted by the naturalist, Alec H. Chisholm, in *Walkabout*, September 1947.

[17] In 1611, Hendrik Brouwer, a commander of marked ability who subsequently became Governor-General of the Dutch East Indies, made a discovery. He found that if, after leaving the Cape, he steered due east for about 5000 kilometres, and then set course north for Java, he had the benefit of favourable winds . . . from the year 1613 all Dutch commanders were under instructions to follow Brouwer's route. (Ernest Scott: *A Short History of Australia*, Oxford, 1950.)

[18] The Black Swan is *Cygnus atratus*. Juvenal (A.D. 60–130) writes typically of the ancients' belief that a black swan was an impossibility: *Rara avis in terris nigroque simillima cycno*.

[19] 5 May 1770, at Botany Bay. It is, of course, just possible, in view of the extract below from *Governor Phillip's Voyage to Botany Bay* (15 April 1788) that the birds Cook saw included some black swans; however Cook was so excellent an observer that this conjecture is scarcely valid.

[20] See previous note.

[21] Aboriginal names varied greatly with district and dialect. The black swan, for instance, was also called, in Victoria, *koon-war-ror*; and in Tasmania *kelangunya* and *pugherittah*. The lyrebird, in Victoria, was *bulln-bulln*. (*The Aborigines of Victoria*, Brough Smyth, 1878).

[22] A. B. (Banjo) Paterson, the famed writer of Australian 'bush ballads,' 1864–1941.

[23] Boobook owl: *Ninox boobook*. The tawny frogmouth: *Podargus strigoides*.

[24] The discovery of the wreck of *Batavia*, and the recovery of many relics from the Dutch vessel, occurred in 1963. On 4 June 1963, 334 years to the day after the wreck, a skin-diver saw her long submerged guns. The find was largely the result of much patient research by the late Mrs Henrietta Drake-Brockman whose fully documented account, *Voyage to Disaster* (Angus & Robertson, Sydney, 1963) includes translation of Pelsart's 'Journals.' A fascinating summary by the same author, *Dead Men's Silver from the Sea*, was published in the Melbourne *Age*, 1 May 1965. Mrs Drake-Brockman's novel, *The Wicked and the Fair* (Angus & Robertson, Sydney, 1957), also is based on the events leading up to, and

following, the wreck and mutiny. Mrs Drake-Brockman herself visited the underwater wreck; she showed the author one of the large silver coins which had been recovered in perfect condition. It bore the date 1628.

[25] Quoted by Ellis Troughton in *Furred Animals of Australia* (Angus & Robertson, Sydney)—a comprehensive, illustrated account of this division of our fauna.

[26] A detailed account of the birth of a kangaroo, and its entry, unaided, into the mother's pouch is given in a letter in *Walkabout*, 1 March 1948. It corroborates the evidence of other eye-witnesses, that the offspring is minute, 'not unlike a small, stumpy-tailed lizard, about the size of a man's thumb,' and that when born it is deposited on to the tail of the mother whence it travels several centimetres through the fur until it finds the pouch.

[27] Macropodidae, the family name, is derived from macropus, a large foot. It was used to describe the great grey kangaroo of the east coast, before the close of the eighteenth century.

[28] Great grey or forester kangaroo, *Macropus major* Shaw; western forester or grey kangaroo, *Macropus ocydromus* Gould. The heavy kangaroo that gave its name to Kangaroo Island, South Australia, is *Macropus fuliginosus*; and the large red kangaroo, the female of which is grey, is *Negaleia rufa*. Both the latter were described by Desmarest in the early nineteenth century. Troughton remarks of the red kangaroo: 'This powerful but gracefully built and richly coloured species is undoubtedly the most striking member of the group of large kangaroos. Fortunately it is one of the best known also; no description or small illustration could do justice to the brilliant wine-red colour of the male, or the soft-tinted smoky-blue of the lightly built doe, whose colour and speed have earned it the appropriate name of "blue flyer".'

[29] It has been observed by many naturalists that similar geographical conditions seem to reveal numerous superficial resemblances between creatures of entirely different families. Thus marsupial mice might be mistaken easily enough for true rodents, and larger members of their family, the native cats and the Tasmanian devils and tigers bear some outward resemblance to well-known carnivora of the Old World.

[30] *Dasyuridae*, with sub-families *Phascogalinae* (marsupial mice), *Dasyurinae* (native and tiger cats, Tasmanian devil), and *Thylacininae* (Tasmanian wolf or tiger).

[31] The marsupial family *Peramelidae*.

[32] Excluding the bats, and the flying-foxes which, in the sense used, are not terrestrial.

[33] See Henry G. Lamond's account in *Walkabout*, April 1953. Lamond actually cites a weight of 135 kilograms for an 'old man' in Queensland.

[34] Monotreme: The word refers to the single opening through which the animal expels its eggs and eliminates bodily waste. Reptiles and birds are also in this respect monotrematous (Gk. *monos*, single; *trema*, -*atos*, a hole).

[35] A. H. Chisholm, in his Melbourne *Herald* account of the first breeding of the platypus in captivity, 4 January 1944, wrote that the event was 'comparable, perhaps, with the sensation of 1884, when W. H. Caldwell, a young Scottish scientist working in Australia, electrified the British Science Association, then meeting in Canada, with a cable message revealing his personal discovery of the fact that the platypus laid eggs.'

An early account of *Ornithorhynchus paradoxus* (*The Penny Magazine*, 13 June 1835) states: 'The question, whether the ornithorhynchus is viviparous, or oviparous, is not yet settled; one thing is certain, that if the young are produced alive, they are at least excluded from eggs, hatched, as in many of the snakes, while yet within the body of the mother: and this indeed, as recent observations and investigations tend to show, appears to be the fact.'

[36] *The Saturday Magazine*, 29 September 1832.

[37] Sir Everard Home, in 1802, 'proved beyond all doubt the existence of the quaint creatures' (E. Troughton). Home was a celebrated anatomist.

[38] Baron Cuvier is the subject of a footnote, chap. 5 (note 10), 'Tasmanian Lakelands.' Dr Shaw's name and that of Nodder are commemorated in the accepted scientific name: *Ornithorhynchus anatinus* Shaw and Nodder, 1799.

[39] Alexander Collie, a naval Surgeon on the sloop, *Sulphur*, gave a detailed written account to the Zoological Society of London. It was published in the *Zoological Journal*, in 1830. A quarter of a century earlier, an American scientist had noted the unaided movement of embryo opossums, also marsupials, to their mother's pouch. (See note 26.)

[40] *Tachyglossus aculeatus* Shaw and Nodder, 1792. Another species, *setosus*, larger than the mainland species, but with shorter spines, is found in Tasmania.

[41] The Phascolarctidae. The koala is *Phascolarctos cinereus* Goldfuss, 1817. It is said (*Walkabout*, May 1963) that in 1924 2 million koala skins were exported.

[42] David Fleay, now of the Fauna Reserve, West Burleigh, Queensland, first bred the platypus in captivity, at Healesville. I am indebted to Mr Fleay for much information on the platypus.

[43] Tasmanian Wolf, Tiger, or Hyena: *Thylacinus cynocephalus*, as Troughton points out an appropriate description meaning 'the pouched dog with the wolf head.'

In September 1965, I was informed by Dr Eric Guiler (Chairman of the Tasmanian Birds and Animals Protection Board) of recent evidence of the continued existence of Thylacine in south-western Tasmania. Almost twenty years later no specimen had been captured and it seemed probable that the animal had become extinct.

[44] Large quantities of kangaroo meat are exported annually as 'pet food,' and the slaughter of kangaroos is numbered in tens of thousands annually. It was reported that 125 000 kangaroos were shot in 1960 in N.S.W. alone. The Australian Conservation Foundation and other concerned bodies, in consort with State Authorities, have made some progress towards implementing a reasoned policy of conservation of all our resources, *including* wildlife and the material needs of our civilisation. National Parks have been greatly augmented, and new reserves established. Forest management, including the milling and wood-chipping of native timbers is under constant surveillance. Total protection of wildlife in our new ecology would be completely impracticable.

[45] There is no evidence of any members of this primitive group having existed in other parts of the world later than, at the latest, the oldest division (Lower Eocene) of the Tertiary period . . . There is good evidence from the resemblance in their tooth-structure to the living *Ornithorhynchus* that the small European Mesozoic Mammals known as the *Multituberculata* were the ancestors of the Australian Monotremes. (From Prof. W. A. Haswell's address to the British Association for the Advancement of Science, 1914.)

[46] Prof. Haswell (see note 29): 'Thus the Kangaroo and Wallabies, herbivorous Mammals with the limbs adapted for swift locomotion on the ground, are the Marsupial parallels of the Deer and other Ruminants. The arboreal Phalangers and Koalas may be compared to the arboreal Lemurs and Monkeys. The Flying Phalangers are comparable to the Flying Squirrels. The Bandicoots, on the one hand, and the Wombats on the other, mimic some of the families of Rodents. The carnivorous Native Cats, Tasmanian Devil, and Thylacine, parallel some of the groups of the true *Carnivora*, while the Moles among the Insectivora find an analogue among the Marsupials in the *Notoryctes* or Marsupial Mole of the Australian desert.'

[47] 'Worm Giants of South-Eastern Gippsland,' by David Fleay (*Walkabout*, January 1953). See also *Earthworms*, by E. C. Pope, in the *Australian Encyclopaedia*.

In Alec H. Chisholm's Anthology, *Land of Wonder* (Angus & Robertson, 1964), is an account of Fleah's discovery of related earthworms in Queensland. Describing the sounds is a particularly graphic passage: 'he had heard loud groaning gurgles and weird, bubbling sounds. With previous experience of the mammoth Gippsland worm in mind, on top of recent local discoveries, there was really only one answer to the question—the sounds must be emanating from giant earthworms contracting in their tunnels.'

'A Giant Among Worms,' by Balcombe Quick, was published in *Walkabout*, February 1963.

[48] Charles Darwin calculated that an acre (0·4 hectares) of earth might house 53 000 common earthworms whose casts would deposit 25 millimetres of soil on the surface in five years.

[49] *Hamitermes meridionalis.*

[50] Quoted by Alec H. Chisholm, *Land of Wonder*, op. cit.

CHAPTER 11

The New Australia: I

So pass the years, till history enfold
An evil system with a venture bold:
The First Fleet flies its ensign in the Cove
And worthy Phillip founds a colony.
Appraise his fame, who in its purpose deemed
A larger destiny than England dreamed!

—*from* WIDE HOMELAND

THIS BOOK IS MAINLY CONCERNED with the Australia that the explorers discovered, whose peculiar creatures and vegetation in their brilliant and varied landscape settings we now wish somehow to preserve. That the land was originally uncompromisingly anti-European, if not anti-human, in its paucity of shelter, food, and water is apparent from the records of all who first scraped their boats upon our shores. When observing the human 'commoners of Nature,' even Tupia, the native Tahitan whom Joseph Banks had added to his suite almost a year before, 'with an air of superiority and compassion, shook his head, and said that they were *Taata Enos*, "poor wretches."'[1] This particular view was not invariably sustained by the later explorers, some of whom considered the Aborigines well enough endowed; though few indeed were the white men who had either the desire or the capacity to emulate their way of life. However, the qualities of Aboriginal happiness, fulfilment, and freedom would scarcely have been recognised by invaders for whom wealth was measured by material possessions. And, because the white man in the bush was liable to starve and perish, he thought the Aborigines must live in equal jeopardy.[2]

For the men of the First Fleet, and for innumerable settlers for many years to come, the land was inimical to their whole way of life, and the sooner their imported crops, imported animals, and they themselves could supplant everything Australian the better. For many years, almost all that made *terra australis incognita* habitable for Europeans was imported. Whatever could be done to reduce the 'world of difference' and implant an alien culture and agriculture was given official blessing: only when the settlers felt secure did interest in the indigenous cover and creatures of the land develop.

Few of the historic utterances of the first-footers really prophesied the future. The magnitude of the work that lay ahead could never have been foreseen, since to have established two of the greater cities of the world, which by their second centenaries might each be supporting populations approaching 5 millions, would have seemed beyond fantasy; the whole of Britain, in 1800, contained fewer people.[3]

When Europe's ancient cities were as old as Sydney or Hobart are today, they were fords or fortresses, barbarous, unclean, unlit, and insanitary. By slow, unhurried degrees, but always under privilege, they grew through strife, plague, and fire, gradually accumulating what seemed most worthy of

262

preservation in ages before electricity, concrete and steel, swift transport of every kind, communications, television, air-conditioning, plastics, and refrigeration were considered, until they attained, substantially, their present form and much of their existing character.

The cities of Europe and Asia were founded by centripetal necessity gathering together the threads of roads and rivers bearing the marketable produce of the regions they served, long before the notion of overseas trade had arisen, when no floating craft larger than a galley or longboat was imaginable, when the sea existed as a barrier, and its fishermen lived in unaspiring coastal villages. There was no reason for large towns to be on the coast; much better that they were central, preferably by a river, at a bridge or ford, where travellers might pause and require sustenance. A ford usually meant converging tracks and market sites propitious for sale and barter. To the majority of people the sea was a myth, and they lived and died without ever seeing the coast. Naturally, where peninsulas jutted into the Mediterranean, coastal shipping developed, and short sea-roads were linked to the caravan routes from Hither Asia.

Because roads and communication generally were so restricted, villages throughout Europe were seldom more than a day's walk or ride apart; people lived very largely from the land they farmed. The pattern of life in the ancient world has left signs that are visible to this day. By the time Sydney was founded, the world was on the brink of a maelstrom by which all conceptions of time and space were to be engulfed, and flung out completely transformed. In any case, Australia could not conceive her embryo cities within the continent; not only was she unable to wrest a living from the land, she was completely dependent on life-lines floating all the way back to England. She suffered under, and finally triumphed over, 'the tyranny of distance'.[4]

So Australia had all her principal towns founded from the sea, until, after more than a century, the vision of a Commonwealth of the six separate colonies might be focused in plans for an inland city of capital proportions. To understand Australian State capitals, all astride broad estuaries or with their backs to the ocean, it is necessary first to look to their origins; to consider them as beach-heads where the invaders of an immense continent could take breath and stock, lay out their gear, establish their bases, and then, without benefit of rivers, push back from the coast to discover exploitable territory.

The absence of navigable rivers—even the largest, the Murray, ended indecisively in Lake Alexandrina from which it flooded through inconstant sandhills to an unsheltered coast—was to some extent compensated for by such drowned valleys as Port Jackson, the Derwent, and King George Sound which carried the sea a few kilometres inland and provided shelter from the unbroken fetch of three oceans.

Naturally, the greatest changes in the Aboriginal landscape, the factors that most disturbed and displaced the old Australians—and the wildlife—and which today (although possibly with an Australian accent) speak a world-wide language, are our cities. Though they are, of course, continually growing, I am here concerned with qualitative change in these final decades of the twentieth century; not the vital statistics of industry and employment and such—important, but properly to be found in the annual State and Commonwealth Year Books. Australian cities are now mature enough to thrust back the pollution of the motor, increase underground transport, and make spacious malls for people, where they may walk and talk, shop, relax, and be entertained. Increasingly, they provide facilities for out-of-door living; for barbecues by rivers and beaches; celebrations in the streets; safe routes for walking and biking. New festivals are established, with new centres for

Overleaf: Sydney Opera House, situated on Bennelong Point, near Government House and the Botanic Gardens. The white sail-like forms relate naturally to the harbour

263

the performing and graphic arts, for games and athletics.

I have no intention of attempting to emulate any of the numerous topographical guide-books—though there is room indeed for an Australian Baedeker. Nor, generally, do I feel impelled to personify our cities: 'Sydney is a trollop . . . Melbourne is a prude'; or even to expand the familiar aphorisms such as that which affirms that when a stranger arrives in Perth, the first question he is asked is, 'Where do you come from?'; in Adelaide, 'What Church do you belong to?'; in Melbourne, 'What school were you at?'; in Sydney, 'How much money have you got?'; while in Brisbane they merely say, 'Come and have a drink.'[5] Rather my purpose in adding two chapters on urban development is to describe the lovely sites of some of our cities, and the way we have used them. If I linger on history here and climate there, it is because they are facets of a complex Australian whole greater than its individual parts.

> Thus, under the blessing of God, was happily completed in eight months and one week (the whole fleet being safe at anchor on 20th of January 1788) a voyage which, before it was undertaken, the mind hardly dared venture to contemplate, and on which it was impossible to reflect without some apprehension as to its termination . . .[6]

So David Collins described the arrival of the founders in Botany Bay, previously visited by Cook almost eighteen years before. For several reasons, but mainly because the shores of the bay were 'deficient in the grand essential, fresh water,' Phillip decided to explore the inlet about 16 kilometres to the north which Cook had reported might provide shelter for a boat. The high shattered sandstone cliffs were inhospitable, and the Aborigines greeted the little fleet of three open boats 'with shouts of defiance and prohibition,' but Governor Phillip was:

> . . . most agreeably surprised at discovering, on his entrance, a harbour capable of affording security for a much larger fleet than would probably ever seek shelter or security within its limits.
>
> In one of the coves of this noble and capacious harbour, he determined to fix the future seat of his government, it having been found to possess a sufficiency of water and soil . . .
>
> The spot chosen for this purpose was at the head of the Cove near a stream of fresh water, which stole silently through a very thick wood, the stillness of which had then, for the first time since the creation, been interrupted by the rude sound of the labourer's axe, and the downfall of its ancient inhabitants . . .

Today the site is occupied by the metropolis, the heart of the huge urban complex that is Sydney. Phillip's little 'Tank Stream' has long since been lost beneath the city pavements.[7] The very estuary has been built over, and the city extended beyond Phillip's wooden bridge and Governor King's subsequent stone arch up to which the tide flooded until contested by the expanding foundations of the town.[8] The Circular Quay that was formed between the Governor's side of the Cove and the historic area known as The Rocks, has itself been straightened out in effect by the elevated expressway[9] that facilitates the daily flow and ebb of the great human tide from across the harbour.

The Governor's side still has room for his 'mansion,' although, on a different site further east, it is a much grander affair than Phillip's generous barns, and the Farm and most of his gardens are now Royal Botanic and Public. On Bennelong Point, commemorating the Aboriginal friend[10] of the first Governor, now rises one of the architectural wonders of the world, the Sydney Opera House,[11] its soaring white sails as great a triumph of the age of steel and concrete as was the vault of Durham Cathedral when men were still

266

trying to overcome the seemingly insuperable problems of spanning a huge space in stone. The precise geometry of the tinted laminated glass seals the vast arches so unobtrusively that nothing of their soaring effect is lost. The totality is an architectural consummation, and supremely beautiful.

From the Rocks side of the Cove springs the heavy steel arch of the Harbour Bridge,[12] straight, high, efficient . . . and not half as bad as its detractors aver . . . 'See to it that it is removed before morning!' said the late Sir Thomas Beecham . . . but more than half as good as its least critical admirers affirm. In any event it is one of the great single arch bridges of the world, and there are lights in which it appears quite ethereal, and angles from which it is truly majestic.

Criticism of the four great 'pylons' defining the ends of the lower arch, rising like cenotaphs at the water's edge, may be justified, in that structurally they are exaggerated; that they are heavy civic status symbols rather than aesthetic flourishes to a remarkable steel structure. However, by bridge-users they may be appreciated in their own right—as portals through which they may enter or leave a beautiful and distinctive city larger than any of Western Europe except London, Berlin, and Paris.

Always in Sydney—as in all the capitals—the use of steel and prestressed concrete continues to produce notable structures. The Gladesville Bridge,[13] Australia's largest single arch concrete span, is one of the most graceful additions to the city's complex pattern of freeways and expressways; the high Centrepoint mast [1980], braced by many cables, promises to remain for some time Sydney's tallest structure [259 metres]. It rises high above the circular 50-storey Australia Square Tower with its revolving restaurant, and the Mutual Life Centre (1978). Sydney's towers command views of 300 kilometres of harbour foreshores and of Greater Sydney, occupying 4000 square kilometres. At least one tall building has broken away from the glass-wall principle, and is surrounded at each storey with a sloping concrete awning.

In the Rocks area, up behind some solid and essential modern buildings— shipping terminals and the Maritime Services Board building—are still to be found some of the inns, cottages, and terraces of early Sydney, though most will perhaps eventually disappear, or, in a few cases, be moved to park sites where they will be more visible and more revered.[14] The original excavation of Argyle Street passes westward under the Bradfield Highway, southern approach to the Harbour Bridge, and leads to an area of great historical interest, containing many early colonial houses—the Observatory, opened in 1858; the oldest inn in Sydney, *The Hero of Waterloo*, built in 1815; and the Garrison Church, commenced in 1840.

In the Argyle Precinct[15]—the historic Rocks area—over which passes the southern bridge approaches, are many early churches, terraces, inns, old cottages, and bond stores. Careful repairs and reconstruction have placed them all at premium as townhouses, shopping arcades, arts centres, offices, and fashionable flats and apartments. Many crafts—spinning, weaving, pottery, glass-blowing and beaten metalwork—are practised at the Argyle Arts Centre; yet the whole area is still imbued with flavours of docks and the sea. Every big city in Australia, of course, has old terrace houses in its inner suburbs, as part of its Victorian heritage. Once scorned almost as slums, renovated and restored they have become both convenient and desirable residences. Up in the Observatory Park, seagulls and pigeons flock together in the sun, assiduous in their attentions to all who voluntarily feed them; and they are quick to swoop on unconsidered trifles left behind.

There are certain aspects of Sydney which will shine through all the centuries. Her fretted harbour, though it runs back only thirty kilometres from the sea to Parramatta, has a meandering shoreline ten times as long,

Facing page top: A general view of commercial Sydney, rising high into the sky. *Bottom:* The Sydney Harbour Bridge is among the longest single-arch bridges in the world; opened in 1932, it links Dawes Point near the city to Milsons Point on the north shore. *This page, right:* Buskers and street entertainers, sellers of jewellery and toys, have found places to vend their talents and wares in the ever-expanding malls of the city

with scores of sequestered coves and beaches as lovely as the golden afternoons that so often lie upon it. From thousands of homes, flats, and offices in Sydney you may see sunlight revelling on water for most of many days, and evening lights twinkling and beckoning. If you spent a lifetime in small craft, skimming into every reach and examining her nine history-thronged islands,[16] you would never come to the end of delight in Sydney Harbour. If by some incredible chance, you did, within 20 or 30 kilometres, there are the other complex estuaries of the Georges River and the Hawkesbury, larger, and in many parts as heavily wooded as when Cook first sailed by, completely oblivious of their magnitude.

Sydney is a city imbued by the sea. John Douglas Pringle, describing the city's natural setting, wrote: 'Physically Sydney is a sketch for one of the most beautiful cities in the world. Neither Rio de Janeiro nor San Francisco nor Naples nor Istanbul which geographically it most resembles, can match the splendour of its site. The vast harbour, with its innumerable bays and coves and inlets surrounded by low wooded hills, is the dream of the town planner.'[17]

Ships from all the world tie up at the ends of her streets. The continuation of Pitt Street which becomes the western arm of Circular Quay occupies space originally held by the waters of Sydney Cove. The largest cruise ships may be berthed literally at the bottom of the street. An area of about 13 square kilometres of the harbour where depths range from 10 to 16 metres is navigable by ocean liners.

As in pre-bridge days, the painted ferries maintain their services and never lack custom. There are many to whom the morning and evening tranquillity of the ferry crossings is as necessary as breakfast and supper. They probably wouldn't admit the fact, for it is fashionable to grumble about transport, nor acknowledge their pride in the double-enders, bright as parrots and gleaming like the brass of an admiral's pinnace, but time on the ferries is always an emollient for tired or tattered nerves.

The sea seduces the metropolis and all the suburbs that lie beneath the old high road to Parramatta, all the streets of the northern side from Mosman to Dundas. Many Sydney children live within easy walking distance of an exciting roadstead linked with the Pacific Ocean. Alas, not all! The growth of this vast city has distanced many from its chief delight. No city in the world has more or lovelier beaches, some safe for children, others tumbled by the eager Pacific surf whose rhythm and challenge capture the heart of youth. One imagines that every one of Sydney's millions, surfs, swims, sails, or in some other way worships the sun and the sea. Even in Martin Plaza or Macquarie Street which between them blend shades of Paris and San Francisco, there is a pervasive sea-freshness and, in the background of indeterminate sound one may also distinguish the crash of the Bondi combers, inaudible since dawn.

Visitors from Europe or America find in Sydney a great international city in whose streets dress is eclectic, though it may be as formal as in Threadneedle Street, deportment is cheerful though it may be sedate, and amid English with a characteristic Australian tone many languages are spoken. They will find sufficient of the flavour of modern international architecture — the glass-houses on stilts, the big rectangular buildings with a general unifying texture of façade in pattern of light and shade, still not quite knowing whether to stress a soaring verticality or their multiple horizontality on the human scale, buildings that are outward viewing as well as upward looking. If they are sensitive to such things, they will discover more rather clever or silly desire for effect than in the reminiscent streets of Scandinavia or California, but, from any high place, looking out over Sydney as a whole through clean, clear air, they will not be given to unfavourable comparisons.

270

Eastward the green gardens that wisdom has preserved since the days of Phillip, Hunter, and King—the Domain, the Royal Botanic, and Hyde Park—will invite them, and there they will find memorials and monuments, the great libraries,[18] the Art Gallery, the Conservatorium of Music,[19] Government House, and the Opera. Between the arms of the harbour, as far as the eye may see, lie the usual blocks of flats and apparent cubic bric-a-brac that distance makes common to all big cities, but this is more diversified than most, with patches of dark trees and shining water. The air is generally clearer and in this respect distance does not inevitably lend enchantment as it does, for instance, to the desolate areas of some European cities. Sydney is not the only Australian city that seems to be extended in ponderous suburbs of red and yellow brick and terra-cotta tiles in planned bad taste.

In parts of Sydney, stairways have been cut through the brown or reddish sandstone to connect differences of level which often occur unexpectedly. Every step is a lookout. I particularly like the sudden gap of Moore Stairs[20] looking down to the ferry boats of Circular Quay, with the modern façade of The Rocks behind, and all sorts of intriguing glimpses of old Sydney showing through the gaps. There is an old and elegant swan-necked lamp-post halfway down, and although it is now electrically lit, it has probably stood there for all of a century.

At the top of the stairs is Macquarie Street flanking the city proper on the eastern side and promenading from the Opera House, past Government House to Queen's Square, where one of the innumerable effigies of the late Empress of India with orb and sceptre, but more youthful and resolute than some, gazes rather severely across the dignified street that has had the temerity to compare much of its old world charm with the 'filing-cabinet' utility of skyscrapers, and contrast it with the abomination of yellow traffic signs and parking meters. Some of the best Greenway architecture survives at this end of Macquarie Street: St James' Church, with its brick stained by time to a rich chocolate, its clean, round arches and symmetrical porches, and graceful copper spire, pale with verdigris, round which the pigeons have circled for more than a hundred years. Almost opposite are his splendidly proportioned Hyde Park Barracks, now used as District Courts and so cluttered inside with the partitions and furniture of their essential but dingy purposes that all dignity is obscured. Queen Victoria's son on his noble stallion—another of the numerous near replicas of the old Empire—is not very far away, watching out from his space in front of the Conservatorium.

Macquarie Street symbolises much of the character of Sydney, at the bottom end combining sun and sea with lovely gardens, and, throughout its length, much visible history with the continuing city. At the southern end you may diverge at Hyde Park for the Town Hall, the Sydney Central Station, Kingsford-Smith Airport on Botany Bay; or Parramatta and the Great Western Highway over the Blue Mountains; or the Princes Highway to Victoria in the south; or you may keep in Sydney and branch east and find all the cheerful delights of Woolloomooloo and Darlinghurst. You may find a place to live somewhere near Kings Cross and become, in the fullness of time, a typical cosmophile, as much a Sydneysider as those who live within the sound of Bow Bells are likely to be Londoners.

In the evenings you may seek the bright lights near the enchanting thistle fountain[21] or the Village Centre, where you encounter the friendly truculence of a people given to fraternity that must be matched by equality, over a pot of beer or in a garish milk-bar. Or, in the same area, you may discover an excellent restaurant which in wine list, menu, and service could scarcely be bettered.

At the weekends you may run out to Coogee and Maroubra, or cross one of the Georges River bridges—the taut Captain Cook Bridge is, in itself

worth visiting—and discover Cook's Memorial and landing place in Botany Bay. You may find delight in going further south down into the Lawrence coast, nearing imposing Bulli and Thirroul. In Richard Aldington's introduction to D. H. Lawrence's *Kangaroo*, he quotes Adrian Lawlor as saying that he had never seen the coast south of Sydney, but 'after reading Lawrence, God! I've *been* there.'

All this from the focus of Macquarie Street from which anyone, however well he knows it, would certainly wish to pass more slowly. He would desire to pause at the remaining sections of the old Rum Hospital[22] of Governor Macquarie's day, Parliament House which was the surgeons' residence, and the Mint Building, another wing of the original. From within its white double colonnades with their square entablatures, the well-proportioned windows look out calmly at the passing parade, perhaps at the helmeted band as it processes to the Changing of the Guard at the Cenotaph in Martin Plaza. This section of Macquarie Street is conservatively professional, mainly medical, with any number of sedate buildings variously dated but with balconies, columns, and curtained or shuttered third floor rooms where the pace of Georgian Sydney may still be maintained.

Sydney is a virile city, as free and democratic as its sunshine and sea; well into its second century, it is conscious of its seniority in Australia, and proud of its heritage of historical links with the earliest days of settlement. It would, of course, be impossible to delineate in a work of this size the history of our cities or their most important monuments. None of their origins is lost in antiquity; no cities in the world are better documented from the moment the first Europeans lifted a sod or felled a tree. There is the stuff of an endless library of creative literature based on available source material. The motto of Sydney University, oldest in New South Wales, *Sidere mens eadem mutato*, proclaims 'the same spirit' under another sky, and deep down, beneath speech, mannerisms, and lack of compromise, a culture in which western traditions will always exist, ultimately, one believes, incorporated in a broader ethos that will also integrate us with Asia.

In the Introduction to Phillip's *Voyage to Botany Bay*,[23] some remarkable verses appear. They may be considered more typical of the mannered style of the period than of their general quality of prophecy. Hope speaks:

> 'Hear me,' she cried, 'ye rising Realms! record
> Time's opening scenes, and Truth's unerring word—
> *There* shall broad streets their stately walls extend,
> The circus widen, and the crescent bend;
> *There*, ray'd from cities o'er the cultur'd land,
> Shall bright canals, and solid roads expand—
> *There* the proud arch, Colossus-like, bestride
> Yon glittering streams, and bound the chafing tide . . .'

In the same volume, the first general design of Sydney is mentioned:

> The principal streets according to this design, will be two hundred feet wide; the ground proposed for them to the southward is nearly level, and is altogether an excellent situation for buildings. It is proposed by Governor Phillip that when houses are to be built here, that grants of land shall be made with such clauses as will prevent the building of more than one house on one allotment, which is to consist of sixty feet in front, and one hundred and fifty feet in depth.

Few would deny that Phillip's city of today, in general, fulfils this vision; but, more widely, the whole conception of individual house blocks, with gardens back and front, that spread out into the suburbs of all Australia's cities, and the wide highways that link them, owe a great deal to our first governor.

Melbourne, nearly fifty years younger than Sydney, lacked both a Macquarie with architectural zeal, and the endless convict labour that was freely available to him and his predecessors. And, of course, the times had changed. Apart from Collins's unenthusiastic settlement among the sandhills on the south-eastern side of Port Phillip Bay, lasting about four months, from October 1803, the beginnings of Victorian settlement in 1835 were unofficial and, from the Crown's point of view, illegal. The belated arrival of Governor Bourke on his tour of 1837, when he named Williamstown at the mouth of the Yarra, preceded the beginnings of Victoria's reign by only three months. He was not impressed with Batman's village further up the river; he named it after the Prime Minister, Lord Melbourne, best remembered perhaps for his midnight visit to the young Victoria to announce her accession.

John Batman, the engaging third son of William, of Parramatta, probably heard of the Port Phillip region directly from Hamilton Hume after his return from the expedition with W. H. Hovell, in 1824–25.

> The results of this important undertaking were the discovery of a vast range of country, invaluable for every purpose of grazing, and of agriculture—watered by numerous fine streams and rivers, and presenting an easy inland intercourse, extending from Port Phillip, and Western Port, to the settled districts of Bathurst . . . fully adequate to receive, at the lowest estimate, the entire *supposed* present surplus population of the Mother Country.[24]

And so he set out from Van Diemen's Land in the 8-tonne schooner, *Rebecca*, carrying the hopes of many land-hungry settlers, and made his famous treaty with the Aborigines, bartering blankets, knives, tomahawks, clothes, flour, and scissors for 'half a million acres,' and writing in his journal the memorable phrase, 'This will be the place for a future village . . .' In April 1836, after reporting to his shareholders, John Batman returned and found John Pascoe Fawkner who, as a boy in 1804, had been with Collins, already taking up land. There was bitter enmity between the joint founders of Melbourne. John Batman set up his house on a site that is now lost in the trucking depots of Spencer Street Railway Station; he brought his good wife, Eliza, and their eight children. Within a year free colonists were pouring in with their flocks and herds, and Bourke was forced to recognise the *fait accompli* of a new colonial bridgehead. But, three years later, poor Batman had died of a chill, and his wife was subsequently dispossessed of even the title to his cottage.

Two further extracts from contemporary writings might stand as background to the sober and noble city of Melbourne:

> Early in the Forties (wrote the author of *The 'Garryowen' Sketches*), when my good or evil genius led me to this land of promise, Melbourne bore some resemblance to a large *kraal* of houses, huts, and tents. Stonewalls, slates, or even corrugated iron were almost unknown as building materials. The present *Herald* office was on the boundary of civilisation, and the site of the Parliament House was far away in the bush. Stores and shanties and cribs of buildings, composed of brick, shingle, and 'wattle and daub,' represented the real property of the nascent city, and the now fashionable 'block' was, after a shower of rain, such a 'glue-pot,' that when one passed through it, he might fairly claim to have matriculated in bog-trotting . . .[25]

From *Australia as it is*, by F. Lancelott,[26] we may glean the situation just ten years later, when gold had been discovered, and the greatest wave of expediency ever to break over Australia was being generated. Incidentally, Mr Lancelott seems to have detected a generic quality shared by Melbourne and Adelaide for, apart from the reprehensible desertion of Melbourne by

276

the first 'diggers,' he uses the same description, word for word, for the two cities:

> The city is the seat of a bishopric, and governed by a mayor, four aldermen, and twelve town-councillors. No regular system of lighting the city after dark has yet been adopted; but by a government regulation, a street lamp must be kept burning, from sun-down to sun-rise, over the door of each public house; and these lamps are so numerous that, at night, the principal streets present all the appearance of well-lit thoroughfares. Educational institutions and public and mercantile associations abound. Of newspapers, five were printed before the gold discoveries; now their number is diminished, the printers having gone to the diggings . . .

A century and a half later, Melbourne and Sydney are close rivals in size and population but differ markedly in atmosphere. Melbourne is perhaps quieter, more sedate, less unified in opinion but also less vocal, divided geographically and socially by its westward-flowing River Yarra, a stream where regattas may be held and the city seen beautifully reflected, rather than an integral part of it. In Melbourne the most fashionable suburbs are south of the river, though the city itself, the University, and its principal sports grounds and arenas are on the northern side; and, in fact, the best areas on the south side are confined by industrial suburbs which effectively shield them from the pleasant sea-breezes and contact with the popular Melbourne beaches. As far as sand and sun are concerned, Melbourne's affluent society requires these to be taken with surf, at Portsea, or at Lorne on the south coast, and that makes these basic Australian pastimes less democratic than in Sydney. There are about 120 kilometres of lovely beaches inside the bay, and the innumerable fern glades and hillside resorts are again delightfully incidental, their prodigality having long since caused them to be taken for granted.

Government House, high above the Botanical Gardens, is a white turreted mansion that overlooks the Albert Park Lake and the Bay, or smiles down on the prosperous residential suburbs following the south bank of the river. Here there are still many peaceful old Victorian homes with sequestered gardens, and innumerable suave yellow brick or concrete blocks of flats, invaders that are found in similar circumstances in all State capitals, and indeed in all modern cities.

Perhaps there is a certain secretiveness about Greater Melbourne. When it is scanned from the air, or from a high building—and there are some where you may have a meal almost in the clouds—it is all beautifully apparent, occupying a considerable plain that stretches between the deep blue ranges of hills, such as the Dandenongs, and the edge of the big, calm bay. Almost all its streets except those of the city, and the original trunk roads that have refused to be regulated, are cardinally aligned[27] but, from the surface, where buildings and traffic have their proper dimensions, you have little idea of their lateral extent. Frequently neither sea nor mountains are visible, but with a minimum number of right-angle turns you may travel anywhere within the 500 square kilometres that are occupied by the city and its closer suburbs. Where roads dip down to the Yarra or its tributaries they may be visible, far away on the other side of the valley where they eventually return to the general suburban level, rather than rise to genuine hilltops. Somehow, in Melbourne, the by-passed suburbs seem anonymous, introspective, and aloof; and people do not stray far from their accustomed routes through the labyrinth.

To the east of the city the mountains become more frequently visible over many square kilometres of dull, prosperous, and respectable suburbs with

Facing page: The Treasury Building, Melbourne; when the plan was first made public it was criticised because 'it was so devoid of the graces of architecture'. *This page, top:* Bourke Street, Melbourne, and one of the well-known Melbourne trams. *Bottom:* Parliament House, Melbourne, has been the home of the colonial parliament of Victoria, the Federal Parliament (1901–1926), and the State parliament of Victoria; it lacks the north and south wing and the dome of the original plan

disciplined gardens and tidy backyards. The older houses are mainly of timber with galvanised iron roofs, the newer of red or yellow brick, tiled, and self-sufficient. A few colonial suburban houses survive, with broad verandas, perhaps with a canopy of iron lace, and a certain spaciousness and individuality inimical to the plans of all subdividers of old estates.

If the people of Sydney are unified by pride in their city as a whole, their proximity to the rhythmic Pacific Ocean, and by a common nonchalance towards other people's business, Melburnians share a positive delight in some superb individual features of their city; they have a stronger adherence, perhaps, to organised sport—especially to Australian Rules football; they are conscious of snow-covered mountains which may be reached easily on Friday night after work, and reluctantly vacated in time for Monday morning. Skiing in Sydney is what surfing is to Melbourne: compared with the wealth of pastimes immediately at hand, relatively expensive. In Melbourne (and Canberra) anyone who really wants to do so may ski almost weekly for three or four months of the year.

Some of the individual streets of Melbourne possess an unmatchable quality: upper Collins Street, for instance, still sometimes assumes a Renoir air, a dappled sunshine and a great dignity and calm that the whirring traffic, by contrast, and the skittish canvas awnings and the pavement tables and the spreading trees, accentuate. Even when the flagstones shine with autumn rain, and the plane trees are bare, there is a quiet and confidential air as though the atmosphere of the consulting rooms wafted into the open, or the discretion of the clubs screened all passers-by . . . and perhaps turned some meandering steps towards idlers' Bourke Street, where you may window-shop to your heart's content, and glance at the pretty girls without feeling indecorous. Huge towers, their walls set obliquely to the pavements, have added an exigent air to the upper eastern ends of Melbourne's streets, though they provide very large areas of bright, totally dependable shelter, unlike the capricious winds and weather that so often furl the kerb-side umbrellas and dismiss the coffee-tables. Collins Place has been called 'a city within a city', and it exemplifies, perhaps, with the malls and city squares, a *fin de siècle* confidence and mastery at variance with the social and economic problems that beset our world at large.

Bourke Street, of course, has its mall, not so tranquil as Adelaide's Rundle Street, or as sedate as Hay Street, in Perth; but just as indicative of a respect for people rather than traffic that has permeated all our capital, and most provincial, cities.

Melbourne's City Square, with its homage to our brisk and brusque weather, makes a similar statement: that human ends are more important than mechanical means. If the car is being a little restricted within the bounds of city streets, see how the freeways grow without, racing away over the West Gate Bridge,[28] elevated high above the Yarra near its mouth, to the western suburbs, Werribee and Geelong, and cutting through the eastern suburbs to the hills.

From far out along any of Melbourne's radiating freeways, the city stands in blue or grey silhouette like a gigantic San Gimignano. Towers, malls, freeways . . . the new Australia exemplify vigorous growth in them all.

At the top of Collins Street is Spring Street, rather like Sydney's Macquarie in places, with gardens and fine public buildings such as the Treasury, an excellent piece of architecture in the Renaissance manner that would give pleasure anywhere in Europe. In detail it is somewhat reminiscent of the Farnese, though the five high frontal arches occupying the unequal upper storeys are more Venetian in character. From the tiers of the stepped terrace with its charming triple lamps, one may look westward down the tree-lined boulevard of Collins Street, through the part often unnecessarily called the

'Paris' end, where medical consulting rooms are spaced by discreet shops selling expensive merchandise, and by equally circumspect restaurants, past spires and towers to the traffic torrents of Swanston and Elizabeth Streets, with the heart of Melbourne between. Even in the distance something of the solidity of the commercial end is revealed as it lifts a little to Spencer Street.

The next canyon to the north is unselfconscious Bourke Street, its prosperous mall filled with surging crowds, suitcases and string bags, parcels and baskets, stores and cinemas, milk-bars and bistros—a rowdy street full of good humour and bargains, with big department stores into whose air-conditioning you may escape only to be impaled on the horns of cornucopia and dilemma . . . there are so many wonderful unwanted things to buy. Better perhaps if the day is sunny, to sit for a while on the classical steps of Parliament House, or seek a higher stance on the podium, between the Doric freestone columns of a grander example of Victorian Renaissance than exists anywhere else in the city. State Parliament has met here for well over a century, except when the building was used by the Federal Parliament from 1901 until 1927, when it assembled for the first time in Canberra.

Melbourne is a wealthy, conservative city which by taking herself a little too seriously, is jealous of Sydney's sophistication, and perhaps of Adelaide's growing international reputation for festivals of the arts, and perhaps of her vintage festivals in the Barossa Valley, too. This faintly provincial attitude should have passed long ago, with any false pride she might have in the remnants of an Establishment, or in any other of the catchword complexes about which she likes to mutter so knowingly. Her cultural endowments— universities, libraries,[29] theatres, galleries, concert halls—are sound and are attempting the almost impossible task of expanding with the population explosion. Her grand 'Cultural Centre,'[30] provides galleries, an art school, a theatre, and a concert hall, all of world standard, and crowned spectacularly by a slender open-structured spire. She possesses a magnificent modern music bowl[31] in the King's Domain, where thousands may gather for concerts, plays, pageants, and other entertainment; her Exhibition Building, in spite of its Victorian sprawl, unified by a wholeness of conception and a superb dome, has no parallel in any other Australian city. To theatre, ballet, music, literature, sculpture, and the graphic arts, she has made significant contributions. Australia, for so long renowned for her singers and sportsmen, has now achieved a place in international ballet and painting.

Even the annual late summer festival of Moomba, with its catch-cry, 'Let's get together and have fun!' has confounded the critics of twenty years ago and, at least once a year, filled Melbourne with unselfconscious crowds, dancing and processing through the streets, with ingenious and often splendid 'floats', picnicking in the gardens, strolling through open-air exhibitions and listening to concerts in the parks. To Moomba the so-called 'ethnic' groups, Asian, Mediterranean, Balkan, and Baltic, have contributed much, as they have in general to Australia's most cosmopolitan city. Of Melbourne's multicultural society, in the 1980s it was estimated that about half had been born overseas, or had parents born outside Australia.

The city skyline, in Melbourne as in all the capitals, changes constantly, as old buildings are replaced by multi-storeyed skyscrapers. Usually they exemplify the twin dignities of size and simplicity. There will be an impressive improvement in the intersection of Flinders Street and Swanston Street when the Princes Gate developments are completed. The roofing over of the railway marshalling yards may be accomplished, to provide building space, and to permit, incidentally, the triple-spired St Paul's Cathedral to be viewed in better perspective. Probably, the present Flinders Street station will be replaced, and the famous old hotel of Young and Jackson's[32] on the fourth corner of the intersection of Flinders and Swanston Streets will disappear.

Overleaf: The spire of the Victorian Arts Centre dominates the skyline, looking down St Kilda Road to the city of Melbourne

281

The Melbourne Cup, the famous 'two-mile' horse race run annually in November at Flemington before an average crowd of 100 000 people, focuses the attention of all Australia on Victoria's capital city; she first attracted world interest when she was host for the Olympic Games of 1956.

Melbourne is Australia's most sport-minded city and yet, at the same time, tranquil, dignified, and aloof. She has more than her share of the bits-and-pieces 'featurism,'[33] especially in her suburbs, of ugly overhead wiring, and of vulgar out-of-doors advertising; yet she possesses extensive public gardens as lovely as any in the world, imposing modern buildings in broad streets and boulevards, and some delightful lanes and arcades. In the morning and evening, from 'under the clocks' of her Flinders Street Railway Station, surge a hundred thousand workers from all the conservative garden suburbs of the east and south-east; for two hours beginning and ending the day, every road and freeway is turgid with streams of traffic.

Being one or two generations older than the other capitals, Sydney and Hobart possess, to a surprising degree, a greater historical perspective. Melbourne has fewer of the simple, succinct, and unpretentious statements in stone that are paralleled by some of the buildings in Sydney's Rocks area, for instance. In her Fitzroy Gardens is Captain Cook's Cottage, brought out and erected brick by brick to commemorate the centenary of the city, in 1934.[34] But, generally, by the time Melbourne ceased to be a frontier town, and to consider an enduring future as capital of the rich and fertile State of Victoria, the new age of democracy and expansion were upon her, and she began to acquire all that money could buy.

David Collins does not seem to have been attracted by the broad waters of Port Phillip Bay. In 1804, when he left its eastern shores and crossed to Van Diemen's Land, he founded Hobart on the estuary of the Derwent, on a site of great natural beauty dominated by the craggy mass of Mt Wellington rising more than 1200 metres directly behind the future city. A month before Collins' arrival in Port Phillip, in September 1803, Lt John Bowen had established a small settlement at Risdon Cove on the Derwent, but Collins moved it and included this settlement in the lovely littoral below his Table Mountain, as it was then called.

Modern Hobart is justly proud of her high bridge, replacing the remarkable concrete floating arch[35] between Government House Point and Montagu Bay which defied for twice as long as was intended, the fierce storms that occasionally blow up the estuary as though directly from the Antarctic.[36] The Tasman Bridge,[37] spanning a wide and deep estuary, is a notable structure capable of handling the great volume of traffic that now enters the city from Bellerive and the eastern side of the valley which is now thrusting its suburbs high up the slopes of the mountain, and along the estuary in every direction.

Whether you view the mountain from Bellerive, with the placid waters of the Derwent like a broad blue lake flooding across to the city; or gaze down from the spiky dolerite summit of Wellington at the buildings of Hobart encrusted like bright crystals at the water's edge 8 kilometres away, it would be hard to conceive a lovelier place for a city. It is difficult to believe that anything so fair was also the scene of fifty years of harsh repression; that without convict labour the lingering grace of Georgian Hobart would never have existed.

From 1853, when Van Diemen's Land ceased to receive convicts, there was a great decline in energy and public works:

> Now the Tasmanians declare themselves to be ruined (wrote Anthony Trollope[38] less than twenty years later), and are not slow to let a stranger know that the last new name given to the island is that of 'Sleepy Hollow.' When the stranger asks the reason of this ruin, he is told that all the public money has gone with the convicts. . . .

Yet something of the horror of the early days of Hobart may be judged from other extracts from the second volume of the great traveller and novelist:

> The period was a hanging period. The system was one to which flogging was necessary. Tenderness had no part in the thing . . . Either the government must keep down the convicts, or the convicts would put down the government . . .
>
> As I have said before, there was very much comfort in the system. Good roads, handsome buildings, clean streets, and public gardens are very comfortable; and when they are produced almost without apparent expense they are heavenly. Such was the case both at Hobart Town and at Launceston. . . . The things are done and no disagreeable questions arise about the money. There were soldiers with uniforms, and officers with many titles. The hangmen and the flagellators were only the undignified extremities of a long tail of repressive but dignified officials . . .
>
> There is a story in the island that the gaol chaplain at Hobart Town once remonstrated—not against hanging in general or the number that were hung—but as to the inconvenient celerity with which the ceremony was performed. Thirteen men, he said, could be comfortably hung at once, but no more . . . The hangman was a great and well-paid official.

The modern city of towers, malls, and freeways still expands so fast outwards and upwards that, proportionately, the mellow freestone, delightful churches, inns, and offices, stern, uniform old warehouses, wrought iron, ivied walls, coach-lamps, and brass knockers, seem to be decreasing too rapidly . . . Franklin Square, bright with flowers; the city centre, with solid old Town Hall, General Post Office, Museum—where Australia's oldest scientific society still meets[39]—and the Ingle Hall; St David's Park, with the weather-worn headstones of the old cemetery propped round the wall; the antiquarian charm of Battery Point or Constitution Dock . . . are all becoming relics of a different world in a city that has suddenly sprung to life. A city where the Cat and Fiddle Square, with its animated mural and modern fountain completely overlies an old, evil alley where once ran the town's drinking water . . . where the roar and smell of traffic in the city streets overpowers the comfort of apples whose aroma, with those of hops, tar, and shell-fish, once seemed to pervade the town.

Salamanca Place, with its accents of trade and entertainment, its puppets and fiddlers, is still the most attractive waterfront street of any of our cities. For every contemporary urbanism—the Wrest Point Hotel, with revolving restaurant and casino (1978), the Tasman Bridge, the Elizabeth Mall, the high-rise buildings of Battery Point—Hobart retains at least one historic foundation. The Anglesea Barracks (1814–50), oldest surviving military barracks in Australia, are typically colonial with their long, columned verandahs; the Theatre Royal survives through close on 150 years; with Frankland's Secheron House on Battery Point (c. 1831), the mellow old sandstone Customs House (c. 1840), which became Parliament House, and the Town Hall (1866). There are numerous old churches, hotels, and houses, many set in very beautiful gardens. Always there is the mountain, Wellington (1270 metres) above, and the Derwent River estuary close on hand. One may well imagine the satisfaction with which David Collins exchanged Port Phillip for Sullivans Cove, in February 1804.

The convict masons, the red-coats, and the crinolines gave way to the oaths and clatter of a whaling township; then to apples, cider, and lotteries; and the atmosphere of all these combined and lingered almost to the middle of the twentieth century. Now it's hydro-electric power, electrolytic zinc, skyscrapers, expressways, bistros, and restaurants lit by candles in the modern style, pre-stressed concrete, industry of many kinds, including the weaving of exclusive fabrics, banking, insurance, the brewing of beer, and shipping.

Top: Hobart city and Mount Wellington; Hobart is the southernmost and second oldest Australian city. *Bottom:* Mount Wellington in winter, seen from the Fingerpost Track; it is 1270 metres high

Top: Hobart Town Hall, built in 1866, one of many historic buildings in the city. *Bottom left:* Modern Hobart—the Cat and Fiddle Arcade. *Bottom right:* The well-known Tasman Bridge over the Derwent, a vital link for metropolitan Hobart

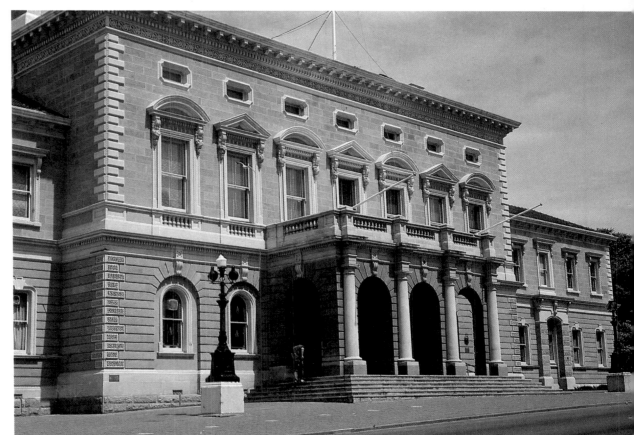

Yet the scale and quality of the natural beauty of Hobart will not be changed; still the big ships will slide into their berths at the foot of Elizabeth and Argyle Streets, scarcely 500 metres from the civic centre, still the competitors in the great Sydney–Hobart yacht race, Australia's major ocean racing event, will, at its end find anchorage in Constitution Dock, feted by thousands, and each February the Hobart Regatta will continue to be one of the fairest sights ever man made of wind and water.[40] Over the high bridge the streams of traffic will flow into the city; but still, against the sky, commuters and travellers will often glimpse the organ-pipes of Wellington[41] buttressing its snowy plateau.

At the end of January 1777, William Bligh,[42] a junior officer on Cook's Third Voyage, planted an apple tree on Bruny Island which helps shelter the Derwent Estuary. There is no record of its survival, yet it might be considered a symbol for the great apple harvest of today, that rolls down to the cold stores of the world from the Huon and Derwent valleys, and from the Tasman Peninsula, between February and August.

In those busy few days, when Cook charted so much, the great navigator wrote:

> The inhabitants whom we met with here, had little of that fierce or wild appearance common to people in their situation; but, on the contrary, seemed mild and cheerful, without reserve or jealousy of strangers.[43]

None of the Tasmanian Aborigines survives either. Few ancient cities ten times older than Hobart have seen more of man's inhumanity to man, nor experienced the vicissitudes of Australia's smallest but perhaps most beautiful State capital.

[1] *Cook's First Voyage: Journal* (London, 1773): Extract from entry for 23 May 1770.

[2] Such was William Buckley, a convict who escaped from Collins's uneasy settlement at Port Phillip in 1804, and lived with the Aborigines for thirty-three years. See also *The Triumph of the Nomads*, by Geoffrey Blainey [Sun Books, 1976.]

[3] At the census (the first taken) of 1801 the population of England was 8 331 434, of Wales, 341 546, and of Scotland 1 599 068 (*The Reign of George III* by J. Steven Watson, Oxford, 1960).

[4] *The Tyranny of Distance*, by Geoffrey Blainey (Sun Books, 1966), is a brilliant analysis of the many factors in the History of Australia to which distance from England (and Europe) contributed.

[5] *Australian Accent*, by John Douglas Pringle (Chatto & Windus, London, 1958).

[6] This quotation, and that which follows, are from *An Account of the English Colony in New South Wales* (1788–1801), by Lt-Col. Collins, of the Royal Marines, published in London, 1804. The same David Collins, in 1803, was not so lyrical about Port Phillip, the site of the future Melbourne, but he scarcely penetrated the bay, and his settlement was withdrawn in the next year.

Phillip's convoy, of course, was primarily for the transport of convicts of whom 565 men and 192 women were embarked, with 160 marines, and the ship's companies. By the end of the century (16 April 1800), 37 convict ships had transported about 5000 men and women in the proportion of four to one. Incidentally, in the eighty years of convictism, a total of 160 663 British were deported to the various convict settlements in Australia. In the eighteenth and early nineteenth centuries in Britain there was inevitable poverty, and deportation could often be traced directly to its effects.

[7] The effluent is conducted through a brick sewer under the city, and pumped out to sea. When the foundations of the high circular tower (157 metres) in Australia Square were being laid in 1964, the Tank Stream had to be diverted.

[8] Bridge Street marks the position of the old bridges. The flood tide reached the site of Macquarie Place, where the pedestalled anchor and a cannon from Phillip's flagship, *Sirius*,

288

make a fitting monument. The vessel, incidentally, was wrecked in 1790 on a reef at Norfolk Island, when Captain John Hunter was attempting to land stores in heavy weather. The loss of the *Sirius* when the youthful colony was desperately short of food caused great consternation in Sydney, and Tench's account states how 'all the officers of the garrison, both civil and military, were summoned to meet the governor in council' to discuss the crisis.

[9] The Cahill Expressway allows bridge traffic between the south-eastern suburbs and North Sydney to by-pass the city.

[10] Bennelong, Baneelon (W. Tench), or Bennillong (as given by Collins, and some other contemporaries) was a Port Jackson Aboriginal. Between Governor Arthur Phillip and the Aboriginal developed a strong bond of mutual confidence. When Phillip sailed for England in *Atlantic*, 11 December 1792, according to Collins's account: 'With the Governor, embarked, voluntarily and cheerfully, two natives of the country which he was about to quit, Bennillong and Yem-mer-ra-wan-nie, two men who were much attached to his person, and who withstood at the moment of their departure the united distress of their wives, and the dismal lamentations of their friends . . .' When he returned, nearly three years later, 'On his first appearance, he conducted himself with polished familiarity towards his sisters and other relations; but to his acquaintance he was distant, and quite the man of consequence. He declared, in a tone and with an air that seemed to expect compliance, that he should no longer suffer them to fight and cut each other's throats, as they had done; that he should introduce peace among them, and make them love each other. He expressed his wish, that when they visited him at Government-house, they would contrive to be somewhat more cleanly in their persons, and less coarse in their manners . . . he conducted himself with great propriety at table, particularly in the observance of those attentions which are chiefly requisite in the presence of women . . .' Eleanor Dark, in *The Timeless Land* (Collins, 1941) produces a very sympathetic portrait of Bennillong.

[11] The Sydney Opera House, designed by the Danish architect, Jørn Utzon, and which began under his supervision, 'involves an almost transcendental concept of architectural imagination.' (John Larkin, Melbourne *Age*, 29 July 1964). On its exposed peninsula the huge structure is sculptural in effect, and contrasts markedly in form with the square skyscrapers of Sydney. The magnificent building was completed and opened in 1973, at a cost exceeding 100 million dollars—subscribed very largely by the public through a series of government lotteries.

Jørn Utzon left Sydney in 1966 as the result of a political controversy. Later work was carried out by architects, Hall, Todd, and Littlemore, and the original engineers, Ove, Arup and Partners. A famous French firm, Boussois, Souchon, Neuvesel provided the glass, laminated both for strength and safety.

The Norman quadripartite nave vault of Durham Cathedral (A.D. 1133) is probably one of the earliest complete stone vaults of the period in Europe.

[12] Sydney Harbour Bridge: Designed by Dr J. J. C. Bradfield, the bridge spans the harbour between Dawes and Milson's Points. The two halves of the bridge were joined, after eight years' construction, in August 1931. The span of the bridge is 503 metres, the top is 133 metres above sea-level, and the shipping clearance 53 metres. The steel used weighs 53 000 tonnes. Sixty thousand or more vehicles use the bridge daily, and it serves 100 million passengers in a year. The structure has been called variously 'a steel jungle' and 'the great coat hanger,' but such metaphors are facetious and half-affectionate. At the Opening on 19 March 1932, a comical diversion occurred when the ceremonial ribbon was prematurely slashed by a mounted demonstrator flourishing his sword.

[13] The Gladesville Bridge, opened by H.R.H. Princess Marina, on 2 October 1964, comprises a concrete arch with a span of 305 metres and a total decking length of 580 metres. The bridge has a central clearance of 41 metres.

[14] 'Cadman's Cottage,' George Street, which once stood almost on the edge of the Cove, will be re-erected in a garden site at Dawes Point. It has been so surrounded by built-up concrete as to be almost lost. It was occupied in 1816 by James Cadman, the official Superintendent of Boats, who had served as boatman to the earliest governors.

[15] The Argyle 'Precinct', containing many historic buildings, is well illustrated and catalogued in *The Heritage of Australia* (Macmillan, 1981). This compendious volume annotates and illustrates such areas all over Australia, in Sydney, for instance, including such fashionable and historic suburbs as Glebe and Paddington; or in Melbourne, Carlton and Fitzroy. Provincial and capital cities are fully listed.

[16] The nine islands are: Fort Denison, Clark, Shark, Garden (between this and the shore at Potts Point is situated the capacious Captain Cook floating dock), Goat, Cockatoo, Spectacle, Snapper, and Rodd. Fort Denison, or Pinchgut, now used as a Tidal Station, recalls the unhappy days of convicts sentenced to shocking confinements. It was also fortified for the defence of Sydney. When the work on the Martello Tower began, Sir William Denison (later Governor 1855–61) wrote (1841): 'I have gone into the question of

the defence of Sydney for the purpose of keeping off much more unpleasant neighbours than the Russians; namely our friends the French and our relations the Americans. The access to this harbour is so easy that unless we have some batteries ready to open upon vessels lying off the town, a few frigates might run in under cover of the night and the first notice I should have of their arrival would be a 32-lb. shot crashing through the walls of my house. Of Russia I have no fear.'

[17] See note 5. Pringle was for some time editor of the *Sydney Morning Herald.*

[18] The Library of New South Wales possesses valuable adjuncts in the Mitchell and Dixson Libraries and Galleries which are repositories, founded on great private collections, for all significant Australiana. In addition to rare volumes on early Australia, many historical documents are housed there.

[19] The Conservatorium of Music building, in its original form, was completed in 1821 as the government mews and servants' quarters, by Francis Greenway, Governor Macquarie's talented architect. Its present purpose, for which interior alterations were necessary, dates back to 1916.

[20] Named after a Mayor of Sydney, in the 1860s. At one end of the tall I.C.I. Building is an interesting piece of applied bronze sculpture, at the other these old Moore Stairs.

[21] The El Alamein Memorial Fountain, a memorial to the Ninth Division of the A.I.F. in the second World War.

[22] Parliament House and the Mint Building: These are the wings remaining from Macquarie's Rum Hospital, completed in 1816, and paid for by the costs of licences granted to import 205 000 litres of rum. Lachlan Macquarie was Governor from December 1809 until December 1821—a period in which Sydney gained much of its architectural character. The hospital which replaced the central building is solid and ornate, but it is reminiscent of Brighton Pier, or the lesser features of the Melbourne Exhibition, without the latter's overall grandeur of design.

[23] Phillip's *Voyage*, 1788, produced by John Stockdale, dedicated to the Marquis of Salisbury—'containing all that is yet known of the Settlement at Sydney Cove.' The poem quoted, 'Visit of Hope to Sydney Cove, near Botany Bay,' is given as 'written by the Author of *The Botanic Garden.*'

[24] Bland's *Journal of Discovery to Port Phillip, New South Wales, by Messrs W. H. Hovell and Hamilton Hume, in 1824 and 1825* (A. Hill, Printer, George Street, Sydney, 1831?).

[25] *The 'Garryowen' Sketches*, by An Old Colonist (M'Kinley & Co., Printers, Queen Street, Melbourne, 1880), were the collected writings previously published in the newspapers.

[26] *Australia as it is*, by F. Lancelott, Mineralogical Surveyor in the Australian Colonies (Colburn and Co., London, 1852).

The discovery of gold in Australia was no isolated occurrence. Chance finds had occurred even in the 1820s. W. B. Clarke, a Sydney geologist discovered gold near Bathurst, and Count Strzelecki and others were enjoined not to reveal their discoveries for fear of causing unrest among the convicts. Edward Hargraves, with Californian experience of gold diggings, recalled the similarity of the Bathurst country, returned there, and discovered payable gold in 1851. Later he received a grant of £10 000 for his discoveries. By the end of 1851, about a million pounds' worth of gold had been taken from Victorian goldfields, and gold-fever was spreading not only through Australia but in many countries overseas. For many years the price of gold was standardised at $31·25 per fine ounce (£15 12s 6d). In the 1980s it fluctuated between $436 and $750 (approx.) per fine ounce. It is hard to translate the £ of 1851 to the $ of the late twentieth century.

[27] Robert Hoddle, Assistant Surveyor-General of New South Wales, came to the infant Melbourne with Governor Bourke in 1837. On Robert Russell's first plan he laid out streets 30 metres wide, dividing the future city into 4-hectare squares. The city streets run N.E.-S.W. and S.E.-N.W., but the main suburban graticule is aligned to the cardinal compass points.

[28] The West Gate Bridge, with an overall length of 2591 metres, and a central span of 336 metres, crosses the lower Yarra, linking the south-western suburbs of Melbourne, and the Geelong Road, directly with the city. It was commenced in 1968 and opened for traffic in November 1978. In October 1970, a section of the bridge under construction fell, with the loss of 35 lives. The cost of the bridge will eventually be met by tolls, the total being amortised in a period of forty years from the opening.

[29] The La Trobe Library, officially opened 6 September 1965, segregating Victorian and Australian historical material from the main library, is the latest of the series that includes the distinguished Mitchell and Dixson Libraries in Sydney, the Battye Library of Perth, Brisbane's Oxley Memorial Library, and the National Library, Canberra.

[30] Cultural Centre: Designed by Architect the late Roy Grounds (who also designed the Academy of Science building in Canberra).

[31] The Sidney Myer Music Bowl is a memorial gift to the City of Melbourne. It com-

memorates the founder of a famous retail store, and a noted Melbourne benefactor. The unique structure of the Bowl comprises a canopy of aluminium-faced laminated panels, suspended upon steel cables, covering a stage of 560 square metres. An audience of more than 2000 may also be sheltered beneath the canopy, but the lovely sloping lawns of the immense excavation can accommodate more than 20 000 people.

[32] Apart from its central position, Young and Jackson's has a special fame in housing the picture 'Chloe,' a nude by Jules Lefebvre. It gained high honours in the Paris Salon of 1876 and was a special attraction at the Melbourne Exhibition of 1880.

[33] In Robin Boyd's *The Australian Ugliness* (F. W. Cheshire, Melbourne, 1960) there is a chapter on Melbourne entitled, 'The Featurist Capital.' It is probable that 'the feature' was originally thought of as an antidote to cold functionalism, although, of course, it has always existed and may be as fitting and beautiful, as it is so frequently unnecessary and unfortunate. I recall a lecture by Le Corbusier in which he said: '. . . the most fitting and functional object ever designed . . . was the human skull. But,' he went on, 'I pray you remember that the Almighty endowed it with features.' Words are necessary; it is a pity that some become so specialised in use as to acquire exclusively unfavourable connotations. Le Corbusier (Charles Edouard Jeanneret, b. 1887) is perhaps best remembered for his 'a house is a machine for living in.'

[34] Captain Cook's Cottage, from Great Ayton, Yorkshire, was presented to the City of Melbourne by Sir Russell Grimwade. It is doubtful whether Captain Cook ever lived in the pleasant cottage, but it is certain that he visited his parents there. Incidentally, one of the early partners in the enterprise with which Grimwade was associated, was Sir Alfred Felton whose Felton Bequest has provided the Melbourne Gallery with a collection unrivalled in Australia. At one time it was said to be the richest art bequest in the world.

[35] The Floating Bridge was conceived and built by A. W. Knight, who later helped direct the affairs of the important Hydroelectric Commission of Tasmania. Its length was 1161 metres comprising linked concrete pontoons with a broad roadway only a metre or so above water-level. It was built in 1943, with an intended life of only ten years. Twenty years later it was still in operation, when the population of the eastern suburbs had risen fivefold to 25 000 (the total population in 1976 was approximately 132 000). The bridge pontoons have been towed away, but they may find other uses.

[36] The Antarctic Division, of the Department of Science and Technology, was transferred from Melbourne to Hobart in 1979–81. It controls the Australian National Antarctic Research Expeditions in Australian Antarctic Territory.

[37] The Tasman Bridge is 1418 metres long, and provides four 3·5 metre traffic lanes, and two 1·5 metre sidewalks. The navigation span at the eastern side is 95 metres, providing for a clear channel of 76 metres width, and a clearance height of 48 metres.

152 000 tonnes of concrete, and 6100 tonnes of steel reinforcing were used. Considerable problems were overcome in bridging the estuary which is up to 37 metres deep, with the bed-rock 15–20 metres lower. On the western side, the basalt ends 305 metres from the bank and major technical difficulties had to be overcome in the sinking of foundations. The bridge is designed to carry 35 000 vehicles per day. It was first opened for traffic in August 1964. On the night of 5 January 1975, a cargo vessel collided with piers of the bridge and caused three spans to fall, with serious loss of life. The bridge was restored by 1977.

[38] Anthony Trollope: *Australia and New Zealand* (Chapman & Hall, London, 1873).

[39] The Royal Society of Tasmania was founded in 1845.

[40] Sir John Franklin (later lost with his North-West Passage Expedition in the Arctic), Lieutenant-Governor of Van Diemen's Land, 1834–43, staged Hobart's first 'aquatic carnival' in 1838. The Regatta has become one of Australia's great annual events. As for the Melbourne Cup, vessels of the Royal Australian Navy have made a tradition of finding exercises each year in the vicinity.

[41] The organ-pipes of Wellington are volcanic columnar formation, of black or buff dolerite similar to the packed vertical hexagonal columns of the Tasman Peninsula.

[42] William Bligh, after his *Bounty* voyage, and other adventures, became Governor of New South Wales in 1806. His stormy career there, and his endless quarrels with John Macarthur, culminated in his arrest by the commanding officer of the New South Wales Corps, Major George Johnston; yet history shows him always to have been a courageous man of principle.

[43] Cook sighted the coast of Van Diemen's Land on 24 January 1777, and sailed for New Zealand on the 30th. Some of his most interesting observations concerning the Australian Aborigines occur in his first volume of *A Voyage to the Pacific Ocean* (the Third Voyage), published in 1785. On 14 February, two years after his visit to Tasmania, Cook was killed by natives at Hawaii; the volume cited was published posthumously.

CHAPTER 12

The New Australia: II

Big eucalypts from little gum-nuts grow—
Where Moreton Bay took Sydney's overflow;
And Adelaide was founded on decisions
Hatched by a fertile brain in Newgate prison!
Where Collins failed, came Batman, Fawkner, Henty
To barter trifles for a land of plenty;
A groundless fear inspired Albany—
While such the haste, that Perth's munificence
Per acre, cost the settler eighteenpence!

—from WIDE HOMELAND

The Rotunda in Elder Park, Adelaide, a fine example of cast-iron filigree; the Festival Centre is in the background

ADELAIDE AND CANBERRA ARE EVEN MORE PLANNED cities than Melbourne, and, as such, are more open, predictable, and unified than Sydney or Hobart. There is a dignified wholeness about central Adelaide's broad sun-drenched squares, its boulevards, malls, and its inner suburbs, supported by an unaffected use of local stone that has survived to the present day. Whereas in the older cities, any unsophisticated use of ashlar is rare and

generally historical, in Adelaide it is plentiful and as natural as her vines, oranges, and peaches. Adelaide and Canberra share, too, a terrestrial rather than a marine flavour, as though they were more conscious of the hills and the plains, the 7·7 million square kilometres that is Australia, than the oceans that separate her from the rest of the world.

Adelaide, of course, is only 10 kilometres from the Gulf of St Vincent, but her river,[1] like that of Canberra, is purely an ornament that helps to make the city beautiful. The visions of Edward Gibbon Wakefield[2] which led to the founding of Adelaide, named after William IV's Queen, preceded the opening of Canberra's first Federal Parliament by almost a century.

Just as Melbourne was given a basic graticule which remains substantially unvaried, so Adelaide received much of her character in her foundation year when Colonel William Light arrived in the *Rapid*, in August 1836, and, in the face of considerable opposition, insisted on the present site on the Torrens[3] and proceeded to lay out a four-square city. From the beginning it was planned to preserve round the future city a belt of open country, originally a 'cannon-shot' in width. This green belt remains to the glory of the city and in the north, on the other side of the Torrens, completely encloses the residential area of North Adelaide.

All the streets of the South Australian capital run north and south, or east and west but are pleasantly interrupted by several tranquil squares which give the city a generosity of open space and sunlight to match that of her nominal perimeter. The parklands themselves are now confined by the sprawl of suburbs that grow constantly from the sea to the Adelaide Hills. Bridges are being widened and new freeways built. Suddenly it seems as though the last decades of the twentieth century promise Greater Adelaide's most fertile period, in which she may put on such growth that only her spacious central city area will be recognisable.

Instead of the tall, straight-grained mountain ash and other easily milled and easily split timbers, South Australia had only the tough, magnificent old redgums, by no means so suitable a material for building, especially when planks were still sawn by hand, as was available in the other States.[4] Accordingly, even without cheap or forced labour, widespread use of the freestones from the uplands was made, with the result that Adelaide learnt early to build from stone, and so avoided the expediency of the eastern States.

The early and continuing stone architecture of Adelaide, both urban and domestic, that remains, gives a more general appearance of old-fashioned stability than is found in any other Australian city. Houses, churches, and city buildings . . . the list retains an attractive admixture of basalt and figured sandstone, with solid old walls and wrought iron.

North Terrace is justly famous for the manner in which it fuses the academic world of the University and the Teachers' College and the general intellectual atmosphere of the Art Gallery, Museum, and Public Library, all set in gardens, with the bustle and commerce of the city. Splendid shade trees and beds of bright flowers bound the city pavements in North Terrace; even more easily than from Sydney's Macquarie Street, and Melbourne's Spring Street, you may exchange the stress of a city for broad lawns by merely crossing the road. If you have time, you may stroll in Elder Park or dine by the lake, with a sweep of water and parkland holding the city at a proper viewing distance, visually enchanting and just pleasantly audible.

From Kings Park, in Perth; on certain days along Melbourne's Yarra down beyond the Music Bowl; and from the edge of Torrens Lake or up by the Light Memorial on Montefiore Hill, quite as often as from the famous more elevated viewpoints of the other capitals, I have found myself thinking, 'Earth has not anything to show more fair . . .'

294

To the traditional stability of Adelaide, for so long reputed to be a calm cathedral city, solid, but as undisturbed as the peace of her summery gardens, the last few decades have added all the visible signs of material change in upward rising city buildings, outspreading suburbs, and an increase of industry. Yet, more significant from a national, and even from a world viewpoint, has been the wonderful success of her two biennial festivals, in alternate years respectively dedicated to the Muses, and to Bacchus.

Adelaide, as with all our cities, has exchanged much of the cacophony of unrestricted traffic for quiet pedestrian malls; in this no city has been more successful. There has been an urbane realisation of the necessity for calm breathing spaces in city squares; in this Adelaide has always led the way. It is no coincidence that such tranquillities have come while many established values were being reconsidered, if not questioned—our attitude to conservation of man's world; to man himself, including Australia's original people. That there are, in each State and, reflecting the world at large, especially in the capitals, industrial and social unrest and, periodically, much unemployment, gives all Australians reason to examine basic tenets, for we are still 'the lucky country'.

It has been suggested on many occasions—I well recall John Masefield saying just this in the old Wilson Hall, when he visited Melbourne in the 1930s—that all the climatic factors aiding ancient Greece to fulfil a special destiny, existed in southern Australia; that from men and women owning the cicada-shrill sunshine and the dry grass, the endless leaping surf on broad uncrowded beaches; from boys and girls walking under the bright southern stars . . . must eventually sound voices dedicated to all the liberal arts; that there would be just such festivals, joyous and spontaneous, as those for which Adelaide has been able to supply both the time and the place.

Something profound and at the same time lighthearted characterises the white assembly of planes that reveals the Festival Centre. It intrigues and it pleases as part of the prismatic decisiveness of so much contemporary sculpture; it is not crowded for space; it may be seen from near and far in its proper setting. Not only at festival time, it houses immense activity; paying audiences in number approaching three-quarters of a million annually, attend an aggregate of a thousand performances. Like the Sydney Opera House, Adelaide's Festival Centre is to be appreciated outside as well as in. The great enchanting ludo-board terraces and coloured blocks—endless places to play, to read, to dream, to rest—of the German sculptor Hajek, are not only attractions for children in their odd-year festivals.

My chapter must be too brief even to summarise the triumphs of music, ballet, opera, drama as well as of the graphic arts, sculpture, and literature that delight the city every second March and, increasingly, attract both national and international talent in many spheres. Someone has suggested that the vision of William Light, who was an artist and musician as well as a surveyor, has at last been fulfilled; but I think he would also be glad to see, looking down over the city from Montefiore Hill, that, with all the mantles and masks of culture, there is plenty of jollity. In the Elder Park the carnival is simultaneous; the Festival also includes dancing and flower girls, flares and torchlight processions, folk singing as well as opera, jazz as well as ballet, world premières and the age-old fun of the fair.

For most of the time since the honest wranglings of Hindmarsh and Gawler, vines have been grown in the Barossa Valley, 65 kilometres northeast of the city. Over 150 or more square kilometres they make virile square or linear patterns that are highly productive under the hot sun. It is not, of course, the only wine-producing area of Australia, nor possibly even the best; nor is Adelaide the only city which might have staged a Festival; but perhaps the old Silesian love of folk-songs and pageantry, and its curious,

Top: The festival city of Adelaide, seen from the north. In the foreground is the University Sports Ground and the winding Torrens River. *Bottom:* The dominating white structure is Adelaide's Festival Centre complex; in the foreground is Government House, at the left Parliament House, and at the top of the picture Adelaide's Railway Station.

Facing page, top and bottom: The Barossa Valley, South Australia, produces over one-third of Australia's wines. The first settlers in 1842 were Silesian Lutherans, and the Lutheran influence is still evident in the 16-kilometre long valley

sincere, serious belief in dignified merry-making was retained round the avenued focus of Nuriootpa, Angaston, and Tanunda, where, every second year, for three days, the streets are full of revels.

It is not easy to stage imported pageantry under the full Australian sunlight without its seeming rather overdone and faintly ridiculous. But there are all sorts of genuine grape-picking and grape-pressing functions, and time for dances and balls and exhibitions, the singing of choirs, and strange mixtures of the atmosphere of Sherwood Forest and the medieval courts . . . and, of course, there is wine-tasting. About the whole Vintage Festival there seems to be less of the rapacity that characterises the usual trade fair or the margins of the great agricultural shows which annually prove that the cities are only the outlets and counting-houses for the country at large.

No Australian city can boast a real river except Brisbane. And that is a great, brown stream that may become angry and swollen, though it may never again tear away the bridges and eat away part of the city as it did, in 1869 and 1893, before it had been estimated and confined in a dredged channel.

> . . . but I think that the river
> Is a strong brown god—sullen, untamed and intractable,
> Patient to some degree, at first recognized as a frontier;
> Useful, untrustworthy, as a conveyor of commerce;
> Then only a problem confronting the builder of bridges . . .[5]

I always feel that Brisbane is still dominated by her river, though now it runs in an ordered channel under half-a-dozen steel or concrete bridges, describing a great 'W' below Indooroopilly, and a fine 'M' to cover the two arms of the City and Merthyr almost 30 kilometres upstream from Moreton Bay, the first settlement founded about ten years before Batman considered a village at the head of Port Phillip Bay.[6]

Up on Wickham Terrace is the old windmill of 1829 which failed to work as such for eight miserable years until a mechanical fault was corrected. In those bitter convict years the tower was used as a treadmill, and occasionally as a suitable eminence from which to hang the lonely malefactors, black or white, who jibbed too strenuously at the system. It has had many uses since, including that of Observatory, signal station, store-house, and radio tower.

There are not many such old buildings left in Brisbane, but Wickham Terrace is an excellent vantage point for overlooking the colourful city and suburbs that have grown on the ten low spurs that twist the river between the Oxley district and the sea. An even better eminence is Mt Coot-tha from which one may distinguish the whole sweep of the valleys from the Darling Downs to the big islands that virtually make Moreton Bay.

Brisbane is prodigal of space and includes almost 24 square kilometres of parklands within the municipal boundaries; it spreads languidly, flooding the broad acres and slowly rising up the hill-slopes, as though gravity exerted a greater force nearer Capricorn. There are, of course, a number of modern four-square buildings—tall twin, conjoined glass towers, and that vast pile at the corner of Greek and Charlotte Streets, reflecting the city broken in marvellous patterns, and the river front freeway looping round tall blocks, from any viewpoint like the setting for a gigantic game of snakes and ladders. Still, the main city area from a height or a distance has something of the general anonymity of the modern commercial centre. Graceful parallel structures, each springing five clean-cut arched spans over Brisbane's river, constitute the Captain Cook Bridge (1972). Like Sydney's older bridge of the same name, across the Georges River, it exceeds 500 metres in length, and is of pre-stressed concrete.

A quite astonishing *tour de force* exists in the Brisbane City Hall which surmounts a huge classical complex, faceted with fluted Ionic columns rising above a romanesque arcade, with a square clock tower and campanile 94 metres high. In the centre of the building, facing King George Square, a heavy Corinthian portico, rising from a pediment elevated to the same level as that of the Ionic columns, with a deeply sculptured tympanum is appropriate to the 'finest city hall in Australia.' The raised colonnade has ample classical precedent, but in the case of the Brisbane City Hall, it has the effect of resting an entire building on an elevated crypt. The down-to-earth columns and pilasters of, for example, the modest Customs House, or of Adelaide's Parliament House may seem aesthetically more satisfying.

Although the general effect from close by is rather overpowering — as though Brisbane's motto, *Meliora sequimur*, in popular translation, 'We aim at higher things,' were displayed too literally — from most parts of the city the dominating square tower is very impressive. Similarly, from the Square, it is possible to isolate the civic temple from the tall tower, and again, fronted by palms in their proper latitude, it is admirable. Just across Victoria Bridge is the modern cultural centre, housing art gallery, State library, performing arts centre . . . the lot, all in a garden setting overlooking the Brisbane River, and with a 60-metre *jet d'eau* in the best Geneva (and Canberra) tradition. The growth of art galleries, concert halls, and 'cultural centres' in the 1980s is some sort of extension of the energy that saw the foundation of new universities in the previous two decades.

It would not be difficult to list a great many interesting and varied architectural features of Brisbane; there are churches ranging, from conventional gothic to featured 'austeric,' government buildings in solid Victorian renaissance, a considerable quantity of blended red brick and yellow stone, a topless vestal temple housing the eternal 'Flame of Remembrance' of the Anzac Memorial, an eagle-headed column commemorating the contribution of the United States' servicemen in the second World War, and some spacious and unified modern freestone in the University of Queensland. There is also the fine market at Rocklea[7] . . . but these might exist in any great rich city. Old Government House (1860–62), in sandstone and Brisbane 'tuff' (porphyry), with its double-columned arcade, and the older first unofficial governor's residence, Capt. John Wickham's Newstead House — now restored as a colonial museum — are worth seeking out. Some fine old buildings, such as Bellevue Hotel, have been demolished, inevitably, and many mourn the houses on stilts, once claimed as Australia's principal contribution to tropical architecture.

Brisbane's special character rests in her turgid, serpentine river, her girdered bridges and — some would say more than in anything else — in her palms and sub-tropical trees, especially the purple jacarandas, the flaming poincianas, and the poinsettias. Brisbane's climate is also the most equable of those of all capital cities: she has no frosts, and her warmest temperatures only exceed those of the other capitals in winter; she has fewer heat-waves than either Melbourne or Adelaide. The Commonwealth Games complex of 1982, and the manner in which the contests were organised, was in the tradition of the Melbourne Olympics of 1956.

Queenslanders have a reputation for an easy, indolent manner, a languid interest in anything that does not directly concern them, for unconventional dress and speech, and for generosity and hospitality. Some of these qualities seem to have rubbed off on the city itself.

Darwin is the only city on the north coast of Australia, on a tropical littoral hard to define, for, greatly indented, it measures at least 7000 kilometres from Cape York to Broome. Otherwise, only the small but vital ports of Derby and Wyndham, between them supporting only a few thousand people,[8] ship the rich produce of the Kimberleys.

299

Top: The Brisbane Anzac Memorial was built by public subscription and dedicated on Armistice Day, 1930. The Memorial sits in Anzac Square, the subject of much debate regarding its redevelopment potential. In the background can be seen the Central Railway Station. *Bottom:* Brisbane's General Post Office on Queen Street, erected in the 1870s. It was built on the site of the Female Convict Factory

Top: A general view of Brisbane, with the City Hall tower (91·5 metres high) in the centre. To the right of the tower can be seen the dome of the circular concert hall.
Bottom: King George Square, with the Brisbane City Hall in the background

Struck by a hurricane of appalling force on 24–25 December 1974, nine-tenths of the city was destroyed, with the loss of many lives. About 30 000 people, two-thirds of the population, were flown to southern cities; a national disaster organisation was set up by the Commonwealth Government, and, from all over the country, Australians subscribed aid of various kinds.

Less than ten years after Cyclone Tracy—as the hurricane was called—Darwin had made a major recovery, her population greater than ever, and the city almost completely rebuilt.

Port Darwin was discovered in 1839 by John Lort Stokes who, since 1825, had been an officer on the *Beagle*. The site was named by Captain J. C. Wickham after the great biologist, Charles Darwin, who had sailed with them on an earlier voyage. However, the settlement, for many years—until 1911—to be known as Palmerston, was established by G. W. Goyder,[9] the Surveyor-General of South Australia, and his intrepid team, in 1869, to hold one end of the Overland Telegraph Line which, after immense difficulties, by 1872 would be stretched across the continent from south to north.

Its value was incalculable, for it linked Port Augusta, 2900 kilometres distant, with a newly laid submarine cable to Java—which already had telegraphic contact with Asia and Europe. For the first time, in 1872, amid great celebrations, messages were transmitted, and Australia was no longer dependent on monthly shipping services for news of the world.

Communication, the supreme quality of human existence, made Darwin. After many years, co-axial cables, high frequency radio, and communication satellites have supplanted the old Java connection. Still, though some of the international jets may now bypass her, Darwin is the estuary of aerial tributary routes, outward from Australia and inward from the world. Still, occasionally, small planes fly in almost at the end of their tether, just as in the heroic days when Ross and Keith Smith landed with the first airmail ever to arc the hemispheres. The 'boat-people', too, have come, refugees from Viet Nam, nearer by sea than any of our southern capitals.

Like so many other Australian cities, though the primary inaugural reasons have decreased or disappeared, Darwin has an assured and growing strength from marshalling and distributing a once undreamed-of potential. For Darwin, it was the wealth of her tropical seas and hinterland, ranging from uranium, iron, and many other metallic ores, to beef cattle, prawns, pearl-shell, and fish. Yearly, Darwin attracts more and more lotus-eaters to her brilliant, palm-barred shores, to her assured sunlight, and a whole range of excitements from crocodiles to casinos, in a land with the fastest growing population, the highest birth rate, and the lowest death rate in Australia, and where perfect weather coincides in time with the southern winter.

Alone of all cities in Australia, Darwin, for obvious reasons, has not built high towers; her buildings do not exceed ten or twelve storeys, and most are of three or four, occupying correspondingly larger ground areas. Three cyclones have devastated the town in the last century, at about forty year intervals, and each has taught her more about hurricane-proof building. She shares not dissimilar problems with some of our Antarctic bases.

The second World War brought to Darwin, alone of all Australian cities, death and destruction from the air. Hundreds of Japanese aircraft bombed the town repeatedly, with heavy consequent loss of life.

It's not function alone that has caused Darwin to rise from each disaster. She is truly an Austral-Asian city. She is closer to Djakarta than to Brisbane, Sydney, or Melbourne; to the Philippines than to any Australian capital. Her citizens include men and women of all nations—European, Asian, and Aboriginal. She is capital of an independent territory that has recognised, more fully than any other, its debt to, and the rights of, Australia's original owners. Before 1990, it is probable that at last the railway will link her with

Alice Springs and the south. Assuredly, she knows her place on the surface of the globe, and it's prepared to contribute to its benesphere.

Flying from London, you could be in Latvia, the Ukraine, Finland, Rumania, Greece, Algeria, Morocco, or Iceland . . . and still have travelled a shorter distance than between Perth and the nearest city of at least her size. In population she is a little smaller than Adelaide or Brisbane, about twice the size of Hobart, and a fifth that of Sydney or Melbourne.[10] Parts of Cuba, Texas, and Hudson Bay are closer to New York than Perth is to Adelaide. If you wish to consider the width of the Australian continent in the same sort of terms—say, in a great circle route skimming the head of the Bight from Perth to Brisbane—the distance is a little greater than from London to Cairo, or from New York to Caracas or Mexico City.

Perth has been called the most isolated city of its size in the world.[11] And whatever problems may exist for her in this fact, Australians in the other capitals consider her distance a disadvantage. Mary Durack once described Perth as 'sighing for the progress she at once envied and despised'. Certainly, until certain links with the eastern states and the outside world were established, the 'tyranny of distance' made Perth one of the most isolated of the world's cities. In 1877, the telegraph connection was made with Adelaide, Melbourne, and Sydney; the Trans-Continental Railway linked Port Augusta with Kalgoorlie in 1917. It was not until late in the 1960s that the east-west road was fully sealed. The Indian-Pacific Railway, a joint-State venture, now runs 3961 kilometres between Sydney and Perth via Port Pirie and Broken Hill. Perth is the civilised capital of a State whose potential is still being revealed, whose 'European' history is older by more than a century and a half than that of any other,[12] and whose flora is unique. Except Brisbane, she is the most northerly of the Australian capitals[13] and has a warm, dry Mediterranean climate and more clear days than any of the other capitals.

Dirk Hartog, in his *Eendracht*, touched the most westerly coasts in 1616, and was followed by other Dutchmen including Vlamingh (*Geelvink*), 1696, who removed the weather-scarred pewter plate[14] nailed to a tree by Dirk Hartog and, as we have seen, put Perth on the edge of history by naming the Swan River. In 1829, Captain James Stirling's gallant colony was established and, for nearly twenty years struggled to break even. Close to the period, the following opinion was stated:

> Western Australia was founded in 1829, on the banks of the Swan River, by a party of gentlemen who desired to establish a colony without the aid of convict labour. It is the least active and progressive of the Australian colonies. Its lands generally are so poor and sandy, that great difficulties are experienced in procuring pasturage for the comparatively few sheep and cattle possessed by the settlers. Its mineral riches are not great, or if so, they are not yet developed, as no mines of metals or valuable minerals are at present worked. Of late years the settlers have increased their trade from the exportation of guano and of sandal wood, a plentiful and valuable indigenous timber. The colony, however, is ill-suited for a settlement of enterprising British emigrants.[15]

Men like Thomas Peel risked all they had in the venture, and were bitterly disappointed, but Stirling's enthusiasm, leadership, and courage sustained the colony which was islanded by desert sands and by the Indian Ocean.

Between 1850, when the population first exceeded that of the optimistic first year, and 1868, Perth, at the request of the colonists, became a last Australian penal settlement, and maintained this status after transportation of convicts had ceased elsewhere. There can be little doubt that the additional labour helped develop the south-west; by agreement with the British Government, the number of convicts was equalled by that of free passage-paid immigrants.

Top: Darwin in the 1980s; an aerial view of Australia's northern outpost. *Bottom:* The busy port of Darwin; over a quarter of a million tonnes of cargo are moved through the port annually. *Facing page:* Smith Street Mall, Darwin. On the left is the restored Victoria Hotel which was ravaged by Cyclone Tracy in 1974

Some of the qualities engendered by the struggle to found an English settlement on the Swan River may be the continuing ethos of Perth. If there is any mistrust or envy of 'the Eastern States' it is quite impersonal, for visitors from every State in Australia, no less than those from overseas, are quickly conscious of Perth's hospitality and friendliness. In discovering and transforming the beautiful, hot dry land; in exploring the harsh, high shield, arid and unsubmerged for longer than almost anywhere else on earth; in the finding of the richest goldfields,[16] and in the comprehension of basic needs in sustenance and comradeship that nuggets could never buy, men and women were strengthened in their purpose and confirmed in their humanity. In the versatility and resourcefulness which—while common to all the colonies—developed most strongly in the most isolated, was blended a calm self-sufficiency that has tempered openheartedness with dignity and possibly still preserved a less materialistic sense of values.

Architecturally, like Sydney, with whom she vies in the beauty of her setting, Perth has two faces, that of a contemporary city of soaring concrete, steel, and glass; and that of an aesthetically attractive colonial settlement built in local stone. In the opulent rectangle between Wellington Street and St Georges Terrace she shows both; in Fremantle, at the mouth of the Swan, 18 kilometres downstream are the West's oldest buildings, now, as those in the city, likely to be preserved.

The prismatic towers multiply; they reflect the vast mineral wealth, discovered and exploited in the post-war period. During that time the State's population has more than doubled,[17] and that of Perth almost trebled. It now approaches its first million; no Australian city or state has grown more swiftly. Perth, with the driest summers and wettest winters of any Australian city, with an annual arts festival, a great circular entertainment centre, and an art gallery both very 'contemporary' in style, with every other facility the east may offer, but in better weather and cleaner air, need no longer sigh. Someone said, 'She is every Australian's second city!'

From Perth, backed by the Darling Scarp, beyond which four-fifths of the State is virtual desert, it is tempting to trace back to its physical sources the country's immense prosperity. Nickel and gold from the Kalgoorlie area; gold from distant Telfer; iron from Pilbara, Yampi, Tom Price, Newman—immense, seemingly inexhaustible deposits in the harsh red wilderness; and diamonds, too—apparently of great value,[18] and thousands of pearls and half-pearls, round and baroque—all from the illimitable north-west; then there is still timber, marvellous jarrah and karri, milled, and there is much wood-chipping,[19] and the mining of bauxite from south of Perth; wheat from 3 million hectares of arable land, also apples and wine; wealth from 34 million sheep, more than 2 million cattle; the produce of the Ord, Kununurra, Wyndham, in the north-west; oil and gas from the North-West Continental Shelf. Slowly the scene would change, from the temperate south to the tropical north, from the golden beaches of the Indian Ocean to the stark, terrible beauty of the deserts—the Gibson, the Great Victoria, and the Great Sandy, beyond the Stirlings, the Glengarrys, and the Hamersleys. And what wonders in passing! Great gorges of the Fitzroy, a noble Baobab, the Wolf Creek Meteorite Crater, probably the world's second largest. We might stand silent, at Djilgu, or some other overhanging wall, out of Dampier, and wonder; think of the people who had different values, who shared equally what they thought important.

Facing the clear shallows of tranquil Perth Water, across a broad parkland, from any high vantage point, the sun-drenched city may seem wholly modern. Senior to both Melbourne and Adelaide, Perth reveals historic relics: fine stone and brick buildings ranging from the old Round House on Arthur Head (1830), constructed as a gaol only a year after Captain Fremantle's annexation

306

(2 May 1829), to Perth's Victorian Gothic Government House (1861), and the odd but attractive Town Hall (1867–71), with everything from lancet windows and battlements to classical Corinthian columns. In the area bounded by St Georges Terrace, Barrack Street, William Street, and the waterfront are several other historic buildings. The earlier ones—Perth's Town Hall, the Barracks Arch, at the west end of St Georges Terrace, and Government House, are mostly of brick. E. Y. W. Henderson's notable museum building at Fremantle (originally an asylum), as many old houses, hotels, and courthouses were of sandstone, or of limestone.

All visitors are attracted by Perth's crowded Hay Street Mall and its tributary arcades, including the pseudo-Tudor London Court (1937) which, it must be said, successfully captures an unusually sunny old-world atmosphere. The city is up-to-date, yet comprehensible, with excellent roads and bridges, and a firm desire to refurbish what is old and to increase what is new. The Narrows Interchange, ribbons of steel and concrete, matches other such apparently essential extravagances.

Of Australia's score of universities,[20] the proliferation of which was a marked movement of the 1960s and 1970s, Perth possesses two, the Murdoch University (1975), named after one of Perth's most famous and well-loved scholars and essayists, and the University of Western Australia (1913), at Nedlands, on the Swan, about 4 kilometres downstream from Perth, but well connected all the way by parklands to heights overlooking the city. The University of Western Australia is distinguished by some of the most suitable and attractive stone architecture in the land. Again, as in parts of the University of Queensland, the buildings are reminiscent of the style of the old Spanish missions down the Californian coast, and of their Romanesque and Islamic antecedents. But, certainly, we discover in their shadowed arcades, their warm stone, whether smooth or rusticated, in their clean, uncluttered lines, something that is certainly Mediterranean, that is assuredly right under the golden western sunlight. If, originally, the people of Perth were a little uneasy about the buildings which rose as a result of the munificent bequest of Sir Winthrop Hackett—breaking away from the familiar Victorian revivals of Gothic and Renaissance—they since have rightly become proud of their senior university. Once distinguished by being the only 'free' university in the British Commonwealth, the University of Western Australia has expanded its courts and cloisters and its magnificent garden setting surrounding the Octagon Theatre and the Winthrop Hall, with its 'landmark' clocktower.

A city is never so becoming as when reflected in water or viewed from under the arched boughs of a great tree. If there is some elevation, so much the better. These elements exist in varying combinations in all Australian capitals, but nowhere more felicitously than in Perth. Stirling seems to have chosen his site almost entirely for its beauty, for the broad placid waters of the estuary are too shallow for commerce but ideal for white sails and relaxation. And still Vlamingh's swans are mirrored in its quiet reaches.

The climb up to Kings Park, a reserve of natural bushland more than 400 hectares in extent, where some of the distinctive Western Australian flora may still be seen, reveals the quiet, sunny city beyond the clever geometrical freeways[21] and the Narrows Bridge, a sweep of water that floats the tall white buildings, and contrasts with the soft distance of the Darling Ranges. There is nowhere in Australia where I like meeting a friend more for an *al fresco* meal than in the restaurant in Kings Park on Perth's Mt Eliza. How often one recalls in Kings Park the words of Sir John Forrest, spoken in 1879. 'This will enable the children a thousand years hence to see what the bush was like when Stirling came to found a city.'

How all those lonely, uncertain bridgeheads grew! All the primary coastal

Top: The Perth city skyline at night, taken across Perth Water from South Perth. Perth earned the name 'City of Lights' when it left its lights on all night to aid an early U.S.A. space mission. *Bottom:* The Barrack's Archway, all that is left of the original Tudor style, Flemish bond brickwork, constructed between 1863 and 1867

Top: The floral clock at Kings Park; most of the 400 hectares of parkland is untended scrubland, famous for its wildflowers in the spring. *Bottom:* London Court was built in the 1930s and gives a sixteenth-century atmosphere to the arcade

colonies had attained the dignity of cities, and sent out tenuous roads, railways, and telegraphs, forming a kind of complex continental consciousness within a hundred years of the First Fleet's arrival; however, so vast the land, and disparate the lights in the darkness, that it had taken more than forty years, often egged on by fears of French colonisation, even to lay claim to 'all the territory outside New South Wales.'[22] It was not until 1803 that Matthew Flinders' circumnavigation had finally proved that Australia was one great island; another sixty years were to pass before the State boundaries were fixed, by which time the majority of the States had responsible government.[23]

It is almost incredible, looking back, that ultimately the boundaries of the States should have become barriers, with customs duties, separate postage stamps, and interstate wrangling over riparian ownership and bridges. However, fifty years after Earl Grey had first proposed a General Assembly of Australia,[24] the Commonwealth of Australia came into being, on and after the first day of January 1901.[25]

A federal capital existed in men's minds from the 'creation time' of the Commonwealth: explorers, convicts, pioneers, settlers, roadbuilders, linesmen, legislators . . . all these, and their women, had spun a web of communication, denser around the coast and in the more fertile south, taut and tenuous over the mallee and mulga, through the whole Mercator grid which had previously existed over inchoate space within the shoreline connecting the capes and bays of first contact. The foundation stones of a federal capital territory were laid by Major Mitchell, Hume and Hovell, Leichhardt. Forrest, Eyre, Burke and Wills, Sturt, Stuart . . . as much as by Matthew Flinders, George Bass, or James Cook, who outlined fact in a whole hemisphere of fantasy.

The federal capital had been started long before ceremonial blocks were set on Capital Hill by the Governor-General, the Prime Minister, and the Minister of State for Home Affairs, on a hot March day in 1913;[26] long before even a site had been found, or a locality determined.[27] Who knows how long was the period of gestation? Canberra was conceived slowly, but it was born big. Not for a federal capital the earth track and bark hut, the general store of split palings, the garrison, or the gallows; but a splendid white city reflecting the maturity of a nation.

Perhaps the truth of the matter is that Canberra was born as a vision possessing dimensions rather than detail. A worldwide competition was held to see who might best explore and chart the vision, and this was won, as all Australians know, by a Chicago architect and landscapist, Walter Burley Griffin.[28] He discovered in the contours of hills and valleys a series of foci round which concentric avenues and radial roads made a complex but unified pattern. He delineated the central areas of the broad valley of the Molonglo, a tributary of the Murrumbidgee. The entire region comprised levels close to 600 metres above the sea. Visualised by Griffin was the dam below the old mansion which would fulfil its destiny by becoming Government House; there was a wonderful bounding bunyip of a lake, crossed by bridges radial from Capital Hill,[29] where eventually one of the most noble centres of any garden city in the world would gleam as white as the snow on the surrounding foothills of Kosciusko.[30]

Griffin also descried the place in the plan of the discreet, traditional, and highly respectable pioneer church of St John. He did not focus all the surrounding future; but, across the visionary lake would be the Parliament Houses—both of them, the temporary and the permanent . . . It would stand at the foot of Capital Hill where, among the ancient scribbly gums,[31] near the extraordinary inconformity in the ancient strata, the symbolic stones of the future capital were to be laid. The future would modify his vision.

The fabric, the size, the wealth, the sheer bulk of steel and stone that is Canberra today is a function of the population of Australia, just as much as the spread of suburbs along the beaches or into the foothills of any of our cities. 'For here we have no continuing city but we seek one to come.' The Pauline text on a grave in the churchyard of St John, so often quoted as though it had been a prophetic forecast, is, in the same sense, both true and false when applied to the present federal capital. The primary plan and its modifications—the mapping of the vision—have crystallised sufficiently to provide continuity for a thousand years. Though Capital Hill[32] become a veritable citadel of marble, it will still be the centre of concentric circles and radial spokes; the lake will float white pleasure craft; tall obelisks and massive memorials will still enshrine solemn records and memories of courage and tragedy;[33] and, doubtless, the loveliness of a million trees blossoming in spring and changing colour in autumn will remain.

But there will always be a Canberra yet to come, for a city without a future must be dead. Every wonder has its day, and becomes part of the accepted scene; acceptance, alas, blunts criticism, and both praise and blame. The Australian Academy of Science, that straddles a circular building and dips fourteen semi-circular arches into a surrounding moat;[34] the Administration and Treasury buildings; the Australian National University, now comprising fifty units by the West Lake, between the Civic Centre and Black Mountain; most of the embassies; the Mount Stromlo Observatory;[35] the complex of the Commonwealth Scientific and Industrial Research Organisation, the headquarters of innumerable government authorities, and the War Memorials; these and so much else become old.

Now there are, still in the focus of opinion, the National Library, mainly in ashlar,[36] the High Court and the National Gallery, solid, silent, prismatic structures which attempt to blend an appreciation of function with that of design. The trouble with concrete and steel is that they may achieve the impossible, piling together huge masses to capture intriguing lights and shadows. Just as the bulldozers on Capital Hill can effortlessly remove mountains, so the architects of the late twentieth can too easily cast roofs and walls, with any geometrical featurism they fancy, adding platforms and obelisks, jumbling together cubes and piercing them with lightwells and wall-high apertures, stressing here a buttress, there a recession, and often facing surfaces with natural stone that denies their true nature. The same virtuosity allows the towering carillon on the shores of the lake, though this may be most successful in its simplicity; just as, some would consider, the library is more satisfying from without than the gallery. And, from within, the gallery has been criticised for its lack of natural lighting, and for the super-human height of its walls. Many lively trees, and the jet-fountain leaping 130 metres to remember Captain Cook; the moving waters of the lake and a sail skimming up one of its reaches; the fluttering of flags and banners, and plenty of animated cars and people, relieve what some have called a mortuary air. It is true that trees frequently soften and screen the rather empirical architecture of some of the sixty embassies, and of the innumerable arcades and buildings on stilts.

Most cities, with age, become more concentrated and centralised, sending up their towers to obtain more floor space where little uncovered ground remains. Then, when the traffic becomes too dense, it is excluded, and pedestrian malls give space back to people who must park their cars further away, and even, perhaps, use public transport to reach them.

Canberra is not like that; it is designed to be disparate; it has built a dozen malls and shopping centres, including Belconnen, north-west of Black Mountain, reportedly the biggest, most advanced, automated shopping centre in the southern hemisphere. Canberra has no 'down-town', no absolute centre.

The national capital is a vast maze, and when you come to the edge of its

311

Top: Canberra City, a panoramic view from Mount Ainslie. *Bottom:* The Carillon and its promenade on an autumn morning

Top: A Japanese submarine in front of the Australian War Memorial: the memorial is visited by over half a million people annually and has what is regarded as Australia's largest art collection in addition to its relics, books, and film. *Bottom left:* The National Library is designed to eventually house 11 million volumes. *Bottom right:* The Commonwealth Avenue Bridge over Lake Burley Griffin links Capital Hill with Canberra City

newest suburb, if you are not lost on the way, there will already be set out in curved concrete pavements, all services at the ready, the permissible limits of the next extension of housing. Unlike in four-square graticuled cities like Melbourne or Adelaide, there is no hope for finding your way without a map. It is impossible to 'run your northing (or any other direction) down'.

Few Canberra residents, even, easily find their way beyond their local malls and shopping centres, their places of work, the Civic Centre, Parliament House, the great national amenities already mentioned, and, of course, the Telecom Tower on Black Mountain, from the galleries and the revolving restaurant of which, may be obtained outstanding views of a city which so becomes comprehensible as a vast disparate metropolis, extending in tongues one may never penetrate. In 1980, not without vocal criticism mourning the great natural beauty of the bush-clad heights and their clear skyline, the tower, rising 195 metres above the summit, received the first of hundreds of thousands of visitors.

The National Gallery, opened by Queen Elizabeth II in October 1982, houses a coherent collection of recent and contemporary Australian painting, and some proclaimed masterpieces of modern art from overseas, such as the controversial *Blue Poles*, by Jackson Pollock, the Léger *Trapeziste*, and *Birds in Space*, exquisite marble abstractions by Constantin Brancusi. Very valuable donations of Australian painting have been made to the gallery, including hundreds of works by Arthur Boyd, and the Ned Kelly series by Sidney Nolan.

At this period in the creation of major public collections, the works of innumerable artists, even representatives of some Schools, may virtually never be acquired. Paintings by some of the earlier Australians such as Conder, Buvelot, Roberts, and of some of the topographical artists, are rarely on the market; by far the majority are already in public galleries. It has been suggested that some of millions spent on the modern overseas masters might have been better spent by creating a superb, and completely represent-ative, display of full-size copies and reproductions, virtually indistinguishable from the originals, covering not only the best of the collections of all the Australian capitals and provincial towns, but of the great galleries abroad. By this means Canberra might hold a marvellous synthesis, though, of course philosophic, rather than aesthetic considerations are involved. It is a fact that, although there are undoubted satisfactions in possessing a First Folio Shakespeare, no one ever appreciated *Hamlet* more by such ownership. It is possible for a reproduction of the *Mona Lisa* to appear identical with the original at an ordinary viewing distance, for an El Greco to be fully appreciated a world away from Toledo or Madrid. Moreover, original contemporary art might be encouraged by the scheme.

Visitors to Canberra, from all over Australia and overseas, outnumber the local residents by ten to one. It is, of course, a unique complex of people and buildings whose essential functions are government, the Public Service of and to a nation, Australia's security, and the maintenance of good relations with the rest of the world. To these are added ancillary attractions and virtues, cultural, academic, aesthetic, and a whole army of tradesmen and purveyors, teachers, doctors, transport workers, lawyers, writers and artists of various kinds. Social status and wealth are important in Canberra; without one or the other, life is drab. Poverty, where it does exist is harsher and harder to hide than in the other cities.

Canberra has been described by Donald Horne, in *The Lucky Country*, as 'a power complex of officials isolated from the Australian people,' as the 'centre of the administrative power game'; it has also been called 'the most un-Australian city in the Commonwealth.' These may all be partly true, for a city that exists as a federal capital cannot be representative of the general tenor of the Australian way of life; the other part of truth may include her best and deepest purposes.

Capital Hill, in the very centre of Canberra, is a scene of great activity. With the completion of the new Parliament House, in 1988, to mark the bi-centenary of the arrival of the First Fleet, the stresses of government and the corridors of power will be transferred from the old, crowded building standing in the foreground, between Administration and Treasury, and what has seemed a symbol of Canberra for almost sixty years will disappear. But Capital Hill, with its arresting discontinuity in the basic Silurian strata, which makes of cities and men, forms and figments as ephemeral as the massed clouds over the Brindabellas, will not entirely disappear. I have camped on Capital Hill in years past; I liked its ant-ridden earth, scribbly gums, native grasses, and natural rock. Some will abide, and there are, I suppose, other places from which it will still be possible to find *terra australis originata.* Only in Canberra, of all the cities I have mentioned, may you sense the vast, half-settled, half-charted continent. Melbourne, Sydney . . . all the capitals of the States are sea-board cities, civilised by ships and foreign men. Here, in Canberra, you are suddenly conscious of the great, blue-distanced dry continent which will never be fully tamed.

Although all Australian State capitals were founded before the Industrial Revolution had gathered much impetus—James Watt's most important steam-engine improvements had been invented only between Cook's landing and the arrival of the First Fleet—and therefore show felicitous vestiges of the prevailing Georgian and Regency styles, they were still small, in a continent that supported a population averaging, up until the end of the nineteenth century, less than 'one person to the square mile'.[37] There was ample room for expansion and endless need for expediency. The idea of individual home ownership, with garden plot in front, and a backyard, was a natural corollary of freedom. And individual freedom was a burning torch, ignited by the friction of an age of squalor, which could flare in Australia while it only smouldered in Europe.

Today we hear almost constant voices decrying the appalling ugliness of the mass achievement in Australia in the age of the common man. Brilliant essays[38] have been written on the Australian ugliness, the Australian luck, the Australian smugness, and the Australian discord. It is usually stated that Australia follows the trends of America rather than of Europe, but that even in her note of imitation, sophistication is lost and improprieties are magnified. Most people who read these criticisms agree with them; those who disagree do not read works on aesthetics, but they will follow any accepted standard of which they are conscious. Like most other progress, the improvement of taste becomes a matter of the education of children. Fortunately the education of the educators in Australia is proceeding apace, and teachers are becoming familiar with the best critical opinions. Less frequently expressed are the reasons, the extenuating circumstances, and the cures . . . all of which exist.

When the Great Melbourne exhibition of 1888 was mooted to celebrate the hundredth anniversary of the arrival of the First Fleet, it already had the building provided for its precursor of 1880. With the necessary extensions, it expanded to cover an area of 15 hectares—this in a city only fifty years old. The most extensive electric lighting ever used for a public function was installed; hundreds of kilometres of wiring and thousands of bulbs lit by power generated by special steam engines were set up for the occasion. The people of Melbourne were enchanted. The idea that soon they might have electric lighting in streets and houses ran triumphantly through the town, outstripping the pauser, aesthetics. The telegraph, too! In 1877, just eleven years before, telegraphic communication had become possible between all

Top left: Sculpture garden, Australian National Gallery. *Top right:* Sculpture garden with High Court building in background. *Bottom:* The High Court viewed through a sculpture. *Facing page, top:* High Court building and waterway. *Bottom:* Australian National Gallery

316

the capital cities of a new continent twenty-five times the area of Great Britain and Ireland. In the year after the exhibition, it became possible to travel by rail all the way from Adelaide to Brisbane. In the interests of lighting, power, and communications, the network of metal—wire, cable, rail—was strung right across the continent. My childhood home in Melbourne was electrically lit thirty years before anyone got round to stringing wires into my pseudo-Georgian stucco rooms a few kilometres north of London.

There will come a time when every overhead wire will be pulled down, and all power and telephone installations join the discreet water mains and sewers underground. The cost at present for this dewebbing of the skies is three to four times that of overhead transmission; the sooner it can be met, in every Australian city, the better. But the day will come when one of the major causes of ugliness, not only the 'loops and tangles of overhead wires,' but the horrible dead posts and standards, visually so redundant, will disappear, and with them, doubtless, a great area of acquiescence in lesser ugliness. Had the population of Greater Sydney or of Greater Melbourne been that of Greater London, most of the wire would already be gone. Ultimately, this particular example of expediency which, on the credit side, has made our cities and suburbs among the most brilliantly lit in the world, will no longer be tolerated. The inevitable process will be speeded by every voice raised in protest; and though none may feel sufficiently strongly to have his light, power, and phones cut off in the meantime, many will continue to criticise aerial insulation until it is used only for high voltage major transmission lines, where it achieves a certain dignity.

Hoardings, posters, and stickers, blatant and rampant, disfigure our cities and suburbs; the meaningless frames for electric signs occupy our sight for much longer than the strident, flashing vulgarities they bear. It is our own fault; we tolerate them. We permit advertising companies to erect huge billboards at the entrances to our cities, and plaster them with discordant, shrieking commands. The facades of shops carry a dozen jarring styles of outsize lettering tangled with man-size reproductions of cartons of salts and soap, or gargantuan bottles of sauce or stout. Perhaps there should be a concerted effort on everyone's part to buy the brand of petrol that advertises least—perhaps with a single, well-designed symbol indicating where it might be purchased. It is not impossible that a few enlightened companies lead the way. But mainly the civic authorities must restore to us the freedom of seeing as much as possible of a clear, worthwhile world and its achievements. While individuals are free to commit such public nuisance, even though they may be in a minority, there will be no end to it. Such ugliness as they perpetrate is temporary and, sooner or later, like the frontier wiring, it will disappear.

The new Australia is most attractive where it is most homogeneous. Much of the earliest building was either quite fugitive, or else used stone, traditional proportions, and necessary constructional disciplines. The local stone blended with its surroundings and the architecture was unified, partly because it had to follow the dictates of stone, and partly because it preceded democracy in Australia. As Adelaide so often shows, it is difficult to serve expediency in stone.

Most modern building materials are more versatile, and some may be used in extravagant simulation of more rigid media, often disguising the basic functional principles and ordered purpose in meaningless curves and vapid 'beautification.' Heterogeneity occurs when the general effect of buildings, with their differing styles, materials, colours, textures, and proportions, is not considered. The unity of an individual structure may similarly be destroyed by applied 'effects' and frills, out of harmony with the underlying form, and by dishonest use of materials to make them seem what they are not. Additionally, in shops, office buildings, and service stations, garish, dominating, and badly designed advertising may completely ruin buildings which, in themselves, are at least tolerable.[39]

The rapid growth of British communities in Australia, the opening up of new country for agriculture and grazing, the ease with which settlers could be self-determining on their own land, created conditions unmatched anywhere in the Old World, where, though feudalism was dead, its traditions still lingered, where there was no virgin land, or at least none for selection and free settlement. The freedom of Australia was imposed on what was so justifiably considered *terra nullius* just when the mightiest revolution in the social history of man—the age of steam, circular saws and power presses, cast iron, extruded wire and steel bar, sheet metal, and the new industrial magnates—could cater most perfectly to the maw of colonial expediency. What has happened, especially since a dozen new building materials might find empty suburban blocks and 'building estates' to spawn upon, would have happened under similar conditions anywhere in the western world. The eloquent voices pleading against ugliness, vulgarity, the laissez-faire heterogeneity of suburbia, the insensitivity of local government, the desecration of a natural beauty and buildings of historical value, are being heeded, as never before, and, for the first time in history, the gap between good taste and the general opinion is being bridged voluntarily. If this takes time, it must be remembered that the process is uniquely of the New World, and that it constitutes a major advance in the effectiveness of society. In the meantime, conservation of all our resources, including the best of the past, and open space for the future, exercises the minds of an increasing number of enlightened people determined to preserve and engender universal values in our world of difference.

[1] Both Canberra's Molonglo, and Adelaide's Torrens, were unimpressive until they had been dammed.

[2] Edward Gibbon Wakefield published his imaginative 'A Letter from Sydney' in 1829 (he had never visited Australia). His theories, of colonial land at 'a sufficient price,' rather than settlement being encouraged by free grants, found special favour with the public at a time when Thomas Peel's colonial plans in Western Australia were obviously unsuccessful. The Wakefield theory, however, was not permitted to be fully implemented, and, in fact, His Majesty's Government was opposed to colonial expansion which was 'always liable in the end in becoming in some way or other a source of expense to the revenue of the country' (Chief Secretary, Colonial Office, 1830). However, Adelaide was ultimately founded, after a false start on Kangaroo Island, and in a general atmosphere of disagreement and doubt, in 1836. Land speculation nearly ruined the infant colony; two early governors, Captain Hindmarsh and Colonel George Gawler, were recalled within five years, and only the firmness and energy of Captain George Grey 'extricated the colony,' as the British Prime Minister, Sir Robert Peel, expressed it, and 'gained the good-will and confidence of both settlers and aboriginals.'

[3] 'Having rejected Port Lincoln owing to its environment, and made an examination of St Vincent's Gulf, he (Light) determined that the best available site was that upon which the City of Adelaide was afterwards reared. When Governor Hindmarsh arrived in the *Buffalo* in December (1836) he was ill-pleased with the choice. A muddy creek, sending its trickle of water through a mangrove swamp afforded no fitting spot for the capital of a colony.'—Ernest Scott: *A Shorter History of Australia*.

[4] It was discovered that imported timbers were frequently attacked by termites.

[5] T. S. Eliot: *The Dry Salvages* (Faber & Faber, 1941).

[6] The discovery of feasible routes over the Blue Mountains by Oxley, 1817–18, causing New South Wales to be revalued as a most favourable field for free immigrants, led to a change of policy in the classification of convicts, and it was Oxley again who found a suitable site for another convict colony. This time, coasting in the *Mermaid*, in 1823, he learnt from ship-wrecked sailors, Messrs Pamphlet and Finnegan, of the existence of a large stream entering the sea in Moreton Bay.

319

Top: Gardens of the Japanese Embassy, Canberra. *Bottom:* Papua New Guinea embassy, Canberra. *Facing page:* Yachts on Lake Burley Griffin, a man-made lake stretching 11 kilometres across Canberra

With Finnegan, John Oxley followed the stream for some kilometres inland and named it the Brisbane River after the Governor of New South Wales (1821–25). Here, from 1824 onwards, were dispatched the more incorrigible characters from the settlement further south. No convicts were sent after 1839, and within a year or two, the area was opened to free settlers. In 1859, the Moreton Bay district became the separate colony of Queensland, administered by the first Governor, Sir George Bowen.

[7] The Rocklea market covering 50 hectares of land was officially opened in August 1964.

[8] The populations of Broome, Derby, and Wyndham at the 1976 census were respectively 2920, 2411, and 1383.

[9] See *The Surveyors: the Story of the Founding of Darwin* (1971), by M. Goyder Kerr.

[10] *Year Book, Australia, 1982*, gives the following figures for population [1980] of capital cities: Sydney, 3 231 700; Melbourne, 2 759 700; Brisbane, 1 028 900; Adelaide, 934 200; Perth, 902 000; Hobart, 170 200; Darwin, 56 482.

[11] *The Lucky Country — Australia in the Sixties*, by Donald Horne (Penguin Books, 1964).

[12] But see *The First Discovery of Australia and New Guinea*, by George Collingridge (1906; republished, 1982, by Pan Books (Aust.) Pty Ltd); also *The Secret Discovery of Australia*, by Kenneth Gordon McIntyre (Souvenir Press, 1977).

[13] Excluding Darwin, the capital of the Northern Territory. Darwin is beautifully situated on a peninsula facing the Clarence Strait between Melville Island and the mainland.

[14] The original plate is in the Rijksmuseum, Amsterdam.

[15] Lancelott, 1852, *op. cit.*

[16] Gold was first mined in the Kalgoorlie-Boulder region in 1893. Paddy Hannan discovered gold there in 1892. Water is pumped to Kalgoorlie from the south-west, a distance of about 560 kilometres. (See chap. 1, note 18.)

[17] In 1947, the population of W.A. was 502 500. In 1980, it was 1 265 000.

[18] On the basis of diamonds found, a pilot plant to treat Kimberlite has been set up at Ellendale, W.A. There are, also,. in the Kimberley region, diamond-bearing alluvials.

[19] Pulpwood (virtually all in the form of woodchips) exports in 1979–80, totalled 4 479 134 tonnes (green)—sawn timber produced, almost entirely for domestic consumption, in the same period was 3 160 264 cubic metres.

[20] In 1980, total student enrolment at Australian universities totalled 163 156. University staff numbered 11 895. See *University Statistics, Australia.*

[21] Regrettably, the reclamation of shallow water areas for the large car park and the bridge approaches, and the walling of the river, has, in fact, caused some water birds to desert the city area. There was, of course, strong opposition to the extension of filling for any purpose into the reeds and rushes where much wild-life nested and found food; scenically and practically, the effect probably justifies what was done.

[22] The original settlements of both Victoria and Tasmania were made to counter possibilities of the French claiming territories, and, as late as June 1825, Sir Ralph Darling, Governor of New South Wales, sent Major Lockyer, with a party numbering about 75, to found a settlement at King George III Sound, in Western Australia. On 2 May 1829, Captain Fremantle hoisted the British flag on the south head of the Swan River, and took possession of 'all that part of New Holland which is not included within the territory of New South Wales.' A month later, Captain James Stirling arrived with the first settlers.

[23] The State boundaries were fixed as follows: Tasmania (Van Diemen's Land), 1825; Western Australia, 1829; Victoria, 1851; Queensland and South Australia, 1861; and the Northern Territory (at first administered by N.S.W., then by S.A., and finally by the Commonwealth), 1863. Responsible Government had been conferred on all States by 1861, except Western Australia (1890). The Northern Territory was established as a self-governing territory in 1978, with its seat of government in Darwin.

[24] Earl Grey's proposal was that an Assembly be elected by the Parliaments, to take charge of 'matters affecting the common interests of Australia.' These, it was proposed, should include customs and excise, postal business, roads, railways, lighthouses, etc.

[25] In the second Referendum of 1899, of a total of 377 988 votes, 236 602 were in favour of Federation. The Commonwealth Bill was submitted to the Imperial Parliament on 14 May 1900, and the Royal assent was given on 9 July 1900.

[26] Bertram Keith has expressed the matter succinctly and well (*Walkabout*, March 1963): 'On that hot, late-summer day—the original "Canberra Day," 12 March 1913—the Light Horse and the carriages of the principal guests raised clouds of dust as they moved across the plain to Capital Hill, where a crowd of 5000 people had gathered. Uniforms and pretty parasols added colour to the prevailing dignity . . .

'The beginnings were simple enough. Foundation stones were laid in the base of the Commencement Column by the Governor-General (Lord Denman), the Prime Minister (the Rt Hon. Andrew Fisher) and the Minister of State for Home Affairs (the Hon. King O'Malley) . . .'

[27] *Whitaker's Almanack*, 1903, stated: 'The final decision as to the site of the New

Australasian Commonwealth has not yet been arrived at, but the question has been narrowed by the selection from among a number of claimants of five sites, on one of which the ultimate choice will fall.' A sketch showed these to be: Orange, Lake George, Tumut, Albury, and Bombala.

The final selection, in 1908, was that near Lake George, in the broad Molonglo Valley south-east of Yass. After a great deal of argument and bitter disagreement, the actual site was determined in 1909. On 1 January 1911, an area of 2300 square kilometres was ceded to the Commonwealth by the Government of New South Wales.

The area had been pastorally developed since 1820, and contained several old homesteads, including the properties of the Campbells and Webbs, Moores and McPhersons. Canberry was the name given by John McPherson to his property—it might have been an Aboriginal name meaning 'meeting place,' and Duntroon belonged to Robert Campbell, who helped build the church of St John, dedicated 11 May 1841. Duntroon is now the name of the Military College, and the suburb of Campbell lies between it and the little church.

[28] Walter Burley Griffin: In the 1913 competition, Griffin's design was chosen from a total of 126 submitted by Australian and overseas architects, and he won a prize of £1750. The original plan has been much modified. The National Capital Development Commission is now responsible for the further planning and growth of Canberra.

[29] The Commonwealth Avenue Bridge and the Kings Avenue Bridge now carry almost incessant streams of traffic. They are simply and beautifully designed, although from some angles the approach obelisks may seem redundant. Their system of lighting, from concealed sources along the balustrades, is both effective and aesthetically satisfying, and one hopes, optimistically, that the method might ultimately be extended to street illumination. Since the filling of Lake Burley Griffin, the whole city of Canberra has realised a new splendour.

[30] Kosciusko, the highest mountain in Australia, 2228 metres, was named after the Polish patriot (1746–1817) who before distinguishing himself against the Russian invaders of his own land, had fought with the American colonists in the American War of Independence.

[31] The common name of *Eucalyptus rossii* is scribbly gum, from the calligraphic markings that occur on the white trunks.

[32] For long a natural breathing space in the heart of Canberra, Capital Hill is now largely occupied by Parliament House, to be completed for the bi-centenary celebration of the arrival of the First Fleet, mainly bringing convicts from gaols overcrowded since the loss of the American colonies.

[33] The Australian War Memorial, on the foothills of Mt Ainslie, and visible from much of the city, contains vast galleries of exhibits and dioramas representing every phase of Australia's part in the World Wars. It is visited annually by hundreds of thousands. The names of Australian Servicemen are recorded in bronze in the Hall of Remembrance.

[34] Australian Academy of Science: A Charter of Incorporation was presented to the first Council of the Australian Academy of Science on 16 February 1954, by Her Majesty Queen Elizabeth II. The building, from a distance, appears like a huge mushroom. It was designed by the late Sir Roy Grounds, the architect of the Melbourne 'Cultural Centre.'

[35] The Mt Stromlo Observatory, of the Research School of Physical Sciences, The Australian National University, is important by world standards because it covers certain areas of the southern skies better than any other existing observatories. Mt Stromlo was opened on 1 January 1924, with W. G. Duffield as Director. Dr R. van der R. Woolley was Director from 1939 until he became Astronomer Royal and Director of Greenwich. Prof. O. J. Eggen is present Director. The complex includes several major telescopes of up to 3·9 metres. There are visiting guest observatories, both American and Swedish.

[36] The National Library of Australia will ultimately hold up to 11 million books. The main building is by the shores of Lake Burley Griffin, in Canberra's Parliamentary triangle between the southern approaches to the bridges. The whole building is framed with Carrara marble. Paving stone was imported from Norway, but Australian trachyte and granite were used for walls and steps.

[37] The population of Australia in 1830 was 62 190. By decades to 1900, it grew as follows: 180 626; 405 660; 1 141 563; 1 650 172; 2 245 448; 3 167 976; 3 745 840. For the first half of the twentieth century, the growth was about 1 million per decade, but it now exceeds 2 million, and the present population approaches 15 million.

[38] Such works include Robin Boyd's *The Australian Ugliness* (Cheshire, 1960); J. D. Pringle's *Australian Accent* (Chatto & Windus Ltd), and *The Lucky Country* (Penguin, 1964). Implicitly, also, the autobiographical novels include a quantity of the restless criticism which has become so vocal in the second half of the century.

[39] On the south side of Sydney Harbour bridge, the skyline has changed vastly with each decade. The majority of buildings in the central office core, bounded by King, Clarence, Macquarie, Bridge, and Grosvenor Streets, have been constructed since 1960. See *The Council of the City of Sydney Central Business District Study, 1978.* The recession of the early 1980s left almost a million square metres of Sydney floor space [18%] vacant.

Photo Credits

Index